Intellectual Property Rights, Copynorm and the Fashion Industry

This book traces the development of the fashion industry, providing insight into the business and, in particular, its interrelations with copyright law. The book explores how the greatest haute couture fashion designers also had a sense for business and that their attention to copyright was one of the weapons in protecting their market position. The work also confronts the peculiarities of the fashion industry as a means of demonstrating the importance of intellectual property protection while pointing out the many challenges involved. A central aim is to provide a copyrightability test for fashion goods based on detailed analysis of the legal regulations in the USA and EU countries, specifically Italy, France, the Netherlands, Germany and Poland. The book will be of interest to researchers and academics working in the areas of Intellectual Property Law, Copyright Law, Business Law, Fashion Law and Design.

Marlena Jankowska is an international lawyer specialising in intellectual property law and business, with a particular interest in fashion, sustainability and supply chains. She is an author, an advocate, a professor of Law and Director of the Center for Design, Fashion and Advertisement Law at the University of Silesia in Katowice, Poland. She is also Director of Intellectual Property Department with Pawełczyk legal office, Warsaw-Katowice. She advises on Intellectual Property and Business Law as well as Brand and Supply Chain Management.

Intellectual Property Rights, Copynorm and the Fashion Industry

A Comparative Analysis

Marlena Jankowska

Routledge
Taylor & Francis Group
LONDON AND NEW YORK

First published 2024
by Routledge
4 Park Square, Milton Park, Abingdon, Oxon OX14 4RN

and by Routledge
605 Third Avenue, New York, NY 10158

Routledge is an imprint of the Taylor & Francis Group, an informa business

British Library Cataloguing-in-Publication Data
A catalogue record for this book is available from the British Library

Library of Congress Cataloging-in-Publication Data
Names: Jankowska, Marlena, author.
Title: Intellectual property rights, copynorm, and the fashion industry : a comparative analysis / Marlena Jankowska.
Description: Abingdon, Oxon [UK] ; New York, NY : Routledge, 2023. | Includes bibliographical references and index. | Summary: — Provided by publisher.
Identifiers: LCCN 2023038462 | ISBN 9781032452265 (hardback) | ISBN 9781032452272 (paperback) | ISBN 9781003376033 (ebook)
Subjects: LCSH: Design protection—United States. | Design protection—European Union countries. | Copyright—United States. | Copyright—European Union countries. | Fashion design—Law and legislation—United States. | Fashion design—Law and legislation—European Union countries. | Intellectual property—United States. | Intellectual property—European Union countries.
Classification: LCC K1490 .J36 2023 | DDC 346.2404/82—dc23/eng/20230929
LC record available at https://lccn.loc.gov/2023038462

ISBN: 978-1-032-45226-5 (hbk)
ISBN: 978-1-032-45227-2 (pbk)
ISBN: 978-1-003-37603-3 (ebk)

DOI: 10.4324/9781003376033

Publication financed under the program of the Minister of Science and Higher Education under the name “DIALOG” in the years 2019–2023 as part of the project “Excellence in Legal Research. Promoting Polish Achievements in the Area of Legal Sciences Abroad” implemented under the leadership of Celina Nowak by the Institute of Law Studies of the Polish Academy of Sciences.

DIALOG

This book is dedicated with much love to my parents, for whose support and guidance I will always be grateful.

Contents

Tables

Boxes

Figures

Preface
The why

"Seductive and craftsmanly qualities stand for originality in fashion".

A fashion product is a mix of multifaceted creative processes that take much more effort than meets the eye. There is a general belief that, on the one hand it takes a lot of exertion and investment to secure intellectual property protection for such goods, and that, on the other hand, copyrightability of fashion goods is ephemeral and very uncertain. This book tells a story of the fashion realm, sheds light on its nuances and history and defines it, while providing insight into the fashion business and its interrelations with copyright law. The book demonstrates that fashion goods are created out of loving emotions, and these emotions are subsequently contagious for the consumers of the products. A deep analysis of the legend of French couturiers gives rise to a focus on their innovation and genius beyond their established fame for the fashion itself. The reader will discover that the greatest *haute couture* fashion designers also had a great sense for business and that their attention to copyright was one of their weapons to copper-fasten their market position. The narrative presents the contemporary fashion industry and its interconnections with intellectual property rights, with a special focus on copyright law. The book confronts the peculiarities of the fashion industry as a means of demonstrating the importance of intellectual property protection in the industry while pointing out the many challenges involved. However, the core aim of the book is to provide a copyrightability test for fashion goods based on detailed analysis of the US and EU (Italy, France, Netherlands, Germany and Poland) legal regulations and doctrinal approaches. For this reason, at the heart of the book are many pictorial illustrations of copyright disputes over fashion goods and their elements.

The conceptual framework of this book is grounded in the theoretical foundation of the intellectual property rights system. A conceptual synthesis approach was adopted to integrate the extant fashion-related research perspectives: philosophical, historical, social and economic. This study offers a novel conceptualisation of fashion and its tiers, including *haute couture* and *petite couture*, the TCLF (textile, clothing, leather and footwear) sector and fashion copyrightability. Surprisingly, there are no well-established definitions for these; therefore, this author explores many angles and discusses the nuances of these topics in pursuit of the necessary clarity. The fashion sector is defined by defining the TCLF sector, by distinguishing it from related sectors and moving beyond the usual considerations of production, sales and marketing mix elements. The book offers a solid background for the legal analysis, that cannot be undertaken without regard for the intricacies and externalities of the fashion business. In order to offer a synthesis of existing copyright theory with regard to fashion, this author reviewed the legal texts, national bodies of doctrine and case law with the hope of identifying a revised approach. This allowed identification of an emerging phenomenon in fashion copyrightability. This study uses a qualitatively driven mix of methods of legal analysis: historical, systemic, systematic, literal, teleological and functional. This body of expertise offers also in-depth interviews with fashion designers and supplementary survey research. The book covers fashion-related copyright cases and reflects on them in detail.

Most of all, the book provides vital insight into the copyright protection for fashion goods under selected legal systems to give a better understanding of how copyright premises work for fashion and to offer a new approach to the understanding of originality in copyright law for such goods.

This book has many fathers. The in-depth analysis would not be possible without the contributions of many people, who acted as inspiration, trigger or sounding board. The first and foremost acknowledgement goes to the rectors and deans of the University of Silesia, who made my dream of the Centre of Design, Fashion and Advertisement Law a reality. This author would also like to thank Prof. Celina Nowak (the head of this scholarly project), Prof. Guillermo C. Jimenez and Dr Piotr Szaradowski for their insightful comments, and Wojciech Kowalski and Wojciech Popiołek for the intellectual journey I have undertaken since I became a student. The realisation of this book owes much to the unwavering and steadfast support of professor Mirosław Pawełczyk. This research would have not been possible if it was not for the very kind help of presiding judges of courts in Poland in locating and accessing case files during the pandemic (especially the District Courts of Nowy Sącz, Opole, Poznań, Katowice and Sieradz). Equally vital were the personal insights of fashion designers and their permission to use many unique copyrighted materials (special thanks to Mariola Turbiarz, Dominika Nowak, Justyna Ołtarzewska, Ewa Stepaniuk, Paweł Węgrzyn, Viola Śpiechowicz and Marzena Chełmińska). Words of gratitude also go to Dermot McNally, who as proofreader, dug deep to help create new names for continental law concepts that are without counterparts in the common-law system.

1 What is fashion? How social and cultural norms make the world of fashion glimmer and mesmerise

1.1 Fashion – social phenomenon. Social and cultural norms

1.1.1 Anthropological roots. Consumer as a social animal

A variety of studies and a number of philosophers have shown that clothes constitute a system of signs and a system of norms in which human beings have been immersed since time immemorial.[1] The number of clothes-related proverbs may be considered the epitome of the significance accorded to garments in our social and cultural contexts. Among others, a Dutch proverb holds that "A smart coat is a good letter of introduction", and Vietnamese people quote the saying "The dog will always attack the one with torn trousers". In Ghana, people say "When a man is wealthy he may wear an old cloth".[2] What these dicta have in common is that, no matter how local they may seem, they are understood across the world and can be easily applied by any society. They concomitantly prove that fashion can be perceived as a self-contained system, though its nooks and minutiae are hardly ever translated into pure and applied sciences. In 1753, William Hogarth published his book *The Analysis of Beauty*, where he too made a clear point in the same vein: "not only . . . ladies of fashion, but that women of every rank, who are said to dress prettily, have known their force, without considering them as principles".[3] Immanuel Kant was one of many to opine that fashion has anthropological roots that unveil themselves through the human aspiration to follow one's superiors and imitate the values associated with success, mirrored in better social status and better financial standing.[4] Attire became the *medium* allowing for externalisation of

1 I. Loschek, *When Clothes Become Fashion: Design and Innovation Systems*, Berg Publishers, 2009, pp. 8, 13, 21; cf. A. Görke, A. Scholl, *Niklas Luhmann's Theory of Social Systems and Journalism Research*, "Journalism Studies", 2006, pp. 644 and ff.; M. Butor, R.G. Elliott, U. Lehmann, *Fashion and the Modern*, "Art in Translation", 2015, vol. 7 no. 2, pp. 266 and ff.

2 https://proverbicals.com/clothes (accessed: 06.01.2023).

3 W. Hogarth, *The Analysis of Beauty. Written with a View of Fixing the Fluctuating Ideas of Taste*, 1700 p. 33, available at: www.gutenberg.org/files/51459/51459-h/51459-h.htm (accessed: 26.01.2023).

4 R. Meinhold, *Fashion Myths. A Cultural Critique*, Transcript Verlag, 2013, p. 37.

DOI: 10.4324/9781003376033-1

one's image,[5] status, views and desires. Denis Diderot, Immanuel Kant and Mark Twain are only a few among many to hold the dictum "clothes make the man" to be a universal truth.[6]

To start the long story about the fashion ecosystem – its concepts, history, rules and regulations – it must be recalled that human interactions consist of relationships having many facets: moral, cultural, social and legal. These are systematised by translating them to norms that reign in nearly every aspect of our lives. The fashion ecosystem, too, is made of many norms, e.g. specific expected apparel for men and women, respectively (cultural norms), expected and acceptable behaviour (moral and social norms),[7] protection of creativity and designs as well as of clusters of fashion professions (legal norms). In previous societies, what an individual wore and its colour was not solely a matter of taste or resources but also of hierarchy (social and legal norms).[8] Over time, style became a matter of individual sensibility, not necessarily of wealth or upper-class credentials. Fashion, including the history of fashion-related laws, has evolved over centuries in many ways. So much so, that fashion became not only a popular and social phenomenon but also a legal one.

As this book's aim is to identify a problem for investigation and discussion, to set forth a few generalisations looking for solutions based on the *threshold of originality establishing protection for fashion design*, it is justified, indeed desirable, to review the state of fashion's literature and social perception. It is, above all, important to note that fashion, as a 'social fact',[9] is itself a little more complex,[10] so restricting this research to mere legal concepts would not only incorrectly narrow down the subject matter of this research but would misrepresent and undermine the notion of fashion.

Suffice it to say that, unlike in any other sector of creative business, *imitation is exceptionally common, prosecution of counterfeits interestingly weak and the line between original and imitation extremely delicate.*[11] So much so, that it is often hard to draw lines between *copying*, on the one hand, meaning slavish 'cloning',[12] and on the other hand *legitimate inspiration* or a grassroots *trend/style hitting the streets.* Many authors, though not lawyers, have a good deal to say about the

5 E. Coccia, *Sensible Life. A Micro-ontology of the Image*, Fordham University Press, 2016, p. 89.

6 I. Kant, *Anthropologie in Pragmatischer Hinsicht*, Leipzig, 1912, [side number 137–138], p. 25; Cf. L. Salamo, M.B. Frank, V. Fischer (eds.), *Mark Twain's Helpful Hints for Good Living*, University of California Press, 2004, pp. 140 and ff; M. Erlhoff, T. Marshall, *Design Dictionary: Perspectives on Design Terminology*, Birkhäuser Basel, 2008, p. 161.

7 J.K. Burgoon, J.K. Guerrero, K. Floyd, *Nonverbal Communication*, Routledge, 2016, p. 39.

8 Cf. M. Agbahoungbata, *Elements of Flair and Fashion*, "Chemistry International", October–December, 2019, pp. 29 and ff.

9 P.H. Nystrom, *Economics of Fashion*, Ronald Press Company, 1928, p. 30.

10 E.J. Kang, *A Dialectical Journey through Fashion and Philosophy*, Springer, 2019.

11 A. Janssens, M. Lavanga, *An Expensive, Confusing, and Ineffective Suit of Armor: Investigating Risks of Design Piracy and Perceptions of the Design Rights Available and Perceptions of the Design Rights Available to Emerging Fashion Designers in the Digital Age*, "The Journal of Dress, Body and Culture", 2018, vol. 24, no. 2, p. 233.

12 The concept of "cloning", introduced and applied by I. Loschek, will be put forward and developed by this author in this book, see Loschek, *When Clothes . . .*, p. 127.

reception of fashion in modern society. A few reflections will frame our understanding of fashion, giving a point of departure for both legal and business fashion-related research. Paul Nystrom asserted, in a point later reiterated by Richard A. Lancioni, that the consumer is "a social animal composed of a group of complex and interrelated needs that either singly or collectively interact to change the direction of fashion".[13] In other words, there is plenty of room for numerous styles and trends, but only a few will gain the final acceptance of consumers, who will vehemently follow one particular fashion trend, rejecting others. And external forces, be they advertisement or the designers themselves, sometimes have no direct influence on this phenomenon. A strong illustration of this point is a business experience associated with the failed 'Midi' dress. The fashion industry complacently marketed the new dress length as a whole new style trend for the 1970s.[14] By the same token, during the Spanish flu epidemic (1918–1920), the US media tried in vain to introduce the prudent habit of wearing face masks,[15] which could cause the influenza bug to diminish faster and take a lesser toll.[16] Interestingly, even a hundred years later, during the Covid-19 pandemic, the same effort to establish a fashion-driven social norm of mask wearing, at times adopting edgy or aspirational themes, also came to naught.[17] It boils down to the competing social norm driving people to want to look attractive. Psychologically speaking, people with an attractive and smiling face are found more appealing than others, placing face masks at odds with the desire for beauty and aesthetics.[18] Moreover, one of the recent studies revealed underlying variables regarding the choice to wear a mask during the Covid-19 pandemic, such as the making of a statement or an enthusiasm for fashion. It was measured how attitudes to fashion can influence decisions regarding wearing masks. In general, it was found that people hardly find face masks fashionable, but, since there was an obligation to wear them, people had a preference

13 R.A. Lancioni, *A Brief Note on the History of Fashion*, "Journal of the Academy of Marketing Science", 1973, vol. 1, p. 129.

14 G.B. Sproles, *Analyzing Fashion Life Cycles: Principles and Perspectives*, "Journal of Marketing", 1981, vol. 45, no. 4, p. 118.

15 Regarding making a face mask a *must-have* trend in the event of Covid-19 see: M. Jankowska, E. Błach, A. Warmuzińska, Coronavirus Couture. *Maseczka w czasach zarazy przedmiotem ochrony prawnej?*, "ZNUJ. PPWI", 2021, no. 2, pp. 147–179.

16 *Girls Wear Masks on Streets Pioneers of Precaution Step*, "Rocky Mountain News", 17 October 1918, p. 3, http://hdl.handle.net/2027/spo.7970flu.0003.797 (accessed: 20.01.2023), *Too many Clothes – and Often Too Few – Will Give IT to You!*, "Chicago Herald and Examiner", 6 October 1918, pp. 1–2, http://hdl.handle.net/2027/spo.5480flu.0001.845 (accessed: 20.01.2023).

17 Emily Gerstell, Sophie Marchessou, Jennifer Schmidt, Emma Spagnuolo, *How COVID-19 Is Changing the World of Beauty?*, "McKinsey & Company", March 2020, pp. 2 and ff., www.mckinsey.com/~/media/McKinsey/Industries/Consumer%20Packaged%20Goods/Our%20Insights/How%20COVID%2019%20is%20changing%20the%20world%20of%20beauty/How-COVID-19-is-changing-the-world-of-beauty-vF.pdf (accessed: 15.03.2022); Sarah Spellings, *Face Masks to Shop Now*, 3 March 2022, www.vogue.com/slideshow/stylish-face-masks-to-shop-now (accessed: 16.03.2022).

18 Eleanor Mills, Kun Guo, *Impact of Face Masks on Female Body Perception Is Modulated by Facial Expressions*, "Perception", 2022, vol. 51, no. 1, pp. 52 and ff.; Cornelia Betsch, Lars Korn, Philipp Sprengholz, Robert Böhm, *Social and Behavioral Consequences of Mask Policies During the COVID-19 Pandemic*, "Psychological and Cognitive Sciences", 2020, vol. 117, no. 36.

for face masks with the logos of brands or school teams or those conveying a political message. On the one hand, it was found important to match mask with outfit, but on the other, people were reluctant to maintain different face masks for different occasions and about expressing themselves through the use of masks.[19]

Item of note 1.1 Face mask fashion tips during the Spanish flu epidemic[20]

An article about face masks was published in the "Seattle Daily Times" on 18 October 1918, p. 9:

> The *en vogue* tip took the approach: "Have you seen the veils worn by Seattle women to protect themselves from the influenza? Chiffon is the prevailing material, and all styles seem to be in vogue, from the swathed-like-a-mummy effect of a thick motor veil, to the fluffy fine-meshed veil with a chiffon border pinned in back of the hair to keep the heavier portion over the nose and mouth".[21]

Another article promoting the new face mask style, was published in "The Cleveland Press" on 11 November 1918, p. 22:

> It coaxed readers to wear one with the words "This looks like a hold up, but it's only a flip, flu fashion! . . . This is positively the latest edition of the flu mask, and it is worn in the full glare of the public eye and called a veil".[22]

In that instance, the trend for wearing veils never became as contagious as the influenza itself. But many prestige goods are doomed to be sales failures, too. Why is that? Because, as Nystrom noted as early as 1928,

> if there were any kings or dictators of fashion in the past, there are certainly not any that are making a success of it today, except those who are able to forecast what consumers are going to want and then give it to them.[23]

19 Denise Nicole Green, Frances Holmes Kozen, Catherine Kueffer Blumenkamp, *Facemasking Behaviors, Preferences, and Attitudes Among Emerging Adults in the United States During the COVID-19 Pandemic: An Explanatory Study*, "Clothing and Textiles Research Journal", 2021, vol. 39, no. 3, pp. 225–229.

20 Marlena Jankowska, Miriam Meghaichi, Mirosław Pawełczyk, *Illustrated Fashion Law*, Instytut Prawa Gospodarczego sp. z o.o., Series of Design, Fashion and Advertisement Law, vol. 10, Katowice, 2023.

21 *Influenza Veils Set New Fashion*, "Seattle Daily Times", 18 October 1918, p. 10, http://hdl.handle.net/2027/spo.1170flu.0010.711 (accessed: 20.01.2023).

22 *Don't Flee! It's Flu Veil*, "The Cleveland Press", 11 November 1918, http://hdl.handle.net/2027/spo.5480flu.0002.845 (accessed: 20.01.2023).

23 Nystrom, *Economics . . .*, p. 35.

A topical example was the Gillette Safety Razor advertisement campaign, which turned out to be extremely successful. By way of background, it should be known that smooth shaving was fashionable at the time of the advertisement, it was just the improved razor qualities that became highly demanded.[24] As noted by Kaiser in 1985,

> The purchase and use of clothing (symbolic consumption) by collective groups of people largely reflects cultural norms and social values. Clothing norms are forms of collective behavior. . . . Collective clothing behavior has implications for the manufacturing and marketing of apparel products, as well as for a basic understanding of cultural aesthetics.[25]

Blumer, too, famous for his human collective theory, articulated in 1969 that fashion is a process of collective selection and formation of collective tastes among a mass of people.[26]

Therefore, this chapter sheds light on some social clothing norms that aroused a debate over societal expectations, imitation, aesthetic presentation, common decency and associations related to a profession or a status, to mention just a few. This very broad, descriptive approach, allowing for better understanding of the existence of a 'self-referential system of apparel' will pave the way to answering the lingering question of what fashion is and what it encompasses.

1.1.2 **Imitatio prominentis et imitatio naturae.** ***Imitation in fashion – socially and evolutionally approved?***

Another anthropological finding is that people zealously ascend the schematic ladder of needs with every step they successfully take. Once they fulfil their basic physiological and safety needs, they aspire for love and belonging, esteem (both self and social, as well as reputation) and self-actualisation (including creativity).[27] The importance of clothing to our species arises in large part because our dress rounds out the picture of ourselves that we present to the world. As much as this assumption seems to be true in this day and age, the scholarship has given us a detailed commentary on philosophers' accounts of fashion. To wit, the phenomenon of humans craving expensive things did not escape the attention of the greatest philosophers of our civilisation. One of the first to slam fashion's sumptuousness was Plato, who despised "costly raiment, or sandals, or other adornments of the body".[28] This surge in expensive accessories, often irrational,

24 Nystrom, *Economics . . .*, p. 82.

25 S.B. Kaiser, *The Social Psychology of Clothing*, Macmillan, 1985; cf. A. Shan-Hsin, *A Comparative Study of Apparel; Shopping Orientations between Asian Americans and Caucasian Americans*, master's thesis, Oregon State University, 1991, p. 20.

26 H. Blumer, *Fashion: From Class Differentiation to Collective Selection*, "Sociological Quarterly", 1969, vol. 10, no. 2, pp. 275–291; Shan-Hsin, *A Comparative Study . . .*, p. 20.

27 A.H. Maslow, *Motivation und Persönlichkeit*, Reinbeck B. Hamburg, 1999, pp. 62 and ff.; cf. G. Simmel, *Fashion*, "International Quarterly", 1904, vol. 10, no. 1, pp. 130 and ff.

28 Plato, *Phaedo*, p. 64 d-e; cf. Meinhold, *Fashion Myths*, transl. J. Irons, p. 10.

is the effect of the double face of human nature: striving for individuality on the one hand and imitating more important people on the other. *Mimesis* was believed by Aristotle to enhance creativity,[29] but, according to Kant, imitation is part of human nature.[30] Kant's opinion that a human being ceaselessly compares themself to others and enthusiastically mimics prominent members of society was shared by many philosophers, including Friedrich Schiller, Friedrich Theodor Vischer, Eugen Fink and Jean Baudrillard. Christian Garve wrote that "many people endeavour to resemble someone whom they feel is excellent, because they hope thereby to increase their own worth".[31] Roman Meinhold coined the term *imitatio prominentis* to define this phenomenon. He opines that, by the act of *imitatio prominentis*, the human being satisfies their most elitist needs pinpointed by Maslow: self-realisation, prestige, increase in self-esteem, affiliation, love.[32]

Imitation, therefore, emerges as one of humankind's inherent features to follow and copy the 'rich' with their aptitude for demonstrative consumption and expensive taste for aesthetics.[33] As already mentioned, one of the most influential philosophers to dwell on the idea of fashion and imitation – Immanuel Kant – made the observation that people's proclivity for comparing themselves with others of greater age or wealth is inherent.[34]

Item of note 1.2 Paul Nystrom on imitation

It is worth going back to 1928, to quote at length Paul Nystrom, who, even then, opened this subject for discussion by stating that

> *imitation* is of course second-rate origination. Origination of style takes time, energy, art and courage. It is also expensive. Most of us are lacking in the artistic ability to originate; most of us have neither the time nor the energy to devote to this kind of work. As already indicated, it would take a high degree of courage to originate and use styles quite different from those employed by the social groups of which we form a part. All that most of us can do is to imitate. Creation and origination are usually left to the so-called style leaders, those who have the time and money, artistic knowledge and, last but not least, the courage to try out new things.

29 Aristotle, *Poetics*, 1448b, pp. 4–9. Aristotle, *The Poetics of Aristotle*, transl. Samuel Henry Butcher, Macmillan and Company, 1902.
30 Kant, *Anthropologie . . .*, p. 25.
31 Meinhold, *Fashion Myths . . .*, pp. 47, 50.
32 Meinhold, *Fashion Myths . . .*, p. 49.
33 Meinhold, *Fashion Myths . . .*, p. 11.
34 Meinhold, *Fashion Myths . . .*, p. 12.

> In imitation there is, therefore, the desire to be like the group in order to be one of its members, but there may also be a competition within the group in which early imitation not only results in proving one's equality with the leaders, but also one's superiority over the poorer members of the group.[35]

Nystrom's observations, notwithstanding their truth, are not earth shattering. Let us reflect on a fact, articulated by Adam Smith in *The Theory of Moral Sentiments* in 1759, that eminent artists "bring about a considerable change in the established modes of each of those arts, and introduce a new fashion of writing, music or architecture". He even specifically cited examples of dress modes that, in his time, used to be introduced by men of high position in society, then admired and imitated.[36]

Among many approaches to fashion and ideas for comprehending it, there are two, dating back to 1906 and 1908, that this author would like to put forward and develop in this chapter. Louis W. Flaccus saw apparel styles as a mirror of society's goals and ambitions. He also believed that understanding fashion was a key to decoding society.[37] And William I. Thomas pointed out that a human being is an animal of no spectacular aptitudes, refined scent or glitter of their own. This is why humans relish external flamboyant goods to adorn themselves and luxuriate in them.[38]

Fashion can, furthermore, be perceived as a *fusion of self-expression and the successful introduction of a new style*, working as a causal relationship between both.[39] Anat Helman noted that

> Sociologist Georg Simmel describes fashion as simultaneously enslaving and liberating the individual. On the one hand, it dictates unified lines of dress for all its followers; on the other hand, within the limits of these dictates, it allows each person to choose specific nuances, which can express and manifest one's own personality.[40]

On the other hand, those humans not prone to bathing themselves in the social spotlight evolutionally opt for mimicry that lets them blend into the rest

35 Nystrom, *Economics of Fashion*, pp. 80–81.

36 A. Smith, *The Theory of Moral Sentiments*, 1759, reprinted (eds.) D.D. Raphael, A.L. Macfie, Liberty Funds, 1984, p. 197, available at: https://christiandemocraticunion.files.wordpress.com/2013/04/the-theory-of-moral-sentiments-by-adam-smith-1759.pdf (accessed: 25.01.2023).

37 L.W. Flaccus, *Remarks on the Psychology of Clothes*, "Pedagogical Seminar", 1906, vol. 13, pp. 61–83, cf. Lancioni, *A Brief Note . . .*, p. 130.

38 W.L. Thomas, *Psychology of Imitation*, "American Magazine", 1908, vol. 67, pp. 66–72.

39 Lancioni, *A Brief Note . . .*, p. 130.

40 A. Helman, *A Coat of Many Colors. Dress Culture in the Young State of Israel*, Academic Studies Press, 2011, p. 52.

of society. As found by James Laver in 1937, clothes are "both self-protective and self-assertive. They serve to merge the individual into his environment".[41] Through fashion, people adjust to the changing world. Imitation in fashion was the subject of deeper reflection in the philosophy of Georg Simmel. He concluded that imitation allows one to identify with the rest of society, that it helps to unify social strata. Thus, it has a socialising function:

> Fashion is the imitation of a given example and satisfies the demand for social adaptation; it leads the individual upon the road which all travel, it furnishes a general condition, which resolves the conduct of every individual into a mere example.[42]

It is very likely that he got this idea from Gabriel Tarde, *Les lois de l'imitation*, which stated: "que l'être social, en tant que social, est imitateur par essence, et que l'imitation joue dans les sociétés un rôle analogue à celui de l'hérédité dans les organismes ou de l'ondulation dans les corps bruts".[43] Therefore, fashion itself is also a very complex social and psychological phenomenon that lets humans survive in the hostile world through both individualisation and socialisation (cf. Chapter 1, section titled "Dualistic nature of fashion. The cycle of life makes the merry-go-round").[44]

1.1.3 Popularisation of fashion. A trickle-down effect

A somewhat interesting approach is taken by Eva-Maria Ziege, who touches upon the imitation of haute couture and upon the motivation for this imitation. She believes in the 'popularisation effect' (or 'trickle-down effect'), whereby high fashion designs become popular through copying or stealing. Just after the seasonal fashion weeks end, the mass production begins.[45] Ironically, Ziege advocates for the retention of this 'merry-go-round', which, in her opinion, is the main reason that high-fashion designs are made so "unwearable". She eagerly explains that *haute couture* is to blame for this problem, requiring the designs to be remade, remodelled and reoffered to the mass public. Would that approach actually mean no copyright protection for the finest *haute couture* houses simply based on established practice or *usus*? This question, she leaves unanswered. The situation tends to be counterbalanced by bringing in the elements of *haute couture* collections, their styles and inspirations, from the bottom, which results in the 'trickle-up' effect. On the other hand, to

41 J. Laver, *Taste and Fashion: From the French Revolution to the Present Day*, George G. Harrap, 1937, p. 248; Y.H. Kwon, *Effects of Situational and Individual Influences on the Selection of Daily Clothing*, "Clothing and Textiles Research Journal", 1988, vol. 6, no. 4, pp. 6–12.

42 G. Simmel, *Fashion*, "American Journal of Sociology", 1957, vol. 62, no. 6, p. 543.

43 G. Tarde, *Les lois de l'imitation*, 1890, p. 12.

44 Blumer, *Fashion*, vol. 10, no. 3, pp. 275 and ff.

45 E.-M. Ziege, *Die Kunst der Unterscheidung. Soziologie der Mode*, "Leviathan", 2011, vol. 39, no. 1, p. 154.

make high fashion more affordable, the world's leading fashion houses accept vulgarisation of fashion by signing contracts with warehouses and bringing to market 'lighter' lines of cheaper products.[46]

Paul M. Gregory also admitted that "fashion could not exist without imitations of high styles in lower price ranges".[47] A similar observation was made by Niklas Luhmann, who said that art as such does not tolerate copies, but that, in fashion, copies serve as a motor and accelerator in one.[48]

1.1.4 Dualistic nature of fashion. The cycle of life makes the merry-go-round

Fashion is a phenomenon built of many contradictory tensions. First, it allows for *individualisation and socialisation*. As V. Pouillard correctly observed, fashion meets two aims: it satisfies human need for imitation while, at the same time, fulfilling the desire for self-individualisation. As contradictory as that may seem, we delve sufficiently deeply into the true nature of fashion to find yet more incongruities than this.[49] Second, it makes the *acts of creation and imitation* exist alongside each other, increasing and eroding creative value at the same time. Third, it is both *static and dynamic*. Regardless of these apparent contradictions, most of all these features work together to the benefit of fashion's inscrutable nature. Simmel presented the view, reiterated later by Meinhold, that fashion is both *constant and elusive*. It is constant due to its suprahistorical manifestation; however, its contents change with every season in accordance with the governing styles.[50] Meinhold compares it to the Platonic dualism of *body and soul* that share the same dilemma. He goes on to say, "from a Platonic point of view just as the body experiences death and birth, but not the soul, which is immortal. Applied to fashion, a fashion style 'dies' when a new one is born".[51] Styles[52] thus become *functions of time*, driven by *culture* and by *society's openness* to experimentation with one's looks and even with stark deviations from established norms. As early as in 1792, Christian Garve, in his essay *On Fashion*, commented, that 'change' is built in a human's mind, which is also the natural reason that trends come and go.

46 Ziege, *Die Kunst der Unterscheidung*, pp. 153 154.

47 P.M. Gregory, *Fashion and Monopolistic Competition*, "Journal of Political Economy", 1948, vol. 56, no. 1, p. 72.

48 N. Luhmann, *Das Kunstwerk und die Selbstreproduktion der Kunst* [in:] H.-U. Gumbrecht, K.L. Pfeiffer (eds.), *Stil. Geschichie und Funktionen eines wissenschaftlichen Diskurselementes*, Suhrkam, 1986, p. 655 [after:] J. Gronow, *Taste and Fashion: The Social Function of Fashion and Style*, "Acta Sociologica", 1993, vol. 36, no. 2, p. 98.

49 V. Pauillard, *Design Piracy in the Fashion Industries of Paris and New York in the Interwar Years*, "The Business History Review", 2011, vol. 85, no. 2, p. 320.

50 Meinhold, *Fashion Myths*. . ., p. 60.

51 Meinhold, *Fashion Myths*. . ., p. 60.

52 As a cliché, note that a study dating back to 1968 found that "[in] the western civilisation the predominant norm with respect to sex differences in dress is that the female is *supposed* to have an interest in dress, while the man is *supposed* to have little or none". See M.J. Horn, *The Second Skin*, Houghton Hifflin Co., 1968, p. 132.

A *special role* in this process is ascribed to the *fashion creator*, who, again, adopts a dual role: birth giver and life taker. Meinhold observed that

> The designer, as the one giving birth, is responsible for the creation of the new fashion and thus indirectly like an executioner for the death of the old one. The new fashion ousts and 'kills' the old one because of its increasing presence. The 'murder' of the old fashion by the new one is inevitable, for the cycles of fashion and their alternation have assumed an autopoietical nature.[53]

Fashion can be easily viewed, in terms of Niklas Luhmann's approach, as an autopoietic system. That is, it changes over time with structures, elements and procedures transforming each other. In Luhmann's words, systems must innovate to survive, and they reproduce themselves through recursive communication, linking back to previous communications and continuously reinterpreting them.[54] Fashion survives through regular style change. But how fast should the pace of change be or to what extent should a change to the latest style be allowed? Every new fashion trend is an outgrowth or elaboration of the one that previously dominated. Those who understand the pace of change and the rhythm of fashion can quickly become fashion dictators. The history of fashion has proven that not many have earned this prestigious title over the centuries.[55]

As the key driver of fashion is innovation, the fashion designer enjoys a high social standing as their bank of creative ideas and experiences can be cashed in once turned into tangible product. In the late 19th and early 20th centuries, it was these designers themselves – strongly convinced of the merit of their creations and acutely aware of the revenues dependent upon them – who provided a key trigger for enhancement of the intellectual property regime to accommodate their works. The dynamics of the fashion economy are based on the momentum of the product being 'in' or 'on the street', which is tantamount to letting more money exchange hands. Stylists, fashion journalists and fashion buyers gauge the major fashion houses to know what will be in next season. Who is to fight for protection of these works if not the creator themself? A court adjudicating upon such matters must address such minutiae of fashion and design and can be ill-equipped to assess the relative merits. ***As such, it falls to the designers to press home the importance of elements that may not be obvious to the outside observer.*** Is it the form or is it the contents? In particular, the designer's role is vital in driving wider social

53 Meinhold, *Fashion Myths* . . ., p. 60.

54 K. van Assche, M. Duineveld, G. Verschraegen, R. During, R. Beunen, *Social Systems and Social Engineering: Niklas Luhmann* [in:] S. Vellema (ed.), *Transformation and Sustainability in Agriculture*. Wageningen Academic Publishers, 2011, pp. 35–48, cf. I. Loschek, *When Clothes Become Fashion*, p. 21.

55 Sproles, *Analyzing Fashion* . . ., pp. 117–118.

acceptance of the importance of their works/designs and, to some extent, fashion trends themselves.

Yet again, the dual character of fashion is plain to see at this level. On the one hand, it is earnestly claimed that *fashion industries*, with the fashion house designers on top, set trends for a malleable society. On the other hand, this approach is strongly attacked in favour of the contention that *consumers* are the ones who dictate fashion trends by picking up the trends they like, not necessarily the ones they are offered by the industry. It seems that the centre of balance is the *latitude of choice given to consumers by the fashion industry*. The wider this latitude, the lesser is the chance of taking a consumer into any one trend. This dualistic nature of fashion, the tension between industry and customers, must be carefully navigated by the designer, who will foresee the currents of fashion to come. Some guidance can be offered by academic theories, a number of which compete to predict the likely course of new trends and their reception among consumers. Among many such theories, four are predominant: the upper-class leadership theory, the mass market theory, the subcultural innovation theory and the collective selection theory.[56] At the same time, it can suffice to be an individual of great resolve and (most of all) to possess a keen hunch for fashion and its trends. Christian Dior, the founder of the New Look, was astonished and bewildered to see how much money women would spend on his designs, often ordering the same dress design in more than ten colours. Here we observe another dual character of fashion. Trends can be *planned*, but the signature fashion designs were *unplanned*.

1.2 Cultural norms and customs in fashion

1.2.1 Fashion as a cultural fact

Fashion is a cultural fact in many ways. That is to say, it unwittingly builds upon customs which evolved along with human needs and activities. These customs may be addressed here from at least three points of view: one is the practice of making clothes based on their usefulness or practicality; another is pursuing what is beautiful, in vogue or of good style (let alone appropriate or legally allowed); finally, fashion can indicate social trust and reliance. The very wearing of apparel or having women's wardrobes much more embellished than men's is also attributable to the influence of custom.[57] So much so that ceremonial attire or garments worn in the course of specific work (e.g. in medical care, courts or military forces) illustrates this point. That said, "fashion is a particular species of it [custom]".[58] Adam Smith recounted that modes of dress

56 Sproles, *Analyzing Fashion . . .*, pp. 118–119.

57 Cf. C. Geertz, *The Interpretation of Cultures. Selected Essays*, Basic Books, 1973, pp. 265 and ff.

58 Smith, *The Theory . . .*, p. 194.

continually change and are consigned to history as he was "experimentally convinced that it owed its vogue chiefly or entirely to custom and fashion".[59]

1.2.2 Buttons

As unusual as it may seem, the manner of placing buttons on the right or left side of clothing as an indication of men's or women's attire builds on customs. The story goes that when a man's right hand was occupied with tools or weapons, buttons on the right side could best be fastened with the left hand. Women's apparel is designed the other way around, as since anybody can remember, women have tended to carry their babies on their left arms, keeping the right hand free to do some work. Another theory relates to the fact that fine women's garments were often so elaborate as to require the assistance of a maid when dressing. In such cases, a right-handed maid would find it easier to fasten buttons on the left side. The same is true of placement of buttons on cuffs and waistbands on the thumb side for men and the little finger side for women. Nearly all oriental costumes originate from ritual ceremonies, an example of which may be turbans or apparel worn in India.[60] To keep this part succinct, it suffices to say that probably no aspect of garments is untouched by the hand of customs.[61]

1.2.3 High heels

The reader may not be aware that high heels were genuinely termed 'French heels', as they originated in France. In the 19th century, they were worn by Parisians, as Paris had no pedestrian pavements. Initially, women simply walked on tiptoe, since the streets in Paris were wet in both summer and winter. Over time, a heel to formalise this gait became an item of adornment and was also found to enhance a woman's silhouette.[62] This trend also triggered publicity on innovations in the manufacturing process of high heels.[63]

1.2.4 Trousers – women's trophy

The apparel used in everyday life often carries cultural elements, though these are not always recognised at first glance. One such garment is trousers as worn by women. It was introduced by Paul Poiret in 1911 in Paris under the oriental label 'harem shirt', however it took a lot of time and mental change for it to gain acceptance. The cultural attitude was influenced by many factors,

59 Smith, *The Theory . . .*, p. 195.
60 E. Harms, *The Psychology of Clothes*, "American Journal of Sociology", 1938, vol. 44, no. 2, p. 245.
61 Nystrom, *Economics . . .*, pp. 129–132.
62 *Origin and Evolution of French Heels*, "Scientific American", 1882, vol. 47, no 2, 8 July, p. 21.
63 *Machine for Forming Heels for Ladies' Shoes*, "Scientific American", 1885, vol. 53, no. 1, 4 July, p. 6.

including the two world wars (which let women wear comfortable garments for work), new leisure such as cycling or swimming (which let women embrace leisurewear) and liberated Hollywood stars who opted for change (Marlene Dietrich and Katharine Hepburn wore trousers in the 1930s). Trousers were formally adopted in 1964 with André Courrèges spring collection.[64] As trousers have traditionally been believed to symbolise male power and sexual independence, in 2009, the Sudanese journalist Lubna Ahmed al-Hussein was put on trial for wearing trousers under Article 152 of the Sudanese Public Order Law.[65] It took ten more years to abolish this morality law in November 2019. It may be amusing that France itself only in 2013 repealed its old law, dating back to 17 November 1800, banning women from wearing trousers. Though French values and fashions had changed significantly, the old rule was still technically in force.[66] This is how we arrive at the issue of fashion as influenced by culture, social morality and laws, which conversely define what is 'in good style' as coherent with morality and laws. It is somewhat staggering to see how many emotions and antithetical attitudes can be triggered by one's dress. Quite recently, in July 2017, Uganda attracted attention with regard to the Ministry of Public Service Establishment Notice No. 1 of 1017 on Dressing Code for the Non-uniformed Officers in the Public Service, which constitutes an interpretation directive of the Uganda Public Service Standing Orders, 2010, Sections F–J, which provide for dress code. The new directive introduced a new definition of "dressing decently", which means that women are not allowed to wear a skirt or dress that is above the knees; wear sleeveless, transparent blouses and dresses; show cleavage, navel, knees or back; have bright-coloured hair (natural hair, braids or hair extensions); have nails longer than 3 cm (1.5 in.), or have bright or multi-coloured nail polish. And men must wear neat trousers, long-sleeved shirts, jacket and tie; not wear tight-fitting trousers; not have open shoes, except on health grounds/recommendation; have well-groomed, short hair.[67] The enactment of such a legal interpretation triggered a public debate on human and women's rights.

1.2.5 Bikini

A two-piece swimming suit, called the bikini, was released by two French designers, independently of each other: Jacques Heim in May 1946 and Louis Rénard in July of the same year. The bikini became the subject of heated moral discussion. In the beginning of the 20th century, it was culturally acknowledged

64 Hoskins, *Stitched Up . . .*, p. 157.

65 Hoskins, *Stitched Up . . .*, p. 157.

66 *Paris women finally allowed to wear trousers*, BBC News, 4 February 2013, www.bbc.com/news/world-europe-21329269 (accessed: 20.01.2023).

67 P. Atuhaire, *Mini-Skirts and Morals in Uganda*, BBC News, 9 July 2017, www.bbc.com/news/world-africa-40507843 (accessed: 20.07.2020); *Public Service Ministry Issues Strict Dress Code for Employees*, "BusinessFocus Reporter", 4 July 2017, https://businessfocus.co.ug/public-service-ministry-issues-strict-dress-code-for-employees/ (accessed: 20.01.2023).

that swimming suits should be modest. The 1907 case of Annette Keller, an Australian swimmer, paints a strong picture of the situation, as the sportswoman was arrested for wearing a fitted, sleeveless, one-piece bathing suit on the beach in Boston. It was later clarified that the beach apparel she was wearing was approved in both the UK and Australia but not in the US.[68]

The bikini is a good example of the cultural change that societies undergo. July 2020 saw the social media action *#MedBikini*, triggered by an online debate as to whether women employed in the health-care system should care about their image. In other words, the question was whether they should be allowed to post so-called unprofessional content, that is, pictures in lingerie, Halloween costumes or bikinis. The response was not long in coming. Huge numbers of women posted their bikini pictures to protest against sexual harassment.

1.2.6 High heels and suits. Apparel as stimuli

There is a great deal of scholarship for how colours, clothes styles or ways of dressing serve as a message in the cognitive process. It is argued that formal clothing can affect the external perception of a person as more competent, rational or professional. It also increases the social distance between parties.[69] Therefore, attire can be the determining element for a person's position, success or influence. High heels have also received a lot of scholarly attention as to why women choose them. Most of the studies proved that high heels increase feminine lumbar curvature, causing women to be perceived as more attractive.[70]

If we consider that, every day, we are presented with a bewildering number of choices and decisions, a careful observer might wonder which of them have the capacity to help steer us towards our objectives. It is legitimate to suggest that one's choice of apparel could indeed qualify. In the *Clothing and Fashion Encyclopedia* of 2009, it was noted that women's "conservative dress-for success" style in the 1980s was a sign of their intention to ascend the corporate ladder. As long ago as 1985, a study investigated the effect of job applicants' dress on interviewers' selections. The experiment's goal was to observe whether an applicant's choice of clothing could influence interviewers.[71] To this end, 77 human resource managers were asked for hiring recommendations based solely on the apparel of the persons applying for management

68 RMN's Blog, *The Law of Bathing Suits*, www.thermnagency.com/the-laws-of-bathing-suits/ (accessed: 31.01.2023); https://fotoblogia.pl/15660,medbikini-lekarki-pokazuja-sie-w-bikini-to-protest-przeciwko-seksizmowi (accessed: 31.01.2023), cf. Jankowska, Meghaichi, Pawełczyk, Illustrated . . . ,.

69 D. Kodzoman, *The Psychology of Clothing: Meaning of Colors, Body Image and Gender Expression in Fashion*, "Textile & Leather Review", 2019, vol. 2, no. 2, pp. 92–96.

70 Kodzoman, *The Psychology of Clothing* . . ., pp. 92–96.

71 S.M. Forsythe, M.F. Drake, Ch.E. Cox, *Influence of Applicant's Dress on Interviewer's Selection Decision*, "Journal of Applied Psychology", 1985, vol. 70, no. 2, p. 374.

positions. According to the concept, they viewed videotaped, muted interviews in order to make hiring choices based on one of four outfits:

- a light beige dress in a soft fabric, with a small round collar, gathered skirt, and long sleeves (least masculine outfit),
- a bright aqua suit with a short, belted jacket and a white blouse with a large, softly draped bow at the neck,
- a beige, tailored suit with a blazer jacket and a rust blouse with narrow bow at the neck,
- a dark navy, tailored suit and a white blouse with an angular collar (most masculine outfit).[72]

A framing assumption for the experiment was that there were no fixed business dress norms for female executives. This allowed application of an empirical approach to exposing the unwritten and unconscious reactions to apparel choices in a business setting. In articulating these reactions, the experiment provided insights that ultimately led to the emergence of new norms for female business apparel.

The research concluded that the most favourable outfit was the third one, moderately masculine. The study showed that it is better for a woman to risk wearing clothes that are too masculine than too feminine when applying for a management position. This proved that a person can dress up to improve their impression on others and thereby increase the chances of success.[73] It must be stressed that the research was performed in strictly laboratory simplified conditions, with an ideal assumption that every interview is the same, without considering any personal cues, like conversational manner, eye contact or merits.[74] There has been widespread agreement with Y. H. Kwon's assessment that "clothing improves people's self-perception of different occupational attributes, such as knowledge, intelligence, competency, efficiency responsibility, honesty, and reliability; by wearing appropriate clothes a person's sense of these traits is enhanced".[75] Tombs also noted that "fashion has an effect on internal feelings and self-concept of the wearer".[76]

72 Forsythe, Drake, Cox, *Influence of Applicant's Dress . . .*, p. 375.

73 Forsythe, Drake, Cox, *Influence of Applicant's Dress . . .*, pp. 377, 378.

74 Cf. S.M. Forsythe, M.F. Drake, Ch.E. Cox, *Dress as an Influence on the Perceptions of Management Characteristics in Women*, "Home Economics Research Journal", 1984, no. 13, pp. 112 and ff.; P.N. Hamid, *Style of Dress as a Perceptual Cue in Impression Formation*, "Perceptual and Motor Skills", 1968, no. 26, pp. 904 and ff.; H.I. Douty, *Influence of Clothing on Perceptions of People*, "Journal of Home Economics", 1963, no. 55, p. 197.

75 Y.H. Kwon, *The Influence of Appropriateness of Dress and Gender on the Self-Perception of Occupational Attributes*, "Clothing & Textiles Research Journal", 1994, vol. 12, no. 3, pp. 33–35; cf. B.S. Gillani, S.K.F. Haider, Z. Qazi, *The Relationship of Clothing with Self-Image: A Study of Working Women in Peshawar*, "PUTAJ Humanities & Social Sciences", 2015, vol. 22, no. 2, p. 174.

76 *A.G. Tombs, Do Our Feelings Leak Through the Clothes We Wear? [in:] Y. Ali, M. van. Dessel* (eds.), *Australian and New Zealand Marketing Academy Conference: Advancing Theory, Maintaining Relevance*, "Australian and New Zealand Academy Conference", Queensland University of Technology, 2006, vol. 1–8, pp. 4 and ff.

This study flagged dress code as worthy of scientific investigation, and its results were found to have stood the test of time 20 years later, proving to some extent that social norms around one's appearance are firm and well-established. Rigid rules of apparel prevail. Research undertaken in the 1990s observed that employers value 'fashionable conservatism'[77] or 'logical creativity' in their employees,[78] which is visible through attachment to a conservative look, rather than a penchant for aesthetic details.[79]

Item of note 1.3 Christian Dior black suit

Fredrik Eklund, a real-estate agent, known worldwide from the "Million Dollar Listing New York", confessed in his book that he bought his first *haute couture* suit only because he was put in an awkward situation by his client, Carson Kressley, who insisted he buy it. Both embarrassed and hoping for good business relations, he bought something that was far beyond his budget. He reminisced later:

> Spending [US]$2,100 on a suit was insane for me at the time. But over the next few years, I realized something. My expensive suit gave me superpowers. I've probably done more sales in that black armor than any other, and it is still hanging in my closet. Let's say the peer pressure from Carson was a divine intervention. . . . I've made millions of dollars wearing that suit.
>
> See F. Eklund, B. Littlefield, *The Secrets of Selling Anything to Anyone. The Sell*, New York 2015, p. 75.

There are also studies on uniforms that prove that they are associated with increased trust, competence, reliability, intelligence or helpfulness, not to mention status and authority.[80]

1.3 Identifying the self

1.3.1 System of signs. Symbolism. Communication

Societies are rich in social norms of behaviour and clothing, and social studies have done a great deal of work on the phenomenon of dressing. The

77 Cf. A.B. DeMello, C.S. Pagragan, *Development of Professional Excellence Puts Best Foot Forward*, "AORN Journal", 1998, no. 67, pp. 214–221.
78 L.A. Gibson, C. Balkwell, *Effects of Harmony Between Personal and Apparel Clothing on Perception of a Woman's Employment Potential*, "Clothing and Textiles Research Journal", 1990, vol. 8, no. 2, pp. 23–28.
79 K.J. Schmalz, *Marketing Yourself, Part 2: The Unwritten Dress Code: How to Dress for the Job Interview*, "Health Promotion Practice", 2000, vol. 1, no. 3, p. 229.
80 Kodzoman, *The Psychology of Clothing* . . ., p. 93.

socio-anthropological approach considers clothing to serve aboriginal people not only as body ornamentation but also as a means of seduction,[81] or as trophies and good luck charms. Since time immemorial, people have recited incantations and worn talismans, including bones, feathers, leather, tattoos, body painting and masks.[82] People believed in their magical spirits just as much as some still do. Even in modern times, when people buy *joaillerie*,[83] they often ask about the meaning of the gems and their alleged effect on the wearer. It seems like the things we wear have an idea or story behind them, hide a sweet mystery about their owners and can be the key to decode the meanings associated with them.[84]

The first to analyse fashion as a system of signs was Roland Barthes,[85] who wrote that

> clothing is one of these objects of communication, like food, gestures, behaviors, conversation, which I have always had a deep joy to question because, on the one hand, they have a daily existence and represent for me a possibility of knowing myself at the most immediate level because I invest myself in my own life, and because, on the other hand, they have an intellectual existence and offer themselves to a systematic analysis by formal means.[86]

Barthes sees clothing as a whole as a set of signs, rules and codes, which change over time. Altogether they convey a message, which can be decoded by other members of society.[87] This turns fashion into a means of communication. Barthes compared couturiers to poets. An inverted approach to fashion was represented by Hegel, who perceived garments as the linkage between the human body and spirit. Clothes, in his view, are an 'instrument to overcome shame' and let the spirit establish a relation with the external world. That is

81 R. Radford, '*Women's Bitterest Enemy': The Uses of the Psychology of Fashion*, "Journal of Design History", 1993, vol. 6, no. 2, p. 117.

82 Ziege, *Die Kunst der Unterscheidung*, p. 149; F. Anderson, *Exploring Visual Culture: Definitions, Concepts, Contexts*, Edinburgh University Press, 2005, p. 68. E. Wilson, *Adorned in Dreams: Fashion and Modernity*, Virago Press, 1985, p. 3.

83 In contrast to *bijuterie*, *joaillerie* is a set of jewellery made of gems.

84 See K. Kuruc, *Fashion as Communication: A Semiotic Analysis of Fashion on 'Sex and the City'*, "Semiotica", 2008, vol. 171, no. ¼, pp. 193 and ff.

85 R. Barthes, *Système de la Mode*, Éditions du Seuil, 1967, p. 24; Meinhold, *Fashion* . . ., pp. 14 and ff.

86 Barthes, *Système* . . ., p. 45:

> Le vêtement est l'un de ces objets de communication, comme la nourriture, les gestes, les comportements, la conversation, que j'ai toujours eu une joie profonde à interroger parce que, d'une part, ils possèdent une existence quotidienne et représentent pour moi une possibilité de connaissance de moi-même au niveau le plus immédiat car je m'y investis dans ma vie propre, et parce que, d'autre part, ils possèdent une existence intellectuelle et s'offrent à une analyse systématique par des moyens formels

cf. O. Burgelin, *Barthes et le vêtement*, "Communications", 1996, vol. 63, pp. 81 and ff.

87 Ziege, *Die Kunst* . . ., pp. 150–151.

the idea of the freedom of the expression of the spirit. In the body, Hegel sees only sentience, deprived of any meaning.[88] Nudity appears in Hegel's approach as spiritual beauty, the emanation of strengths and ingenuity in one. The way he perceives clothing is at odds with Barthes. Inspired by perfect human forms from Greek times, he criticised contemporary garments for not holding their shape and not following the human body. Hegelian perfect clothing was 'formless'.[89] Since that time, *fashion as a system* has been addressed by many scholars.[90]

1.3.2 Self, identity and well-being in the communication process of fashion etiquette

The psychology of fashion deems fashion to be the "vehicle for enhancing well-being"[91] but also a medium to manifest one's high status in society.[92] According to some studies, our clothes reveal who we are, our personality and our identity through non-verbal communication.[93] Elisabeth Wilson coined a term for that, 'unspeakable meaningfulness'.[94] Ingrid Loschek took the view that "clothing, as well as body painting and other designs of the body, makes 'the person' into a social addressor".[95] According to Carolyn Mair, people make judgements about others in a time span of under one second. However, these are often flawed, as the interpretation of the clothing (the message) is influenced not only by the wearer but also by the observer, as well as by the social and cultural context.[96] Tansy E. Hoskins observed that fashion aspires to a system of communication in which people express chosen meanings through their clothes.[97]

Valerie Steele, the director and chief curator of the Museum at the Fashion Institute of Technology in New York, advanced a definition of fashion that relates it to the individual, an angle we go on to discuss at greater length. Her description was "a cultural construction of the embodied identity".[98] From her

88 B. Terracciano, *The Contemporary Fashion System* [in:] G. Motta, A. Biagini (eds.), *Fashion Through History: Costumes, Symbols, Communication*, vol. I, Cambridge Scholars Publishing, 2017, p. 402.
89 R. Barthes, *The Language of Fashion*, Bloomsbury, 2013, p. 148.
90 Ch. Battisti, L. Dahlberg, *Focus: Law Fashion and Identities*, "Pólemos", 2016, vol. 10, no. 1, pp. 1 and ff.; P. Heritier, *Fashion as an Institutional System*, "Pólemos", 2016, vol. 10, no. 1, p. 26.
91 C. Mair, *The Psychology of Fashion*, Taylor & Francis, 2019, audiobook, Chap. 1.
92 Hoskins, *Stitched Up*, p. 151.
93 Cf. J.C. Lauer, R.H. Lauer, *The New Encyclopedia of Southern Culture: Volume 4: Myth, Manners, and Memory*, University of North Carolina Press, 2006, p. 61.
94 Anderson, *Exploring* . . ., p. 68; Wilson, *Adorned* . . ., p. 3.
95 I. Loschek, *When Clothes* . . ., p. 26.
96 Mair, *The Psychology* . . ., Chap. 1.
97 Hoskins, *Stitched Up* . . ., p. 150, cf; Harms, *The Psychology* . . ., p. 246.
98 Mair, *The Psychology* . . ., Chap. 1.

perspective, fashion attracts attention because of its intimate relation with the physical body and, therefore, with the identity of the wearer.

This all allows us to reiterate after Hoskins that "dress can influence the ability to gain employment, rent a flat, avoid assault or arrest, be found 'not guilty', get a visa, appear in the media, win elections, get on planes, make friends or marry the person you love".[99]

1.4 Emotion is the name of the game

1.4.1 Emotional identity

If we were capable of returning to the mediaeval age, or even further back still, the social behaviours, attitudes and values would, as they still do today, confirm that

> fashion as communication is a cultural phenomenon: the garments that we wear are not us but they are things we use to represent or stand for ourselves. A garment, then, is something that stands for, or represents, something else – oneself, the self, one's emotions, identity and so on.[100]

So much so, that the boost in one's status and mood and one's sheer delight in consuming fashion products serve as a daily motivator for many in their daily toil; they drive us to scale the career ladder, and observed at the level of an entire society, this triggered effort is an actual driver of economic improvement.

At the time when this author was just commencing work on this book, *TIME*'s list of *100 Women of the Year* was announced, labelling Coco Chanel the most influential woman of 1924.[101] Chanel is the one reputed to have said: "dress like you are going to meet your worst enemy today" and "then, you never know, maybe that's the day [you have] a date with destiny. And it's best to be as pretty as possible for destiny".[102] It is an undisputed psychological fact that apparel takes on social meaning in relation to its wearer and displays our image to the world. It is the "first social interface" and "a social tool that interfaces our bodies with society".[103] Apparel tells its owner's story: status, occupation, mood, preferences and beliefs. All these features can be gauged

99 Hoskins, *Stitched Up . . .*, p. 151.

100 M. Barnard, *Fashion Theory: An Introduction*, Routledge, 2014.

101 *TIME*, in its tribute to great women and their achievements, created 100 covers and selected 100 women, awarding each the title "woman of the year" for each year from 1920 to 2020. Each was given a label describing her outstanding achievement. Coco Chanel was captured with the line "Refashioning style". Cf. https://time.com/5792683/coco-chanel-100-women-of-the-year/, https://mymodernmet.com/time-100-women-of-the-year/, accessed: 2.01.2023.

102 Cf. www.news18.com/news/indiwo/work-and-career-coco-chanel-quotes-that-make-you-two-things-classy-and-fabulous-1609633.html, accessed: 2.01.2023.

103 Kodzoman, *The Psychology of Clothing . . .*, p. 91.

from a multitude of perspectives: social, psychological, legal, commercial and historical. Indeed, in previous eras, the close relationship between dress and the social status of a woman was very evident.[104] It is said that our appearance creates our "social identity".[105] But fashion also builds our 'emotional identity'.

1.4.2 Designer-2-Consumer. Emotion is the bridge

What should be noted at the very beginning of our research is the role of emotions and their under-appreciated juridico-social significance. There are some accounts in the psychology literature showing that it is not the quality of a design itself or of its finished product that catch people's attention and make it a desirable commodity, but rather, the way the components are processed and perceived together.[106] A great deal has been discovered by identifying intimate relations between the consumer and the product.[107] One of the ways of generating a surge of emotions on the part of the consumer was through fashion journals, which became popular as early as in the 18th century.[108]

That the designer pours *emotions* and life experience into a product plays a major part in creating a linkage between the author and consumers – the so-called bridge.[109] The emotional approach to clothes is expressed in fabrics, patterns, colours, shapes and the manner of presentation (including movement and sound). As noted by Masae Nakanishi and Masako Niwa, the right fabric and wearing comfort alone make clothing look beautiful. From their perspective,

> this includes the color, pattern and texture of a fabric surface, the fitness of a garment to the wearer's body shape, tailoring technique, and the

104 M.J. Horn, *The Second Skin: An Interdisciplinary Study of Clothing*, Houghton Mifflin, 1968, p. 134.

105 S.E. Asch, *Forming Impressions of Personality*, "The Journal of Abnormal and Social Psychology", 1946, vol. 41, no. 3, pp. 258 and ff.

106 Cf. Z.O. Ertekin, B.S. Oflac, C. Serbetcioglu, *Fashion Consumption During Economic Crisis: Emerging Practices and Feelings of Consumers*, "Journal of Global Fashion Marketing", 2020, vol. 11, no. 3, pp. 270–288.

107 Cf. Kuruc, *Fashion . . .*, p. 199.

108 U. Lehmann, *Fashion and Materialism*, Edinburgh University Press, 2018, p. 75; cf. Erlhoff, Marshall, *Design Dictionary . . .*, p. 162. The two first reported fashion journals were "Mercure" (1692) and "Journal des Luxus und der Modern" (1786).

109 R. Sinclair, *Textile and Fashion Materials, Design and Technology*, Woodhead Publishing, 2015; N. Kongprasert, *Emotional Design Approach to Design Teak Wood Furniture* [in:] V. Kachitvichyanukul, H.T. Luong, R. Pitakaso (eds.), *Proceedings of the Asia Pacific Industrial Engineering & Management Systems Conference*, 2012, pp. 806 and ff. Some of the research addresses the manufacturing parameters such as quality, time, cost and environmental impact, which may help designers meet customers' expectations. Cf. N. Kongprasert, D. Brissaud, C. Bouchard, A. Aoussat, S. Butdee, *Contribution to the Mapping of Customer's Requirements and Process Parameters*, "Kansei Engineering and Emotion Research International Conference", 2010, Paris, France, pp. 2426. ffhal-00478678f.

> beautifully-styled silhouette. In addition, especially for ladies' clothing, the dynamic silhouette of a garment or fabric's swaying, caused by the wearer's motion or the wind, also affects the beauty of the appearance of the clothing.[110]

They examined the relationship between the beauty of a dress and the manner of its movement using a mannequin simulating walking and a test set of 25 different kinds of fabric.[111] The research also considers the link between the beauty of skirts in motion and fabric properties such as shear and bending.[112] On that same topic, there was a study undertaken at the Gazi University in Ankara by Pınar Göklüberk Özlü and Serap Dengin Sevinir to examine consumers' aesthetic and emotional response to different fabrics used to produce the same design of a garment.[113] It was a half-circle skirt cut the same way and presented in the same navy-blue colour, but made of four different fabrics: artificial leather, chiffon, denim and combed cotton.

The study was twofold, designed to establish the general response to the fabrics and the relationship between the fabric and the design. To that end, it measured the following consumer reactions: 1) aesthetic effects of the fabric, 2) aesthetic effect of the relationship between the fabric and the design, 3) emotion statement associated with the fabric and the relationship between the fabric and the design, and 4) themes associated with the reason for which it is liked or not. The bottom line was that artificial leather scored highest (score interval of 27–37) followed by chiffon (24–31) and denim (16–32).

110 M. Nakanishi, M. Niwa, *Fabric Mechanical Parameters Related to the Beauty of Fabric Movement of Ladies' Garments Brought about by Human Motion*, "Journal of Home Economics of Japan", 2001, vol. 52, no. 3, p. 251.

111 Nakanishi, Niwa, *Fabric . . .*, p. 251.

112 M. Matsudaira, *Vibrational Property of Filament Woven Fabrics Based on Shear Deformation. Part 3: Relationship between Shear and Bending Vibrational Properties of Fabrics and Beautiful Appearance of Skirt in Dynamic State*, "Journal of the Textile Machinery Society of Japan", 1993, vol. 39, no. 2, p. 33; J. Hu, *Structure and Mechanics of Woven Fabrics*, Woodhead Publishing Ltd and CRC Press LLC, 2004, p. 190. As noted by J.E. Berkowitch, convergent needs, interests, and technical advances are coalescing into a new discipline aimed at improving human well-being by optimizing physiological and psychological environments. One aspect of this all-encompassing objective is the design of products – including textiles – with an eye on observable physiological responses to the stimuli they engender. . . . The three-step approach being followed seeks to (1) develop techniques that permit the quantitative characterization of physiological responses (e.g., brain signals, electromyographs, hormone releases, and so on); (2) generate statistically significant correlations between such measurements and stimuli magnitudes; and (3) design products that trigger improved consumer responses. Correlations are emerging between preferred sensory perceptions (tactile, visual, auditory), brain-wave patterns, and stimulus dimensions.

Cf. J.E. Berkowitch, *Trends in Japanese Textile Technology*, Office of Technology Policy, 1996, p. 75.

113 P. Göklüberk Özlü, S: Dengin Sevinir, *Aesthetical and Emotional Effects of Material on Clothing Design*, "The Turkish Online Journal of Design, Art and Communication", 2019, vol. 9, no. 1, p. 43.

In summary, there is general consensus that a product's market success will be a function of its aesthetic appeal, the pleasure it generates, and the customer satisfaction it yields.[114] A number of studies show undeniably that a fashion design is a complex and demanding body of work for its creator, based, as it is, very much on the personal preferences of the client, which are in turn based more on the garment's appearance than on its utilitarian function (though in theory the latter is of greater importance), and on the overall aesthetic impact it makes.[115] This is also the reason for observing customer behaviour and for following the trends set for a season. In this way, the fashion designer encounters many unexpressed limits when feeding their creative core. This is not the place to dwell on the social and psychological aspects of consumers' choices, which also should not be overgeneralised, but it is important to observe that one of the strongest stimuli for a purchase is the symbolic meaning of the product, along with its function and emotional value. As noted by Hüsne Demirel, "power, prestige, approval and acceptance, which the purchased product will bring symbolically, are among the important factors".[116] There is also a study showing that consumers' loyalty towards a brand/fashion designer is moderate and amounts to 30% of respondents. At the same time, 62% declared openness towards novelty and new brands. Traditional types of consumers admitted to making fashion choices in line with their own personality (32%). Furthermore, 25% showed interest in fashion trends in general (but without adopting these in their own clothing), 18% showed interest in adopting new trends and 36% expressed the desire to try new fashion styles.[117]

1.4.3 Levels of consumers' emotional interaction with design

It is claimed that people consume life 80% through emotions and 20% through intellect.[118] In other words, the interaction between a product and the consumer can be reduced to an 'emotional situation'.

114 H.M. Khalid, M.G. Helander, *Customer Emotional Needs in Product Design*, "Concurrent Engineering: Research and Applications", 2006, vol. 14, no. 3, pp. 197–206; M. Bruce, L. Daly, *Buyer Behaviour for Fast Fashion Journal of Fashion*, "Marketing and Management", 2006, vol. 10, no. 3, p. 329.

115 N.A. Neacsu, C.A. Băltescu, S. Bălăsescu, D. Boscor, *The Influence of Design and Aesthetics Elements in Choosing Clothing*, "Industria Textila", 2017, vol. 68, no. 5, p. 375 [spelling special signs].

116 H. Demirel, *The Influence of Personality Traits and Psychological Characteristics of Individuals on Their Clothing Purchase Behaviors*, "Journal of Textile & Apparel/ Tekstil ve Konfeksiyon", 2013, vol. 23, no. 1, pp. 67 and ff.

117 Surprising at the same time is that only 30% of respondents find their appearance important. See D.T. Dragonici, *The Degree of Interest for Consumers Regarding Fashion*, "Review of Management & Economic Engineering", 2015, vol. 14, no. 1, pp. 117–118.

118 C. Wrigley, *Design Dialogue: The Visceral Hedonic Rhetoric Framework*, "Design Issues", 2013, vol. 29, no. 2, p. 82.

Julie Khaslavsky and Nathan Shedroff argue that

> the seductive power of the design of certain material and virtual objects can transcend issues of price and performance for buyers and users alike. To many an engineer's dismay, the appearance of a product, or the way it feels physically, can sometimes make or break the product's market reaction . . .. Audrey Hepburn's black dress in the movie *Breakfast at Tiffany's* [is an example] of seductive experiences going beyond beauty and efficiency.[119]

These authors' findings, that the audience craves an *'emotional bond'* with products or designers, are *intuitive* rather than *groundbreaking*. They provide a list of elements that add up to the *'seductive quality'* which establishes the bond. Based on an example from those authors taken from the realm of design, this author undertook the challenge of applying the same criteria in an assessment of a piece of fashion (a Louis Vuitton bag).

Item of note 1.4 Emotional experience with a physical product. J. Khaslavsky, N. Shedroff test – transposition to fashion, own approach[120]

Seductive Quality	*Philippe Starck's Juicer*[121]	*LV Crafty Collection Bag, Neo-expressionist Twist*[122]
Entice by diverting attention	It is unlike every other kitchen product by virtue of the nature of its shape, form and materials.	There are many iconic LV bags. However, their forms and shapes are a cliché. This design is a clean break from the other LV model.
Deliver surprising novelty	It is not immediately identifiable as a juicer, and its form is unusual enough to be intriguing, even surprising when its purpose first becomes clear.	The printed pattern introduces expressionist elements, and the enlarged LV logo commands the attention of the viewer.

(*Continued*)

119 J. Khaslavsky, N. Shedroff, *Understanding the Seductive Experience*, "Communications of the ACM", 1999, vol. 42, no. 5, p. 45.

120 Khaslavsky, Shedroff, *Understanding* . . ., pp. 47–48.

121 www.metmuseum.org/art/collection/search/491871 (accessed: 23.01.2023).

122 https://us.louisvuitton.com/eng-us/magazine/articles/lvcrafty-collection# (accessed: 23.01.2023).

Item of note 1.4 (Continued)

Seductive Quality	*Philippe Starck's Juicer*[121]	*LV Crafty Collection Bag, Neo-expressionist Twist*[122]
Go beyond obvious needs and expectations	To satisfy these criteria – of being surprising and novel – it need only be bright orange or all wood. It goes so far beyond what is expected or required, it becomes something else entirely.	The back employs the colours black, beige and white, which, surprisingly, match any kind of clothing.
Create an instinctive response	At first, the shape creates curiosity, then emotional responses confusion and, perhaps, fear, since it is so sharp and dangerous looking.	Neo-expressionist elements create curiosity and confusion about one's knowledge of art.
Espouse values or connections to personal goals	It transforms the routine act of juicing an orange into a special experience. Its innovative approach, simplicity, and elegance in shape and performance create an appreciation and desire to possess not only the object but the values that helped create it, including innovation, originality, elegance and sophistication. It speaks as much about the person who owns it as it does about its designer.	Wearing this LV bag amounts to a new experience. The bag is simple but very feminine and makes an impression that the wearer has an interest in art.
Promise to fulfil these goals	It promises to make an ordinary action extraordinary. It also promises to raise the status of the owner to a higher level of sophistication for recognising its qualities.	With the extraordinarily large LV logo, it promises to raise the owner's status.
Lead the casual viewer to discover something deeper about the experience	While the juicer does not necessarily teach the user anything new about juice or juicing, it does teach a lesson that even ordinary things in life can be interesting and that design can enhance living. It also teaches the user to expect wonder where it is unexpected – all positive feelings about the future.	The bag has an artistic twist that imparts positive feelings to the viewer.

Fulfil these promises	Every time it is used, it reminds the user of its elegance and approach to design. It fulfils these promises through its performance, reconjuring the emotions originally connected with the product. It also serves as a point of surprise and conversation by the associates of its owner—and is another chance to espouse its values and have them validated.	It allows the wearer to show their special relationship with art. It also serves as a source of surprise and as a talking point.

I believe that these features establishing the "seductive quality" of a product can be easily linked with both legal expertise and the legal perspective on copyrightability of fashion design. Despite the fact that legal analysis is ruled by its own concepts and premises, it is fair to say that law cannot exist in a vacuum. A deeper insight into the categories of 'work of authorship' proves that different categories may be assessed differently as to the modicum of creativity needed to assure copyright protection. Having established agreement that fashion is a phenomenon that combines social, cultural, psychological and anthropological features, it is hard to assess it from the copyright perspective in a clear-cut way. Imitation, which in other areas of life would be tainted with negative characteristics, gains a new connotation and an ambiguous meaning in fashion. Given that society follows fashion trends, which is a natural state of affairs, it is not easy to draw a line between *copycatting*, *borrowing*, *reproducing* and *following the trend*. How much originality is sufficient to render a fashion design appropriate for copyright protection, and by contrast, what does it mean to simply render a style? A *problem is that the doctrinal copyright questions regarding the distinction between a manner of expression and an idea* do not fit the process of creating fashion (cf. Chapter 5). The previously discussed test for "emotional experience" seems relevant and helpful for copyright discussions. Obviously, *haute couture* or 'artisan fashion' (also referred to as *petit couture*, 'small fashion studio' or 'small fashion atelier') do not pose as many problems as everyday (including *prêt-à-porter*) fashion does. As Chapter 4's copyright analysis proves, this understanding of originality for the purpose of fashion varies across national legal systems, and even a multitude of cases at a national level does not help to establish simple and clear-cut criteria.

Donald A. Norman boils down the *'emotional situation'* to three levels of consumer response:

- the visceral level: the look of the product is evaluated by sensory perception; it allows for quick assessment in terms of good/bad, attractive/unattractive;
- the behavioural level: sensory data are interpreted to make judgements about the product's usability, its functions and the pleasure provided by it;
- the reflective level: the consumer estimates how the products makes them feel; it is about the consumer's identity, image and the message conveyed.[123]

The three-level system approach is neither novel nor unique. There are a variety of accounts that correspond to Norman's view of the emotional situation.[124]

Item of note 1.5 Emotional situation: the three-level system approach

Author	*Level 1*	*Level 2*	*Level 3*
Donald A. Norman	Visceral level	Behavioural level	Reflective level
Zdzislaw Lewaski	X-values	Y-values	Z-values
Ray Crozier	Response to form	Response to function	Response to meaning
Mike Baxter	Intrinsic attractiveness	Semantic attractiveness	Symbolic attractiveness
Gerry Cupchic	Sensory/ aesthetic response	Cognitive/ behavioural response	Personal/symbolic response

Obviously, the functionality and utilitarian character of a work cannot sustain a claim to copyright, but rather the aesthetic or creative elements. *Sensory perception and emotion are triggered by good design (or good fashion design), and that is what makes a design copyrightable.* Despite how hard to measure this may seem, the concept of originality itself does not prove to be any easier.

1.5 Functions of fashion design. Approaches to interest in clothing

1.5.1 Philosophical account. Roland Barthes' approach

The previously discussed research appears to be in line with the findings of Roland Barthes, who defined fashion as a complex system of meanings and

123 D.A. Norman, *Emotional Design: Why We Love (or Hate) Everyday Things*, Basic Books, 2004, pp. 125–162; Wrigley, *Design Dialogue* . . . , pp. 85–86.

124 Wrigley, *Design Dialogue* . . . , p. 85.

who claimed that, behind clothes, there is a visual part which can be "read" like text.[125] According to his premise, a garment can be perceived and discussed from three significant perspectives:

- technological – given the creation of a product, from concept to tangible item;
- spatial – regarding its shapes, lines, surfaces and colours;
- verbal – relating to the visual message of the garment, as it delivers an experience in a certain context.

Barthes' concept assumes that a fashion design, as a product, is special and very different from other creative products, as the consumer is more strongly invested in it. It reveals some cues of the person, the wearer, their status in society, their lifestyle and personality.

1.5.2 Socio-psychological account. K. Young's and Edmund Bergler's approaches

There are many social and psychological approaches to fashion and its role in society. They have been addressed at length earlier in this chapter. Here, I mention just a few. The first two date back to the 1950s and are referenced just for the sake of curiosity. Kimball Young made an appealing comment that "men's clothing, made to be uniform, does not readily indicate one's financial standing, this role falls to women's clothing due to the Fashion through which a man expressed his economic status".[126] It seems to derive from Veblen's theory that the upper class displays its status through products symbolising wealth and that the most visual of this evidence is one's apparel.[127] Edmund Bergler expressed a somewhat disputable view that the primary function of fashion was *seduction*, the surge in anxiety filled with fear, modesty and transgression.[128] From his standpoint, fashion is irrational and ridiculous as its main purpose is the stimulation of male libido. Women, on the other hand, have no choice but to surrender and submit to fashion in a constant effort to meet its demands. The hypothetical pleasure of buying is presented as a tyranny, a terror and an addiction to ever-more-extravagant clothes of bad taste, serving only to provoke their husbands to anger. To quit the quest for the latest fashion seems not to be an option, as women deviating from prevailing tastes in dress and personal appearances are deemed to be revealing psychological problems.[129] There are a few more voices that incline to the view that fashion is detrimental: Ray L. Gold defined fashion "as irrational and transitory items or patterns of behaviour" and L. L. Bernard believed it to be "the same order of instability and irrationality as fads".[130]

125 R. Barthes, *The Fashion System*, University of California Press, Berkeley, 1990, p. 8; Neacsu, Băltescu, Bălăsescu, Boscor, *The Influence of Design* . . ., p. 375.
126 K. Young, *Handbook of Social Psychology*, Routledge & Kegan Paul, 1951, p. 420.
127 Sproles, *Analyzing Fashion* . . ., p. 119.
128 Radford, *Women's* . . ., p. 117.
129 Radford, *Women's* . . ., pp. 117, 119.
130 Radford, *Women's* . . ., p. 120 and the literature cited.

A more scholarly approach is represented by Gilles Lipovetsky, who inclines to the view that fashion merges *three aspects of human nature*: the *desire for the new*, the application of *aesthetic judgement* and *seduction*.[131]

1.5.3 Social account. James Laver's account

A fashion product, according to James Laver, should be designed to meet three criteria,[132] which are labelled 'functions':

- utility – pragmatic aspect of a garment; a cursory examination of the literature reveals that this is of least importance;
- hierarchy – status obtained and demonstrated in society;
- seduction – garment allows a person to evoke social attraction.

Under this concept, that dates from the 1950s, a successful creator should address all three aspects in his design. At that time, women's interest in clothing was subject to extended research especially in masters' and doctoral dissertations in the US, by, to mention just a few, Lewis R. Aiken Jr. (1963), Anna M. Creekmore (1963, 1966 and 1971), Betty Brady (1963), Kay S. Griesman (1965), L. C. Taylor and N. H. Compton (1968) and Lois M. Gurel (1974) each of whom built on the conclusions and methodologies of each other in connection with consumers' apparel-related stimuli.[133] The following are eight factors influencing women's fashion preferences, that were determined over time by A.M. Creekmore and five of her students: 1) personal appearance, 2) experimentation with clothing, 3) conformity, 4) modesty, 5) psychological awareness, 6) self-concept, 7) fashion interest

131 G. Lipovetsky, *L'Empire de l'éphémère: la mode et son destin dans les sociétés modernes*, Gallimard Paris, 1987.

132 J. Laver, *Pleasure of Life. vol. 5, Clothes*, Horizon Press, 1952, p. 23; cf. Neacsu, Băltescu, Bălăsescu, Boscor, *The Influence of Design . . .*, p. 375.

133 L.R. Aiken, *The Relationship of Dress to Selected Measures of Personality in Undergraduate Women*, "Journal of Social Psychology", 1963, vol. 59, pp. 119–128; A.M. Creekmore, *Methods of Measuring Clothing's Variables*, Michigan Agricultural Experiment Station Project, 1971, pp. 96–97; B.L. Brady, *Clothing Behavior: Refinement of a Measure and Relationships with Social Security and Insecurity for a Group of College Women*, master's thesis, the Pennsylvania State University, 1963; K.S. Griesman, *Clothing Behavior Related to Attitudes Toward Certain Clothing Standards, Clothing Interest, Orthodoxy, and Conformity*, master's thesis, the Oregon State University, Corvallis, 1965; L.C. Taylor, N.H. Compton, *Personality Correlates of Dress Conformity*, "Journal of Home Economics", 1968, vol. 60, pp. 653 and ff. L.M. Gurel, *Dimensions of Clothing Interest Based on Factor Analysis of Creekmore's 1968 Clothing Measure*, doctoral dissertation, the University of North Carolina, Greensboro, 1974; Cf. E.S. Toerien, *Dimensions of Clothing Interest: A Cross-Cultural Study*, thesis submitted to the Faculty of the Virginia Polytechnic Institute and State University, Virginia, 1987, pp. 6 and. ff., available at: https://vtechworks.lib.vt.edu/bitstream/handle/10919/80058/LD5655.V855_1987.T637.pdf?sequence=1 (accessed: 2.01.2023).

and 8) comfort.[134] Gurel arrived at the definition of 'clothing interest' which she perceived as

> the attitudes and beliefs about clothing, the knowledge of and attention paid to clothing, the concern and curiosity a person has about his own clothing and that of others. This interest may be manifested by an individual's practices in regard to clothing himself – the amount of time, energy, and money he is willing to spend on clothing; the degree to which he uses clothing in an experimental manner; and his awareness of fashion and what is new.[135]

At the same time, the research proved that men's interest in clothing is much more limited, though it was not always so. Prior to the nineteenth century, upper-class men were much more fashion oriented.[136] Capitalism and industrialism made them pivot towards uniformity and conservatism in dress code. Also, work took the place of pleasure and of the time-consuming interest in fashion.[137] A study on that topic proved that the factors exerting major influence on that shift were 1) a cultural pattern for masculinity, 2) the pattern of work and 3) pressure towards conformity.[138] Here we should note the survey conducted in 1958 by Lundeen, who wanted to identify the stimuli behind men's choice of wear. It comes as a surprise that only 12% of men had specific knowledge of and high interest in fashion. This group also confessed to relishing better outfits and shared the belief that good-quality apparel was always worth the investment. Then, an overwhelming 70% of respondents expressed some interest in clothing but without feeling anxious about their apparel or the status it might symbolise. The remaining 18% of men confessed to having nothing but a pragmatic interest in clothing. Finally, the literature review shows that these framing findings can only serve as a starting point for detailed research delving deeply into consumers' interest in fashion, as the results will vary from country to country and from culture to culture. In the literature, we see a number of works addressing these cross-cultural aspects.[139] It is worth

134 Creekmore, *Methods . . .*, pp. 96–97.

135 Gurel, *Dimensions . . .*, p. 36; cf. Toerien, *Dimensions . . .*, pp. 7–8.

136 L. Langner, *The Importance of Wearing Clothes*, Hastings House, 1959, p. 185; cf. Paeth, *Body Awareness . . .*, p. 31.

137 C. Kidwell, M.C. Christman, *Suiting Everyone: The Democratization of Clothing in America*, Smithsonian Institution Press, 1974, p. 37; cf. Paeth, *Body Awareness . . .*, p. 32.

138 G. Millstein, *Man of Mouse or Butterfly*, "New York Times Magazine", 2 April 1950, pp. 17 and 63; cf. Paeth, *Body Awareness . . .*, p. 32.

139 D.J. Tigert, C.W. King, L. Ring, *Fashion Involvement: A Cross-Cultural Comparative Analysis*, "Advances in Consumer Research", 1980, pp. 17 and ff (the survey considered the cultures of English Canadian, French Canadian, United States and Netherlands); H.L. Schrank, A.I. Sugawara, M. Kim, *Fashion Leadership: A Two-Culture Study. Part 2: Comparison of Korean and American Fashion Leaders*, "Home Economics Research Journal", 1982, pp. 235 and ff. (the author examined American and Korean women); M. Lee, L.D. Burns, *Self Consciousness*

mentioning that, in this day and age, we witness a kind of fashion politics, in which major fashion and design entrepreneurs issue different lines for, e.g. US and European consumers, accepting the fact that their respective consumption expectations and desires vary.

1.5.4 Legal account. We are what we wear? Miss Pearl Pugsley

It may come as a surprise, but the function of fashion was also a subject of juridical research. A US court made a great many observations from an examination of the role of clothes when deciding on primary First Amendment rights akin to 'pure speech', but in public school settings (*Diana Canady v. Bossier Parish School Board*, 2001 January 23).[140] The US Court of Appeals had to establish whether one's choice of apparel may convey sufficient communicative content to elicit First Amendment shelter. It assessed that

> [a] person's choice of clothing is infused with intentional expression on many levels. In some instances, clothing functions as pure speech. A student may choose to wear shirts or jackets with written messages supporting political candidates or important social issues. Words printed on clothing qualify as pure speech and are protected under the First Amendment.[141]

The court made an observation that clothes may serve as a symbol of one's ethnic heritage, religious beliefs or political or social standing. Clothes not

and Clothing Purchase Criteria of Korean and United States College Women, "Clothing and Textiles Research Journal", 1993; K. Kwon, *Korean and U.S. College Women's Fashion Information Seeking*, a thesis submitted to the Oregon State University, 1993–1994, available at: ir.library.oregonstate.edu › downloads (accessed: 22.01.2023); H. Park, *Global Advertising of Apparel Products: U.S. vs. Korean Consumer* Response, Iowa State University Digital Repository, 1996, available at: https://core.ac.uk/download/pdf/38931231.pdf (accessed: 22.01.2023); L.F.C. Hao, *A Cross-Cultural Study: The Relationship between Clothing Behaviors and General Values*, thesis at the University of Tennessee, 1971 (the author compared behaviours of Chinese and American women), C.C.C. MacKay, *Clothing Behavior in Relation to Selected Cultural Differences: A Cross-Cultural Study*, master's thesis, The Pennsylvania State University, 1967 (compared Puerto Rican and American students), A.R. Mendoza, *Clothing Values and Their Relation to General Values: A Cross-Cultural Study*, doctoral dissertation, The Pennsylvania State University, 1965, (compared Philippine and American female students). See Cf. Toerien, *Dimensions of Clothing* . . . , pp. 16–21. Cf. Y. Wang, *A Cross-Cultural Study of Consumer Attitudes and Emotional Responses of Apparel Purchase Behavior*, Florida State University, 2007.

140 *Diana Canady v. Bossier Parish School Board*, 23 January 2001, US Court of Appeals, 5th Cir., No. 99–31318.

141 See *Cohen v. California*, 403 U.S. 15, 18, 91 S.Ct. 1780, 29 L.Ed.2d 284 (1971); *Board of Airport Comm'rs of the City of Los Angeles v. Jews for Jesus, Inc.*, 482 U.S. 569, 575, 107 S.Ct. 2568, 96 L.Ed.2d 500 (1987).

only let people exude confidence when loudly conveying their ideas and opinions, they can also silently express a message. With regard to the latter, there is a flag judgement of the US Supreme Court as of 1969 February 24, deciding in the case *Tinker v. Des Moines Independent Community School District et al.*[142] The court noted that students were legitimately wearing black armbands two inches wide at school in protest against the Vietnam War.[143] In the case of *Canady*, the court went on to say that

> students in particular often choose their attire with the intent to signify the social group to which they belong, their participation in different activities, and their general attitudes toward society and the school environment. While the message students intend to communicate about their identity and interests may be of little value to some adults, it has a considerable effect, whether positive or negative, on a young person's social development. Although this sort of expression may not convey a particularized message to warrant First Amendment protection in every instance, we cannot declare that expression of one's identity and affiliation to unique social groups through choice of clothing will never amount to protected speech.

A number of arguments that underlie the pursuit of liberty by students to wear their choice of clothing to school are connected to the Fourteenth Amendment of the US Constitution. It is widely contended and strongly believed that a reasonably considered school dress code serves to maintain school discipline and has a positive effect on student's health and on the decorum of the institution.[144] However, in order to meet that aim, the code must have sufficient balance and limitations. Surprisingly enough, a rule banning powder on students' cheeks was apparently intended to ensure this same discipline and decorum. The use of face powder at school made legal news in the 1920s, while also becoming the subject of lively attention in the newspapers, including *The New York Times*.[145]

142 393 U.S. 503, 89 S. Ct. 733, 21 L. Ed. 2d 731, 1969 U.S. LEXIS 2443.

143 The decision was taken on the grounds that they wore it to exhibit their disapproval of the Vietnam hostilities and their advocacy of a truce, to make their views known, and, by their example, to influence others to adopt them. They neither interrupted school activities nor sought to intrude in the school affairs or the lives of others. They caused discussion outside of the classrooms, but no interference with work and no disorder. In the circumstances, our Constitution does not permit officials of the State to deny their form of expression. *Supra*.

144 *Farrell v. Dallas Independent School District at al.*, 392 F.2d 697 (5th Cir. 1968).

145 *Defies School Board Anti-Cosmetic Rule; Arkansas Girl Brings Suit to Test Her Right to Powder Her Nose*, "The New York Times", 18 December 1921; Pearl Pugsley, *"Joan of Arc" of the Lipstick War*, 23 May 2016, available at: www.oldstatehouse.com/collectionsblog/pearl-pugsley-joan-of-arc-of-the-lipstick-war (accessed: 09.01.2023).

Item of note 1.6 A tale about how Miss Pearl Pugsley became 'Joan of Arc of the Lipstick War', testing her right to powder her nose[146]

The case was decided in September 1921, the Knobel School Board had passed the rule: *The wearing of transparent hosiery, low-necked dresses and any style of clothing tending to immodesty in dress, or the use of face powder or cosmetics, is prohibited.* An American 17-year-old student, named Pearl Pugsley, was expelled from school for refusing to remove powder from her face. She brought the case before the court but lost in two instances, the second by a 2:1 vote. She earned a vote from Jesse C. Hart, Arkansas Supreme Court justice, who dissented and said that

> I think that a rule forbidding a girl pupil of her age from putting talcum powder on her face is so far unreasonable and beyond the exercise of discretion . . .. "Useless laws diminish the authority of necessary ones." The tone of the majority opinion exemplifies the wisdom of this old proverb.

She lost in court, but "earned admiration of people across the country. Her battle also led school officials to rescind the lipstick ban"

D.L. Hudson, Let the Students Speak!: A History of the Fight for Free Expression in American Schools, Beacon Press, Boston 2011, p. 13–14.

At that time, the story was sensational, and journalists compared her to the patron of France, Joan of Arc. Pearl Pugsley of Knobel, Arkansas, not only became known as 'Pretty Pearl' but received thousands of letters from all over the US and even a US$1,000 a week contract offer from a motion picture company.

In terms of freedom of speech, the US courts recognise two types of speech: pure and symbolic. In defining symbolic speech, a two-step helps determine whether 1) there was an intent to convey a particular message, and 2) there is a great likelihood that the message would be understood by those who viewed it. As observed by Harold W. Mitchell and John C. Knechtle:

> [the] individual selection of dress satisfies both prongs of the test; therefore, it constitutes symbolic speech. Studies show that dress is conduct

146 *Pugsley v. Sellmeyer*, 158 Ark. 247, decided 1923 April 9.

> where it conveys messages about the self and suggests countless qualities about identity, attitudes, values, and moods . . .. Studies also indicate that individuals' dress communicates nonverbally to others and that this can affect the way others view individuals, and quite possibly, the way that individuals view themselves.[147]

A number of legal cases have established that personal appearance, in addition to being a social and cultural phenomenon, can also fall subject to legal discussion. There is a record of cases of employers that wanted to establish their *reputation* or *corporate image* through a dress code.[148] The apparel restrictions, however, were not always supported by the employees themselves, which became the subject of legal dispute as to the permissible to which a dress code be the subject of an employment contract. One of the remarkable cases concerned Austicks Bookshops that had a rule forbidding female bookstore staff from wearing trousers. In a workforce consisting of 20 women and only 2 men, Ms Schmidt refused to comply with the requirement and argued it was sex discrimination. The Employment Appeal Tribunal (further: EAT) deciding the case in 1978 dismissed the claim.[149] Later, in 1994, there was a case regarding female nurses who were obliged to wear a cap as part of their uniform despite the fact that men were not. EAT dismissed the claim based on sex discrimination and followed the same reasoning as in Schmidt. It found that as the rule to wear a uniform applied to both male and female nurses, the fact that the uniforms varied and that the applicant questioned one part of the uniform, was not tantamount to less favourable treatment under s. 1 (1)(a) of the Sex Discrimination Act 1975.[150] In the *Hutcheson* case, the plaintiff, a senior female employee, was obliged to wear a nylon overall, whereas the men's dress code was lounge suits. The plaintiff managed to prove that her outfit was uncomfortable and therefore discriminatory.[151] These cases are just the tip of an iceberg showing that so much importance is given to apparel that clothing can even land people in court.

147 H.W. Mitchell, J.C. Knechtle, *Uniforms in Public Schools and the First Amendment: A Constitutional Analysis*, "The Journal of Negro Education", 2003, vol. 72, no. 4, p. 489; cf. N. Reschler, *Metaphilosophy: Philosophy in Philosophical Perspective*, Lexington Books, 2014, p. 2018

148 Ian Smith, Aaron Baker, Owen Warnock, *Smith & Wood's Employment Law*, Oxford University Press, 2017, pp. 294–295. Robert Wintemute, *Recognising New Kinds of Direct Sex Discrimination: Transsexualism, Sexual Orientation and Dress Codes*, "The Modern Law Review", 1997, vol. 60, no. 3, pp. 334 and ff.

149 Schmidt v Austicks Bookshops Ltd [1978] ICR 85; cf. a case regarding man's ponytail in a workplace (grooming code), *Smith v. Safeway plc.*, [1996] ICR 868, [1996] IRLP 456, CA.

150 *Burrett v West Birmingham Health Authority* [1994] IRLR 7; cf. Olga Hay, Sam Middlemiss, *Fashion Victims, Dress to Conform to the Norm, or Else? Comparative Analysis of Legal Protection against Employers' Appearance Codes in the United Kingdom and the United States*, "International Journal of Discrimination and the Law", 2003, vol. p. 72.

151 *Hutcheson v Graham and Morton Ltd* case no S/626/83.

1.6 What is fashion?

1.6.1 A crop of definitions

In this chapter, we arrive at the heart of the matter, and we confront the question of what fashion is. Recent scholarship related to a definition of fashion proved it to be very elusive.[152]

It was observed in the literature that the concept of fashion goes back to the 17th century, when the French coined a term: *à la mode*. It meant modern, up to date or topical.[153] Roman Meinhold reiterated the points of Günter Wiswede, Hans Freyer and Roland Barthes, that fashion was "born as a child of industrialisation, commercialisation and the democratisation of consumption of luxury".[154] The research taken by this author, partly presented in Chapter 2, strongly endorses this observation. The industrial revolution triggered an invigoration that was seen in many aspects of life. A zealous drive for innovation (also in textiles), fledgling sweatshops and numerous patent applications are just some examples of the changes the revolution brought. It proved pivotal in popularising fashion and looks. As noted by Valerie Steele, notwithstanding the fact that France was the birthplace of fashion and that its lifeblood was industrial modernisation,[155] in 11th-century Japan, describing someone as *imamekashi*, translated as "up-to-date", was already considered a great compliment.[156] It appears from advanced historical studies that the premodern Eastern cultures of Japan, India and China were not ignorant of fashion. Reportedly, a Chinese scholar named Chen Yao used the term *shiyang*, meaning fashion, in the 1570s. The term referred to "the look of the moment".[157]

The French, German and Polish words (such as Fr. *la Mode*, Ger. *die Mode*, or Pol. *Moda*) derive from the Latin term *modus*, meaning "measure, extent, quantity proper measure, rhythm, song, a way, manner, fashion, style".[158] It is also used as a synonym for "ratio" in the sense of method or rationale.[159] The English term *fashion* seems to be more complex. The term *fasoun*, reportedly used in the 12th century, used to mean "physical make-up or composition; form, shape; appearance". This concept corresponds with the French terms *façon, fachon, fazon* meaning "face, appearance; construction, pattern, design; thing done; beauty; manner, characteristic feature".[160] These terms are close to the

152 Mair, *The Psychology . . .*, Chap. 1.

153 Meinhold, *Fashion Myths . . .*, p. 19, cf. www.etymonline.com/word/modus (accessed: 16.03.2023).

154 Meinhold, *Fashion Myths . . .*, p. 20.

155 D. Slater, *Consumer Culture and Modernity*, Polity Press, 1997.

156 V. Steele, *Paris Fashion. A Cultural History*, Bloomsbury Academic, 2017, p. 22.

157 Steele, *Paris Fashion*, p. 23.

158 See www.etymonline.com/word/modus (accessed: 16.03.2023); cf. Erlhoff, Marshall, *Design Dictionary*, pp. 161–162.

159 R.A. Muller, *Dictionary of Latin and Greek Theological Terms. Drawn Principally from Protestant Scholastic Theology*, Baker Academics, 2017.

160 See T.L. Tu, *Fashion* [in:] B. Burgett, G. Hendler (eds.), *Keywords for American Cultural Studies*, 2nd ed., NYU Press, 2014, p. 104; cf. P. Aspers, F. Godart, *Sociology of Fashion: Order and Change*, "Annual Review of Sociology", 2013, vol. 39, pp. 173 and ff.

Latin *factionem* and Italian *facere*, both denoting action or making. Beginning in the 17th century, *fashion* gained a new meaning: good style.[161] As observed by Thuy Linh Tu, fashion is a term used for a "relatively new cultural form".[162] With the introduction of the French couturiers' guild in the 17th century, tailors were free to make clothes for non-aristocrats, which was the turning point in fashion history, since anybody who could afford to could now be *à la mode*.[163]

Paul Poiret disdained the word 'fashion', which he connoted rather with 'tedious uniformity' than 'tasteful and creative individuality'.[164] His counterparts, Madame Lanvin and Lucien Lelong, when asked about who creates fashion, would respond, respectively: "les couturiers, évidement, mais aucun n'a pu définir exactement dans quelles conditions" (the couturiers, obviously, but nobody can define exactly under what conditions) and "C'est un truisme de dire que la Mode est faite autant par les femmes que par les couturiers" (It is a truism to say that fashion is made as much by women as by couturiers).[165] Marcel Rouff recounted in 1946 that

> la Mode est le résultat de la combinaison du goût artistique du couturier, plus ou moins influencé lui-même par les conditions économiques ou sociales de l'époque, et du désir de la femme qu'il veut habiller. Or, la femme que le couturier veut avant tout habiller est la Parisienne, depuis toujours sa plus fidèle collaboratrice, l'incarnation, si l'on veut, du *Goût*, avec un grand G.
>
> (Fashion is the result of the combination of the artistic taste of the couturier, who is more or less influenced by the economic or social conditions of the time, and the desire of the woman he wishes to dress. However, the woman he wants above all others to dress is the Parisienne woman, who has always been his most faithful collaborator, the incarnation, if you will, of Taste with a capital T).[166]

Thorstein Veblen expressed the view in 1899 that "fashion is created when garments undergo changes that, although not strictly necessary, are integral to the aspirational nature of fashion".[167]

Later, in 1967, James Laver noted that:

> Everybody knows what fashion is; it hits us in the eye every time we go into the street. And most people are convinced that they know what

161 See www.etymonline.com/word/fashion (accessed: 16.01.2023).

162 Tu, *Fashion . . .*, p. 104.

163 Tu, *Fashion . . .*, p. 104.

164 N.J. Troy, *The Logic of Fashion*, "The Journal of the Decorative Arts Society", 1850 – the Present, 1995, no. 19, p. 2.

165 M. Rouff, *La haute couture parisienne et son évolution*, "Annales. Histoire, Sciences Sociales", 1ère Anné3, 1946, no. 2, p. 116.

166 Own translation. Cf. fn. 165.

167 V. Pouillard, *Design Piracy in the Fashion Industries of Paris and New York in the Interwar Years*, "The Business History Review", 2011/6, vol. 85, no. 2, p. 320; T. Veblen, *The Theory of the Leisure Class*, Macmillan, 1899.

> art is, although they would be hard put to define it. Beauty then! For it is the obvious purpose of art to produce beauty; and it is the obvious purpose of fashion to make women beautiful. Fashion, art, beauty must surely mean the same thing, or so nearly the same thing that we can swallow them all in one gulp and rest content.[168]

Rik Wenting opined that "fashion design, like many other cultural products, relies upon its aesthetic component to confer value . . .. The aesthetic component reflects the designer's ability to understand and incorporate symbolic knowledge from its environment into a commercial product" and added that "a variety of pre-entry experiences is beneficial to the creative potential of a designer".[169]

From the earlier discussion it can be seen that philosophers, sociologists and psychologists have a good deal to say about fashion and what it denotes. One commentator to take account of the multiplicity of possible definitions of fashion was Roman Meinhold, who took all the possible 'fables and follies' of fashion to differentiate between four various concepts:

- the broadest: trends and tendencies in human actions and their results since time immemorial, including styles and methods of architecture as well as trends governing things made for sale; it covers more, including painting, dancing, medicine, business management or even scientific research[170];
- fairly broad: trends and tendencies in human actions brought on by the democratisation of consumption (a record of this influence is the purchase of specific types of electronics, which is the example of R. Meinhold);
- fairly narrow: styles of clothing in the wider spectrum of time, that is characteristic of an epoque, like the wearing of togas in Ancient Rome;
- narrowest: "periodically changing commercialised, present-day-oriented style of democratised luxury clothing".[171]

Meinhold narrows down the proper definition of 'fashion' to the sphere limited by three elements: clothing, proletarisation of luxury and contemporaneity. Still, his conclusions can be disputed on two points. First of all, fashion is a concept that arrived with the industrial revolution. Second, fashion in the narrowest of its meanings will occasionally draw inspiration from or have interplay with the three wider meanings.[172]

168 J. Laver, *Fashion, Art, and Beauty*, "The Metropolitan Museum of Art Bulletin", New Series, 1967, vol. 26, no. 3, p. 117.

169 R. Wenting, *Spinoff Dynamics and the Spatial Formation of the Fashion Design Industry, 1858–2005*, "Journal of Economic Geography", 2008, vol. 8, no. 5, Geography and the Cultural Economy, p. 595.

170 Aspers, Godart, *Sociology of Fashion*, p. 175; cf. N. Luhmann, *Die Gesellschaft der Gesellschaft*, Suhrkamp Verlag, 1997; Blumer, *Fashion*, pp. 275–291.

171 Meinhold, *Fashion Myths . . .*, pp. 20–22.

172 Meinhold, *Fashion Myths . . .*, pp. 24–25.

Recall that Valerie Steele defined fashion as "a cultural construction of the embodied identity".[173] Emanuele Coccia similarly claims that it

> is a process of imaginal identification performed through nonpsychological means. It is not only the interiorization of the image in the mirror that allows us to become an 'I', but any kind of taking on of an image that is capable of making us appear in a certain way.[174]

Therefore, fashion encompasses all forms of personal style, from high-street to high couture. However, the term 'fashion' is mostly used to refer to the prevailing style of dress or behaviour.

1.6.2 Scholarly conundrum about the term

It appears from the research undertaken that the glut of definitions of "fashion" results from the fact that fashion has always been a subject of interest in many disciplines,[175] even though, in the beginning, the pure sciences refused to acknowledge it as a scientific area of study. Although a united definition of fashion accepted by all commentators would be very helpful, in practice, the variety of approaches represented across the many sciences make this very challenging. Fashion became subject to research in economics, sociology, history, anthropology, philosophy and literature.[176] More recently, psychology and law also put fashion on their radar. *Normativity of the phenomena of fashion*, a term coined by Paolo Heritier, demonstrates the ever-increasing legal commentary on fashion.[177]

Fashion has also proved to be strongly interdisciplinary, with many inter-referential elements having their roots in different disciplines. E. Sapir made a very accurate point about this by saying,

> The chief difficulty of understanding fashion in its apparent vagaries is the lack of exact knowledge of the unconscious symbolism attaching to forms, colours, textures, postures and other expressive elements in a given culture. The difficulty is apparently increased by the fact that the same expressive elements tend to have quite different symbolic references in different areas.[178]

173 Mair, *The Psychology* . . ., Chap. 1.

174 Coccia, *Sensible Life*, p. 89.

175 Cf. T.L. Tu, *Keywords for American Cultural Studies, Second Edition*, NYU Press, 2014, p. 104.

176 P. Gregory, *An Economic Interpretation of Women's Fashion*, "Southern Economic Journal", 1947, vol. 14, p. 148; Gregory, *Fashion* . . ., pp. 69 and ff.

177 Heritier, *Fashion* . . ., p. 26.

178 E. Sapir, 'Fashion', The Encyclopaedia of Social Sciences, vol. VI, p. 141 [after:] R.T. Horowitz, *From Élite Fashion to Mass Fashion*, "European Journal of Sociology", vol. 16, no. 2, 1975, p. 283.

1.6.3 *Fashion versus clothes*

Some candidate definitions rely on the antithetical relationship of clothes and apparel *versus* fashion. Tansy E. Hoskins proposes a somewhat discriminatory and audacious idea that items of personal style (garments, accessories, etc.) produced in Paris, Milan, London and New York deserve to be labelled 'fashion', with the rest created outside of these centres regarded merely as 'clothes' or 'apparel'.[179] As previously acknowledged, there are many approaches to the relationship between what we choose to call fashion and what we choose to call apparel. Hoskins' approach is specific to an extreme and unhelpful degree and would have the effect of requiring complete separation in our treatment of two areas which in fact have a very natural overlap. George B. Sproles offered the observation that "clothing is clearly the classic product of fashion-oriented behaviour, but fashion also touches consumers' aesthetics choices ranging from autos and housing to foods and music".[180] It should be agreed with C. Mair that fashion should be observed from the perspective of change, while clothing is an umbrella term, covering both functional and decorative items.

A somewhat more meta-level explanation is offered by Ingrid Loschek. In her view, clothing serves as a *form*, whereas fashion serves as a *medium*. To use her own words, "since the form of clothing represents the foundation for the medium of fashion, fashion is form and medium".[181]

To recap, Patrick Aspers and Frédéric Godart observe that fashion is a social phenomenon that is not restricted to the domain of clothing. However, the voluminous literature related to fashion proves that the term is most frequently applied to clothes.[182]

As shown in coming chapters, fashion is not only apparel, despite being wrongly, sometimes carelessly, equated with it. Fashion also encompasses, or more precisely intersects with, the areas of textiles, furnishings, furniture, jewellery, beauty products and everything that entails elements of attractive appearance and lifestyle (cf. Chapter 1, section titled "Fashion versus design or 'fashion design'" and Chapter 2). It is an oversimplification to assume that fashion is tantamount to apparel. This research nonetheless mostly reflects on sartorial design and accessories (with elements of design for comparison).

1.6.4 *Fashion versus style*

As expressed by April Calahan, in fashion it is extremely risky to make "sweeping generalizations that any one designer was the 'first' to do anything".[183] She

179 Hoskins, *Stitched Up* . . ..
180 Sproles, *Analyzing Fashion* . . ., p. 116.
181 Loschek, *When Clothes* . . ., p. 25.
182 P. Aspers, F. Godart, *Sociology* . . ., pp. 175, 187; cf. A. Janssens, M. Lavanga, *An Expensive* . . ., p. 232.
183 A. Calahan, *The Myth of Poiret as Debunked by 1906*, "A Fashion Institute of Technology Blog", 9 July 2015, https://blog.fitnyc.edu/materialmode/2015/07/09/the-myth-of-poiret-as-debunked-by-1906/ (accessed: 17.01.2023).

points to David Prown's thesis that "once a group of objects produced in the same place at the same time begin to exhibit similar motifs or properties, then one can claim a style has been established". It means that the direction dictating fashion is not monopolised by one person extraordinary at their time, but rather that fashion is the product of a shared bank of experiences, stimuli and materialisation of ideas.[184] Some have portrayed fashion as an epidemic, going 'from home to home' to 'take its victims'.[185]

In the literature, it is argued whether fashion and style are synonyms. A style can be defined in two contexts: clothing and fashion. The first denotes style as any distinctive mode of tailoring, whereas the latter applies it to the prevailing mode at any given time.[186] Aspers opines that style constitutes a "multidimensional self-referential aesthetic system produced and extended over time".[187] N. Luhmann, however, claimed that it is hardly possible to draw a line between fashion and style.[188] This intersection is the crux of the problem of copyrightability of fashion products, because trends and styles are inherently intertwined in this ecosystem. As much as copyright law inevitably tries to draw a hard line between idea (style) and its expression (a product in the style), this distinction will be challenged in Chapter 4, in which, by example of a great many legal cases, it will be proven that fashion – to the despair of lawyers – cannot be accommodated within this legal axiom of copyright law. Although style itself clearly cannot be monopolised by copyright protection and belongs to the public domain, a fact generally recognised and accepted by fashion trendsetters (e.g. distinctive fashion houses), it is style that fashion builds upon. The line between idea and form can be very weak and rather conventional. Fashion and industrial design are two areas of creative work badly served by the axiom that many other creative areas fit well (e.g. fine arts, music, architecture).

1.6.5 Model versus design

The term 'model' is, in many ways, misleading, as it is blurred and wide with many connotations. As observed by C. Evans,

> the idea of a model is many centuries old; derived from *modulus*, the Latin word for measure or standard – the diminutive of which was *modellus*, from which came the old Italian *modello*, meaning the mould for producing things – the word drifted into French, *modèle*, in the sixteenth century, and then into English shortly afterwards, in the sense of a small representation of an object, like a sculptor's maquette for example or an

184 Calahan, *The Myth . . .*

185 M.L. Roberts, *Samson and Delilah Revisited: The Politics of Women's Fashion in 1920s France*, "The American Historical Review", 1993, vol. 98, no. 3, p. 657 [after:] R. Rambaud, *Les fugitives: Précis anecdotique et historique des coiffures féminines à travers les âges des Egyptiens à 1945*, 1947, pp. 250–251.

186 Gregory, *Fashion . . .*, p. 69.

187 Aspers, 2006, p. 75; Aspers, Godart, *Sociology . . .*, p. 174.

188 Luhmann, *Das Kunstwerk . . .* , p. 655; Gronow, *Taste . . .*, p. 98.

> architectural model. Its usage to connote a mathematical model only developed in the twentieth century, as did the term fashion model.[189]

The meaning of 'model' can vary depending on the area of art, such as fine art, design, architecture, fashion, photography or new media, and can denote: a rudimentary sketch, an idea, a miniature, a set of instructions, a maquette or a prototype.[190] Fashion is an area in which contradictions in meaning are easy to see, as it may refer to either a dress model or a human model. Only in fashion is it acceptable to apply the term to a human being. The idea of human models goes back to the 18th century and the manner of promoting sartorial work using dolls. These were about 75 cm high and were sent around Europe. Then, in the 19th century, human models came to be more commonly used, though it may come as a surprise that these models were men and were referred to as 'mannequins'.[191] Because, until the end of the 19th century, fashion models continued to be men, the masculine denomination of the term was never considered to differentiate between male and female models.[192] It is claimed that the House of Worth had its fair part in coining these terms, as, according to Caroline Evans, a journalist working for *La Vie Parisienne* in 1870 saw a *vendeuse* at Worth's modelling a dress for a client, and so wrote an article about 'the *Entrée de Mlle Mannequin*'. That was the first occasion of which the term "mannequin" was applied to a woman.[193]

According to the *Dictionnaire de l'Académie Française* of 1762, 'model' denoted three items: 1) an exemplar, something to aspire to, like a model of behaviour; 2) an architectural model or sculptor's maquette; and 3) an artist's model, either male or female.[194]

1.6.6 Fashion versus design or 'fashion design'

It is important to note that this subsection of the book was added at the refinement stage. Initially, there was not sufficient attention given to the border between fashion and design. Intuitively, these areas may seem to be close but nonetheless competing areas of 'art'. This presumption can be drawn based on observation of people engaged in these two areas, their activities and approach to the process of creation. Whereas fashion seems to be flamboyant, colourful, easy-going, sometimes hedonistic and cartoonish, contemporary design is by comparison quite minimalist, simple, low-key and ultimately serious. The many discussions this author has on a daily basis with representatives of these

189 C. Evans, *The Ontology of the Fashion Model*, "AA Files", no. 63, 2011, p. 58.
190 Evans, *The Ontology . . .*, p. 58.
191 Their work was to attend places occupied by high-society men and to present latest trends and designs. Evans, *The Ontology . . .*, p. 59.
192 Evans, *The Ontology . . .*, p. 61.
193 Until this point, she had been referred to as an "*essayeuse*" or "*demoiselle de magasin*". Evans, *The Ontology . . .*, p. 61.
194 Evans, *The Ontology . . .*, p. 65.

two professions has also led her to think that fashion and design should be afforded separate treatment and analysis. Deeper legal analysis of copyright cases regarding applied art let her conclude that, from the legal point of view, courts' discussions and findings regarding copyrightability of designs can be directly transferred to the area of fashion. This led her to ask the question: "what is the true relationship between fashion and design?" Design itself has been analysed from many angles leading to the conclusion that there is no single definition that would gain international and universal acceptance.[195] Walsh asserted in 1996 that "the term 'design' covers a wide range of activities: architecture, ***fashion design***, interior design, graphic design, industrial design, engineering design" (emphasis mine – MJ).[196] Based on this quite wide definition of design, this author found a supporting argument for her claim that "fashion is design", which further allows us to embrace the concept of "fashion design". Therefore, fashion is a subcategory of the wider conglomerate of concepts called design. It is remarkable that international institutions have attempted to define design for legislative or regulatory purposes.[197] The European Commission defined 'design' as "the appearance of the whole or a part of a product resulting from the features of, in particular, the lines, contours, colours, shape, texture and/or materials of the product itself and/or its ornamentation".[198] To support this claim, this definition entirely fits the understanding and purpose of fashion. Others have also attempted to define "design", in both very broad and narrow ways. The EU's Office for Harmonization in the Internal Market claimed that 'design' is "an art and a science, it forms our homes and our workplace, and it is all around us, wherever we are. Design is the surface of the man-made-environment".[199] A more specific attempt was made by the World Intellectual Property Organization, which opined that the general concept of 'industrial design' "constitutes the ornamental or aesthetic aspect of an article. A design may consist of three-dimensional features, such as the shape or surface of an article, or of two-dimensional features, such as patterns, lines and colour".[200]

195 G. Gemser, M. Leenders, *How Integrating Industrial Design in the Product Development Process Impacts on Company Performance*, "Journal of Product Innovation Management", 2001, vol. 18, pp. 25–38.

196 V. Walsh, *Design, Innovation and the Boundaries of the Firm*, "Research Policy", 1996, vol. 25, no. 4, pp. 509–529.

197 Ch. L. Tucci, T. Peters, *Design and Design Frameworks: Investment in KBC and Economic Performance* [w:] OECD, *Enquiries into Intellectual Property's Economic Impact*, 2015, p. 325.

198 European Commission, *Council Regulation No. 6/2002 of 12 December 2001 on Community Designs*. Official Journal of the European Communities, 2002.

199 OHIM, *Design Definition*, Ohimportal. https://oami.europa.eu/ohimportal/en/design-definition, 2013 (accessed: 18.03.2022); OHIM, *Designs in the European Union*, https://oami.europa.eu/ohimportal/en/designs-in-the-european-union 2013 (accessed: 18.01.2023).

200 WIPO, *Industrial Designs*, www.wipo.int/designs/en/ (accessed: 18.01.2023).

As noted by D'Ippolito and reiterated by Christopher L. Tucci and Tilo Peters, design can be viewed from four different angles, which have also been evolving over time.[201] These are as follows:

- design as a creation of artefacts,
- design as a problem-solving activity,
- design as a reflective practice and design as making sense of things,
- design as a key input to strategy.

All of these guideposts can be easily extended to fashion. Chapter 2 elaborates on point 1 and Chapter 3 on point 4. Chapter 4 provides a legal analysis building on points 2 and 3.

1.7 Shades of fashion

1.7.1 Segments of sartorial designs and democratisation of art. From **haute couture** *to ultra-fast fashion*

Fashion comes in a variety of forms and expressions – from more sublime and meticulously well-thought-up to preparations of standard garments designed for quick profit. If we were to segment the various types of clothing products, five categories can be distinguished, including both artistic and non-artistic fashion: 1) avant-garde/wearable art, 2) costumes, 3) haute couture, 4) ready-to-wear and 5) mass market. This categorisation[202] was introduced by Allison DeVore and will serve as a structure for further research of the fashion spectrum. The multitude of definitions of fashion formulated using a multi-academic (sociological, psychological, anthological and legal) approach creates uncertainty as to how broadly the term should be applied. As long as we are striving to create a spectrum of consideration for the use of law and its legal protection, fashion cannot be understood in the narrowest sense, such as that proposed by Roman Meinhold. The legal protection of fashion, given the teleological and functional interpretation of copyright law, should encompass clothing as such, notwithstanding whether it is *en vogue* or luxurious. To wit, it might indeed be the case that it is mostly modern and more luxurious garments that are subject to copying, but this observation cannot be considered

201 Tucci, Peters, *Design . . .*, p. 325; B. D'Ippolito, *The Importance of Design for Firms' Competitiveness: A Review of the Literature*, Technovation, 2014; H.A. Simon, *The Sciences of the Artificial*, MIT Press, 1969; U. Johansson-Sköldberg, J. Woodilla, M. Çetinkaya, *Design Thinking: Past, Present and Possible Futures*, "Creativity and Innovation Management", 2013, vol. 22, no. 2, pp. 121–146; K. Krippendorff, *On the Essential Contexts of Artifacts or on the Proposition That "Design Is Making Sense (of Things)"*, "Design Issues", 1989, pp. 9 and ff.

202 A. DeVore, *The Battle between the Courthouse and the Fashion House: Creating a Tailored Solution for Copyright Protection of Artistic Fashion Designs*, "Thomas Jefferson Law Review", 2013, vol. 35, pp. 193, 228, p. 197.

an ironclad definition of imitation. Therefore, *the juxtaposition of fashion segments by Allison DeVore gives an interesting, but introductory, impression of what should be protected as 'fashion'.*

The first category of fashion according to DeVore includes 'innovative fashion' and 'wearable fashion', where, to put it in its authors' words, "the body is the canvas". Put differently, the human body becomes a model on which the design is to be moulded. It is a nucleus of form yet to be born. It is about the creative work of an artist whose medium is fashion. The works are artistically driven and generally created with an emphasis on art and creativity instead of functionality. One of the many examples is the dress made of raw meat that was worn by Lady Gaga at the 2010 MTV Video Music Awards. After the debut, the dress was taken to a taxidermist, chemically preserved, dried, painted and then sent to the Rock and Roll Hall of Fame exhibition. Another example of innovation is Rihanna's dress made of LEDs, which changed between various coloured patterns during the concert. Thanks to that idea, she did not have to change outfits to perform.

The definition of costume relies on intuition – it is an outfit designed to create a look characteristic of an era, person, place or thing. Costumes are meant to give the wearer a completely different look. As an example, one can think of a costume worn for Halloween or during carnival. According to R. Meinhold, a costume is "a *vestimentary* precursor of fashion". It was an outfit worn for a special occasion, related to tradition and therefore belonging to the past. Fashion, on the contrary, belongs to the future.[203]

In fashion, there are several types of tailoring. *Haute couture* is also known as 'high tailoring', 'high fashion', 'artistic creation', 'couture création' or 'élite fashion',[204] and is characterised by the dominance of manual work and the creation of individual designs for individual clients. Haute couture designs are elegant fashion, including underwear and corsetry. The works are made in limited quantities, and professionals sometimes grant the right to reproduce them. The cradle of *haute couture* is France, where the term has been protected since 1945.[205] Legal regulations oblige haute couture designers to comply with certain standards.

Both *prêt-à-porter* and wholesale tailoring (mass market) are branches of the clothing industry. *Prêt-à-porter* is also known as 'ready-to-wear' or tailor made for the industry. They are characterised by serial and mechanically prepared collections, not made-to-measure for the client. Sometimes there are options like 'half measure' or 'industrial measure', which enable the customer to choose the goods from a variety of sizes and even materials. *Prêt-à-porter* are clothes available in ready-made form, popularised in the US as cheaper and faster in the mid-19th century due to the invention of the sewing machine. Thanks to this, it was possible to produce high-quality clothes to wear every day.

203 Meinhold, *Fashion Myths*. . ., p. 25.

204 Horowitz, *From Élite Fashion* . . ., pp. 289–290.

205 A. Manfredi, *Haute Copyright: Tailoring Copyright Protection to High-Profile Fashion Designs*, "Cardozo Journal of International and Comparative Law", 2012, vol. 111, p. 116.

The last category – mass market – covers clothes of standard sizes and designs, manufactured in cheap production cycles and within a fast fashion policy.[206] It is common for whole collections to reflect the latest trends and designs, inspired by catwalk creations, or just slavishly copying them.

1.7.2 Allison DeVore's legal concept of fashion – discussion. Petit couture. *Seductive and craftsmanly quality*

Allison DeVore's well-known and widely quoted attempt to introduce a distinction between different kinds of fashion is not as flawless as it may seem.

First, the division between *haute couture* and *prêt-à-porter* goes back to the French couturiers who advocated for precisely this clear-cut delineation (cf. Chapter 2, . . .). The distinction was always an uneasy one, and nowadays there is really no ironclad line between the two. The best exemplification of this is that the categories merge at the upper end of *prêt-à-porter* and that most respectful fashion houses offer both categories of apparel. The line between them is delicate.

Second, the usage of the term *haute couture* is somehow wrong due to its overgeneralisation. The use of this word in its widest understanding is very common in literature, but to use it in the legal context a lot more nuance should be included. The in-depth analysis leads to the conclusion that there are many shades of *haute couture* and that it is not a monolith. The term became a legal one in 1945 to secure the legal and business standing of Parisian fashion houses, that, in this way, were exclusively granted the right to be labelled as *haute couture* and to use the term in marketing and sales.

Item of note 1.7 *Chambre Syndicale* criteria for *haute couture*

In order to be considered *haute couture*, an atelier has to meet a set of criteria from the *Chambre Syndicale* that were established by the *Règlement intérieur de la Commission de Contrôle et de Classement "Couture Création"*.[207] The commission is held under the aegis of the Ministry of Economy and Finance. To be eligible for this label, an atelier must

206 P. Aspers, *Orderly Fashion. A Sociology of Markets*, Princeton University Press, 2010, pp. 34 and ff.

207 Décret no 45–147 du 29 janvier 1945 portant création de l'office professionnel des industries et métiers d'art et de creation, JORF, 30. Janvier 195, p. 426; *Règlement intérieur de la Commission de Contrôle et de Classement "Couture Création" de la décision VIA 29 du 23 janvier 1945 validée par arrêté ministériel du 30 juin 1947 et de l'arrêté du 6 avril 1945*; CAEF, DCE, B-8409/1, *Classification couture-création – Règlement d'application du décret 45–147 du 29 janvier 1945*; Voncent Dubé-Senécal, *La mode française. Vecteur d'influence aux États-Unis* (1946–1960), pp. 136–137; Eleni Koutsopoulou, *Haute Couture as a Work Protected by Copyright*, master's thesis, Thessaloniki Greece, January 2017, p. 7.
C. Barrère, W. Santagata, *La mode. Une économie de la créativité et du patrimoine, à l'heure du marché.* Ministère de la Culture – DEPS, pp. 53–77.

make designs that are cut-to-size for private clients with at least four or more fittings and are not available for sale off-the-shelf;

establish a workshop or atelier in Paris with at least 15 staff members employed full time;

employ 20 full-time technical people in at least one workshop;

offer fashion design that is by hand, by superiorly skilled seamstresses and tailors;

every season, present two specific collections of at least 35 (some sources mention between 25 and 50) original designs, of both day and evening garments.

After becoming a member there are even more regulations to follow, which are closely regulated by the Fédération de la Couture, du Prêt-à-Porter des Couturiers et des Créateurs de Mode, such as 1) collections are private events and presented to accredited press only, 2) the Fédération controls the list of press accredited for each event and 3) fashion shows are not open to the public.[208]

There are permanent members and correspondent members of the *Chambre Syndicale de la Haute Couture*, approved each year.[209] As of 2022 there were 16 permanent *Haute Couture* members:

Adeline André
Alexandre Vauthier
Alexis Mabille
Bouchra Jarrar
Chanel
Dior
Franck Sorbier
Giambattista Valli
Givenchy
Jean Paul Gaultier
Julien Fournié
Maison Margiela
Maison Rabih Kayrouz
Maurizio Galante
Schiaparelli
Stéphane Rolland
The correspondent members are
Atelier Versace
Elie Saab

(*Continued*)

208 *Doing Couture? Why You Might Be Breaking the Law*, www.createafashionbrand.com/doing-couture-why-you-might-be-breaking-the-law/ (accessed: 20.01.2023).

209 https://fhcm.paris/en/haute-couture-2/ (accessed: 20.01.2023).

Item of note 1.7 (Continued)

Fendi Couture
Giorgio Armani Privé
Iris Van Herpen
Miu Miu
Ulyana Sergeenko
Valentino
Viktor&Rolf
There are also over 120 brands that are guest members.

Altogether, there are three associations: *Chambre Syndicale de la Haute Couture* whose members consist only of those fashion houses that are labelled as *Haute Couture*; *Chambre Syndicale du Prêt-à-Porter des Couturiers et des Créateurs de Mode* accepting members from *Haute Couture* houses and ateliers that produce *prêt-à-porter* fashion. Finally, there is *Chambre Syndicale de la Mode Masculine* that includes men's ready-to-wear brands (cf. Chapter 2, . . .).

Therefore, qualification as *haute couture* can be measured in a selection of ways:

- *legal* (meeting the requirements of the French legal act),
- *institutional* (being listed in the exclusive family of *haute couture* fashion houses),
- *descriptive* (pertaining to the quality criteria that separate the finest kind of apparel from the lesser types).

Haute couture in the descriptive sense is used in a conventional, not to say colloquial, way. To be specific, it should be used in the legal or institutional ways. In fact, what is meant by the descriptive sense is both: *haute couture* and *couture*. There are many prestigious fashion houses in all corners of the world that do not make French *haute couture*, as they do not meet the criteria of the *Loi 45–147*, but which provide work of the same or similar standards. Legally, they are not allowed to be labelled as *haute couture* but may be labelled as *couture*. This intermediate category, bridging the gap between *haute couture* and *prêt-à-porter*, often receives less attention in scholarly discussions, as the emphasis may not always be on such nuanced legal distinctions.

Third, the scope of fashion encompasses more than just clothing, suggesting that DeVore's interpretation may be somewhat restrictive. As an afterthought it is remarkable that the couture label may be applied to design, more precisely to jewellery, interior design and furniture. Surprisingly to this author, the *Loi 45–147* establishing the *haute couture* label mentions not only clothes but also fabrics, clothing accessories, furnishings, perfumes, jewellery (of all kinds: *bijouterie*, *orfèvrerie* and *joaillerie*) and even other kinds of art.

Fourth, as much as it is impossible to deny that wearable art and costumes are apparel, they should be kept away from this fashion spectrum because of the following:

- They are more artistic than utilitarian (or useful), and therefore they neither constitute the core of fashion nor merit consideration as their own category. At the same time, it is not claimed that *haute couture* or *prêt-à-porter* are not artistic, just that they need to serve a functional goal that wearable art and costumes do not.
- The sphere of creative work is wider compared to utilitarian fashion.
- Based on the two previous arguments, that they are inherently artistic, they hardly suffer from the true copyrightability issues that assail utilitarian fashion.
- They are not style/trend-constrained as much as everyday fashion is.
- Wearable art and costumes are not quality related as much as other fashion categories are.

Fifth, fashion segmentation should be based on a differentia, which in this case seems to be quality of goods. Again, wearable art and costumes escape this differentiation as they may belong to any category from *haute couture* to ultra-fast fashion.

Sixth, the *prêt-á-porter* category is a very wide category and should be divided into a few substantial and meaningful subcategories. The ones proposed here are deluxe, premium and basic.

Seventh, the 'mass market' category is misleading in the sense that it can refer to both *prêt-à-porter* and fast fashion. In fact, *prêt-à-porter* is also produced in bulk.

Eighth, in-depth analysis allows contesting of the clear-cut distinction between *haute couture* and *prêt-à-porter* not only because of *couture* but also due to another group of designers. Between the two familiar tiers there is a distinctive number of one- to three-person ateliers (reportedly 90% of fashion businesses operate on this small scale), among which there is an often forgotten group of ***artisan fashion designers*** (***petit couture***, 'small fashion studio' or 'small fashion atelier'). They constitute a significant number of businesses; however, more importantly, they offer a very special kind of work:

- production/creation based on a short supply chain,
- better consumer experience, that is, a special bond between the client and the fashion designer and/or their work,
- a personal and creative approach to production,
- a product based on an artistic and artisanal approach (Explanatory item no. 1.1).

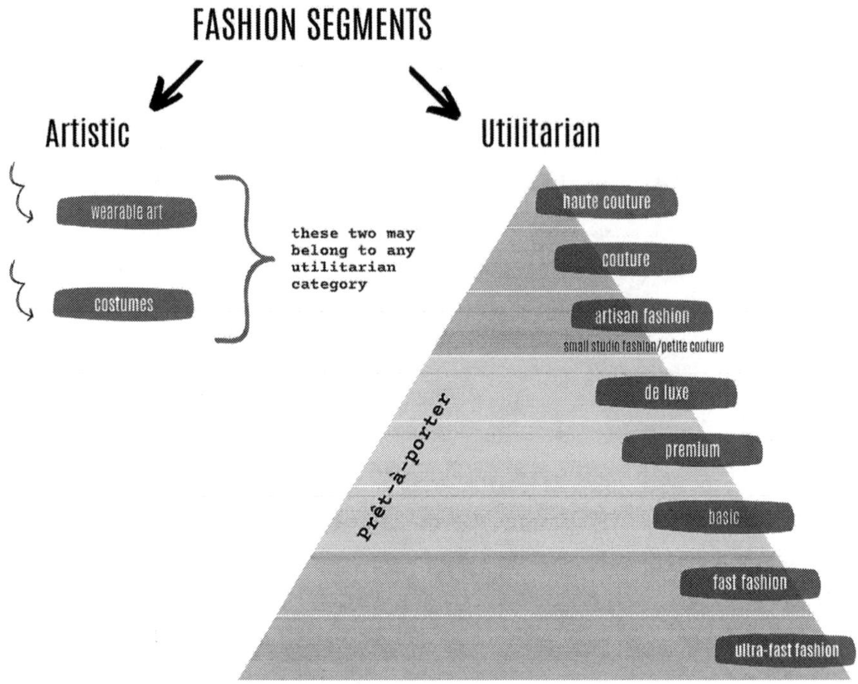

Explanatory item no. 1.1 Fashion segments. Own study

Source: Created by author

Interestingly, the reputable French couturiers at the turn of the 20th century have their origins in this artisan category. They created a new fashion segment, *haute couture*, by injecting into their creation the "touch and feel" approach and by putting their entire heart into the quality. They knew how to evoke *emotions*. They were pioneers, not only in their craft but also in building the very special "*emotional bond*" with the clients, which was possible through the flamboyant interiors of their fashion ateliers and the treatment as well as fulfilment they offered their clients. They mastered the development of an "*emotional situation*" within the realm of fashion. Their businesses proliferated based on the observation that clothing serves many functions. It gives protection to a human body but, most importantly, meets the inner human need to embellish one's appearance, to look good and feel validated in one's surroundings. French couturiers *intuitively* discovered and exploited the fact that, apart from apparel, they were selling emotions. If we examine their way of establishing the concept of fashion, we arrive at a question: can originality also be measured based on intuition? Is it not the case that copyright reasoning pertaining to originality is driven by emotion? As hard as it is to admit, originality itself is a vague and malleable concept.

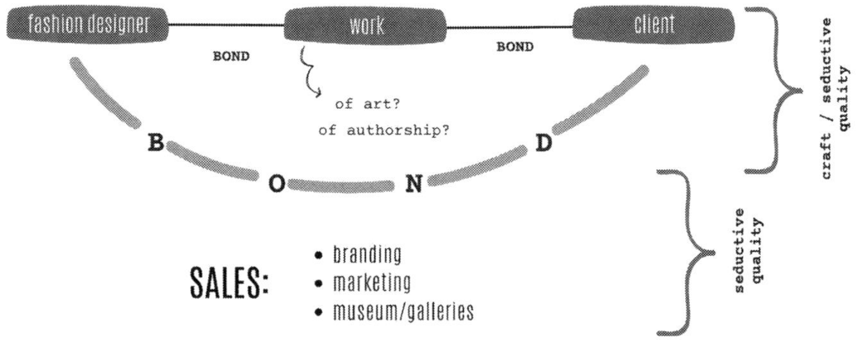

Explanatory item no. 1.2 Seductive and craft quality that constitutes the bond between the author and the audience

Source: Created by author

This author found, based on a lot of observation and analysis, that fashion is a phenomenon that should be discussed in copyright law from the *quality angle*. This quality encompasses

- *seductive quality* (cf. Chapter 1, section titled "Levels of consumers' emotional interaction with design"), that is, *emotional bond*, an interaction between the fashion design and the client based on the work's features as well as the overall package of how the work is offered for sale (e.g. branding, marketing, exhibiting a work in museums/galleries),
- *craft quality*, that is, quality of production, construction, technical aspect of the design.

The picture (Explanatory item no. 1.2) shows that the bond between the client and the good can be maintained in many ways: via the quality of work itself, via the sales strategies, or both.

This means that a work of fashion design may be placed on the scale of copyrightability based on these two complementary elements. A work may also attain the criterion of originality based on only one of these. As much as the idea of fashion is anchored in the seductive quality, its craft quality should not be underestimated, especially given that fashion also encompasses construction. Some products require massive amounts of work that resemble engineering design and detail. It is beyond discussion that this meticulous work can be original as it takes not just technique but creative insight. In assessing overall originality, a shortfall in either of the quality categories can be compensated by a particularly high score in the other. Therefore, fashion design contains a mix of two elements: artistic and technical.

The relationship between quality and originality (and therefore copyrightability) can be illustrated visually (Explanatory item nos. 1.3 and 1.4).

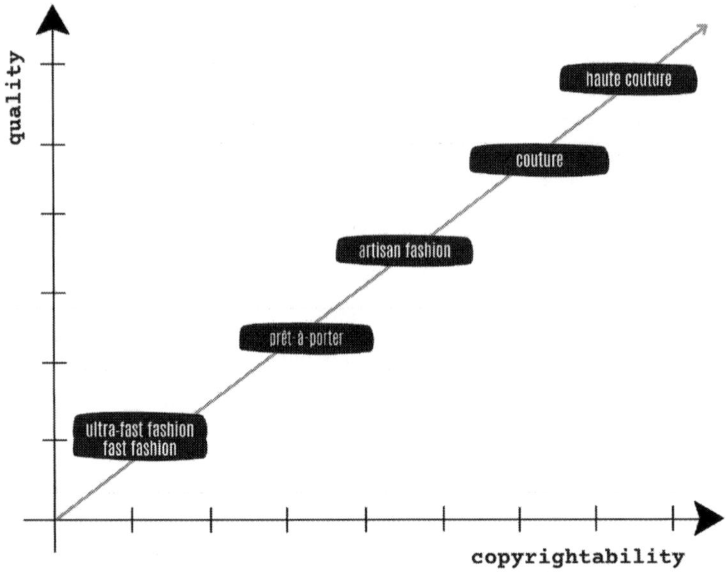

Explanatory item no. 1.3 Relationship between quality and copyrightability in fashion

Source: Created by author

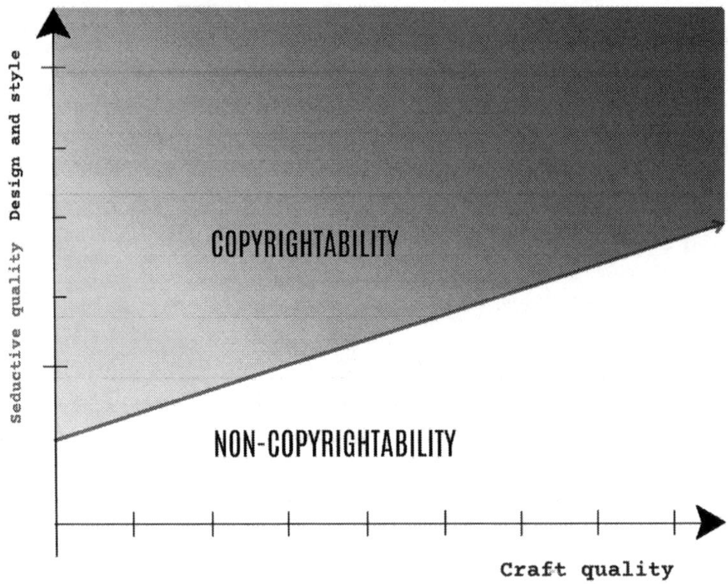

Explanatory item no. 1.4 Relationship between seductive quality and craft quality with respect to copyrightability in fashion

Source: Created by author

These scales may be malleable but offer a suitable starting point for discussions of how to understand fashion based on sartorial quality.

The emotional bond established in the fashion emotional situation makes it hard to judge whether any given work is original enough to merit copyright protection. The emotional bond becomes a double-edged sword. As fashion designers inject mostly emotions supplemented with a varied degree of creativity into their work, they provoke the question of whether this modicum of creativity clothed in emotion is legally adequate to trigger copyright protection. This question is even more complex than it may seem at first glance, as the universe of fashion rests on styles, trends, manners and ideas, all elements that intrinsically fall outside of copyright protection.

And, is it not so, that, in the courtroom, the judge will be guided by their emotions and therefore intuition?

1.7.3 Four capitals of the fashion business

In many ways, Paris will remain the heart of fashion. This is so mostly for the historical reasons that put the French capital on the map of the fashion business forever. Obviously *haute couture* is one of them, but it is worth mentioning that the first journal in the world dedicated to fashion, styling and consumptionism was the *Cabinet des Modes*, which was established in 1785 in Paris.[210]

In 2008, Rik Wenting undertook a body of research[211] comparing 565 of the world's leading fashion designers in the *haute couture* and ready-to-wear (without mass production) universe during the time span of 1858 to 2005, only to discover that there are four creative cities that leave the rest of the world far behind.[212]

Fashion is a fast-growing business with four fashion capitals: New York, London, Paris and Milan. Other fashion clusters include Los Angeles, Mumbai, Shanghai and Rio de Janeiro, however these have not so far maintained a competitive edge. The statistics show that Paris had a market share of 70% in 1923, which was to decrease to 36% in 1941 and to less than 25% in the 2000s. Paris surrendered its position to the other three capitals. It is observed that this loss of position was the result of the growth of the *prêt-à-porter* segment in the 1950s and 1960s. French designers, aligned with the Syndicate Chamber of Parisian Couture, were initially banned from making clothes in this market. In the event, they entered the ready-to-wear market much later and were easily outnumbered by others, especially by ateliers in New York.[213]

210 Lehmann, *Fashion . . .*, p. 75.
211 Wenting, *Spinoff . . .*, pp. 593 and ff.
212 Wenting, *Spinoff . . .*, p. 598.
213 Wenting, *Spinoff . . .*, p. 597; G. Waddell, *How Fashion Works: Couture, Ready-to-Wear and Mass Production*, Blackwell Publishing, 2004.

1.7.4 Inter-segmental interactions and artistic attitude

If one takes the time to view the unfolding of past centuries, it is readily apparent that fashion has undergone the process of becoming available in a mass scale. The 20th century brought industrialisation of sartorial works, standardisation of patterns and democratisation of access to *en vogue* designs through mass consumption. The scholarship in Chapter 2 will give a detailed account of how even the *haute couture* Parisian designers (Worth, Paquin, Poiret and Vionnet, to name but a few) contributed strongly to the popularisation of *prêt-à-porter* fashion. In Green's words it was a one-way clothing transformation from 'made for somebody' through 'made for anybody', finally arriving at 'made for everybody'.[214] These three dimensions of fashion exist side by side and should not be subject to a pecking order, just as the copyright law does not discriminate between them. Indeed, it was Coco Chanel who declared, "I am no longer interested in dressing a few hundred women, private clients; I shall dress thousands of women".[215]

The importance of originality and innovation to 19th-century tailors is apparent from the French term from that time, 'nouveautés', which denoted fashion goods. There is no doubt that *haute couture* is a form of art, a mantra constantly repeated by the French couturiers, including Worth.[216] Making the clientele believe that clothes appeal to the artistic senses meant that more money would change hands in the right direction. With the advent of the *prêt-à-porter* segment, the question was whether designs more approachable by wider groups of society could retain the privilege of being called art. *Haute couture* tailors wanted to separate these two segments into just two areas: art and industry,]; however, ready-to-wear manufacturers refused the indignity of being categorised in merely functional, industrial terms. As advocated by Green:

> whereas the history of ready-to-wear can thus be interpreted as a struggle over the attribution of aura, I would argue further that by the late nineteenth century a new hierarchy of artistic values emerged. The discourse on the garment industry in general, and by its manufacturers in particular, sought to legitimate the more standardized product by maintaining that it still contained an inherent artistic component. The garment-as-art-form persisted in industrial language, both as a holdover from previous ways of perceiving clothes and as an argument destined to ensure appreciation of the newly conceived product. Art, which was

214 M.-H.T. Pham, *The Right to Fashion in the Age of Terrorism*, "Signs", 2011, vol. 36, no. 2, p. 400; N.L. Green, *Art and Industry: The Language of Modernization in the Production of Fashion*, "French Historical Studies", 1994, vol. 18, no. 3, p. 727 [after:] Kidwell, Christman, *Suiting Everyone*, 1974.

215 M.-H.T. Pham, *The Right*. . ., p. 400 [after:] B. English, *A Cultural History of Fashion in the Twentieth Century: From the Catwalk to the Sidewalk*, Berg Publishers, 2007, p. 28.

216 Green, *Art*. . ., p. 727.

> initially relegated to the upper end of the market, continued to provide the cultural norm for thinking about the industry as a whole.[217]

Even the sewing machine evolved in its form to better address the needs of the discerning ready-to-wear industry and its artistic sensibilities. Early machines, having been built to be functional and practical, with these priorities reflected in the poor quality of stitching, were eschewed by the makers of clothing-as-art. The early machines served only to confirm the established prejudice that quality sewing had to be done by hand. Over time, though, 19th-century sewing machines began to be improved to support the finesse and accuracy prized by the high-end operators. Slowly, the artists were won over, in spite of the machines' mass-production heritage. Machine-stitching came to be recognised as stronger and more even, and ultimately it gained wide acceptance.[218]

1.7.5 Fashion as art

This author could not end the chapter without dwelling briefly on the artistic aspects of fashion as the rhetorical question reappears: is fashion art? According to Eva-Maria Ziege, the natural home of fashion is the museum. Indeed, the world's greatest museums, such as the Metropolitan Museum in New York, the Victoria & Albert Museum in London and the Louvre in Paris, take great pride in their garment collections, which can be counted in thousands. By this measure, the Louvre alone possesses over 80,000 pieces of clothes. It was also observed that some clothes, at the time of their production, are intended specifically for museums.[219]

It is important to note that fashion is perceived in a twofold way. It represents itself through its content but also through its form.[220] Not many genres of art function on this multi-sensual level. In the case of garments, there is appeal to the senses of touch and hearing when handling the textile. There is also the feeling of trying it on or the watching of a body moving while clothed in the outfit. The museum setting does not usually cater for all of these aspects, but there are exceptions, like the MET's Alexander McQueen exposition called *Savage Beauty* (2011). There was a separate area, the "Cabinet of Curiosities", where visitors were allowed to approach costumes so closely that they could even touch them.[221]

217 Green, *Art* . . ., pp. 732–733.

218 Green, *Art* . . ., p. 734.

219 Ziege, *Die Kunst* . . ., p. 156; J. Gronow, S. Zhuravlev, *Fashion Meets Socialism Fashion Industry in the Soviet Union after the Second World War,* Finnish Literature Society, 2015, pp. 92 and ff.

220 Ziege, *Die Kunst* . . ., p. 142.

221 K. Weise, *Kleider, die berühren. Über das Verhältnis von Kleidermode, Taktilität und Wissen in Museumsausstellungen* [in:] R. Wenrich (ed.), *Die Medialität der Mode. Kleidung als kulturelle Praxis. Perspektiven für eine Modewissenschaft,* Transcript Verlag, 2015, pp. 286–287;

How far-reaching is the assumption that fashion is art? As with any issue regarding fashion, these concepts are very fluid and malleable. It seems that American copyright law depends more heavily on that qualification than those in Europe. Bearing in mind the US doctrine of useful or utilitarian articles, the artistic qualification seems to be a matter of law in that legal system. As this doctrine was not embraced in European systems of copyright law, the debate over the artistic value of fashion gains less attention. According to Allison DeVore, the distinction between artistic and non-artistic clothes is as simple as placing wearable art and costumes at the artistic end of the spectrum of the fashion spectrum, leaving *haute couture*, ready-to-wear and mass market on the non-artistic end.[222] Upon this contraposition, DeVore built a doctrine of the Wearable Article Test that would help differentiate between work falling inside and outside of copyright protection.[223] This author does not share this reasoning and, in the coming chapters, will try to exemplify her outlook with works of fashion and legal cases that cast doubt whether this factitious juxtaposition can be adopted for the purpose of law.

1.8 Conclusions

This book's aim is to propose the concept of the copynorm in fashion. In order to do so, it is necessary to probe the details of the fashion ecosystem to gain a wider insight. It is well observed that specialised matters of this kind can only be well regulated legally if the legislator is sufficiently informed of the key forces on the industry, especially from the social, moral, cultural and business perspectives. Legal norms are best obeyed when they are socially understood and desired. Likewise, legal protection can only be uniformly and fairly enforced if the legal system fully grasps the issues involved. The research has proved that many sources have a good deal to say about the perception of fashion in modern society, but we should not be surprised that much of this attention was from the social, philosophical and cultural sciences. Fashion is perceived by these disciplines as a self-contained system, though its nooks and crannies are hard to translate into pure and applied sciences. This proves that fashion is an extremely socially anchored phenomenon with many cultural and moral influences. Recently, psychology and law scholars have also paid increased attention to fashion.

J. Birringer, *Performance in the Cabinet of Curiosities. Or, the Boy Who Lived in the Tree*, "Performing Arts Journal", 2016, vol. 114, pp. 19 and ff.

222 DeVore, *The Battle* . . ., pp. 197–198, 200–201.

223 The Wearable Article Test draws copyright protection on five criteria: 1) expert testimony on where the article falls on the spectrum of artistic and non-artistic fashion; 2) the designer's testimony regarding the purpose of the article and where the article was intended to fall on the spectrum of artistic and non-artistic fashion; 3) whether the article's functional aspects outweigh its creative aspects; 4) any reasonably foreseeable effects copyrighting the article would have on the fashion industry; and 5) whether copyrighting the article furthers both the public's and the designer's interests under the copyright policy, cf. DeVore, *The Battle* . . ., p. 220.

Imitation, though deeply embedded in fashion's DNA, must be examined in a wider context. *Mimesis* was already believed by Aristotle to enhance creativity. According to Kant, imitation is part of human nature. This nature motivates people to ascend the social ladder of wealth, status, trust and pleasure and, as proved in this study, they manifest their standing through their apparel. In this way, fashion became a channel of non-verbal expression. As noted by a number of reputed philosophers, including Friedrich Schiller, Friedrich Theodor Vischer, Eugen Fink and Jean Baudrillard, people imitate the styles and identities of the most prominent individuals. Fashion therefore plays a very important part in society. Fashion also allows us to blend into society. People merge with their clothes as though they were a second skin. A special relationship exists not only between an individual and society but also between a consumer and a designer. Consumers select their styles based on their emotions, which can include a desire for designer names and logos. Labels provide undeniable status in society.

This chapter also proves the special role of a fashion designer, who, if successful in predicting the public's desires and new upcoming trends, can be elevated to a status not unlike that of a fashion dictator. The fashion designer enjoys a high social standing based on their bank of creative ideas and experiences. That being so, can the designer be assured of financial gain once their vision is turned into a tangible and successful product? Or might the designer be cut out of the transaction, if fashion, given its utilitarian status, should fall into the public domain? From the sociological perspective, it is agreed that, as much as art does not tolerate copies, in fashion, copies serve as a strong catalyst, a motor and accelerator in one. Sociologists, philosophers, accountants and economists go as far as to claim that fashion could not exist without imitations.

If, however, copyright protection is to be secured for fashion designs, what copyrightability test would be adequate? In the legal literature it is suggested that originality tests do not apply to fashion in the same way as they would to literature or art. The arguments underpinning this opinion are that fashion serves a utilitarian function, that it becomes a social phenomenon engaging whole societies and that imitation is at the core of progress in the fashion industry. But does this mean that top fashion designers' work should be left unprotected? In order to understand where the originality in apparel is to be found, one has to understand the unique character of a garment, its functions, symbolism, emotional elements and the relationship between designer and consumer. This relationship in particular is very different from those found between the creators and consumers of other types of creative work that enjoy copyright protection.

The emotional bond established in the fashion emotional situation makes it hard to judge whether particular works are original enough to merit copyright protection. The emotional bond becomes a double-edged sword. As fashion designers inject mostly emotions supplemented with a varied degree of creativity into their work, they provoke the question of whether this modicum of creativity clothed in emotion is legally adequate to trigger copyright protection. This question is even more complex than it may seem at first glance, as the universe of fashion rests on styles, trends, manners and ideas, all elements that intrinsically fall outside of copyright protection. And is it not so, that, in the courtroom, the judge will be guided by emotions and therefore intuition?

Moreover, particular branches of fashion aspire very strongly to produce works of art, a fact which, in the wider and more theoretical context, justifies consideration of the difference between fashion and mere clothes. This issue must in turn be considered from various perspectives corresponding to the variety of definitions offered for fashion itself. The distinction overlaps with the generally acknowledged segmentation of fashion into *haute couture*, *prêt-à-porter* and mass market fashion. The straightforward division between *haute couture* and *prêt-à-porter* was partly based on the somewhat artificial assumption that the former segment is artistic, whereas the latter is not. Furthermore, some commentators hold that *haute couture* cannot be considered artistic due to its utilitarian function. This glut of differing methods for the systematisation of fashion does not contribute to a unified legal approach but rather poses a bigger definitional conundrum. In this chapter it was argued that fashion is a part of design. This observation will also be useful when discussing copyright protection.

Copyright law, which is often at odds with the theory of art, does not engage with the artistic or utilitarian purposes of garments, nor with any elitist character they may possess. Therefore 'fashion' for the needs of this study will simply be taken to refer to 'clothes' or 'apparel', including accessories (shoes, bags, jewellery, etc., and to some extent, cosmetics). Only such an approach will enable us to consider fashion in sufficient breadth.

To recap, imitation is integral to the fashion business. This author seeks to examine the competing forces surrounding the phenomenon of copying. Notwithstanding the fact that imitation is a generally accepted aspect of the fashion ecosystem, this author will offer a copyrightability test in forthcoming chapters that will take into consideration the history of manufacturers' and designers' drive for recognition and legal protection. Chapter 2 offers an in-depth perspective on the industrial revolution, which ignited the need for protection of clothing and textile innovations in order to safeguard the inventors' ability to earn from their creations. French couturiers similarly had to agitate for intellectual property protection. The chapter also offers a presentation of selected cases that were groundbreaking for fashion creators.

2 House of sartorial genius? History of imitation in the modern fashion industry

2.1 Overview

Over the course of this research, observations were made across the entire history of garments,[1] which led to the identification of some watershed moments which are presented in this book. In the fashion industry, the *current technological and organisational approaches to making and selling fashion* can still be credited to the *original French haute couture designers*. French creators were always highly valued for their creativity.[2] Italian ones, on the other hand, were known for craftsmanship and manufacturing. Americans, who introduced European fashion trends to the US, had a sense for business and brand identity management.[3] This chapter sheds light on how much proliferation of imitation was enabled by innovation. Speaking of innovations, one of great significance occurred in urban industrialised European and American society in the period from 1860 to 1940,[4] which saw a significant transition from manual to mechanised production of garments.[5] The invention of the sewing machine allowed for a speeding up of the clothing production process. Traditionally, the year 1858 is also the time when the French *haute couture* was born. This timing is not a matter of coincidence, but rather, the progress of innovation and the creation of French fashion were strongly intertwined. The objective of this chapter is to identify specific noteworthy instances of imitation and inspiration in the modern fashion industry and the reaction of the early *haute couture* designers to their creations being copied. It aims to provide a closer look at the most prominent

1 Green, *Art*. . ., p. 732.

2 M.L. Djelic, A. Ainamo, *Coevolution of New Organizational Forms in the Fashion Industry: A Historical and Comparative Study of France, Italy, and the United States*, "Organization Science", 1999, vol. 10, no. 5, pp. 622 and ff.

3 D. Crane, *Globalization, Organizational Size, and Innovation in the French Luxury Fashion Industry: Production of Culture Theory Revisited*, "Poetics", 1997, vol. 24, no. 6, pp. 393 and ff.

4 This author however presents the unfolding of events from 1700 onwards to give a better understanding of the events related to intellectual property that allow the *haute couture* to be born in 1860.

5 M.E. Roach, J.B. Eicher, *The Visible Self: Perspectives on Dress*, Prentice-Hall, 1973, p. 176.

DOI: 10.4324/9781003376033-2

early *couturiers*, who, in addition to being very innovative in their design projects, accessories, business plans and branding, were also highly *copyright minded*. The thesis that is the subject of examination is that, as much as inspiration is the backbone of fashion, these designers were pure masters at turning the old-fashion designs and styles into something *subjectively new*.[6] Due to the limited space of this book, this author draws the landscape of fashion innovations, regulations and designers' *ateliers* mostly in the period between the 19th and early 20th centuries.

2.2 Fashion business scenarios by example of French couturiers

2.2.1 Parisian haute couture

Paris was, in the 18th and 19th centuries, the centre of French society. In attaining that status, the city's ideal geography played an important part, as it was clear that wealthy people travelling north and south would not wish to forego the great deal of leisure and fun offered in the fashion capital.[7] Paris was also an industrial region, well-reputed for its textiles, apparel and accessories. In the 1920s, 300,000 workers were employed in the apparel industry in Paris (out of 1,200,000 in France) and 80,000 dressmaking shops in Paris alone, more than in the entire US. It is said in the literature that Parisian couturiers produced at least 25,000 designs each year, with 10,000 garments shown each season.[8] It was also the leading centre for production of perfumes with more than 10,000 perfume shops in Paris.[9]

France had sought to ward off competitors and reassert its position in fashion since at least the 17th century, when Louis XIV was zealously imposing France's supremacy in style and in the fashion business. His general minister Jean-Baptiste Colbert is reputed to have said: "fashion is to France what the goldmines of Peru are to Spain". He was also famous for a strict policy promoting French luxury goods. In that period of time, foreign apparel specialists in all kinds of garments were encouraged to settle in France.[10] That bore fruit a century later, as France became highly valued for its most exquisite quality, a status it owed to workers who had mastered the art of sewing and knitting. This knack for artistic works and handicrafts made of textiles, lace, leather and other materials became so strongly rooted in society that

6 It is often said that works have to be subjectively new in order to be copyrightable. That is opposed to inventions that need to be objectively new in order to be subject to patent protection.

7 Nystrom, *Economics* . . ., p. 167.

8 Nystrom, *Economics* . . ., pp. 168–169.

9 With spectacular organisations such as Roger et Gallet, Isabey, Rigaud, Geurlain, Bourgeois, Houbigant, Côty and Carron to have their headquarters in Paris. Cf. Nystrom, *Economics* . . ., p. 172.

10 A. Rocamora, *Fashioning the City. Paris, Fashion and the Media*, I.B. Tauris, 2009, pp. 25–26.

it was nearly a custom in French families that every teenage girl was trained at home to use scissors. At age 13 or 14 years, home education was supplemented with an apprenticeship system and design schools. The schools taught the history of textiles, the history of art, introduction to designing, cutting, fitting and sewing. This educational basis was the keystone in building the professional fashion industry.[11] These seamstresses were called *midinettes.* Women, soon after getting married and having children, would relocate home, where they would continue to sew designs (often copied) based on customer orders and pass their skills on to their daughters. *Haute couture* houses had their ecosystems, meaning their own formal relationships with suppliers, in particular textile and embroidery manufacturers, feather and flower dealers. France was home to a wide variety of professions that made it unique in the world: 'tailleurs', 'jupières', 'corsagières', 'mancheuses', 'garnisseuses'. The ecosystem of fashion houses was hierarchical with the designer at the top, supported by *premières,* who were experts in sewing according to type: *flou* (dresses), tailoring, coats, millinery.[12] Shops, too, operated according to the recognised hierarchy (première, seconde, mécaniciennes, first and second apprentices).[13]

To fully understand what fashion really is, it is essential to establish an awareness of the fashion houses that established the norms of the fashion business as we know it today, including the *symbiotic relationship entwining designers and their high-status consumers.* As this book is concerned with copyright law, and as the history of fashion is only meant to supplement the legal research, I refrain from a detailed presentation of every game-changing fashion designer (for instance, Gianni Versace, Tommy Hilfiger, Vivienne Westwood are not examined). Rather, in order to present the best picture of modern fashion's origin story, the focus is on significant French couturiers. The *scenario* is mostly the same: *good old school of sewing* + *appropriation* of existing styles and motifs (to some degree) + *intuitive* response to human desires (e.g. innovation in usefulness or comfort, playing with emotions) + *game-changing marketing* strategies. Subsequently, we return to an examination of this formula.

As for the choice of French couturiers of the turn of 20th century, this author chose the most significant ateliers based in Paris who were members of the *Chambre Syndicale de la Couture Parisienne* and were actively fighting for copyright protection in fashion. It is beyond the scope and aim of this book to cover all existing fashion houses and ateliers of Paris that existed at that time. The choice of ateliers offers a sufficient test of the thesis put at the beginning of the chapter.

11 Nystrom, Economics . . . , pp. 171, 191, 192.

12 Pouillard, *Design Piracy* . . ., p. 322.

13 V. Pouillard, *Early Haute Couture a Historical View*, Slides, October 2017, http://uio.academia.edu/VeroniquePouillard/CurriculumVitae (accessed: 02.01.2023).

2.2.2 French couturiers 1858–1940. A search for creativity and copyrightability

2.2.2.1 The house of Charles Worth

Charles Frederick Worth (1825–1895) was one of the most influential fashion designers and the founder of the modern couture system of fashion production, though it is important to note that his origination of the system would not have been possible without his hard work and many ideas of brilliance. He built his destiny from the ground up, and the prosperity he achieved was attributed to his own hard work and talent. His contemporaries either talked about him with fascination, labelling him a 'wizard of silks and tulle',[14] or regarded him as a scandalous man cutting in on women's business. He was a constant subject of fashion news in magazines, memoirs and books.

He was born and taught the business of selling in England. In 1846, he went to Paris to continue his professional path as a salesman with Gagelin. He soon became a general assistant responsible for retail silk. In 1858, in partnership with Bobergh, he established a tailoring business, which became one of the most reputed high couture fashion houses.

The Metropolitan Museum of Art's pictures illustrate Charles Frederick Worth's reputation-building exquisite simplicity at the early stage of his career.[15]

His business sense and skill in self-promotion caused future generations of fashion lovers to believe that his was the first Parisian fashion house, a belief that does not hold up to scrutiny.[16] The business survived in its initial form until 1870, when, after the Franco-Prussian War, the partners split, and Worth continued alone. It is claimed in the literature that the significant date of 1858 is one of the most important watersheds in the history of fashion, as it was at this point in time that France declared its supremacy in fashion, which it would retain for the next hundred years.[17]

It suffices to mention a few of Worth's inventive ideas. While still working with Gagelin, he devised a so called *manteau de cour*, a court mantle made of antique watered silk embroidered in gold, which soon became the royal fashion.[18] Also at that time, he devised a method of advising his clients on textiles by showing them worn by a living model, Marie Augustine Vernet, who soon became his wife. His sense of business again made many believe he was the first

14 A. Joseph, *"A Wizard of Silks and Tulle": Charles Worth and the Queer Origins of Couture*, "Victorian Studies", 2014, vol. 56, no. 2, p. 252.

15 www.metmuseum.org/art/collection/search/156080?searchField=All&sortBy=relevance&showOnly=openAccess&ft=worth&offset=0&rpp=40&pos=27.

16 At the court of Empress Eugenia, Worth supplied ball gowns, Laferrière casual clothes, Fèlicie coats and capes, Mme Virot and Mme Lebel hats, and Henry Creed riding clothes. Such a set of names shows that in his time there were other fashion houses already operating before him. Cf. Diana de Marly, *Worth: Father of Haute Couture*, Elm Tree Books, 1980, p. 45.

17 V. Pouillard, *The Rise of Fashion Forecasting and Fashion Public Relations, 1920–1940: The History of Tobé and Bernays* [in:] T. Kuehne, H. Berghoff (eds.), *Globalizing Beauty. Body Aesthetics in the 20th Century*, Palgrave, 2013, p. 151.

18 Nystrom, *Economics . . .*, p. 205.

to introduce this innovation.[19] About 1860 he adapted the crinoline,[20] which he was trying to make lighter and more comfortable than before.

He not only changed the perception of fashion with own designs and innovations, he also introduced

> new species of relations between male designer and female clients, one that has remained predominant in high fashion up to the present: intimate but nonsexual relations in which desire does not focus directly on bodies but is, instead, routed through the fabrics that enhance and reshape them.[21]

Designing a dress became a ritual. He also devised and perfected new creative and commercial practices, that, as we would describe it today, evoked emotions and added a sprinkling of luxury and an incitement to spend.

He was the first to establish showrooms that resembled the parlours of the most elegant houses. The interiors were opulently furnished, including expensive carpets and exotic flowers.[22] In addition, the sales girls wore luxurious attire. Previously, designers would pay visits to their clients at their homes.[23] *Haute couture* kept this model but extended beyond that to high street ateliers. When it came to marketing, Worth often encouraged his wife to wear his 'works of art' at social occasions, such as races. He was also the forefather of marking clothes with the designer's label, the purpose of which was at that time perceived in two ways: some took pride in wearing high couture apparel, others reacted with exasperation over the tailor's conceitedness. Beginning in 1867, the House of Worth advertised its apparel in the American fashion press.[24] Although at this time designers often created specially ordered pieces of apparel for clients, Worth was the first, or at least one of first, to prepare a wide variety of designs that the clients could choose from. He also was the first to introduce constant change of forms, fabrics and accessories.[25] Gilles Lipovetsky makes a fair point on that account, that

> Worth implemented the dual principle that constitutes fashion in the current sense of the term: the designer-couturier gained autonomy in

19 C. Evans, *Mechanical Smile: Modernism and the First Fashion Shows in France and America, 1900–1929*, Yale University Press, 2013, pp. 12–13. To wit, of the newest sources also questions whether his wife really served as a model at Gagelin's. Chantal Trubert-Tollu, Françoise Tétart-Vittu, Jean-Marie Martin-Hattemberg, Fabrice Olivieri, *The House of Worth 1858–1954. The Birth of Haute Couture*, Thames & Hudson, 2017, p. 22.

20 Laver, *Fashion* . . ., p. 127.

21 A. Joseph, "*A Wizard* . . ., p. 253.

22 P. Sparke, *Interior Decoration and Haute Couture: Links between the Developments of the Two Professions in France and the USA in the Late Nineteenth and Early Twentieth Centuries: A Historiographical Analysis*, "Journal of Design History", 2008, vol. 21, no. 1, Professionalizing Interior Design 1870–1970, p. 103.

23 V. Pouillard, *Early Haute Couture* . . .

24 V. Pouillard, *Early Haute Couture* . . .

25 G. Lipovetsky, *The Empire of Fashion. Dressing Modern Democracy*, Princeton University Press, 2002, p. 64.

> the theory and in fact, while the client lost the initiative in the matter of dress. This shift marks the unmistakable historical novelty of haute couture: the era in which clients cooperated with dressmakers on a design that was in the final analysis unchangeable gave way to an era in which articles of clothing were invented, created from start to finish, by professionals according to their own "inspiration" and taste. The woman became a mere consumer, albeit at the level of luxury, while the couturier was transformed from artisan into sovereign artist.[26]

Worth was also one of the first to show clothes on live models (fr. *essayeuses*, meaning 'tryer-on'). With this introduction, a new incarnation of *haute couture* was born, *prêtes à essayer*, translated as 'ready to try on, departing somewhat from the classic couture model'.[27] To understand the significance of this innovation, it suffices to note that the first true fashion show is dated to 1900, when the 1900 Paris Exposition took place. It welcomed 20 fashion houses, including Worth itself, Rouff, Paquin and Callot Soeurs.[28]

Worth developed dresses that were pieces of art that executed a flawless interplay of hues and textures made by carefully selected fabrics and trims. His respect for and support of the textile industry can be seen in the vast amount of textile he used to create each outfit.[29]

Worth maintained such values as originality, uniqueness and exclusivity. That did not, however, restrain him from reusing aspects of his work, an approach which was accurately planned in order to keep his house more efficient and identifiable. Worth, as also his counterparts, saw no contradiction between *haute couture* quality and the selective use of sewing machines, which he used for long runs of stitches and topstitching. He introduced cost-effective so called mix-and-match methods of production.[30]

Worth's strategy was to become the royal tailor, which he accomplished to his great financial success.[31]

26 Lipovetsky, *The Empire . . .*, p. 75.

27 Evans, *The Ontology . . .*, p. 61.

28 Lipovetsky, *Empire . . .*, p. 57. *Paris Haute Couture 2012 – Paris Haute Couture*, ed. Olivier Saillard, Anne Zazzo, Flammarion, 2012, p. 50.

29 www.metmuseum.org/art/collection/search/159187?searchField=All&sortBy=relevance&showOnly=openAccess&ft=worth&offset=0&rpp=40&pos=21.

30 Didier Grumbach, *History of International Fashion*, Interlink Books, 2014, p. 31.

31 *Among Worth's clients were Empress Eugénie of France and Empress Elisabeth of Austria (Sisi).*
Franz X. Winterhalter, *The Empress Eugénie*, 1854.
Source: Met's Open Access: Public Domain www.metmuseum.org/art/collection/search/437942?sortBy=Relevance&ft=Franz+Xaver+Winterhalter&offset=0&rpp=40&pos=3.
Franz X. Winterhalter, *Empress Elisabeth of Austria*, 1865.
Source: Kunsthistorisches Museum, Vienna, Austria, Public domain, https://commons.wikimedia.org/wiki/File:Elisabeth_of_Austria,_by_Franz_Xaver_Winterhalter.jpg.
www.metmuseum.org/art/collection/search/437942.
https://commons.wikimedia.org/wiki/File:Elisabeth_of_Austria,_by_Franz_Xaver_Winterhalter.jpg.

Item of note 2.1 'Electric Light' dress

Worth also knew how to conquer American high society. In 1883 he designed a dress for Alice Vanderbilt, the wife of Cornelius Vanderbilt, for the Vanderbilt Costume Ball, known as the 'Electric Light' dress.

> The dress was also embellished at the shoulders with gold metallic tinsel and beaded tassels with golden fringe at the neckline and golden tulle attached at the shoulders that flowed down the back of the dress. The dress cleverly featured hidden batteries so that Alice would be able to switch on to light up the dress like an electric light bulb, which was a recent invention of Thomas Edison.
> B. Jones

Source: B. Jones, *Charles Worth and the House of Worth*, October 2015, available at: http://theenchantedmanor.com/charles-worth-and-the-house-of-worth/ accessed: 3.01.2023.

When it comes to innovation, one of his dresses, as presented in the Metropolitan Museum of Art's pictures, was ordered with three bodices. The mentioned dress could be worn as either a court presentation gown with a spectacular train, a ballgown or a dinner dress, as seen on MET websites.[32]

The magnificent, voided velvet, which was woven in Lyon, is recognisable for its Aesthetic Movement colour scheme. The "greenery-yallery" flowers are depicted in "ciselé" velvet (having a mix of cut and uncut silk loops), which contrast with the light, almost mauve-coloured pink satin background. Thus, Worth transformed the retardataire into the avant-garde by incorporating the advanced "artistic" taste of the time into this court presentation gown, the most formal attire possible for a non-royal.[33]

The House of Worth was continued by his sons, Jean-Philippe and Gaston Worth, who inherited great skills in fashion, and his grandsons, Jean Charles and Jacques. Like his father before him, Jean-Philippe Worth was acclaimed for creating complex artistic gowns with delicate trimmings employing unique textiles.

It was reputed for its style, which was gorgeous, regal and rich with fine embellishments, ornaments and lace. For nearly 100 years it resisted its strong rivals and kept at the forefront of the couture world.[34] His son and grandsons, Jean-Philippe and Jean Charles along with Jacques Worth, fuelled the family

32 www.metmuseum.org/art/collection/search/137479?searchField=All&sortBy=relevance&showOnly=openAccess&ft=worth&offset=40&rpp=40&pos=45.

33 www.metmuseum.org/art/collection/search/137479?searchField=All&sortBy=relevance&showOnly=openAccess&ft=worth&offset=40&rpp=40&pos=45.

34 Nystrom, *Economics* . . ., p. 207.

business with their knack for success.[35] They ensured the growth of the House of Worth by introducing a strict policy, according to which what mattered in *haute couture* designs was 1) the client's body shape and social standing, 2) the client's preferences and 3) a compromise between the client's expectations and the right cut/colour/style. Worth paid a great deal of attention to slimming a body visually by employing advantageous cuts, using stripes and respecting proportions.[36] Contemporary images of his designs are hard to find, as, due to fear of copying, Worth cut back on advertising channels.

2.2.2.2 The house of Jeanne Paquin

Jeanne Paquin (1869–1936) was a leading fashion designer, labelled as "the most commercial artist alive".[37] She is considered the first major couturier and one of the forerunners of the modern fashion business. Unlike other couturières of her time,[38] she is not credited with any specific design innovation but rather with institutional innovation.[39] One account concerned with design innovation reported that she was the forgotten creator of the 'Empire-line dress' made in 1905,[40] with which Poiret made his name a year later.[41] Another design wrongly credited to Poiret was the kimono coat[42] (an evening dress for theatre or opera) that Paquin had made in 1912, a year before her counterpart.

This coat brings up one of the significant observations and ethical problems. The Japanese were always credited for the creation of the kimono, so there is a lingering question over whether it is allowed or ethical to give credit to the Parisian designers who imported this clothing idea into their own fashion. The Japanese trend to make kimonos was *à la mode* for decades, and the garment was subject to transformation in its country of origin.[43] This is one of the first instances of ***fashion appropriation*** that today would be the subject of heated moral debate.[44]

35 Nystrom, *Economics . . .*, p. 207.
36 V. Pouillard, *Early Haute Couture . . .*
37 B. Polan, R. Tredre, *The Great Fashion Designers*, Berg, 2009, p. 17.
38 *The BERG Companion to Fashion* (ed. Valerie Steele), Berg, 2010, pp. 551–552, entry: Paquin Jeanne.
39 J.F. Blanco, M.D. Doering (eds.), *Clothing and Fashion: American Fashion from Head to Toe. Volume One: Pre-Colonial Times through the American Revolution*, ABC – CLIO, 2016, p. 249.
40 Jankowska, Meghaichi, Pawełczyk, Illustrated . . .
41 More information with pictorial explanation see Margareth, *Jeanne Paquin, the Forgotten Dressmaker*, "Bliss from Bygone Days", Blog, 14 April 2020, www.blissfrombygonedays.com/home/2017/4/12/jeanne-paquin; cf. A. Calahan, *The Myth of Poiret as Debunked by 1906*, "A Fashion Institute of Technology Blog", 9 July 2015, https://blog.fitnyc.edu/materialmode/2015/07/09/the-myth-of-poiret-as-debunked-by-1906/
42 Jankowska, Meghaichi, Pawełczyk, Illustrated . . . .
43 Lionel Lambourne, *Japonisme: Cultural Crossings between Japan and the West*, Phaidon Press, 2007.
44 Jankowska, Meghaichi, Pawełczyk, Illustrated . . .

She was trained in sewing at Maison Rouff and, at first, helped her husband run a couture shop that had grown out of a menswear shop established in the 1840s. House of Paquin, established in 1891, ran counter to prevailing trends. Her fashion was perceived as simple but futuristic. She introduced simple, youthful garments, hobble skirts (1908–1909) as well as sheath and directoire gowns (1910–1912).[45] She rejected the *jupe-culotte*.[46] She was the first woman to see black as a colour of elegance rather than of mourning after the times of the Spanish flu and World War I. She made it *en vogue* by blending it with flamboyantly coloured linings and embroidery.[47] In doing so, she attracted a clientele that was edgier than Worth's.[48] After the death of Charles Worth in 1895, she became the most famous designer of ball gowns and sumptuous dresses.[49] She had a predisposition to emulate Greek and Roman style as well as Asian culture but did so in her own recognisable manner.[50]

Paquin made a true wholesale business out of sewing. She is claimed to have been the first to sell clothes to department stores for sale to consumers and to wholesalers for resale to dealers. One of her success formulae was the ability to merge innovation and elegance. She also had a gift of making her clientele take delight in her designs without ever questioning her good taste.[51] As to her innovations, they were recounted in the pages of *Harper's Bazaar* and *The New York Times*, which underlined her knack for 'feminine outlines' and her love for true colours. She "could be credited with inventing what was described as the appropriately tight skirt".[52] Following in the footsteps of House of Worth, and along with Poiret, she was one of the first to understand that in order to reach a mass audience and to enthuse clients to buy her designs, the *Maison* has to be visible during public events like theatre plays, operas or races, where she would send her models regardless of the risk of plagiarism or pastiche.[53] She even organised the first travelling fashion show with a dozen models, who went on a tour in the US.[54]

In 1896, Paquin opened a branch in London while reorganising her business structure into a limited company. She also had branches in Buenos Aires and Madrid. Beginning in 1900, fur coats and fur accessories began to appear

45 Nystrom, Economics . . . , p. 208.

46 N.J. Troy, *The Theatre of Fashion: Staging Haute Couture in Early 20th-Century France*, "Theatre Journal", 2001, vol. 53, no. 1, p. 23.

47 K. Joslin, *Edith Wharton and the Making of Fashion*, University of New Hampshire Press, 2009, p. 126.

48 A. Dymond, *Embodying the Nation: Art, Fashion, and Allegorical Women at the 1900 Exposition Universelle,* "RACAR: revue d'art canadienne"/ "Canadian Art Review", 2011, vol. 36, no. 2, p. 5.

49 M.L. Stewart, *Dressing Modern Frenchwomen. Marketing Haute Couture 1919–1939*, The John Hopkins University Press, 2008, p. 7.

50 Margareth, *Jeanne Paquin* . . .

51 Troy, *The Theatre* . . ., p. 24.

52 Troy, *The Theatre* . . ., p. 24.

53 Troy, *The Theatre* . . ., p. 24.

54 Joslin, *Edith* . . ., p. 126.

regularly in French *confection* collections. House of Paquin was known for fur collections.[55] In 1912, she opened a shop in New York to sell furs. In a city containing much untapped demand for this product, the venture was profitable, aided in no small way by the introduction of fashionable colours and shapes, e.g. white fox.[56] As Henry Poland noted about white fox fur in 1892, "the fur until recent years was of little value . . . but now it is much admired, and exceeds the price of red fox".[57] At that time, Paquin had around 2,000 employees.[58]

As much as Poiret drew inspiration from the Orient, Paquin was less open to oriental style. However, both used fans to advertise their fashion designs. Paquin hired illustrators (Paul Iribe, Georges Barbier and Georges Lepape) to enthuse her clients.[59]

She was highly regarded in the US, a fact that, as in the case of Poiret, resulted in extensive copying and counterfeiting of her designs. She is also known as an activist for copyright and fair protection of her works. For this reason, she joined Poiret's Syndicate for the Protection of the Great French Couture and Related Industries. In the late 1910s, she became president of the *Chambre Syndicale de la Haute Couture*.[60]

Queens of Spain, Belgium and Portugal were clients of Paquin. After Jeanne Paquin's death in 1936, the house remained operational until 1956.[61]

2.2.2.3 House of Callot Soeurs

The House of Callot Soeurs was established in 1895, four years after the opening of the House of Paquin, by four sisters: Marie Callot Gerber (1870–1927), Marthe Callot Bertrand (1895–1937), Regina Callot Tennyson-Chantrell (1895–1937) and Joséphine Callot Crimont. The eldest sister, Marie, received a sartorial education and gained experience with Raudnitz and Co., a reputable Parisian atelier. The Callot sisters were active in fashion marketing, exhibiting their designs at fairs (among others, the 1900 Paris World's Fair and the 1915 Universal Exhibition in San Francisco) and built an impressive client base. American *Vogue* declared them in 1916 "foremost among the powers that rule the destinies of a woman's life and increase the income of France".[62] Today,

55 J.R. Bockstoce, *White Fox and Icy Seas in the Western Arctic. The Fur Trade, Transportation, and Change in the Early Twentieth Century*, Yale University Press, p. 52.

56 Bockstoce, *White Fox* . . . , p. 52.

57 Bockstoce, *White Fox* . . . , p. 53.

58 Dymond, *Embodying* . . ., p. 5.

59 A. Fukai, *The Collection of the Kyoto Costume Institute. Fashion. A History from the 18th to the 20th Century*, Taschen, 2002, p. 352.

60 Blanco, Doering (eds.)., *Clothing* . . ., p. 249.

61 D. Milford-Cottam, Daniel (2 June 2015). *Paquin: Parisian Fashion Designs 1897–1954*, "The Factory Presents". Victoria and Albert Museum, 2 June 2015, www.vam.ac.uk/blog/caring-for-our-collections/paquin-parisian-fashion-designs-1897-1954 (accessed: 17.01.2023).

62 J. Hatcher, P. Dukovic, *Twenty-One Dresses*, "The New Yorker", 16 March 2015, www.newyorker.com/magazine/2015/03/23/twenty-one-dresses (accessed: 27.01.2023).

they remain among the industry's unsung heroes, as despite being more or less forgotten today, their gowns were, in their heyday, among the most sought-after garments by discerning consumers because of Callot's intuition for style, understanding of materials, innovativeness and craftsmanship.[63] The Callot sisters were among the first to use lace and lamé,[64] to reject the corset and to enthuse with light and fluid dress lines.[65] Their designs stood out as daring and original for both their lines and their colours. They also had a sense for matching unusual fabrics. The house of Callot drew on orientalism[66] to create gowns resembling saris, qipaos or djellabas.[67] Today this kind of creation would surely be subject to criticism as an instance of unreasonable cultural appropriation.

In terms of innovation,

> the work of Callot Soeur does not stint the couture's roster of technical skills. Here, sequins vary: some are punched into a filigree pinwheel, others are hammered flat; in some instances metal is overlaid onto faceted crystal. But even this ornamentation is not entirely for the pleasure of diversity, but for the calculated and magical effects of such varied surfaces seen in evening and candle lights.[68]

They were first to use gold and silver lamé to make dresses, first to make straight sheath gowns and first to introduce interpretations of Japanese kimono sleeves to Europe.

According to Paul Nystrom, "They were the first creators of the straight sheath gown".[69] However, this opinion might be an overgeneralisation as this was an interpretation of the Princess Sheath dress that was popular between 1878 and 1880 and was worn by the Princess of Wales.

In addition to asserting ownership of orient-inspired style and extreme (almost theatrical) designs, the house of Callot Soeur created garments for operas and theatre, as did Paquin and Poiret.

Madeleine Vionnet, a *protégée* of the house of Callot,[70] coyly extolled the quality of its designs: "Without the example of the Callot Soeur, I would have continued to make Fords. It is because of them that I have been able to make Rolls Royces".[71] Another of Callot's apprentices was Marie-Louise Bruyère.

63 Jankowska, Meghaichi, Pawełczyk, *Illustrated Fashion Law.*

64 B. Tietzel, Museum fur Angewandte Kunts Koln, "Wallraf-Richartz-Jahrbuch", vol. 56, 1995, pp. 354–356.

65 Jankowska, Meghaichi, Pawełczyk, Illustrated . . . .

66 J. Kim, *1910–14 – Callot Soeurs, Evening Dress,* "Woomans Fasion", 1 December 2019, http://woomansfasion.com/1910-14-callot-soeurs-evening (accessed: 27.01.2023).

67 Hatcher, Dukovic, *Twenty-one . . .*

68 *Evening Dress, 1910–14, Callot Souers,* www.metmuseum.org/art/collection/search/81139 (accessed: 27.01.2023).

69 Nystrom, *Economics . . .*, p. 210.

70 B. Kirke, *Vionnet: Fashion's Twentieth Century Technician*, "Thresholds", 2001, no. 22, fashion, pp. 79.

71 *Evening Dress . . .*

In 1900 Callot hired 200 employees and made 2 million Francs in sales (equivalent to 8 million Euro), which, by 1901, they had tripled and doubled, respectively. In the 1920s, they established branches in Nice, Biarritz, Buenos Aires and London.[72]

Callot Soeurs were well known in Paris for their zealous fight against copying of their style.

2.2.2.4 House of Paul Poiret

Paul Poiret (1879–1944) established his atelier in 1903 at the age of 24 years, after having accomplished sartorial practice with major Parisian fashion houses, such as Jacques Doucet's or Worth's. Like Worth, he took care to cultivate this artist's persona.[73] To American journalists Poiret said, "Ladies come to me for a gown as they go to a distinguished painter to get their portraits put on canvas. I am an artist, not a dressmaker".[74] With that purpose in mind, he hired painters and graphic artists to furnish his new atelier, making artistic announcements of the change of address. He also created two *deluxe* albums of his dress designs, one of which he presented in the Galerie Barbazanges. He had a keen sense of aestheticism and a knack for business, which he successfully linked.[75] He introduced himself to high society class in his self-promoting catalogue *Les robes de Paul Poiret*.[76] One of his creative and business ideas was to hire Edward Steichen to photograph his designs for publication in *Art et Décoration*. He was uncannily prescient in branding 'life style'.[77] As a fashion creator he was a trailblazer in introducing lines of perfume (Rosine 1911), cosmetics (soaps, beauty creams, powders, makeup, lipsticks)[78] and furniture.[79] He was one of the first to make his own *pochoir* prints and encourage interior designers to perceive their own work as part of the fashion system.[80]

72 G.J. Sumathi, *Elements of Fashion and Apparel Design*, New Age International (P) Limited Publishers, 2002, p. 112; E.L. Block, *Dressing Up: The Women Who Influenced French Fashion*, The MIT Press, 2021, p. 67.

73 S. Lissim, *The Decorative Arts Society 1850 to the Present*, "The Journal of the Decorative Arts Society 1890–1940", 1978, no. 2, p. 21.

74 Poiret, quoted in *Poiret Here to Tell of His Art*, "The New York Times" (21 September 1913), p. 1 [after:] N.J. Troy, *The Logic of Fashion*, p. 2.

75 C. Wilk, *Introduction*, "The Journal of the Decorative Arts Society 1850 – the Present", 1995, no. 19.

76 D. Roylance, *Art Deco Paris 1900–1925: Catalogue of the Exhibition of Pochoir Color Prints from the Graphic Arts Collection*, "The Princeton University Library Chronicle", 1999, vol. 61, no. 1, pp. 18–19.

77 L. Cooke, *'Poiret: King of Fashion'. New York*, "The Burlington Magazine", 2007, vol. 149, no. 1253, p. 585; H. Koda (ed.), *Poiret, Exhibition Catalogue*, MET, 2007, pp. 38–41.

78 I. Paris, *Fashion as a System: Changes in Demand as the Basis for the Establishment of the Italian Fashion System (1960–1970)*, "Enterprise & Society", vol. 11, no. 3, 2010, p. 531.

79 S.E. Safer, *Designing Lucile Ltd: Couture and the Modern Interior 1900–1920s*, "The Journal of the Decorative Arts Society 1850 to the Present", 2009, no. 33, p. 47.

80 S. Street, J. Yumibe, *Chromatic Modernity Color: Color, Cinema and Media of the 1920s*, Columbia University Press, 2019, p. 68; P. Sparke, *Interior Decoration and Haute Couture:*

He made his name with such designs as the kimono coat, 'Empire-line dress' or corset-free dress, even though he was not the first to apply these styles. He is credited with the turban, hobble shirts, harem pants, peasant-type blouses (1912–1913) and the minaret[81] or lampshade gown (1913–1914),[82] and he was hailed the father of 'draping',[83] which he mastered to perfection.[84] His rejection of full corsets and his neoclassical-oriented drive to reveal the female body was as much groundbreaking as shocking. Poiret is said to have revolutionised dress colours[85] by introducing violet, red, orange, blue and green in place of pale Edwardian hues and tones.[86] This, in turn, he took from the Russian ballets, so it is hard to attribute to him, although it must be admitted that he was fluent in marketing, which, unfortunately, is why we credit so many innovations to him.[87]

The infatuation with Turkish clothing that developed in Europe and America in the 18th century and persisted into the 19th and early 20th centuries is demonstrated by garments in the Turkish style. Paul Poiret's "harem" pants and the fancy dress ball "1002nd Night", which had a Turkish theme, marked the peak of this fad in 1911.

In his time, Poiret received a lot of criticism from fashion magazines. A great deal of public indignation was prompted by Jean-Philippe Worth, who disparaged Poiret's abandonment of corsets with these words: "They are hideous, barbaric! . . . They are really only suitable for the women of uncivilized tribes. If we adopt them, let us ride on camels and ostriches!"[88] Not content with this, Worth found Poiret's pantaloon gowns "vulgar, wicked and ugly", while, at the same, time these two innovations went down in fashion history as among the most important milestones.[89]

Links between the Developments of the Two Professions in France and the USA in the Late Nineteenth and Early Twentieth Centuries: A Historiographical Analysis, "Journal of Design History", 2008, vol. 21, no. 1, Professionalizing Interior Design 1870–1970 (Spring), p. 103.

81 Jankowska, Meghaichi, Pawełczyk, *Illustrated . . . .*

82 Nystrom, *Economics of Fashion*, p. 213. Cf. M. Antle, *Surrealism and the Orient,* "Yale French Studies", 2006, no. 109, p. 15.

83 Laver, *Fashion . . .*, p. 120.

84 E. Carlson, *Cubist Fashion: Mainstreaming Modernism after the Armory*, "Winterthur Portfolio", 2014, vol. 48, no. 1, p. 10.

85 E. Carlson, *Cubist Fashion . . .*, p. 10, E. Bespalova, *Leon Bakst's Textile and Interior Design in America*, "Studies in the Decorative Arts", 1997–1998, vol. 5, no. 1 (Fall–Winter), p. 13.

86 S. Donaldson, *Followers of Fashion,* "Irish Arts Review", 2005, vol. 22, no. 1, p. 59; cf. S. Blum, *Costume Institute*, "Notable Acquisitions" (Metropolitan Museum of Art), no. 1981/1982, p. 33.

87 As discussed with Dr Piotr Szaradowski.

88 M.E. Davis, *Classic Chic: Music, Fashion, and Modernism,* University of California Press, 2006, p. 26.

89 S. Blum, P.M. Ettesvold, J.L. Druesedow, *Costume Institute*, "Notable Acquisitions" (Metropolitan Museum of Art), 1982–1983, no. 1982/1983), pp. 41–43; J.R. Bockstoce, *White Fox and Icy Seas in the Western Arctic: The Fur Trade, Transportation, and Change in the Early Twentieth Century*, Yale University Press, pp. 53–54. M.L. Roberts quoted Poiret's response to this avalanche of animadversion "It was the age of the corset," Poiret later reminisced,

In fact, Poiret derived his ideas from all around the world. The robes he introduced were worn in Ancient Greece and Rome by young women. He drew also from the orient,[90] for which he was anointed as the father of 'Style Sultane'. He made many references to Asia, the Middle East and Africa.[91] Among other examples, in 1912 he created 'Kazan', a dress closely based on Russian peasant style[92]; in 1920 a dress inspired by *akhnif*, a style of man's cloak from Morocco's High Atlas region[93]; and in 1924 an evening gown called 'Nubian'.[94] We observe a lot of cultural appropriation here – dubious to modern sensibilities.

He was known for labelling his designs with names revealing his inspiration, like 'Joséphine', '1811',[95] 'La Perse'[96] or "Iudree". The criticism of his work was countered with equal measures of approval, notably including *Vogue* dubbing him 'the Prophet of Simplicity'.[97]

After he visited Vienna in November 1911, he used Austrian textiles (Wiener Werkstätte Silks) in his designs.[98] Even *Vogue*, in 1914, devoted publishing space to the art of printed fabrics: "not only do artists create them, they name and sign them, so that one buys a fabric almost as one buys an etching".[99] *Harper's Bazaar* and *The New York Times* also found them 'unusual', 'futuristic' and 'modern'.[100] His bright colours and geometric shapes were well timed for the transition to cubism and were generally perceived as part of the avant-garde.[101]

"I waged war upon it. It was in the name of liberty that I brought about my first Revolution, by deliberately laying siege to the corset." "Poiret here likened himself to a revolutionary storming the Bastille of Victorian fashion, thereby restoring to women their innate right to freedom of movement", see. M.L. Roberts, *Samson and Delilah Revisited: The Politics of Women's Fashion in 1920s France*, "The American Historical Review", 1993, vol. 98, no. 3, p. 666; A.B. Presley, *Fifty Years of Change: Societal Attitudes and Women's Fashions, 1900–1950*, "The Historian", 1998, vol. 60, no. 2, p. 311; cf. J. Fields, *'Fighting the Corsetless Evil': Shaping Corsets and Culture, 1900–1930*, "Journal of Social History", 1999, vol. 33, no. 2, pp. 355–384.

90 D. Roylance, *Art Deco* . . ., pp. 23, 27; Laver, *Fashion* . . ., p. 128.

91 V.L. Rovine, *Colonialism's Clothing: Africa, France, and the Deployment of Fashion*, "Design Issues", 2009, vol. 25, no. 3, p. 52.

92 L. Taylor, *Peasant Embroidery: Rural to Urban and East to West Relationships 1860–1914*, "The Journal of the Decorative Arts Society 1850 – the Present", 1990, no. 14, Turn of the Century Design: Cross Currents in Europe, pp. 49–50.

93 Rovine, *Colonialism's Clothing* . . ., p. 56.

94 Rovine, *Colonialism's Clothing* . . ., p. 57.

95 Davis, *Classic Chic* . . . , p. 28.

96 Cooke, *'Poiret: King* . . ., p. 585.

97 Davis, *Classic Chic* . . ., p. 31.

98 M.L. Wagner, *Fashion and Feminism in "Fin de Siècle" Vienna*, "Woman's Art Journal", 1989–1990, vol. 10, no. 2, p. 32.

99 H. Hess, *Changing Impressions: Wiener Werkstätte Prints and Textiles*, "Art in Print", 2011, vol. 1, no. 3, pp. 24–25; *Fabrics Created, Signed, and Copyrighted*, "Vogue", 1914, vol. 43, 15 April, p. 48.

100 Hess, *Changing* . . ., pp. 24–25.

101 Carlson, *Cubist Fashion* . . ., pp. 9–10; Roberts, *Samson* . . ., p. 666.

In 1911, Poiret founded the École Martine (also referred to as Atelier Martine),[102] an art school with a brand-new approach to creativity. To enhance their intellectual skills, Poiret's students regularly visited gardens, aquariums or the countryside in order to make sketches of plants and animals, which were later used on textiles[103] used for fashion, home furnishings, curtains, wallpaper and carpets.[104]

Poiret was reputed for his oriental style, which he also popularised by supplying theatres with his designs of this kind. He was one of the first to dress actresses and well-known women for no payment, in exchange for which he received publicity at such places as Longchamps, the Opéra or on the stage.[105]

It is worth mentioning that, in June 1911, he organised "The 1002nd Night",[106] to which he invited artists and patrons of art, all of whom he asked to dress in costumes resembling his fashions. As stressed by Nancy J. Troy,

> "The 1002nd Night" helped to solidify Poiret's reputation not only for extravagance but also for audacity, particularly in connection with his controversial designs for culottes and harem trousers, an orientalist style of cross-dressing that brought him dangerously close to violating the vaguely demarcated yet highly charged border between fashion and scandal.[107]

Theatre became his preferred channel for advertising designs. One spectacular success was his tunic worn in the Persian play *Le Minaret* (1913). The garment took its name, the *Minaret-style dress*, from the title of the play. The very morning after the premiere he received phone calls from clients ordering similar garments, not to mention from the American market. The biggest fashion stores – J. M. Gidding, Gimbel's, Macy's and Wanamaker's – jockeyed for position to introduce Poiret's designs first to the American market.[108] When Poiret visited America, he was staggered to see gowns displayed in shop windows falsely under his brand, complete with his label sewn in. He brought a case before the court demanding legal protection

102 It was just like the Vienna Workshops. He had been aware of the Workshop before, before his visit in 1911. He had also seen the Stoclet Palace, near Brussels.

103 Jankowska, Meghaichi, Pawełczyk, *Illustrated* . . . .

104 J. Adlin, A. Peck, *20th Century*, "The Metropolitan Museum of Art Bulletin. New Series", 1995–1996, vol. 53, no. 3, p. 66; Sparke, *Interior Decoration* . . ., p. 103.

105 N.J. Troy, *The Theatre of Fashion: Staging Haute Couture in Early 20th-Century France*, "Theatre Journal", 2001, vol. 53, vol. 1, p. 4 [after:] C. Castle, *Model Girl*, David & Charles, 1977, p. 17.

106 Blum, Ettesvold, Druesedow, *Costume* . . ., p. 42. Troy, *The Theatre of Fashion* . . ., p. 13; Cooke, *'Poiret: King of Fashion'* . . ., p. 585.

107 Troy, *The Logic* . . . , p. 2.

108 Troy, *The Logic* . . . , p. 2; cf. SEM, Le vrai et le faux chic, Paris 1914.

for his designs, since these had become subject to imitation and counterfeit. He sued William Fantell of the Universal Weaving Company, who in 1915 was found guilty of having manufactured and sold Poiret's designs. Seeking protection on the grounds of copying proved costly. The effect of the legal action was the opposite of that intended. Although Poiret managed to win one battle, he did not stem the commercial surge of imitations of his designs. Macy's and Gimbel's were not afraid of selling 'American-made copies of the Imported Gowns'.[109] Poiret publicly threatened to take legal action against anyone copying his label or appropriating his brand on a garment in any other fashion.[110] On his return to Paris, he established the Syndicate for the Protection of the Great French Couture and Related Industries to issue a set of, at that time, controversial rules regarding access to seasonal shows and control of publication of photographs of new designs.[111]

As to Poiret's practice of protecting his designs, this is well demonstrated by a preserved stamped label stitched into the hem of a dress dating back to 1909 with imprinted design model number, copyright registration number (5272), model name ("Maintenon") and collection model number (800).[112] The label indicates that the design was registered at the Paris Industrial Relations Board. The source goes on to say that:

> the dress would have been worn by a mannequin in the fashion show. If ordered by a private client it would be re-made to her measurements; if bought by a trade buyer, the buyer acquired the right to reproduce the dress commercially. Much modified, this would then be mass produced in American garment factories, while the model dress itself was never sold. It was a prototype whose sole purpose was to be copied and adapted for sale. Models were all numbered for internal records, and the couture houses kept careful track of these for their fight against copyright infringement.[113]

109 Troy, *The Logic . . .*, p. 4.

110 P. Poiret, *Warning against False Labels*, "Women's Wear", 14 October 1913, p. 3.
Poiret's warning against false labels:
www.google.com/url?sa=i&url=https%3A%2F%2Fwww.pinterest.it%2Fpin%2F503699539548715167%2F&psig=AOvVaw24ykvMY-xMAA2cwjFjcijr&ust=1589807034468000&source=images&cd=vfe&ved=0CAIQjRxqFwoTCOiwmfT6uukCFQAAAAAdAAAAABAf.
Harper's Bazaar's advertisement demonstrating how sought-after Poiret's designs were. This content reflects garments offered for sale by Macy's, Gimbel's and J.M. Gidding:
http://susannaives.com/wordpress/2019/11/friday-fashions-from-harpers-bazaar-1913/.

111 Troy, *The Logic . . .*, p. 4.

112 Evans, *The Ontology . . .*, p. 65. Cf. Jankowska, Meghaichi, Pawełczyk, *Illustrated . . . .*

113 Evans, *The Ontology . . .*, [after:] G. Le Fèvre, *Au secours de la couture (industrie française)*, Editions Baudinière, 1929, p. 142.

Item of note no. 2.2 ***Paul Poiret v. Jules Poiret* (1920)[114]**

Paul Poiret sued an Englishman, A. F. Nash, for establishing an atelier in London in 1914 under the name 'Jules Poiret'. Some of his dresses were published in *Tatler* and *Sketch*. His designs were initially attributed to Paul Poiret. Even though he published corrections as to the name of the designer, Paul Poiret sued him for using his surname in the brand. The passing-off claim had to meet two premises: local business activity and earned goodwill. Even though P. Poiret did not have a branch in England and even closed his business for the period of World War I, P.O. Lawrence J had no doubt that the defendant "had acquired a considerable connection chiefly, if not exclusively, as a theatrical costumier". The judge took the view that P. Poiret had earned his reputation in the British market as a top *haute couture* label and that an argument of a few years' downtime was of no relevance. In the case, it was also observed that Nash's style was so similar to Poiret's that it could cause confusion and damage his goodwill after re-entering the market.[115] The case may be considered the epitome of protecting one's brand and of the use of a surname as a label.[116]

2.2.2.5 House of Lanvin

Jeanne Lanvin (1867–1946) was initially a *chapelière* (hatmaker) but also sewed dresses for her daughter. As she was often approached because of admiration for her designs, she decided to launch an atelier in 1889, which makes her the first female couturière.[117] As observed in the literature,

> she gained renown for the intimist delicacy and sensitivity of her handling of fabric, color, and ornament, as well as for the then-radial simplicity of the silhouettes of her designs and for their youthfulness. The simple lines of her work prompted comparisons – at this time of interest

114 Paul Poiret v. Jules Poiret et Cie., Ltd., & Nash, 37 R. P. C. 177 (Eng. 1920). One of the pages of *Daily Sketch* from 31 March 1916, showing Jules Poiret designs (www.wdl.org/en/item/19170/view/1/9/).

115 M. Richardson, J. Thomas, *Fashioning Intellectual Property: Exhibition, Advertising and the Press*, Cambridge University Press, 2012, p. 131; C.W.F., *Unfair Competition by the Use of a Surname. The Waterman Fountain Pen Cases*, "University of Pennsylvania Law Review and American Law Register", 1924, vol. 72, no. 3, p. 301.

116 Richardson, Thomas, *Fashioning* . . ., p. 132.

117 S. Laurent, R. Wittman, *Teaching the Applied Arts to Women at the École Duperré in Paris, 1864–1940*, "Studies in the Decorative Arts", 1996–1997, vol. 4, no. 1 (Fall–Winter), p. 81.

in the neoclassical – with the 'Greek tunic,' and identified her with the modernizing tendencies in women's dress just before World War I.[118]

She also created turbans, which were very much *en vogue* at that time.[119] Her dresses were made in bold florals, colours and with appliqué work.[120] She was also known for her romantic style[121] and pearl-embroidered dresses.[122] She also labelled her designs with names, such as: "Roseraie", "Jolibois", "Phèdre", "Fusée", "Cyclone".[123]

As to inventiveness, she is considered the first designer of the 19th century to send costume dolls from Paris to the US. However, dolls were shipped long distances back in the *Ancien Régime* and in the 19th century as well. So although it is hard to acknowledge any invention in this, it is worth observing that the French designer knew how to use her marketing prowess to her benefit.

The dolls were clothed in peasant embroideries. Unquestionably, this gimmick won huge attention.[124] She also opened her own dye factory to produce inimitable 'Lanvin blue' (cornflower blue). Lanvin remains operational today and still successfully makes this colour its totem: "whether azure, sky blue, periwinkle, ultramarine, or indigo, blue has been ever-present at Lanvin since the company's beginning".[125]

The company's success can be validated through its popularity in Paris alone, but it also flourished overseas, where its name was passionately misused for forgery and profit.

Item of note no. 2.3 Matter of Sidney J. Kreiss, Inc. – unfair competitive practices[126]

The House of Lanvin along with Cassini were plaintiffs to a proceeding before the Federal Trade Commission, which, on 13 June 1960, issued an order (no. 7264) banning Sidney J. Kreiss Inc. and Picturesque Hosiery Co., Inc., both based in New York, from selling counterfeited

118 A. Schirrmeister, B. Alberty, *Costume Institute*, "Recent Acquisitions" (Metropolitan Museum of Art), 1985–1986, no. 1985/1986, p. 47.

119 M. Jan, *L'élégance comme signe de résistance*, "Vingtième Siècle. Revue d'histoire", no. 105, L'Amérique latine des régimes militaires (janvier–mars 2010), p. 249.

120 N.J.S., K.C.B., D.E.K., *Textiles and Costumes*, "The Museum Year: Annual Report of the Museum of Fine Arts", 1989–1990, vol. 114, p. 49; A.S. Cavallo, K. Stoddert, *Fashion Plate: An Opening Exhibition for the New Costume Institute*, "The Metropolitan Museum of Art Bulletin, New Series", 1971, vol. 30, no. 1, The Costume Institute (August–September), p. 48.

121 D. Veillon, *La Moda como Patrimonio cultural en tiempos de guerra*, "Historia y Fuente Oral", 1990, no. 3, Esas Guerras . . ., p. 106.

122 Y. Hersant, D. Bellocq, *Letter from Paris*, "The Hudson Review", 1986, vol. 38, no. 4 (Winter), p. 548.

123 Cf. Wikipedia: Jeanne Lanvin. See Jankowska, Meghaichi, Pawełczyk, *Illustrated* . . . .

124 R. Riley, *The Design Laboratory*, "The Brooklyn Museum Annual", 1965–1966, vol. 7, p. 105.

125 Lanvin.com, accessed: 2.06.2020; Jankowska, Meghaichi, Pawełczyk, *Illustrated* . . . .

126 CCH Trade Reg. Rep. no. 28,840 (FTC 1960); S.A. Diamond, *Requirements of a Trademark Licensing Program*, "The Business Lawyer", January 1962, vol. 17, no. 2, pp. 304–305.

women's hosiery under these brands. Commissioner Anderson noted that

> the record clearly establishes that neither of these at any time created, designed or styled the hosiery carrying their names. As shown by the hearing examiner, this hosiery was either purchased by respondents as greige goods and sent to a mill for dyeing and finishing or was purchased in finished form from the mill. In addition, the admission by respondent Sidney J. Kreiss, that identical hosiery was sold under both the Lavin and Cassini names would itself warrant a finding that the representations in question were false.[127]

Lanvin, just like Paul Poiret or Jean Patou, understood that perfume turned into fashion accessory could capitalise effectively on the fame of the brand.[128] With this in mind, she opened Lanvin Parfums SA in 1924. Three years later, she introduced her signature fragrance, Arpège. It is important to observe that this area of business also exposed the company to legal disputes.

Item of note no. 2.4 ***Lanvin Parfums, Inc. v. Le Dans, Ltd.* – unfair competition and antitrust injuries**[129]

The Supreme Court authorised injunction against the sale of misbranded goods, because "the alleged criminal acts also threaten plaintiff's property rights" – injunctions rebottling in violation of Penal Law – complaint which alleged that corporate defendants were purchasing the plaintiff's toilet waters and rebottling or repackaging same and selling them at less than the prices charged by the plaintiff. The injunction states cause of action under section 2354 (subd. 6) of Penal Law, which renders a person who offers goods for sale, which are represented to be the product of another person, firm or corporation, guilty of misdemeanor unless the goods are contained in the original package.[130]

127 Federal Trade Commission, "News Summary", 13 June 1960, no. 39; *The Name's the Same – But Is the Designer?*, "New York Times", 31 August 1964, p. 28.

128 E. Briot, *From Industry to Luxury: French Perfume in the Nineteenth Century*, "The Business History Review", Summer 2011, vol. 85, no. 2, p. 294.

129 9 N.Y.2d 516, 523, 174 N.E.2d 920, 922, 215 N.Y.S.2d 257, 260–261 (27 April 1961)

130 D. Laycock, *The Death of the Irreparable Injury Rule*, Oxford University Press, 1991, p. 227; https://theamazonpost.com/post-trial-brief-pdfs/brief/51cLanvin.pdf, accessed: 2.01.2023.

Item of note no. 2.5 *Janel Sales Corp. v. Lanvin Parfums, Inc.* – alleged violation of the Sherman Act, 15 U.S.C. 1[131]

The Court of Appeals upheld the vertical agreement that imposed resale price and customed restriction – plaintiff demanded prohibition of enforcement by a perfume manufacturer of a resale price maintenance agreement against a perfume retailer where the evidence indicated that the manufacturer was also engaged in retail operations, holding that the contract was prohibited as one "between retailers" even though there was no demonstration that the retailers were in actual competition with each other.[132]

The House of Lanvin remains operational to this day. On 20 November 2013, it became the official tailor of Arsenal FC.[133]

2.2.2.6 *Madeleine Vionnet*

Madeleine Vionnet (1867–1946), a former apprentice of Doucet and Callot Soeurs, opened her atelier in 1912 only to close it again two years later due to the outbreak of World War I. As her fashion house was closed for several years and as materials and funds for making designs were scarce, she spent this time in a spiritual state of mind in her atelier. She practiced her skills with a wooden doll, which became the focus point of her universe. During the downtime and slow period brought on by the war, she used to travel to Italy, where she met Ernesto Michahelles (Thayaht), who came to Paris from Florence.[134] He introduced her to the Futurist movement (also the concept of "dynamic symmetry"), and later, she was also inspired by Cubism.[135] Many of her dresses were

131 67 Trade Cas. no. 72,224 (SDNY 1967); rev'd 396 F.2d 398 (June 5, 1968); cert. denied, 393 U.S. 938, 89 S. Ct. 303, 21 L. Ed. 2d 275 (1968)

132 *Charles W. Bowen, Jr., D/B/A Suburbia News Delivery Service, et al., Plaintiffs-Appellees, v. New York News, Inc., et al., Defendants-Appellants, 522 F.2d 1242 (2d Cir. 1975)*; J.R. Burley, *Territorial Restrictions in Distribution Systems: Current Legal Developments*, "Journal of Marketing", 1975, vol. 39, no. 4, p. 52; J.J. Jacobson (ed.), *Antitrust Law Developments (Sixth), vol. I*, American Bar Association, 2007, p. 147; Legal, *Developments in Marketing*, "Journal of Marketing", April 1968, vol. 32, no. 2, p. 81.

133 M. Russell, *Arsenal and Lanvin: a striking partnership*, www.gq-magazine.co.uk/article/arsenal-football-lanvin-tailoring-suits (accessed: 02.01.2023); *Arsenal welcomes Lanvin*, www.arsenal.com/news/news-archive/arsenal-welcomes-lanvin (accessed: 02.01.2023).

134 P. Golbin (ed.), *Madeleine Vionnet, Exhibition Catalogue*, MAR, 2009, p. 293.

135 B. Kirke, *Vionnet: Fashion's Twentieth Century Technican*, "Tresholds", 2001, no. 22, p. 79; E. Paulicelli, *Fashion and Futurism: Performing Dress*, "Annali d'Italianistica", 2009, vol. 27, A Century of Futurism: 1909–2009, pp. 192, 199; F. Zoccoli, *Futurist Accessories* [in:] C. Giorcelli, P. Rabinowitz (eds.), *Accessorizing the Body. Habits of Being I*, University of Minnesota Press, pp. 75, 79.

geometric and asymmetric.[136] She mastered her skill to bring about feminine lines through the motion of a dress.[137]

She went down in fashion history as the "Queen of the bias cut",[138] "the architect among dressmakers" and the "Euclid of Fashion".[139] She made fashion news and gained a lot of publicity for her 'bias cut', which is considered the epitome of her style. She reflected on her legacy in these words: "Maybe because everyone else made dresses that flowed in the same direction, I saw that if I turned the fabric on an angle . . . it gained elasticity. Everything came from my head. Bias came from my head".[140] Betty Kirke, a fashion expert, wonders, however whether Thayaht's mindset and his futurist thinking might have helped ignite this idea. Either way, the bias cut was made famous by Hollywood film stars.[141] Vionnet is sometimes claimed to be the inventor of the 20th-century woman.[142]

In addition, Vionnet, in common with her counterparts, also eschewed corsets and explored the Grecian style.[143] She is credited with the words: "My inspiration comes from Greek vases, from the beautifully clothed women depicted on them, or even the noble lines of the vase itself".[144] The motion and the worship of the beauty of feminine lines inspired later American style and sports dress. Annamarie Strassel wrote about her:

> the dance aesthetic that accompanied a broader interest in athleticism represents another important dimension of American design that evolved American fashions from the classical referents championed by Vionnet to a sartorial futurism embodied in the minimalism and uniformity of the dance leotard.[145]

Madeleine Vionnet was a designer who strongly pursued legal protection for her designs, which she did in many ways. She declared war on the copyists armed with pen and knowledge and made the press her battlefield. The magazine *Le Moniteur de l'exportation* created a column for her in 1920, where she

136 L.J. Evered, *Folded Fashions: Symmetry in Clothing Design*, "The Arithmetic Teacher" December 1992, vol. 40, no. 4, pp. 204–206; cf. P. Golbin, A. Steta, *La mode ou l'art de conserver l'éphémère*, "Revue des Deux Mondes", February 2014, pp. 67.

137 A. Strassel, *Designing Women: Feminist Methodologies in American* Fashion, "Women's Studies Quarterly", Spring/Summer 2012, vol. 41, no. 1/2, p. 44.

138 Jankowska, Meghaichi, Pawełczyk, *Illustrated* . . . .

139 L.J. Evered, *Folded* . . ., pp. 204, 206 [after:] J. Demornex, *Madeleine Vionnet*, Rizzoli International Publications, 1991.

140 Kirke, *Vionnet: Fashion's* . . ., p. 80.

141 A. Jenkins, *Recent Acquisitions at The Bowes Museum, Barnard Castle*, "The Burlington Magazine", June 2012, vol. 154, no. 1311, Sculpture and design, p. 460.

142 B.G. Telford, *To the Blue Group Marc Jacobs Explains His Haunting*, "Columbia: A Journal of Literature and Art", 2009, no. 46, p. 159.

143 Strassel, *Designing* . . ., pp. 44. 45, 48.

144 Kirke, *Vionnet: Fashion's* . . ., p. 79.

145 Strassel, *Designing* . . ., p. 52.

could educate readers on fashion protection. In this channel she exclaimed: "Mme. Madeleine Vionnet does not sell to agents or to dressmakers. The 1909 law protects models. All Madeleine Vionnet's creations are her property. Copies and reproductions will always result in legal suits against their authors".[146]

Item of note no. 2.6 Vionnet's quest for copyright success

Vionnet admitted that her drive for protecting fashion designs was fuelled by the energy of one of the Callot Soeurs, who helped her understand its importance. Delivering on her promise in magazine news, her first suit was adjudicated on 31 December 1921, against Demoiselle Millet and Veuve Boudreau.[147] The court admitted that her fashion designs were artistic works and therefore capable of protection. She was awarded high compensation and interest on the plagiarists' profits. The judgement was also published in the magazine of her choice.[148] Together with her lawyers, Armand Trouyet and Louis Dangel, she sued literally every copyist of her work.[149] A great deal of scholarship establishes Vionnet's credentials as a copyright law activist, because she committed her heart and soul to fashion and wanted to make people understand that, behind clothing, there is the spectrum of one's originality, which is tantamount to hard work. She is reputed to have said: "It is not so much damages and interests we want: above all, we want respect for our intellectual property".[150]

Vionnet took such care of her reputation that, at the beginning of the 1920s, she introduced her own manner of marking her works. Each dress bore her signature and had a serial number, but, as if that wasn't enough, also her fingerprint.[151]

146 Cf. M.L. Stewart, *Dressing Modern Frenchwoman: Marketing Haute Couture, 1919–1939,* The Johns Hopkins University Press, 2008, p. 131.

147 INPI, 1922, Art. 5431, Tribunal Correctionnel de la Seine, 31 Dec. 1921, Vionnet contre Demoiselle Millet et Veuve Boudreau.

148 M. Jankowska, M. Pawełczyk, A. Warmuzińska, *Prawo designu i mody. Kreowanie produktu,* Warszawa-Katowice, 2020, p. 29.

149 INPI, 1923, Art. 6178, 16 June 1923, Vionnet contre Dames Robillard and Gramond; *La Gazette du Palais,* 8 May 1930, Tribunal correctionnel de la Seine, 10 March 1930, Vionnet contre dame Muraz.

150 P. Tilburg, *Working Girls: Sex, Taste, and Reform in the Parisian Garment Trades,* 188–1919, Oxford University Press, 2019, p. 240 [after:] H. Hugault, *Une campagne d'assainissement, défendos nos artistes,* "Le Figaro", 12 August 1930.

151 Jankowska, Pawełczyk, Warmuzińska, *Prawo designu i mody,* p. 29.

2.2.2.7 *House of Lucien Lelong*

Lucien Lelong (1889–1958) was connected to fashion through his parents, who owned a small fashion house,[152] but he himself graduated from Oxford University and received training at the Hautes Etudes de Commerciales. He managed to merge his twin aptitudes for business and arts through his couture house, which he opened in the early 1910s. He was reputed for modern management of his work premises, including division of labour, proper lighting and safe conditions.[153]

He stands out from the other *haute couture* houses of that time through his hiring of many designers rather than building the house on the signature of just one. Lelong was the 'chêf de maison' rather than a designer, but his atelier was the studio of Christian Dior (1941–1946), Pierre Balmain, Nadine Robinson and Hubert de Givenchy. Dior had a lot of deference for Lelong and recounted his experience with the fashion house with these words:

> It was at Lucien Lelong that . . . I learned the importance of this most essential principle in couture: the grain of the fabric. With the same idea and the same fabric, a dress can be a success or it can be a complete failure, according to whether or not one has known how to direct the natural movement of the textile, which it must always follow.[154]

Despite the fact that Lelong designed through his talented couturiers, he was to receive the final credit, as the style resembled him. Dior recounted later that he never injected his full feeling into the Lelong dresses. He revealed that "certainly at Lelong I was secure and I got along well with everyone, but I was working for someone else and for someone else's taste. My sense of responsibility to Lelong prevented me from expressing myself with total liberty".[155] Lelong's style can be described as kinetic, dynamic and inspired by feminine lines in free movement.[156] Embracing this style, he actively promoted his house's designs in American *Vogue*.[157] He was a fashion activist,[158] though

152 A. Bolton, J. Regan, M. Hubler, *In Pursuit of Fashion: The Sandy Schreier Collection*, Yale University Press, 2019, p. 96.

153 Nystrom, *Economics* . . . , p. 217; L. Font, *Dior before Dior*, "West 86th: A Journal of Decorative Arts, Design History, and Material Culture", Spring–Summer 2011, vol. 18, no. 1, p. 35.

154 Font, *Dior before* . . ., p. 35, cf. Ch. Dior, A. Chavane, E. Rabourdin, *Christian Dior: Je suis Couturier*, Éditions du Conquistador (les Impressions rapides), Paris, 1951, p. 213.

155 Font, *Dior before* . . ., p. 40; cf. Dior, *Christian Dior et moi*, p. 39.

156 M. Rouff, *Une industrie motrice: La haute couture parisienne et son évolution*, "Annales. Histoire, Sciences Sociales", April–June 1946, 1ère Année, no. 2, pp. 116 and ff.

157 H. Crawforth, *Surrealism and the Fashion Magazine*, "American Periodicals", 2004, vol. 14, no. 2, p. 216.

158 A. Settle, *Fashion and Trade*, "Journal of the Royal Society of Arts", 1970, vol. 118, no. 5162, p. 105; Bolton, Regan, Hubler, *In Pursuit* . . ., p. 96. I. Masseli, *Lucien Lelong and the Théâtre de la Mode: The Preservation of Haute Couture during Wartime*, "Journal of Tourism, Culture and Territorial Development", 2018, no. 9, pp. 129 and ff.

not an innovator. Hannah Crawforth reminiscently described him in her fashion studies as an "astute businessman, quickly capable of picking up on the ideas of others and capturing the modes of the moment".[159] In 1924, Lelong graced an issue of *Le Figaro* to share the secret of the modern woman, which, in his opinion, was "to be dressed in such a way so as to live for the speed – I would even say the electricity – of every passing moment . . . *Tout est vitesse prodigieuse* and we appear in a dazzling film".[160] His house was the biggest in Paris with nearly one thousand designs a year. Lelong paid due attention to the artistic representation of beauty products created by his atelier, including perfume and cosmetics. He was inspired by Classicism and especially Surrealism. His lipstick (created between 1935 and 1942) was a homage to Surrealism and, more precisely, to Meret Oppenheim's work (*Objects*, 1936 – fur-covered teacup, saucer and spoon), which is regarded as one of the most quintessential works of that artistic current.[161]

This house's perfume containers were so exquisite that they were noticed by Lelong's counterparts, who modelled their own products after them.

Item of note no. 2.7 ***Lucien Lelong, Inc. v. Lander Co.*** **– a common-law trademark right?**[162]

This case was brought to enjoin Lander from competing unfairly with Lelong by using specific bottles in which it sold its colognes and by using a name for a fragrance alleged to be confusingly similar to the bottles and name of a fragrance used by Lelong in the marketing of its products. The defendant copied the two designs registered, respectively, in 1934 and 1937 (patent No. 91,372 and 106,647). The product shapes were similar as the defendant adopted the specific idea of "glass bottles having globular bases, long, narrow, cylindrical necks, spherical stoppers and labels encircling the entire long, cylindrical necks". Lelong's fragrance name "Whisper" was remade by the defendant as "Garden Whispers" and subsequently as "Whispering Grass". As to the names, the court concluded that they were not deceitful for the clients and that the labels were so dissimilar that they could not have caused confusion. As to the shape, the court made an observation that

159 Crawforth, *Surrealism* . . ., p. 243.

160 M.L. Roberts, *Samson and Delilah Revisited: The Politics of Women's Fashion in 1920s France*, "The American Historical Review", June 1993, vol. 98, no. 3, p. 676, cf. L. Lelong, *Lettre ouverte 'a Madame Camille Duguet*, "Le Figaro", 2 December 1924.

161 Jankowska, Meghaichi, Pawełczyk, *Illustrated* . . . .

162 Official Gazette of the US Patent Office, vol. 438, Jan. 16, 1934, p. 575; Official Gazette of the US Patent Office, vol. 483, Oct. 26, 1937, p. 927; (US District Court, D.S. New York, May 29, 194, 67 F.Supp 997 [S.D.N.Y. 1946]).

> Glass containers with globular bases and long necks have been used for various purposes for centuries and such shaped bottles have been used in marketing colognes prior to plaintiff's use. There is some evidence that Rosine perfumes in bottles similarly shaped were sold in the United States in 1928 or 1929.

As a matter of law, the protection for Lelong's designs expired the year the trial took place. Notwithstanding that, the plaintiff asserted that the shape of the bottle itself was a distinguishing mark of origin under the concept of "palming off"[163] and that it constituted a "secondary meaning"[164] under the common-law trademark regime. The judge dismissed the case, noting that the perfume bottles of both parties were so different in appearance that the defendant's products could not undermine the plaintiff's market. The judgement of the district court was affirmed by the court of appeals.[165]

Lelong succeeded, however, in the case *Lucien Lelong, Inc. v. George. W. Button Corporation* as of 26 April 1943 (50 F. Supp. 708 [1943], no. appeal). The court adhered to the plaintiff's observation that the symmetry of the bottles in dispute was 95% similar and, notwithstanding the fact that the shape of the bottle was not unique, it was the plaintiff who first adopted and marketed it beginning in 1933. In that case, the court admitted that the imitation invades the market as the bottle has an intrinsic value. It is worth noting that these two cases were adjudicated differently based on different facts and findings.

The modern organisational structure of the fashion house was escorted into being by the strict intellectual property policy which often ended in courts. The case *Lucien Lelong, Inc. v. Dana Perfumes* (as of 22 December 1955) is an instance of this.[166] The dispute regarded the use of the word 'Solid', which Lelong struggled to register, as a descriptive trademark for its perfume. Over time, Dana Perfumes, Inc. began to use the phrase "solid cologne" in

163 The term "palming off" regards "the newcomer's act of misrepresenting his product in a manner which confuses the public about the course of origin of the product". See J.T. Caleshu, *Trademarks and the "Free Ride" Doctrine: Unfair Competition*, "Trademark Infringement Stanford Law Review", May 1964, vol. 16, no. 3, pp. 736–737; R. Stern, J.E. Hoffman, *Public Injury and the Public Interest: Secondary Meaning in the Law of Unfair Competition*, "University of Pennsylvania Law Review", May 1962, vol. 110, no. 7, p. 939.

164 "Secondary meaning" is the case of then a consumer identifies a product with its producer. Cf. *Misrepresentation and the Lindsay Bill: A Stab at Uniformity in the Law of Unfair Competition*, "The Yale Law Journal", January 1961, vol. 70, no. 3, p. 409.

165 US Court of Appeals for the Second Circuit – 164 F.2d 395 (2d Cir. 1947), 4 December 1947.

166 Cf. R.F. Dole, *Merchant and Consumer Protection: The Uniform Deceptive Trade Practices Act*, "The Yale Law Journal", January 1967, vol. 76, no. 3, p. 496.

the packaging and advertising of its merchandise (a non-liquid cologne under trademarks 'Tabu', '20 Carats', 'Platine' etc.). Lelong, simultaneously with a court battle, took to warding off his competitor through sinister correspondence. To wit, he sent 5,000 stern letters dated 13 October 1949 to department stores, drugstores, wholesale and retail outlets to assert:

> We are today writing our customers to inform them that we own United States Trade Mark registration No. 500262 for the trade mark "Solid" as applied to stick cologne. Our rights to this mark have been challenged by Dana Perfumes and we have, in turn, filed suit against them in the United States District Court at Chicago for the infringement of this registered trade mark. Furthermore, we expect to do everything necessary to protect our exclusive rights to the trade mark "Solid" in connection with the marketing at wholesale and at retail of stick cologne.

Without going into further extensive detail, the claim was dismissed.

2.2.2.8 House of Chanel

Gabrielle Bonheur Chanel (1883–1971), generally known as Coco Chanel or Chanel or just Coco, carved out a reputation not only as a fashion designer of exquisite reputation but as a true fashion icon. Early in her career she was labelled *Princesse de la haute couture*.[167] Not only are her fashion creations emblems of inspiration for coming generations of artists, her life would fill many motivation talks.[168] She was born into an impoverished family, with her mother dying when she was 12 years old after which her father abandoned her. She grew up in a convent orphanage run by the Congregation of the Sacred Heart of Mary in Aubazine, France. Surprisingly, this sequence of events influenced her further career, as this was the place where she was taught to sew.[169] As a young woman, she worked as a sales assistant in the Maison Grampayre shop in Moulins, at the same time she was also hired as a singer in a café. As her dream was to pursue an artistic career, she labelled herself Coco, a four-letter stage name, that the entire world would later cherish.[170] Rumour has it that this nickname came from the song she used to sing "Qui gu'a vu Coco".[171]

167 Gabrielle Chanel, *Copier la mode: Pourquoi pas? C'est hommage au génie de Paris*, "Le Journal", 22 February 1935, p. 1, gallica.bnf.fr (accessed: 25.01.2023).

168 L. Chaney, *Chanel: An Intimate Life*. Fig Tree, 2011, pp. 14–27; Chanel, Gabrielle (Coco) [in:] V. Steele (ed.), *Encyclopedia of Clothing and Fashion*, vol. 1, Charles Scribner's Sons, 2005, p. 249.

169 H. Vaughan, *Sleeping with the Enemy: Coco Chanel's Secret War*. Knopf, 2011, p. 5.

170 B. Bartlett, *Coco Chanel and Socialist Fashion Magazines* [in:] D. Bartlett, S. Cole, A. Rocamora (eds.), *Fashion Media: Past and Present*, Bloomsbury, 2013; A. Mackrell, *Art and Fashion*, Sterling Publishing, 2005, p. 133; M.H. Guedes, *Quem Foi Coco Chanel?*, Clube de Autores, 2016, p. 31.

171 Jessica, *History of the Brand: Chanel*, 5 June 2020, https://etoile-luxuryvintage.com/blogs/news/history-of-the-brand-chanel (accessed: 25.01.2023).

She started her fashion endeavour in 1910 as a *chapelière* (hatmaker) in her own hat shop "Chanel Modes" at 21 rue Cambon in the centre of Paris. Two years later, in 1912, she opened her first Chanel Boutique in Deauville. As she became quickly appraised for her talents and her business grew, she acquired the entire building at Number 31 in 1918. The premises became the cornerstone of the French fashion history, as in 1921 she began selling textiles, but soon she expanded to fashion accessories and her own first perfume (N°5). Over time, she added jewellery and beauty products.[172]

Interestingly, at the early stage of her business activities, her reputation as a hatmaker grew exponentially because her hats were worn by well-known French actresses of that time. Similarly to Worth or Poiret, she knew how to make her own publicity.

She revolutionised fashion in many ways. From early on, reportedly 1913, she offered women a line of sportswear made of jersey, a textile previously reserved for men's underwear. Menswear inspired her, as she did not intend to follow the norms imposed by the Belle Époque, which offered women wide and draped dresses with multiple underskirts. She was reported to say that fashion is no luxury if it is uncomfortable, but this was just the tip of the iceberg. The use of jersey changed the approach to women's fashion and its relationship with their body.[173] This "poor girl" style attracted the attention of influential rich women who were drawn to the comfortable clothing and its appearance.[174] She recounted once to Paul Morand that her idea for the style came from a dress she tailored from an old jersey, that triggered attention from other people asking her to make the same dress for them.[175] She craved a style that was distinguished by simplicity and elegance, a model that is followed to this day.[176]

In the 1920s, women still wore corsets and other confining garments. Therefore, when, in 1925, she introduced the Chanel tweed suit[177] and, in

172 Mackrell, *Art . . .*, p. 133;. Guedes, *Quem . . .* , p. 31; *31 Rue Cambon. The Story Behind the Façade*, 23 February 2011, www.chanel.com/my/fashion/news/2011/02/31-rue-cambon-the-story-behind-the-facade.html (accessed: 25.01.2023).

173 *The History*, www.chanel.com/us/about-chanel/the-history/1910/ (accessed: 25.01.2023).

174 *Coco Chanel. French Designer*, Britannica Online, www.britannica.com/biography/Coco-Chanel (accessed: 25.01.2023).

175 Jessica, *History of the Brand . . .*

176 M. Ginsburg, *Paris Fashions: The Art Deco Style of the 1920s*, Bracken, 1989; Mary E. Davis, *Classic Chic: Music, Fashion, and Modernism*. University of California Press, 2006. *eBook Collection (EBSCOhost)*. Web. 12 October 2016; Justine Picardie, *Coco Chanel: The Legend and the Life*. It Books, 2010, pp. 14–26, 35, 36.; Vogue, *Coco Chanel: Simply Chic*, www.vogue.fr/fashion/article/coco-chanel-simply-chic (accessed: 12.03.2022); P.N. Danziger, *What's Ahead for Chanel as Virginie Viard Takes Over From Karl Lagerfeld*, www.forbes.com/sites/pamdanziger/2019/02/20/whats-ahead-after-chanel-passes-the-torch-to-virginie-viard/?sh=4bc36d0622d3 (accessed: 11.03.2022).

177 Coco Chanel drew inspiration to use tweed from the Duke of Westminster, the richest man in England, known for his extravagant receptions for passion for hunting.

1926, her famous "little black dress" (or LBD) she went beyond the social norms, but, in doing so, offered a new style that survived decades. In 1926, American *Vogue* called her dress "Chanel's Ford" likening it to the Model T.

In the October 1927 issue of American *Vogue*, Chanel was featured in an article bearing the symbolic title "Scottish Tweed is a New Godchild of French Couturiers".[178]

As noted by Penny Goldstone,

> her timing was of course, perfect. Because the dress was released in the Great Depression era, where simple and affordable was key. Later, during the war, textiles and fabrics were rationed, and the simple black dress remained the outfit of choice, as you could be elegant without breaking the bank.[179]

"The Chanel jacket is a man's jacket which has become typically feminine. It has definitely come to symbolise a certain nonchalant feminine elegance that is timeless, and for all times," said Karl Lagerfeld, creative director of Chanel since 1983. It became the "must have" for icons of that time such as Brigitte Bardot, Grace Kelly or Audrey Hepburn. A delicate chain sewn into the silk lining ensured the perfect fall.[180]

As noted by Martin Teo,

> The trims are placed gracefully on the tweed to delineate the continuity of the garment while emphasising its shape. A delicate chain is sewn into the silk lining as the finishing touch to ensure a perfect fall. This is Chanel's secret to weighing down the jacket effortlessly.[181]

> The tweed is made by weaving the warp and weft, using a variety of different kinds of threads which creates a unique and somewhat irregular appearance. The warp – vertically strung – is the background of the fabric, the base that will support the assembly of materials. There can be up to 12 different threads used for a single warp. The weft – woven horizontally – gives the fabric its unique character and can have an unlimited number of threads. Tight, perforated, textured, thick, with a relief, plaited, random, twill . . . the potential number of effects is endless.

said the Chanel house; see Ruthie Friedlander, *How Coco Chanel Discovered Her Iconic Tweed*, "Elle", 18 March 2014, www.elle.com/fashion/news/a15402/the-story-of-chanels-tweed/ (accessed: 25.03.2022).

178 *The Success of the Chanel Tweed Suit*, https://vinvoy.com/blog/Chanel-Tweed-Jacket-Success/ (accessed: 25.03.2022).

179 Penny Goldstone, *A Short Yet Comprehensive History of the Little Black Dress*, "Marie Claire Blog", 20 July 2017, ciniba.edu.pl/en/zrodla-elektroniczne-przeglad/79-bazy-danych-dziedzinowo/663-law (accessed: 25.01.2023).

180 Jankowska, Meghaichi, Pawełczyk, *Illustrated* . . . , www.lifestyleasia.com/hk/style/fashion/how-coco-chanel-revolutionised-womens-fashion-with-just-a-jacket/ (accessed: 25.01.2023).

181 M. Teo, *How Coco Chanel Revolutionized Women's Fashion with Just a Jacket*, "Lifestyle Asia" Blog, 23 October 2018, www.lifestyleasia.com/hk/style/fashion/how-coco-chanel-revolutionised-womens-fashion-with-just-a-jacket/ (accessed: 25.01.2023).

Similarly to the other renowned fashion designers, Chanel designed for the theatre, including costumes for Sergei Diaghilev's Russian ballets.[182] At the peak of her entrepreneurship, she employed 4,000 people.[183] That was in 1935. After the outbreak of World War II, she was forced to close her boutiques. However, she kept her business active from 31 Rue Cambon, as fragrances and accessories were still coveted goods, especially by the American soldiers buying gifts for their loved ones at home. Her fashion business activities can be divided into two periods: before and after the war (as her business resumed in 1954).[184] In 1954 she introduced her highly copied suit design: a collarless, braid-trimmed cardigan jacket with a graceful skirt. She also introduced bell-bottomed pants and other innovations while always retaining a clean classic look. In 1955, Chanel introduced the Classic Flap bag, named 2.55 after the year in which it was designed.

Her success can be gauged by the facts that by the end of 2019, Chanel (as a brand) employed exactly 27,018 people across the world and was making US$9.6 billion in annual revenue in 2017.[185]

Coco Chanel was known for her specific approach to copying and intellectual property rights. She strongly asserted the idea that a fashion design cannot be perceived in terms of any other artistic work. Famous for saying "imitation is the highest form of flattery",[186] she had meant a *pale imitation*, which is something similar but not as good. She believed that Paris derived its status as *Fashion Capital* through imitation by *petite couture* players whose copying served to acknowledge the prestige and standing of *haute couture*. To fight copycats or fashion piracy would be like letting go of the reputation of inimitable elegance, which would risk women from other capitals losing sight of the distinction between high fashion (*la grande couture*) and tailoring (*la confection*). Such a loss of prestige would be as damaging to Parisian fashion as even the most cynical and outrageous copying. Just like her forerunners and counterparts, Coco Chanel also tried to influence the public opinion using newspapers.[187]

182 Vaughan, *Sleeping . . .*, pp. 31–32.

183 V. Sherrow, *For Appearance' Sake: The Historical Encyclopedia of Good Looks, Beauty, and Grooming*, Greenwood Publishing Group, 2001, p. 73.

184 T.J. Mazzeo, *The Secret of Chanel no. 5*. HarperCollins, 2011, pp. 176–177.

185 https://craft.co/chanel (accessed: 25.01.2023).

186 Jeannie Suk Gersen, *Chanel 2.55* [in:] C. Op den Kamp, D. Hunter (eds.), *A History of Intellectual Property in 50 Objects*, Cambridge University Press, 2019, p. 249. Earlier, Oscar Wilde similarly had said: "Imitation is the sincerest form of flattery that mediocrity can pay to greatness" [in:] GoodRead (ed.), *Oscar Wilde. Quotes. Quotable Quote.*, www.goodreads.com/quotes/558084-imitation-is-the-sincerest-form-of-flattery-that-mediocrity-can (accessed: 12.01.2023).

187 Gabrielle Chanel, *Copier la mode: Pourquoi pas? C'est homage au genie de Paris*, "Le Journal", 22 February 1935, p. 1, gallica.bnf.fr.

Item of note no. 2.8 Coco Chanel on copying: *Le Journal* as of 22 February 1935

Coco Chanel believed that

> Ainsi, la vertu de la mode tient dans l'inspiration prodigue de mains ingénieuses qui doivent répandre sans compter leurs créations et n'en pas tenir un compte trop jalous, puis-que l'imitation est un hommage rendu à leur génie: *ce génie de Paris qu'on ne volera pas plus qu'on ne peut fixer, dans le ciel, l'eclatante trajectorie d'une fusée qui monte, s'éspanouit et meurt.*[188]
>
> *Thus, the virtue of fashion lies in the lavish inspiration of ingenious hands which must spread their creation without taking them into account and not being too jealous of them, since imitation is, indirectly, a tribute paid to the creator's ingenuity: that Parisian genius, that cannot be stolen any more than one can fix in the sky the dazzling trajectory of a rocket that rises, explodes and expires.*

Item of note no. 2.9 Madeleine Vionnet and Jeanne Lanvin response: *Le Journal* as of 4 March 1935

It did not take long for a response to Coco's words. The reply came two weeks later in the same newspaper and literally in the same placement. Madeleine Vionnet and Jeanne Lanvin vehemently opposed her idea of keeping a *haute couture* house afloat alongside smaller ateliers overflowing the market with their copies and imitations of the quality products.[189] Their position was based on the argument that letting go of strong legal protection would be a *veritable suicide* that would kill the fashion industry. They mentioned how complicated the process was of designing and launching a fashion design, with many specialists involved working towards securing the highest quality. Long months of work can be diminished within a few hours, because this is all it takes to copy a design. Furthermore, a dress can hardly be reproduced without using the original fabric. They emphasised that the fashion business is an *industrie de qualité*, which needs to be secured.

188 Chanel, *Copier*…, p. 1.

189 M. Vionnet, J. Lanvin, *Copier la mode ce serait la tuer*, "Le Journal", 4 March 1935, p. 1, gallica.bnf.fr (accessed: 25.01.2023).

Chanel claimed that illegal copying was not only a tribute but also the best form of advertisement.[190] She used this language of business to address her clientele for Chanel N°5 perfume: “This most copied and popular couturière, ardent sponsor of Youth and designs that keep you enchantingly young looking, had the same idea in mind when she made her famous perfumes”.[191] As juicily recounted by Elisabeth Hawes there was an old tradition in Paris that a designer that is not copied is dead. This urge for designer products was developed in the heated atmosphere of bootleg industry that was subject to raids and elimination”. These two ideas of fashion were alive in Paris of that time and are still today.[192]

For all the reasons pointed out earlier, Coco Chanel was opposed to the overprotective Parisian approach to design piracy.[193] She released the drawings of her designs to the press and let seamstresses come to her atelier to sketch and make notes.[194] She was reputed to have said “If people can’t afford to buy a real Chanel . . . I’d rather they bought a fake Chanel with the idea of Chanel in mind”.[195] As much as she was generous in terms of her intellectual property rights (IPRs) when faced with street copying, she did bring her business partners to court and made efforts to secure her interests against piracy, contract breach or misuse on their part.[196] This reputed generosity changed after her death and the Chanel Inc. business takeover.

2.3 Protection of *haute couture* in France 1868–1945

2.3.1 Origins of the Fédération de la Haute Couture et de la Mode

The watershed moment in the history of protection of *haute couture* was in 1868, with the establishment of Charles Worth’s brainchild, the *Chambre Syndicale de la Couture, des Confectionneurs et des Tailleurs pour Dame* (Chambre Syndicale for Couture, Clothing Manufacturers and Tailors for Women) that to this day protects designers’ rights. On 14 December 1910, his son renamed it *Chambre Syndicale de la Couture Parisienne.*[197] Its main activities were

- exchanging information on the progress of styles;
- preventing copying and style piracy;

190 Pouillard, *Design Piracy*, p. 335.

191 United States. Federal Trade Commission, *Federal Trade Commission Decisions. Findings, Orders and Stipulations.*, 1 June 1939 to 30 November 1939, vol. 29, p. 1022.

192 E. Hawes, *Fashion Is Spinach*, Random House, 1938, p. 46.

193 Suk Gersen, *Chanel 2.55 . . .*, pp. 251–252.

194 Suk Gersen, *Chanel 2.55 . . .*, pp. 251–252.

195 Suk Gersen, *Chanel 2.55 . . .*, p. 252.

196 S. Vaidhyanathan, *Intellectual Property: A Very Short Introduction*, Oxford University Press, 2017, p. 91.

197 Nystrom, *Economics . . .* , p. 189; V. Pouillard, *Managing Fashion Creativity. The History of the Chambre Syndicale de la Couture Parisienne During the Interwar Period*, “Investigaciones de Historia Económica – Economic History Research”, 2016, no. 12, pp. 76–87.

- developing transparent labour contract clauses, including work conditions, wages, working hours, education of apprentices, etc.;
- providing dispute settlement;
- ensuring the proper opening of new seasons;
- supporting sewing schools;
- providing official standing representing the industry before the French government.

On 23 January 1945, it became the *Chambre Syndicale de la Haute Couture*, which coincided with the introduction of the legal framework for the "Haute Couture" designation. Since the end of World War II in 1946, the Chambre gained such members as Balmain, Chanel, Christian Dior, Christian Lacroix, Emanuel Ungaro, Féraud, Givenchy, Hanae Mori, Scherrer, Torrente and Jean Paul Gaultier.[198]

On 8 October 1973, the *Chambre Syndicale du Prêt-à-Porter des Couturiers et des Créateurs de Mode* and the *Chambre Syndicale de la Mode Masculine* were founded. All three chambers merged that same day to become the *Fédération Française de la Couture, du Prêt-à-Porter des Couturiers et des Créateurs de Mode*, which on 29 June 2017 became the *Fédération de la Haute Couture et de la Mode*.

The Fédération also has a fashion school, *L'École de la Chambre Syndicale de la Couture Parisienne* (created in 1927 and still active). Alumni of the school include Valentino Garavani, Yves Saint Laurent, Karl Lagerfeld, André Courrèges, Issey Miyake, Anne Valerie Hash, Alexis Mabille, Tomas Maier, Nicole Miller, Stéphane Rolland and Victor Joris.[199]

2.3.3.1 Legal remedies in the early times of haute couture

To appreciate the significance of the *Chambre Syndicale de la Couture, des Confectionneurs et des Tailleurs pour Dame*, it should be remembered that, under the 1793 French intellectual property law regime, couturiers had previously tried to establish jurisprudence. Later, after World War I, faced with renewed pressure to address the issue, courts revived the old precedent. Under those old rules, if couturiers suspected theft of their designs they could notify the police, who would *then seize any counterfeit garments.* The first infraction was punished with a fine, the second with imprisonment for one to six months.[200]

In addition, the Chambre was concerned with the intellectual property laws and policy, which resulted in the formation of Service of Defence against the Copying of Models (fr. *Service de Défense contre la copie des Modèles*). The idea

198 S. Lutz-Sorg, *Haute Couture: Faiseurs de feu, faiseurs de shows*, "Revue des Deux Mondes", July–August 2002, p. 59; D. Grumbach, N. de Baudry Asson, *Paris, capitale de la mode?*, "Revue des Deux Mondes", July 2001, pp. 76–79.

199 *École de la Chambre Syndicale de la Couture Parisienne.* "*Fashionista*", https://fashionista.com/page/ecole-de-la-chambre-syndicale-2016 (accessed: 25.01.2023).

200 Pouillard, *Design Piracy* . . ., p. 326; Hawes, *Fashion Is Spinach* . . ., p. 20.

behind this was an understanding of the business reality. Legal services were expensive, counterfeiting was rampant and the development of a new mindset about copyright protection in fashion was in its infancy. Following this reasoning, the creators coalesced in their belief that the Chambre would work better than individual actors. As early as 1914, André Allart and Paul Carteron wrote a handbook on case law regarding copying and counterfeiting, which seems to be the cornerstone for the modern fashion law syllabus.[201]

The first efforts to introduce across-the-board decent and *honest rules of conduct in fashion* (in opposition to copying) were taken in the 19th century at the contractual level between Paris and New York designers. At that time, buyers from New York were the largest group of Paris *haute couture* clientele.[202]

The Chambre survived the test of time in all respects. In 1920 its membership surpassed 234 entrepreneurs, between them accounting for 15,000 employees.[203] In the late 1920s, the Chambre found a way to limit illegitimate leakage of ideas and designs to the US market. To that aim, the Chambre established the *concept of 'viewing rights'* (fr. *droit de vision*), that would allow foreign buyers to attend fashion shows (then named season openings). Buyers had to purchase attendance rights in advance on the basis of future purchasing commitment.[204] The business of copying also proliferated in Paris, the birthplace of the original *haute couture* garments. The reason was blindingly simple: French seamstresses were the only ones capable of reproducing the quality of the prototypes. Seamstresses who acquired their skills in the professional sewing business would leave after getting married, only to reopen their own practices (copy houses). Reportedly, in 1929 there were at least 100 such operations.[205] A number of factors facilitated this proliferation. There was social acquiescence towards copying at different levels of society. Copyists took garments home, where seizure was not authorised. Their friends would also let them store the works. Copyists visited clients at home and avoided having fixed appointment hours. The *haute couture* fashion houses' staff would also take part in the fraud, as many of them readily shared the specifics of upcoming designs for remuneration of approximately 50 to 100 French francs (equivalent to US$150 to $300 in 2009).[206] To make matters worse, even rich *haute couture* clients would eagerly lend garments they had just purchased, which brought considerable amounts of money back into their pockets. On

201 V. Pouillard, *Managing*..., p. 82; cf. A. Allart, P. Carteron, *La mode devant les tribunaux: legislation & jurisprudence*, Recueil Sirey, 1914.

202 *Haute couture* designs imported legally by US companies from France were exempted from customs.

203 S. Sirot, Les congés payés en France avant le Front populaire: L'exemple des ouvriers parisiens de 1919 à 1935, Vingtième Siècle. Revue d'histoire, no. 50 (April–June 1996), p. 91.

204 Pouillard, *Design Piracy*..., p. 323; G. Deschamps, La Crise dans les Industries du vêtement et de la mode à Paris pendant la période de 1930 à 1937 (Paris, 1937), 51.

205 5 Bertram J. Perkins, "Klotz Deplores Inefficiency of French Style Piracy Laws," WWD, 22 May 1929, sec. 1, 1.

206 Pouillard, *Design Piracy*..., p. 325.

top of all this, it was even claimed that a mistress of the director of a famous fashion house let others copy her dresses for payment.[207] Within the copying scene, it was common for purchasers to pool their expenditures by buying agreed designs in order to share them for their common profit. French fashion houses tried to take measures to counteract this. They demanded royalties for reproduced goods, and, where these were not forthcoming, offenders would be blacklisted and denied access to the openings.[208] The other threat was sketchers, who, although not permitted to bring sketchpads and pencils into fashion openings, were trained in committing the designs to memory.[209]

Fashion design piracy was a big problem for fashion houses, especially the fact that copies were offered to, often foreign, buyers concurrently with the first displays of the original models at the opening of new seasons. As the protection granted by French intellectual property law (through copyright and design registration) was weak and insecure, *some practical measures* were undertaken. One of these was to secretly keep new models in *safes or locked places.* Designers also strove to keep *supply chains secret*, especially with regard to *fabrics and trimmings.*

One of the measures taken as early as the beginning of the 20th century was *invisible signs sewn into dresses or invisible ink marked inside.*[210]

2.3.2 Fashion protection coalitions: ADAPA, PAIS and others

Paul Poiret, having returned from his trip to the US, and having seen the proliferating business of counterfeits, had the idea of establishing an association that could effectively enforce international protection. To gather the attention of his counterparts, he convinced publishers to make legal news out of his struggles in the US. In June 1915, the Protective Association of French Couturiers was formed by him, Jacques Worth, Jeanne Lanvin, Jeanne Paquin, the Callot Sisters and the textile producers, Rodier brothers. Their promise to fight knock-offs and unlawful use of their brands was put on hold as war took hold.[211]

After World War II, Madeleine Vionnet, together with her business manager, Louis Dangel, and counterparts such as Callot Sisters, Paul Poiret, Madeleine Cheruit, Jacques Worth, Jeanne Lanvin and Drécoll founded the *Association pour la Défense des Arts Plastiques et Appliqués* in 1923 (ADAPA),[212] and in 1928, the *Société des Auteurs de la Mode.*[213] ADAPA's goal was to lobby for international copyright laws. In 1930, Armand Trouyet became the head of the recently established Protection des Industries des Saisonnières

207 Pouillard, *Design Piracy* . . ., p. 326; Hawes, *Fashion Is* . . ., p. 45.
208 Pouillard, *Design Piracy* . . ., p. 325.
209 Hawes, *Fashion Is* . . ., p. 47.
210 Pouillard, *Design Piracy* . . ., p. 329.
211 Stewart, *Dressing* . . ., p. 119.
212 Tilburg, *Working* . . ., p. 240.
213 F. Sterlacci, J. Arbuckle, *Historical Dictionary of the Fashion Industry*, Rowman & Littlefield, 2017, p. 511.

(PAIS),[214] that became revered for its successful counterfeiting raids and its lobbying for new intellectual property laws. The lawsuits brought by designers at that time were supported by these associations as to merits and strategy of handling the case. Reportedly PAIS sued every copier they could find.[215]

In 1930, there was a landmark case involving Vionnet and Chanel against Suzanne Laneil – caught with 48 Vionnet and Chanel knock-offs, in which the court admitted that couturiers were authors of 'real works of art' and therefore deserving of the same copyright protection as artists and writers.[216] As the practice shows, the legal protection sought in courts was gained with a lot of effort and ingenuity in making both legal reasoning and arguments. However, the damages granted were not high enough to put an end to the machinations of counterfeiters.

About the same time, the Fashion Originators' Guild of America was established in New York, founded by Maurice Rentner and his lawyer Sylvan Gotshal. Its aim was to establish connections between entrepreneurs who agreed to label the products they sold and to guarantee the origin of the designs they retailed. French and American cooperation on that basis began in the late 1930s.[217]

2.3.3 *Conseil des Prud'hommes*

The *Conseil des Prud'hommes* is, in English, sometimes termed the Paris Industrial Relations Board. It was a French organisation with many tasks entrusted to it, established in 1847 to keep record of the fashion designs of Parisian creators. It may be interesting to note that, from the 1880s onwards, it stored photographs and pictures of dress designs in order to document their ownership under the old law of industrial property.[218] There is only limited scholarship on its unprecedented role in asserting copyrights. Among many, Jeanne Paquin, Patou,[219] Jeanne Lanvin[220] and Madeleine Vionnet zealously protected their legacy and pressed home the importance of intellectual property rights. They were pioneers in strict IP (Intellectual Property) policy as courts very begrudgingly adjudicated their cases. With the passage of time and plenty of struggles by advocates to convince courts that photographs deposited with the *Conseil des Prud'hommes* could serve as major exhibits in the copyright trials, its archives assumed great importance. Reportedly, in 1924, Vionnet deposited 939 photo graphs of her fashion designs, of which she publicly realised only three.

214 Pouillard, *Managing* . . ., p. 85.
215 Pouillard, *Managing* . . ., p. 85.
216 F. Sterlacci, J. Arbuckle, *The A to Z of the Fashon*, Industry, 2009, p. Iiv; Sterlacci, Arbuckle, *Historical* . . ., p. 20; G. Diliberto, *Vive le knockoff*, "Los Angeles Times", 10 October 2007; Stewart, *Dressing* . . ., p. 130.
217 Pouillard, *Design Piracy* . . ., p. 321.
218 C. Evans, *The Ontology* . . ., p. 66.
219 Cf. Art. 6011, Cour de Paris, 22 June 1926, Patou et Cie contre Touboul (Maison Cyber).
220 Cf. Jeanne Lanvin contre Dames Robillard et Gramond, 1926.

To wit, in 1906 Jeanne Paquin sued *Le Chic* and *Le Chic Parisien* magazines for publishing photographs of her new models before they were shown publicly by the designer. Pictures that had been deposited with the Conseil proved compelling exhibits in the trial. The court in the first instance refused to adjudicate upon the case based on mere reliance on the photographs, but the court of appeals overturned its decision and observed that the publication of fashion models would support copying and promote unfair competition.[221] In the same year, Paquin sued the Beer couture house, also with reference to photographs she had deposited with the Conseil. The court affirmed and ordered Beer to pay 8,000 francs in damages. In the upper instance, however, the defendant managed to create discord by pinning down meanings of its own, with the result that the panels had to reconsider whether minor changes in design preclude charges of privacy and whether fashion designs' protection should be limited to 'servile copying' only. Against this backdrop the courts upheld their decision in Paquin's favour.[222]

2.4 Conclusions

There is a reason why France, and especially Paris, has exerted such an influence on the fashion sector. One needs to consider the spectrum of historical, social and economic aspects to understand how natural it was for France to gain its high standing in fashion. Not only was quality literally celebrated and cultivated, the country benefited from a large pool of seamstresses highly skilled in sewing and knitting, who worked for very low wages.[223] France also became home to a wide variety of professions that made it unique in the world: 'tailleurs', 'jupières', 'corsagières', 'mancheuses', 'garnisseuses'.

By 1930s, Paris dictated fashion in literally every aspect and every sense.[224] As to the success of French fashion houses, the assumption laid out in this chapter was that the highest standards relied on a number of prerequisites: quality old-school sewing + the appropriation of existing styles and motifs (to some degree) + an intuitive response to human desires (e.g. innovation in usefulness or comfort) + game-changing marketing strategies. As set out in Table 2.1, the research has proved that the most exquisite fashion ateliers had to carve their own path while still benefitting from guidance from existing approaches

221 Steward, *Dressing*..., p. 128; INPI, 1909, Art. 80, C. de Paris, 1re Chambre, 11 March 1909, Société Paquin contre *Le Chic* and *Le Chic Parisien,* and *La Gazette du Palais,* 1913, 363 Cour de Cassation (Ch.Civ.), 29 July 1913, Bachwitz et autres contre Sté Paquin.

222 Steward, *Dressing* . . . , p. 128.

223 T. Benton, C. Benton, G. Woods (eds.), *Art Deco: 1910–1939,* V & A Publications, 2005, p. 142.

224 Though tastes may differ across the globe,

> Paris caters to all of these differences. The South American countries are among the best customers of the Paris dressmaking houses. The South American customer may be followed by a Maharanee of India, the later by a woman from Poland, then another from New Zealand, and so on Nystrom, Economics . . ., p. 178

Table 2.1 Creativity and innovation in the times of early *haute couture*

Couturiers	*New fashion designs*	*New style and textiles*	*Innovations*	*Imitations*
Charles Frederick Worth 'wizard of silks and tulle'	• 'manteau de cour'	• Adaptation of crinoline • Fine embellishments, ornaments and lace • Attention to slimming a body visually by employing advantageous cuts, using stripes and respecting proportions	• Advising his clients on textiles by showing them worn by a living model • Reportedly first to show clothes on live models • Close personal client relations • First showrooms • Showing his designs at social events • First designer labels on clothes • Advertisement in American fashion press as early as in 1867 • Clients could choose from a variety of designs • First to introduce constant change of forms, fabrics and accessories • Selective use of sewing machines, made possible the 'mix and match' methods of production • Strong intellectual property (IP) policy	
Jeanne Paquin 'the most commercial artist alive'	• 'Empire-line dress' made (1905) • Kimono coat, an evening dress for theatre or opera (1912) • Hobble skirts (1908–1909) • Directoire gowns (1910–1912) • Tight skirt	• Simple, but futuristic • The first woman to see black as a colour of elegance rather than of mourning • Flamboyantly coloured linings and embroidery	• The first to sell clothes to department stores • The first to sell clothes to wholesalers for resale to dealers • Showing her designs at social events • First travelling fashion show • Branches in London, Buenos Aires, Madrid, New York • First to introduce fur coats and fur accessories (starting around 1900) • Hired illustrators to draw fashion models and enthuse clients • Garments for opera and theatre • Strong IP policy	• Greek and Roman style • Asian culture • Use of fans

(*Continued*)

Table 2.1 (Continued)

Couturiers	*New fashion designs*	*New style and textiles*	*Innovations*	*Imitations*
Paul Poiret "I am an artist, not a dressmaker" he was hailed the father of 'draping', the father of 'Style Sultane'	• 'Empire-line dress' made (1906) • Kimono coat, an evening dress for theatre or opera (1913) • Corset-free dress • Turbans, hobble skirts, harem pants, peasant-type blouses (1912–1913), and the minaret or lampshade gown (1913–1914) • 'Kazan' a dress based on Russian peasant style (1912) • 'Nubian' (1924) • Minaret-style dress (1913)	• The first to make his own *pochoir* prints • Revolutionised dress colours by introducing red, orange, blue and green • New fabrics and patterns • Bright colours • Geometric shapes	• Garment for opera and theatre • Dresses for actresses in exchange for publicity • Artistic atelier • Two *deluxe* albums of his dress designs (contemporary lookbooks) • Branding of 'lifestyle' • Lines of perfume, cosmetics and furniture • Labels and names for fashion designs like 'Joséphine', '1811', 'La Perse' or "Iudree" • In 1911, Poiret founded L'École Martine • Copyright labels stitched into dresses • Strong IP policy	• Ancient Greece and Rome • Orient • Asia, the Middle East and Africa
Callot Soeurs *Marie Callot Gerber, Marthe Callot Bertrand, Regina Callot Tennyson-Chantrell and Joséphine Callot Crimont*	• First to make straight sheath gowns • First to introduce kimono sleeves in Europe	• Intuition for style • Understanding of materials, craftsmanship • First to use lace and lamé (also gold and silver) • Rejection of corset • Light and fluid dress lines • Matching unusual fabrics • Overlayer of ornamentation	• Usage of different kinds of sequins • Garments for opera and theatre • 200 employees • Branches in Nice, Biarritz, Buenos Aires and London	• Orientalism, gowns resembling saris, qipaos, djellabas

Couturiers	*New fashion designs*	*New style and textiles*	*Innovations*	*Imitations*
Jeanne Lanvin		• Known for romantic style • Reputed for pearl-embroidered dresses • Created a style that was a mix of femininity, youth and modernity	• Labelled her dresses, e.g. "Roseraie", "Jolibois", "Phèdre", "Fusée", "Cyclone" • One of the first designers of the 19th century to send costume dolls from Paris to the US • Established own dye factory to produce inimitable 'Lanvin blue' (cornflower blue) • Selling accessories, e.g. perfumes (Lanvin Parfums SA, 1924)	• Greek style • Orientalism • Peasant style
Madeleine Vionnet "Queen of the bias cut", "the architect among dressmakers", "Euclid of Fashion"	• Reputed for her 'bias cut'		• Marked her dresses with her signature, a serial number and a fingerprint • The designer herself wrote monthly columns in "Le Moniteur de l'exportation" • Strong IP policy	• Cubism • Greek style
Lucien Lelong		• Known for a style that was kinetic, dynamic, inspired by feminine lines	• Merged his aptitudes for business and arts • Reputed for modern management of his work premises, including division of labour, proper lighting and safe conditions • Hired many fashion designers to operate under his name and label, maintaining strong core style • Promoted his atelier in American *Vogue* • Strong IP policy	
Coco Chanel	Many fashion designs, including • Little black dress • Tweed women suit • Bag 2.55 N°5 perfume	• Tweed • Jersey	• Chain sewn into the linen to secure the perfect fall • Modern marketing • Weak IP policy as she was not afraid of competition	• Menswear

and patterns.[225] Those early fashion designers were gifted with an enviable talent and understanding of fashion, textiles and clients' desires. The kudos and cachet they earned was often a result of an inner creative instinct, but also of a love of work. This led to the perfect combination of spontaneity, good judgement and drive. This combination led to business strategies that would today rank easily among the cleverest intellectual property strategies. The top French ateliers were smart in introducing innovation and groundbreaking client–designer relations. They made fashion designs coveted goods that led clients to focus less on price or practicality and instead to follow their desires and lay their money down.

As for fashion designers of the early 20th century, there are a couple of takeaways. The fashion designers presented in this chapter made the design process a magnetising, even magical, experience of creating garments that, over time, almost attained an equivalent status as works of art. Designing a dress became a ritual. Garments of the era are noteworthy for their elaborate ornamentation, including embroidery and lace. Many historical fashion designs have their own extraordinary stories to tell, making these dresses unique. Since these works are beyond question both original and individual, they therefore fall under the copyright category of a work of authorship. It is remarkable that these great early designers knew how to inspire themselves with (or how to appropriate) styles (e.g. cubism) and patterns (e.g. of African and Asian origin) and still create something new, bearing their own personal stamp. These works were so characteristic of their creators that we can easily relate random fashion designs to their respective fashion houses. The question that remains unsolved is whether bringing styles, forms and ideas from other époques and other continents was still pure inspiration rather than cultural appropriation of a kind that today would be noticed and criticised. The Parisian *couturiers* must be acknowledged for their ***instinct*** and ***flair for self-promotion***. They painted themselves as artists but were equally exquisite businesspeople who intuitively knew how to market their brand. Designing clothes was only one part of their work. Another was marketing. As Piotr Szaradowski pointed out in one of our discussions, they mastered the skill of falsifying their image presenting themselves as artists and creators. They declared war on copyists while at the same time being copyists themselves. Although it cannot be denied that they developed their own designs (based up to a point on pre-existing patterns) and that they developed inventions in the area of fashion, it is very hard to determine which of these would fall under intellectual property protection and which would not.

225 And yet a detailed account of many more fashion designers is not possible due to the limited space and the subject of the book. A. Bookner, *Paris,* "The Burlington Magazine", July 1957, vol. 99, no. 652, pp. 248–251; J.-P. Daviet, ***Art déco, résonances de l'ancien et du nouveau***, "Vingtième Siècle. Revue d'histoire", octobre–décembre 2014, no. 124, pp. 185–187; Y. Aït-Sahalia, J.A. Parker, M. Yogo, Luxury ***Goods and the Equity Premium***, "The Journal of Finance", December 2004, vol. 59, no. 6, p. 3001.

Notably, these renowned fashion designers suffered from the consequences of their own success. Their elite collections were carefully watched and followed by the copiers, who delivered knock-offs for their middle-class clients, less financially privileged but zealous to imitate the lifestyle of the rich aristocracy. In the early 1930s, Paul N. Nystrom recounted that "the problem of protection of designs is one of the most important ones demanding solution at the present time, not only in Paris, but in all other style centers of the world".[226] This proves that the problem of plagiarism in fashion is as old as fashion itself. It is evident from the research conducted in this chapter that these French fashion designers not only vigilantly tracked down copies of their works but were frantically involved in activities to assert the relevance of existing copyright law to their creations, with many cases undertaken to establish precedent in this regard. This chapter has given us a detailed account of legal suits filed by such designers as Worth, Poiret and Vionnet. Many of these cases were a result of a common designers' understanding that their *haute couture* garments were in every way works of art and works of authorship. Designers' zealous fight for copyright protection proved to be a difficult one, and even when cases were won, the costs of litigation would often exceed the adjudicated damages. In the early 20th century, *haute couture* garments were sold in France and the US (mostly New York) and were therefore affected by these two jurisdictions' regimes of protection. As American copyright law did not grant protection to utilitarian and functional works, actions taken in the US failed utterly. Neither did American patent law secure designers' right. The only option at the time was trademark law, and that protected only the brand itself.

It should also be stressed that despite designers' self-image, courts did not at all acknowledge them as artists, but they did treat them as entrepreneurs. As noted, such litigation was a complex and costly undertaking, and therefore out of reach of all but the very largest and best-resourced designers.

Despite the novelty and significance of these early successful cases taken under copyright law, it is surprising how this topic has been disregarded by legal history and how no real pattern of protection emerged for the benefit of future designers. This was unfortunate particularly for smaller ateliers, for whom legal recourse in such situations remained unfeasible. Therefore, in the next chapter we examine contemporary issues surrounding fashion plagiarism affecting both esteemed fashion houses and individual ateliers, and today's relevant legal intellectual property framework.

226 Nystrom, *Economics . . .*, p. 191.

3 Fashion as creativity- and emotions-intensive sector. Business perspectives and intellectual property strategies

3.1 The fashion business – connecting the threads

3.1.1 Overview

Much of the legal framework of the fashion branch can be best understood when armed with knowledge of how the business operates. A deep dive into this will help us take stock of the strengths and weaknesses of the legal protection relating to and benefitting the fashion business. This applies particularly to the intellectual property (IP) protection of fashion designers. One issue that lies at the heart of this thesis is whether IP tools work in isolation of or without regard to the field of the protected work. In this section we demonstrate that, despite the abundance of books on IP protection, some even on IP protection for fashion goods, they do not address the multitude of social, macro- and micro-economic factors that should be heeded in a *perfect IP policy for a particular sector*. As with quality garments themselves, "one size does not fit all". This chapter sheds light on some different approaches to and instruments of protection, including their malleability with regard to fashion goods, in order to present the pros and cons of the different available legal regimes. It is important to understand that ever-changing styles and trends, and the reality that they will be copied, *are the very elements that make the fashion world go round*. Before we tap into detailed legal expertise (cf. Chapters 4 and 5), let us decode the fashion business landscape to understand its genetics and kinetics.

3.1.2 Parties to the business relationship – La Griffe.[1] *The brand owner*

Most of the time, there are two parties to a (legal) relationship. It is about the tension created between brand owner and consumer (the so-called *emotional bond*, cf. Chapter 1, section titled "Allison DeVore's legal concept of fashion – discussion. *Petit couture*. Seductive and craftsmanly quality"). A purchasing

1 Fr. *la griffe* means one of the hooked nails of an animal or bird. It is also used to denote the ultimate level of luxury, sometimes even out above *haute couture*. In this context it is used as a remote symbol of success, to which all brands aspire.

DOI: 10.4324/9781003376033-3

decision is driven by the aesthetic rapture that can be triggered by the brand owner, capitalising on their ideas, aptitude and cachet.[2]

Historically there is a clear-cut division between *haute couture/couture* (high fashion) and *prêt-à-porter* (ready-to-wear).[3] Mass-market manufacturing also exists as a third tier. My recent research into the theory and empirics of the fashion industry opens a discussion as to whether this division may be too abstract and too far removed from the reality. In this reality, a large group of fashion designers (artisan fashion designers or *petit couture*) do not fall under any of these tiers, as they cannot be counted as part of *haute couture*, nor do they fit into the *prêt-à-porter* category (Cf. Chapter 1, section titled "Allison DeVore's legal concept of fashion – discussion. *Petit couture*. Seductive and craftsmanly quality"). These are individual designers, mostly having a small atelier and hiring a small number of seamstresses. They inject variety into the fashion scene, as their business differs vastly from that of the big players that attract the most attention by scholars. They defy inclusion in the above-mentioned categories in many ways, as they

- create artistic and individual designs, which, despite their elegance, do not meet the criteria of *haute couture* goods;
- do not make typical ready-to-wear designs;
- seldom make designs that will later be subject to mass production;
- do not retain legal counsel, as their atelier is too small to withstand such costs;
- do not have a well-thought-out IP policy;
- do not have a separate budget for IP protection;
- do not get involved in lab-derived textile innovations;
- do not have an interest in registering their designs, as these are often one-offs; furthermore, the cost of registration may surpass the price of their goods or make their work cost-ineffective;

have limited options for fighting knock-offs of their works.

This author emphasises that, between *haute couture/couture* and *prêt-à-porter*, there is a new category of player, that of *individual, artisan ateliers* (also referred to as *petit couturiers* or small fashion studios).[4] They may not hyper-perform

2 There is an account of theories regarding the emotional relationship between a consumer and a brand; cf. Y.K. Kim, P. Sullivan, *Emotional Branding Speaks to Consumers' Heart: The Case of Fashion Brands*, "Fashion and Textiles", 2019, vol. 6, no. 2, https://doi.org/10.1186/s40691-018-0164-y (accessed: 25.01.2023). C. Alvarez, J.D. Brick, S. Fournier, *Doing Relationship Work: A Theory of Change in Consumer – Brand Relationships*, "Journal of Consumer Research", 2021, ucab022, https://doi.org/10.1093/jcr/ucab022 (accessed: 25.01.2023).

3 V. Stelle (ed.) *Encyclopedia of Clothing and Fashion*, "Scribner Library of Daily Life", Farmington Hills, 2005, vol. 2, pp. 186–189 and vol. 3, pp. 84–89. G. Calò, D. Scudero, *Moda e Arte: dal Decadentismo all'Ipermoderno*, Gangemi Editore spa, 2009, pp. 70–73.

4 This group constitutes so called *micro-size companies or small firms*, cf. M. Aakko, K. Niinimäki, *Fashion Designers as Entrepreneurs: Challenges and Advantages of Micro-size Companies*, "The Journal of Design, Creative Process & the Fashion Industry", 2018, vol. 10, no. 3, https://doi.org/10.1080/17569370.2018.1507148; R. Ward, R. Randall, K. Krcmar,

in the field of technical and organisational innovations nor be as rapacious as the French *haute couture* designers who were the focus of the historical research in Chapter 2, but they produce individual designs that are creative, out of the ordinary, individualistic and (up to a point) non-derivative. They constitute an *unacknowledged category of 'fashion makers'* and should be included in any study on fashion. They may even merit extra attention.

In summary, the fashion scene has never ceased to be very competitive, regardless of any change of circumstances. A plethora of individual fashion designers add their spice to the variety of legal problems generated by the fashion sector, with the IP perspective particularly notable.

3.1.3 Parties to the business relationship – La Grippe.[5] *The target*

Styles, trends and designs are of themselves like a flu, they too are contagious. In the literature, we see a streaming of people engaged with fashion, such as creators and consumers, into 'fashion leaders' (also known as 'pioneers', 'market pioneers' or 'first movers')[6] and 'fashion followers'.[7] Fashion leaders are themselves split into two categories:

- *fashion innovators* – creators of new fashion styles. They include the revered fashion designers, but also consumers who have a proclivity to wear or make unique clothes and accessories and who may even provide stimuli for new styles;
- *fashion motivators* – notable and acclaimed persons, who, being consumers themselves, are idols for others and have the potential to influence them to adopt a particular style of dress.

On the other side of the fence are the *fashion followers*, who do not zealously hunt for new apparel, hairstyles or accessories, for reasons including a lack of aptitude for fashion, scarce resources or a lack of time. This group of consumers has always been perceived as the most important category for the fashion industry, as they adopt styles often unwittingly, desiring simply to blend into

Small Firms in the Clothing Industry: The Growth of Minority Enterprise, "International Small Business Journal" 1986, vol. 4, no. 3, https://journals.sagepub.com/doi/abs/10.1177/026624268600400305 (accessed: 24.01.2023).

5 Fr. *la grippe* means a flu. In this context it is used to describe a phenomenon that is contagious, just like a trend, that makes the fashion sector profitable.

6 M.B. Lieberman, D.B. Montgomery, *First-Mover Advantages*, "Strategic Management Journal", 1988, vol. 9, pp. 50–51; G.L. Urban, T. Carter, S.P. Gaskin, Z. Mucha, *Market Share Rewards to Pioneering Brands: An Empirical Analysis and Strategic Implications*, "Management Science", 1986, 32(6), p. 645 et seq.; A.R. Linden, *An Analysis of the Fast Fashion Industry*, "Senior Project Fall", 2016, https://digitalcommons.bard.edu/cgi/viewcontent.cgi?article=1033&context=senproj_f2016 (accessed: 25.01.2023); P.N. Golder, G.J. Tellis, *Pioneer Advantage: Marketing Logic or Marketing Legend*, "Journal of Marketing Research", vol. 30, no. 2, pp. 159–160.

7 P. Khurana, M. Sethi, *Introduction to Fashion Technology*, Firewall Media, 2007, pp. 17–18.

society and not stand out.[8] Their lackadaisical attitude towards clothes can be easily played by the ***mass manufacturers***, who in turn are the ones responsible for marketing mass garments, referred to as 'mass', 'volume' or 'fast fashion'. Consumers from this group do not choose apparel as a statement and therefore do not pose inconvenient questions about ***textile quality, garment origin or the genuine authorship of the design***. One might even speculate that they do not objectively or rigorously consider how the apparel will be used after a few years, or whether its style or colours are classic enough to endure for a long future. This clientele is not apt to choose rarer fashion, including ***haute couture*** or ***prêt-à-porter***. This reportedly makes them the easiest and most desired target of the fashion industry. Mass manufacturers capitalise on original fashion designs and offer goods that are inspired, copied or derived from one-offs or from limited collections of luxurious garments. Mass manufacturers can also be referred to as fashion followers. There is a large variety of options of following one's work, from counterfeits through knock-offs to slavish inspirations, which are especially hard to get off the market. The line between an original work and a mere style or trend can be hard to pin down, which leaves original fashion designers exposed to ***perplexing legal uncertainty***.

It has been demonstrated that contemporary purchasing decisions are influenced by many types of factors, such as personal and demographic, social, cultural, economic and psychological. Social media, with their increasing numbers of users, are shown to have a sweeping influence on consumer preferences. Many recent accounts report that social media are not only a sprawling source of information but also a game changer in consumer choices.[9] The survey conducted by the Polish Chamber of E-commerce (Izba Gospodarki Elektronicznej) in 2016 demonstrated that 61% of users share information about purchased products online, 76% declare that information shared by their friends influences their views on products and brands, 44% actually bought a product they had not intended to and 40% changed their preferences or choices about particular products based on the online opinions of their friends.[10]

3.1.4 Fashionless fashion. Artification of fashion. Creativity in business

However, the fashion business, especially at the luxurious end of the spectrum, works differently. Often, the creative process does not begin with an idea for a product itself but with the ***brand identity***, the crafting of a clear brand personality

8 P. Khurana, M. Sethi, *Introduction* . . ., pp. 17–18.

9 M. Stachowiak-Krzyżan, *Wykorzystanie mediów społecznościowych przez młodych konsumentów w procesach zakupowych*, "Marketing instytucji naukowych i badawczych", 2019, vol. 31, no. 1, p. 86; E. Djafarova, T. Bowes, *'Instagram Made Me Buy It': Generation Z Impulse Purchases in Fashion Industry*, "Journal of Retailing and Consumer Services", 2020, https://doi.org/10.1016/j.jretconser.2020.102345 (accessed: 21.01.2023).

10 Izba Gospodarki Elektronicznej. (2016). *Lubię to czy kupuję to? Jak media społecznościowe wspierają sprzedaż.* https://eizba.pl/wp-content/uploads/2018/07/LubieToCzyKupujeTo_SocialCommerce_Sierpien2016 (accessed: 26.01.2023)

or brand concept that will permit the consumer to identify the brand and its products and not only feel at ease with their purchase but long for it and make the product a part of their own self-image.[11] Clients allocate space in their minds (so-called ***brand share***) for brands to which they remain loyal.[12] Surprisingly, this makes space for ***"fashionless fashion"***, as noted by Miuccia Prada and Patrizio Bertelli. The brand effect is so strong that it easily extends to every fashion product, regardless of its degree of creativity or product segment (e.g. by example of the Prada Group that includes five brands: Prada, Miu Miu, Church's, Car Shoe and Marchesi).[13] On the other hand, top-tier fashion brands successfully capitalise on their earned position by ***"artification"*** of their product.[14]

Item of note no 3.1 Artification of fashion

Artification is an art-based strategy that enhances the public perception of the prestige and originality of fashion products. The relationship between fashion and arts is established through multiple art-related activities, including collaboration with artists, hiring artistic directors, sponsorships, funding and advertising. One of the approaches in a decommodification strategy is to exhibit fashion products in museums and galleries. As shown by example of Italian law, this approach has secured fashion brands the protection of copyright law.

The question is, how does creativity fit into the brand–consumer relationship? For fashion-engaged people, it is easy to recognise a brand on the fly based only on a glimpse of its products. Brands choose a style that is then reflected in their design. The assumption that is made at this stage is that this narrow seam of creativity that establishes the design image is the key to making the design copyrightable.

11 M. Ricca, R. Robins, *Meta-Luxury Brands and the Culture of Excellence*, Palgrave Macmillan, 2012, p. 5; "The essence of the luxury brands is the identity, which is how the customers perceive the brands and who the brands are in reality", M. Nässel, L. Persson, *Characteristics of and How to Maintain a Luxury Brand*; Degree of Master in Fashion Management, The Swedish School of Textiles, 2011, p. 4; S. Geiger-Oneto, B.D. Gelb, D. Walker, J.D. Hess, *"Buying Status" by Choosing or Rejecting Luxury Brands and Their Counterfeits*, "Journal of the Academy of Marketing Science", 2013, Obj. 41; no. 3, pp. 370–371.

12 U. Okonkwo, *Luxury Fashion Branding. Trends, Tactics, Techniques*, Palgrave Macmillan, 2007, pp. 5, 8, 118–119.

13 S. Masè, K. Silchenko, *The Prada Trend: Brand Building at the Intersection of Design, Art, Technology, and Retail Experience* [in:] B. Jin, E. Cedrola (eds.), *Fashion Branding and Communication. Core Strategies of European Luxury Brands*, Palgrave Macmillan, 2017, p. 127.

14 S. Masè, E. Cedrola, *Louis Vuitton's Art-Based Strategy to Communicate Exclusivity and Prestige* [in:] B. Jin, E. Cedrola (eds.), *Fashion Branding and Communication. Core Strategies of European Luxury Brands*, Palgrave Macmillan, 2017, p. 156.

3.1.5 Boundaries of the "spark of creativity" criterion and imitation in the business environment – designers' accounts

Fashion changes but follows economic and aesthetic rules. New trends come every year and are translated into design, which takes a more practical form in terms of making the garment suitable for everyday wear. A lots of fashion ateliers are businesses catering to demand, following trends through research of sources like magazines, fashion shows, movies and city streets.[15] It is noteworthy that a person involved in fashion is easily capable of foreseeing trends in terms of colours and forms. This is partly due to their participation in the ecosystem but more specifically attributable to the *sense for fashion*.

Item of note no. 3.2 Vera Wang on inspiration

Sometimes it's a movie. Sometimes it's a piece of art. Sometimes it's nothing: I just start, and I say, "Where is this going?" The movie *Kill Bill* was an inspiration for one of my collections. That led me to Japanese culture, which I didn't know a lot about. But I tried to keep thinking of touch points, like the big corded rope belts that sumo wrestlers wear to hold up their pants, or how a kimono is about wrapping and wrapping, layer over layer. I take these codes and make them my own. Recently I've been obsessed by Versailles. Louis XIV was the original fashion rock star – a man who loved clothing and forced his courtiers to dress up. He used clothing as power and control. So then I think, *How am I going to make Louis XIV look young and hip and fun and for this generation?* I do research, but not like the kind I had time to do 30 years ago, because fashion's moving so fast. I probably never get more than five weeks of real active working time – from inspiration to visualization – to do a major collection.

Vera Wang's Spring 2011 collection was drawn from the main character from Quentin Tarantino's "Kill Bill", with a mixture of culottes, silk floral print dresses, kimono tops, peasant wrap pants and jersey tunics.[16]

Source: A. Beard, Life's Work: An Interview with Vera Wang, *Harvard Business Review*, July–August 2010.

As for designers, they are concerned with trends but also with consumer expectations. Consumers set the tone for quality, materials and sustainable

15 M. Tungate, *Fashion Brands. Branding Style from Armani to Zara*, Kogan Page, 2004, p. 52.
16 D. Lo, Vera Wang: Inspired by Lucy Liu's Character in Kill Bill: vol. 1, Racked, www.racked.com/2010/9/16/7788239/vera-wang-spring-2011, as of 1.01.2023.

products.[17] Designers and technologists answer this demand by innovating with new styles and techniques in order to outperform the competition.

However, it is noteworthy that they must abide by predictable trends. In other words, they create to sell. There is no place for 'art for art's sake'. Tom Ford once said, "if the collection you designed didn't sell, you were fired the next day". He is also reputed to have said,

> I love to design. I am a commercial fashion designer. I always design jackets with two sleeves. I don't design jackets with three sleeves, or the layers and layers come off like little dolls from Russia. Fashion for me is a creative endeavor, but it is *not art for me* [emphasis mine – MJ].[18]

On the other end of the scale, Vera Wang says she is "never very commercial in her ready-to-wear lines",[19] as her signature is a merging of *an artist and a designer*. Miuccia Prada addressed the *clash between art and business*:

> Ideas can be so pure when you do the fashion show, but my job forces me to see the bad things – "This doesn't work; this isn't selling". It forces you to see the reality, and to understand what people like, even when that isn't always what you like yourself. That is the most relevant point in my work: always to face reality. When it is good that is fine – it doesn't make my life better – but I only care about what doesn't work.[20]

Vera Wang said that "Each design school – Parsons, FIT, SCAD, RISD, Chambre Syndicale in France, Bunka in Tokyo – is different and has its own philosophy on how to encourage talent".[21]

Fiona Dieffenbacher, the director of the BFA fashion design program at Parsons School of Design sums it up perfectly: "Ultimately, it's about creating desire. . . . Whether it's a commercial or conceptual piece, it's about the connection between the product and consumer. That's the magic moment".[22]

17 It is what defines consumerism, which is that trends are created by consumers and that marketers only respond to that demand, see L. Vincent, *Legendary Brands: Unleashing the Power of Storytelling to Create a Winning Market Strategy*, Dearborn Trade Publishing, 2002, p. 12.

18 www.brainyquote.com/quotes/tom_ford_613718; P. Berk, *Tom Ford: Fashion Is Not Art*, "The Star", 17 November 2016, www.thestar.com.my/lifestyle/living/2016/11/17/tom-ford-fashion-is-not-art (accessed: 01.01.2023).

19 A. Beard, *Life's Work: An Interview with Vera Wang*, "Harvard Business Review", July–August 2019, https://hbr.org/2019/07/lifes-work-an-interview-with-vera-wang (accessed: 01.01.2023).

20 J. Wingfield, *There's Something Wrong About This Idea of Big Brands. Miuccia Prada and Raf Simons in Conversation*, https://system-magazine.com/issue8/miuccia-prada-raf-simons/ (accessed: 01.01.2023); cf. Tungate, *Fashion Brands* . . ., p. 57.

21 Beard, *Life's Work* . . .

22 L. Sherman, *The Secret Journey of a Fashion Piece – Part 1: Creativity & Design*, "Business of Fashion", 23 September 2014, www.businessoffashion.com/articles/news-analysis/secret-journey-fashion-piece-part-1-creativity-design (accessed: 01.01.2023).

Item of note no. 3.3 Choice, selection and arrangement (a premise of originality under copyright law)

Miuccia Prada said,

> I like the idea of doing something that is new, that is for sure. At least I tend towards that. But it sometimes feels like everything has been done, so today it is sometimes more about context and how you choose to put things together.[23]

In a creative business, the acme of perfection is earned through many endeavours. Some of the brands even make that part of their advertising agenda, channelling the idea of the endless perfectioning of their products. Columbia Sportswear brought its pursuit of quality and wit to the fashion business by making its slogan, "Trying stuff since 1938".[24] There will be widespread agreement with Steve Dennis' observation that "growth does not spring from the pursuit of instant perfection".[25]

3.1.6 Fashion industry versus TCLF and other sectors on the international and European scene

3.1.6.1 Is the fashion industry only clothes?

Part of the comparative research is the conundrum about definitions and names for institutions (inter alia fashion and fashion industry) that may vary in their scope and understanding not only from one country to the other but also from one area of science to another. The terminology issue is not confined to minor discrepancies in translations and qualifications because fashion is a very vibrant sector of the economy and one that is addressed on many fronts, especially economic, financial and statistical. In legal literature one can find a lot of references to 'fashion industry'; however, I challenge this approach as it is confusing and introduces artificial boundaries where none truly exist.[26] According to Hauge's approach to defining the term,

> (t)he fashion industry is closely related to the clothing industry, but (the two) are not synonymous. In the clothing industry it is the actual

23 Wingfield, *There's Something* . . ..

24 S. Dennis, *Remarkable. How to Win & Keep Customers in the Age of Digital Disruption*, Apple Books, pp. 411–412.

25 Dennis, *Remarkable* . . ., p. 411.

26 A. Reilly, *Key Concepts for the Fashion Industry*, Bloomsbury, 2014. The issues of semiology of the concept of "fashion" [in:] R. Barthes (ed.), *The Fashion System*, University of California Press, 1990; Fashion as a social system [in:] I. Loschek (ed.), *When Clothes Become Fashion:*

garment that is the end product, but in the fashion industry this is only, though vital, one of many inputs that will lead to a symbolically and aesthetically charged product of end consumers. One can say that image is the form and fashion is the function. An analysis of the fashion industry would nevertheless be ridden with major shortcomings, without a thorough understanding of how the clothing industry works.[27]

Notwithstanding the foregoing, this author observed that the term 'fashion industry' is troublesome for a few reasons:

- It is not a term used in internationally recognised industry classification and existing economic literature.[28]
- The term is itself too broad (compare Chapter 1).
- One of the arguments advanced in favour of this term is the idea that the term "clothing industry" does not readily encompass such goods as footwear, accessories (hats, scarves, belts, handbags or jewellery). But conversely, the clothing industry is, in turn, part of a wider TCLF (textile, clothing, leather and footwear) sector which, with the possible exception of jewellery, does include all of the previous goods. The TCLF sector is a more all-encompassing umbrella category for consideration of IP protection than

Design and Innovation System, Bloomsbury Academic, 2009; J. Lange, *Moda: Szkic społeczno – polityczny*, Warszawa: L. Bogusławski, 1912; R. von Jehring, *Der Zweck im Recht*, 1883; R. Burbidge, *What Is Fashion Law?* [in:] R. Burbidge (ed.), *European Fashion Law: A Practical Guide from Start-up to Global Success*, Elgar Practical Guides, 2019, pp. 2–14; V.R. Watkins, *Copyright and the Fashion Industry*, "Landslide", 2011, vol. 3, no. 3, p. 53; Library of Congress, *Fashion Industry: A Resource Guide*, https://guides.loc.gov/fashion-industry (accessed: 21.01.2023); C. Singh, *Role of Intellectual Property Rights in Fashion Industry*, "LexForti Legal Journal", 2021, vol. 2, no. 3, p. 77; R. Burstall, B. Clark, *Blockchain, IP and the Fashion Industry*, "Managing Intellectual Property", 2017, 266, p. 9.

27 A. Hauge, *The Learning Dynamics and Competitiveness of Swedish Fashion: A Theoretical Framework*, Uppsala University, November 2004, p. 3, cf. I. De Voldere, G. Jans, E. Durinck, N. Plaisier, F. Smakman, D., Mirza, A. Szalavetz, *Study on the Competitiveness of the EU Fashion Industries*, IDEA Consult, European Union, 2012, p. 9–10.

28 The basic international classification standards are as follows: International *Standard Industrial Classification of All Economic Activities* (ISIC; the current version is ISIC Rev.4), established by the United Nations. Point C of this document lists manufacturing, which includes, inter alia: 13 – Manufacture of textiles; 14 – Manufacture of wearing apparel; 15 – Manufacture of leather and related products. In the European Union there is the *Statistical Classification of Economic Activities in the European Community* (NACE, rev. 2), that was established on the basis of the provisions of Council Regulation (EEC) No 3037/90 of 9 October 1990 (Journal of Laws UE.L no. 293, page 1). There are sections C, and E (e.g. C.13-Manufacture of textiles; C.14-Manufacture of wearing apparel; C.15-Manufacture of leather and related products, C.31-Manufacture of furniture, C.32 -Other manufacturing (incl. jewellery, bijouterie), G.46-Wholesale trade). Based on these two documents each country has its own classification, e.g. the Polish Classification of Activities (PKD) was created, the provisions of which result from the Regulation of the Council of Ministers on the PKD of December 24, 2007 (Journal of Laws no. 251, item 1885). These classifications show inter-relationships between segments of fashion; however, there is no specific classification for fashion as such.

the concept of a "clothing industry". Therefore, there is a firm basis for the formulating of a new term 'fashion industry'.[29]

- Another argument in favour of this term was rooted in the idea of a 'fashion good' that is defined by five criteria, as they are 1) consumer goods; 2) about personal dress and personal image; 3) a mix of functionality and 'symbolic value'; 4) creative, often a product of artisan work; 5) highly trend sensitive.[30] As much as the idea of a 'fashion good' is worth accommodating into the discussion, it should be kept in mind that defining the 'fashion industry' based on the concept of a 'fashion good' would be an *idem per idem* error.
- By presuming that 'fashion goods' are creative, the fashion industry is seen to encompass only design-intensive goods. Unfortunately, there is no objective measure by which to distinguish between creative and non-creative goods. This difficulty has particular impact from the legal perspective, particularly in the area of IP.[31]

It could be simply accepted that the term *fashion industry* is tantamount to the TCLF industry.[32]

From the foregoing illustration, it is possible to draw some conclusions (Explanatory item no. 3.1). Most notably, people's concept of fashion relates overwhelmingly to fashion designers and their creative products, but in reality, fashion is a multifaceted and multi-layered business involving goods that take a long journey: commencing on the plantation or in the lab (in terms of

29 De Voldere, Jans, Durinck, Plaisier, Smakman, Mirza, Szalavetz, *Study on the Competitiveness* . . ., p. 9; A. Hodge, *Copyrights and the Fashion Industry: Love-Hate Relationship*, "Intellectual Property Brief", 2010, vol. 2, no. 1; I. Tan, *Knock It Off, Forever 21 The Fashion Industry's Battle against Design Piracy*, "Journal of Law and Policy", 2010, vol. 18, no. 2; E. Ferrill, T. Tanhehco, *Protecting the Material World: The Role of Design Patents in the Fashion Industry*, "North Carolina Journal of Law & Technology", 2011, vol. 12, no. 2; N.N. Stone, *Continuity of Production in the Clothing Industry*, "American Labor Legislation Review", 1921, vol. 11, no. 1; B. Emmet, *Piece-Rate Wage Systems in the Men's Clothing Industry*, 5 "Monthly Review of the U.S. Bureau of Labor Statistics", 1917, 857; E. Karpova, S. Marcketti, C. Kamm, *Fashion Industry Professionals' Viewpoints on Creative Traits and, Strategies for Creativity Development*, "Thinking Skills and Creativity", 2013, vol. 10, https://doi.org/10.1016/j.tsc.2013.09.001 (accessed: 21.01.2023).

30 De Voldere, Jans, Durinck, Plaisier, Smakman, Mirza, Szalavetz, *Study on the Competitiveness* . . ., p. 9.

31 Karpova, Marcketti, Kamm, *Fashion Industry* . . .

32 There are organisations and authors that just use the concept of TCLF to address fashion industry, e.g. International Labor Organization (ILO); see [in:] ILO, Textiles, clothing, leather and footwear sector, www.ilo.org/global/industries-and-sectors/textiles-clothing-leather-footwear/lang–en/index.htm (accessed: 01.01.2023); European Commission, *Open Your Mind, Textile, Clothing, Leather and Footwear (TCLF) sectors in the EU*, https://s4tclfblueprint.eu/wp-content/uploads/2021/02/brochure-english.pdf; cf. R. Dziuba, M. Jabłońska, J. Ławińska, Z. Wysokińska, *Overview of EU and Global Conditions for the TCLF Industry on the Way to a Circular and Digital Economy (Case Studies from Poland)*, "Comparative Economic Research, Central and Eastern Europe", 2022, vol. 25, no. 1, p. 75 et seq.

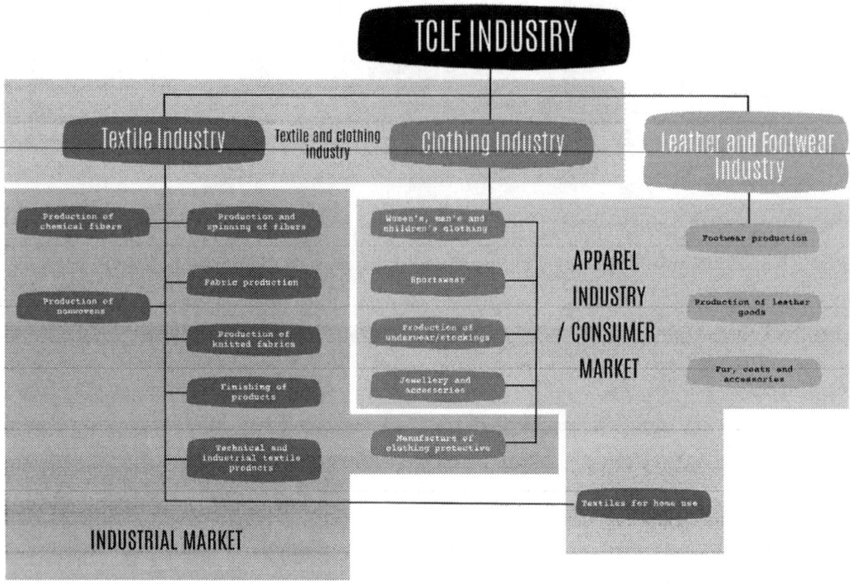

Explanatory item no. 3.1 Textile industry – classification, segments, nature of the market. Own reinterpretation

Source: Created by author

Source: Reinterpretation of a diagram by A. Rudnicka, M. Koszewska, Uszyte z klasą. Przemysł odzieżowy wobec wyzwań społecznych i środowiskowych, Łódź 2020, p. 15.

textiles, including fabrics, fibres, yarns and threads) ending in the hands of consumers, or indeed back in factories for recycling or up-cycling.[33] Moreover, it is a diverse and heterogeneous industry, embracing both private, individual or even cottage industry entrepreneurs and big players, the 'Super Winners'.[34]

33 Complexity of the fashion industry may be presented using its chain segments:
(1) raw material supply, including: natural and synthetic fibers; (2) provision of components, such as the yarns and fabrics manufactured by textile companies; (3) production networks made up of garment factories, including their domestic and overseas subcontractors; (4) export channels established by trade intermediaries; and (5) marketing networks at the retail level.
See K. Fernandez-Stark, S. Frederick, G. Gereffi, *The Apparel Global Value Chain: Economic Upgrading and Workforce Development* [in:] G. Gereffi, K. Fernandez-Stark, P. Psilos (eds.), *Skills for Upgrading: Workforce Development and Global Value Chains in Developing Countries*, Center on Globalization, Governance & Competitiveness, Duke University, 2011, p. 82; M. Pagella, Z. Wub, N.N. Murth, *The Supply Chain Implications of Recycling*, "Business Horizons", 2007, vol. 50, no. 2, https://doi.org/10.1016/j.bushor.2006.08.007 (accessed: 24.01.2023).

34 The so-called "Super Winners", according to McKinsey, who achieved the greatest economic revenues in 2019 and 2020: Nike, Inditex, LVMH, TJX Companies, Hermès or Kering [in:] McKinsey Global Fashion Index (MGFI), www.mckinsey.com/~/media/mckinsey/industries/retail/our%20insights/state%20of%20fashion/2022/the-state-of-fashion-2022.pdf (accessed: 24.01.2023).

3.1.6.2 *What is the fashion industry?*

I believe this question is one of the most compelling in this book. As much as the term *fashion* is very malleable and fluctuating, it is also true that the concept of the fashion industry will not yield to easy definitions. From a deeper analysis of TCLF, and especially of its boundaries, it is clear that the sector extends to decorations and furnishings, which area takes us into the furniture industry itself. The furniture industry is, in turn, part of the manufacturing sector, however it is beyond question that *home couture* can easily be placed into the category of fashion. *Bottega Veneta* (since 1966), *Armani/Casa* (since 1975), *Ralph Lauren Home* (since 1983), *Versace Home Collection Versace Home Lifestyle* (since 1992), *Fendi Casa* (since 1988), *Hermès* (since 2011), Off-White (since 2016), *Gucci Décor* (since 2017), *Berluti* (2019), *Dior Maison* (since 2019), *Dolce & Gabbana Home Décor Line* (since 2021) – these are just some of the fashion brands that offer furniture and decorations as part of a *fashion ecosystem*.[35] The *Dior Maison*'s sneak peak of its 2019 collection was advertised with the words, "your home deserves to be as fashion-forward as you are".[36] That fashion and design would attempt to connect with its customers at this level should not be surprising for a couple of reasons. First, if we consider the historical angle and look back at the French couturiers of the early 20th century, Charles Frederick Worth, with his characteristic sense of fashion, recognised that fashion encompasses not only clothes but also interiors. His business practice of making clients comfortable at his premises was adopted by most prominent fashion designers of that time. It is unquestionable that fashion and furniture are intrinsically linked. In general, both fashion and interiors are about lifestyle, self-image and self-worth. They seem to be rooted in the same human pursuit of happiness and desire for respect and in a love of creativity. Also, as already discussed in Chapter 1, fashion itself is part of the broader concept of design.

Speaking of decorations, fashion also includes jewellery and watches. These belong to their own 'gems and jewellery industry', which is a high-value and growing sector.[37] The importance of creativity in this sector can be gauged based on a survey of members of the Jewellery Manufacturers' Association of South Africa. To the question "how many of your clients are interested in unique designs", 51.3% responded "most", and 12.8% responded "all".[38]

35 *10 Luxury Fashion Brands That Also Make Designer Furniture*, 15 March 2021, www.lifestyleasia.com/bk/living/property-interiors/luxury-fashion-designer-furniture/ (accessed: 15.01.2023).

36 Jade Simon, *The Dior Maison Boutique Opens in Paris Today*, 29 July 2019, www.vogue.fr/lifestyle-en/article/a-new-dior-maison-boutique-is-opening-in-paris (accessed: 15.01.2023).

37 As it was noted by the Gem and Jewellery Skill Council of India (GJSCI) that "Protection of IPR is a key concern and existing safeguards are largely ineffective. Problem of plagiarism, particularly, for designs is a major concern. Pooling a large number of designers is a trend among big manufacturers", see IMaCS, *Skilling Indian Gems & Jewellery Sector*, May 2014, p. 57, www.gjsci.org/reports/IMaCS%20Gems%20and%20Jewellery%20Industry%20Report-May2014-2%20-%20Copy.pdf (accessed: 15.01.2023).

38 Nina Newman, *The Perception of Registered Design Protection in the South African Jewellery Industry*, 7th International DEFSA Conference Proceedings, 2015, p. 242.

Finally, fashion can also encompass the beauty sector that comprises skin care, colour cosmetics, hair care, fragrances, personal care and more.[39] By way of dispelling any possible doubt, in 2000, "across all hair-coloring manufacturers there . . . [were] over five hundred different shades of blond alone, from strawberry blond to platinum blonde and every shade in between".[40]

The in-depth analysis undertaken in the preparation of this book inclines this author to claim that the fashion sector can be understood in a multifold way: 1) The fashion industry is an amalgam of the TCLF, furniture, gem and jewellery and beauty industries as well as everything that involves elements of aesthetics and lifestyle. It expands to a multitude of processes, from research and development (R&D) and design through production and retail and marketing, up to waste and recycling. 2) Fashion could be confined to textiles, clothing, shoes, bags and accessories with elements of jewellery and fragrances. 3) Sometimes it feels valid to use the term even more as a synonym for the ***apparel industry*** (clothing or garment industry), which comprises clothing only: from daywear, evening wear, underwear, sleepwear to shoes, purses and accessories. 4) One could also be tempted to claim that the fashion industry is simply the TCLF industry, an opinion that in fact cuts a number of corners and is erroneous for many reasons, some of which were presented earlier. This author decided to hover somewhere between the first and second approaches to keep the breadth of this analysis within appropriate bounds. In order to represent statistics correctly, some of the data will refer to TCLF (or T/C) as such, which is justified, since TCLF constitutes such a large part of the fashion industry.

These attempts to provide definitions were made at the last stage of preparing this book, benefitting from consideration of the many legal cases that allowed the author to reflect on the scope of the fashion industry and fashion law. Although many definitions have been offered for fashion law, this author would like to frame this book with her belief that fashion law is a set of legal norms that regulate the existence and functioning of the fashion industry understood in the broadest way (as in point 1).

3.1.7 TCLF landscape globally and in Europe

3.1.7.1 Overview and structure

To understand that the TCLF sector is one of the world's largest,[41] it suffices to look at statistics. The global apparel market reached a value of nearly

39 Gerstell, Marchessou, Schmidt, Spagnuolo, *How COVID-19 Is Changing the World of Beauty?*

40 N.L. Etcoff, *Survival of the Prettiest: The Science of Beauty*, Anchor Books, 2000; Katherine T. Frith, *Globalizing Beauty: A Cultural History of the Global Beauty Industry*, paper submitted to ICA for presentation at the Annual Conference Seattle, May 2014, p. 10.

41 It is placed right after the global life and health insurance carriers industry (US$4,384,3 billion), global pension funds industry (US$3,564.4 billion), global commercial real estate (US$3.167,8 billion), global car and automobile sales (US$3,138.5 billion) and global car

US$527.1 billion in 2020, having declined at a compound annual growth rate (CAGR) of –0.6% since 2015. The decline in 2020 can be attributed to the Covid-19 pandemic. The market is anticipated to recover and grow at a CAGR of 9.8% from 2020 and to reach US$842.7 billion in 2025, and US$1,138.8 billion in 2030.[42] Womenswear is the best-selling apparel category globally. Its 2021 revenue amounted to US$876,710 million.[43]

But there is more to tell about the structure of TCLF. Many fashion ateliers have low capital, few employees and no separation between ownership and management,[44] making them prone to threats specific to their business environment (Explanatory item no. 3.2). These are companies of limited resources, low negotiation power and low credit rating.[45] When we dive into the structure of European operators, it may be surprising that a significant majority of firms comprise one to nine employees.[46] In 2017 there were 176,400 entrepreneurs active in the textile and clothing business (T/C), employing 1.7 million workers.

In textiles and clothing, the most striking similarity between the EU and the US is the fact that those two regions are the world's most important importers of T/C products, given their sheer size – in terms of population and income – and their high average purchasing power. The two regions constitute the most important outlets for the so-called exporting countries, which are mainly situated in Asia. Moreover, both the EU and the US remain important T/C producers themselves – with a particular emphasis on high value-added

and automobile manufacturing (US$2,689.0 billion), M. Arsenovic, *31 Absolutely Stunning Fashion Industry Statistics & Facts*, Capital Counselor, 22.01.2023, https://capitalcounselor.com/fashion-industry-statistics/.

42 Global Apparel Market (2020 to 2030) – Key Opportunities and Strategies – ResearchAndMarkets.com; www.businesswire.com/news/home/20210406005828/en/global-apparel-market-2020-to-2030---key-opportunities-and-strategies---researchandmarkets.com, 22.01.2023. Cf. Facts & Key Figures of the European Textile and Clothing Industry, 2020 Edition Euratex; Fashion Industry Report, Shopifyplus, 2021.

43 *Key Figures 2017 – The EU-28 Textile and Clothing Industry in the year 2017*, Euratex 2017, https://euratex.eu/wp-content/uploads/2019/05/EURATEX-KEY-FIGURES-2017.pdf (accessed: 22.01.2023).

44 A. Bencsik, T. Juhász, *Knowledge Management Strategy as a Chance of Small and Medium-Sized Enterprises*, [in:] *Organizational Culture and Behavior: Concepts, Methodologies, Tools, and Applications*, Information Resources Management Association, 2017, p. 585; A. Sadowski, B. Dobrowolska, B. Skowron-Grabowska, A. Bujak, *Polish Textile and Apparel Industry: Global Supply Chain Management Perspective*, "AUTEX Research Journal", 2021, vol. 21, no. 3, p. 269.

45 Tungate, *Fashion Brands* . . . , p. 145.

46 *European Sector Skills Council. Textile Clothing Leather Footwear, Report 2014*, http://europeanskillscouncil.t-c-l.eu/pdoc/22-eng/2014_report_F.pdf (accessed: 22.01.2023); P. Smith, *Apparel and Clothing Market Europe – Statistics and Facts*, www.statista.com/topics/3423/clothing-and-apparel-market-in-europe/#dossierKeyfigures (accessed: 22.01.2023); P. Smith, *U.S. Apparel Market – Statistics & Facts*, www.statista.com/topics/965/apparel-market-in-the-us/ (accessed: 22.01.2023); Joint Research Centre, European Commission, *Productivity in Europe. Trends and Drivers in a Service-Based Economy*, EUR 30076 EN, 2020, p. 8.

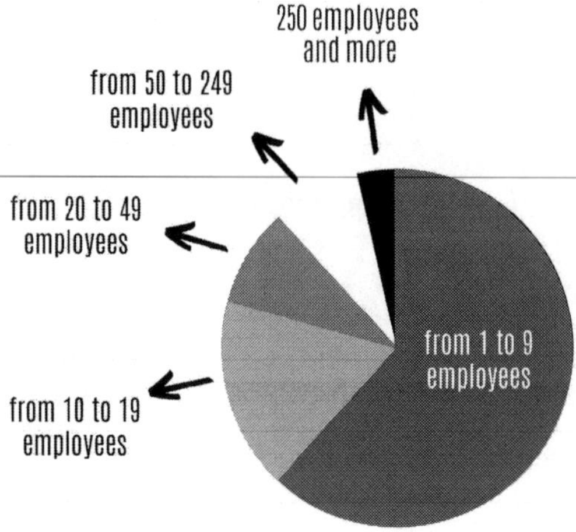

Explanatory item no. 3.2 Structure of European T/C sector by workers' numbers as of 2017

Source: Created by author

Source: CEDEFOP, *European Sector* . . . , p. 33

products.[47] The EU and the US also show similar statistics concerning the relative importance of the T/C industry in total manufacturing output, added value and employment. In terms of productivity, the EU lags behind the US, which benefits from lower production costs (per hour) combined with higher labour productivity (in terms of value added per person employed). The US has also been somewhat faster in adopting new information and communication technologies, especially as far as e-commerce is concerned.

3.1.7.2 Where do creativity and quality stand in the 'ideal' world of TCLF? Creative people in the fashion industry

It is worthy of note that 99% of these companies are "small and medium-sized niche players focusing on quality, innovation, creativity and outstanding customer service".[48] Kotler rightfully opines that brands win through their *superior creativity* and that "one does not win through *better sameness*; one wins through *uniqueness*".[49] Luxurious brands perceive quality as an *inherent*

47 W. Stengg, *The Textile* . . ., p. 28; European Central Bank, Key factors behind productivity trends in EU countries. ECB Strategy review, No 268/September 2021, pp. 5–6. P. Smith, *Apparel and Clothing* . . . ; P. Smith, *U.S. Apparel Market* . . . ; Joint Research Centre, European Commission, *Productivity* . . ., p. 8.

48 Euratex Annual Report, p. 1, https://euratex.eu/wp-content/uploads/2019/05/Euratex-annual-report-2017-LR.pdf (accessed: 12.01.2023).

49 P. Kotler, *Marketing Insights from A to Z: 80 Concerns Every Manager Needs to Know*, Wiley, 2003, p. 27.

facet of identity.[50] Raf Simons, co-creative director of Prada, said that "as times change, so should creativity".[51]

In 2014, it was observed by the European Skills Council, that:

> How TCLF products are manufactured along with their application are evolving as advancements in production processes, techniques and materials are made. For instance, increasingly more sophisticated computer aided design, virtual manufacturing simulators, the laser welding of garments, the production of smart clothing and footwear, the introduction of more ecological sustainable chemicals in the leather sector and new efficient machinery and in some cases robotic manufacturing processes such as in the footwear sector are examples of enabling technologies that can offer new commercial possibilities for manufacturers. Whilst many of these new processes are automated requiring new skills to undertake them, there is also a need to ensure traditional TCLF knowledge and principles are embedded and training requirements are widely understood. . . . As traditional mass textile manufacture moved beyond European borders, there has been a rise in the development of technical textiles, textiles created for performance rather than aesthetics requiring a whole new skill set within the sector. Technical textile development has become a key driver for many producers moving away from traditional textiles markets where knowledge and innovation are required. The leather sector with new innovations, especially within automotive and aeroplane production is increasingly important and are the equivalent to technical textiles in this sector whilst footwear has seen a need for new lighter, stronger, performance and ecological materials. However, technical textiles remain costly to produce, with the ability to commercialise them also important. There also remain substantial intellectual property rights (IPRs) issues which are crucial to the maintenance and growth of this sector.[52]

As mentioned earlier (Chapter 3, section titled "Parties to the business relationship – La Griffe. The brand owner"), a fashion house can choose from

50 A different standpoint represents Laurence Vincent, who observes that clients are drawn to a brand by different features than the quality itself, cf. L. Vincent, *Legendary Brands: Unleashing the Power of Storytelling to Create a Winning Market Strategy*, Dearborn Trade Publishing, 2002, p. 5.

51 N. Levy, *Raf Simons Becomes Co-Creative Director of Prada*, "De Zeen", 25 February 2020, www.dezeen.com/2020/02/25/raf-simons-prada-co-creative-director-fashion-news/ (accessed: 12.01.2023), cf. M. Tungate, *Fashion Brands: Branding Style from Armani to Zara*, Kogan Page, 2008, p. 91; cf. European Commission, *Fashion and High-End Industries in the EU*, https://ec.europa.eu/growth/sectors/fashion/fashion-and-high-end-industries/fashion-and-high-end-industries-eu_en (accessed: 12.01.2023).

52 *European Sector Skills Council. Textile Clothing Leather Footwear, Report 2014*, http://europeanskillscouncil.t-c-l.eu/pdoc/22-eng/2014_report_F.pdf (accessed: 12.01.2023).

a variety of structures. The biggest and most sophisticated hire large numbers of people engaged in creative business at many levels:

- managers: e.g. footwear product development manager, textile product developer, leather environmental manager;
- professionals: textile laboratory technician, footwear quality control laboratory technician, organisational and methods technician;
- associate professionals: clothing product designer, textile technologist;
- skilled trades: garment and related pattern-makers, weavers, knitters, leather craftworkers;
- plant and machine operators and assemblers: pattern-making machine operator, sewing machine operator, leather production machine operator;
- elementary occupations: hand garment presser, warehouse operative.

At the managerial level, what is undertaken is product development, compliance with specifications and policies, keeping up with clients' expectations, market analysis, R&D, construction and quality details. At the professional level, scientific and technological advancements are checked and developed with regard to textiles and products. Other than that, what is planned is distribution. Although the creative process takes place at many levels, the professional level lies at the heart of the fashion house structure, where it is responsible for creativity and innovation. They create master patterns for production of products (garments) and are skilled in marking, cutting, shaping and trimming materials and operating computer-aided design programs, while also possessing excellent freehand drawing skills. They deal with issues related to the process of creation, including sourcing fabrics, conducting quality control tests, experimenting with dyeing and other production processes. The skilled trades are said to be the "backbone" of the TCLF sector. Garment and related pattern-makers interpret designers' sketches and make precise master patterns. At this level, staff need a bank of knowledge related to pattern cutting and material properties that provides the bridge between the designing and manufacturing levels.[53]

Interestingly, the landscape of fashion business and technology is changing, and new roles are emerging, many of which enhance the creativity of the design process. Some expected emerging jobs within the TCLF sector are as follows:

- managers: fashion product manager, e-commerce manager, social media marketing and communications manager;
- professionals: process and production timeline analyst, head of information technology;
- associate professionals: research, development and information textile researcher, product and process innovation systems professional, graphic designer for textiles, 3D design and construction engineer;

53 *European Sector* . . ., pp. 84–100.

- skilled trades: fashion product managers;
- operatives: digital printing machine operator, laser cutting and assembly operators, automatic cutting system operator.[54]

In any scenario a brand chooses to pursue, the bottom line is that

> the successful brands are those that understand the challenge of finding a balance between being timeless through a firm brand concept and heritage; being current and relevant for the moment through strong brand positioning; and being innovative in crafting a future, all at the same time.[55]

3.1.7.3 Intuition outpacing creativity

The TCLF sector is one of the oldest in the history of industrial development, and it is often considered part of 'traditional industry' or the 'old economy'.[56] Nonetheless, it is said that TCLF is a sector that embraces by reorienting production towards innovative and high-quality products.[57] Patrik Aspers rightly observed that fashion is based on the premise that is related to social situations, culture and space, meaning that fashion touches on relationship between man and his environment.[58] In relation to fashion, as the term has been used, it is about the 'gut feeling' (or 'feel for the game', *Fingerspitzengefühl*, literally 'fingertip feel')[59] for what will succeed in the market. Designers can draw from statistics, and from the general belief that trends need to be reinterpreted to sell, but they must also include shared values, history or patterns of thinking.[60] Aspers calls this 'mysterious' knowledge, for which he offers the synonyms 'creativity', 'talent', 'gut-feeling' and 'genius'. Indeed, Sunley et al. argue that

> the market plays a key knowledge formation role; the design market is not a narrow channel that only sends flickering price and demand signals

54 *European Sector* . . ., pp. 102–105.
55 Okonkwo, *Luxury Fashion* . . ., p. 5.
56 W. Stengg, *The Textile and Clothing Industry in the EU, a Survey*. Enterprise Papers, No. 2 2001, Ref. Ares (2014)77487–15/01/2014, p. 1.
57 W. Stengg, *The Textile* . . ., p. 1. A. Hauge, *The Learning* . . . 2005; Aspers, *Orderly Fashion* . . .; V. Ledezma, *Globalization and Fashion: Too Fast, Too Furious*, "Laurier Undergraduate Journal of the Arts", 2017, vol. 4, Art. 9, pp. 74–75; H.B. Zekri, *Globalization and the Fast Fashion Phenomenon: The Impact Upon Labors, Environment and the Consumer Behavior*, "MAS Journal of Applied Sciences", 2021, 8, http://dx.doi.org/10.52520/masjaps.102 (accessed: 12.01.2023); Ch. Barrère, S. Delabruyère, *Intellectual Property Rights on Creativity and Heritage: The Case of the Fashion Industry*, "European Journal of Law and Economics", 2011/12, vol. 32; no. 3, p. 307.
58 P. Aspers, *Using Design for Upgrading in the Fashion Industry*, "Journal of Economic Geography", 2010, vol. 10, p. 196; Cf. the concepts of *situated knowledge* in the paper.
59 Bourdieu P., *The Logic of Practice*, Polity Press, 1980, 1990, p. 66.
60 Aspers, *Using Design* . . ., p. 200.

> but instead acts as a broad, interpersonal and frequently relational channel that carries a great deal of learning and knowledge exchange.[61]

It is often overlooked that the TCLF has always been closely connected with aspects such as the industrial revolution, which brought about the mechanisation and production of textiles, and French couturiers, known for their original designs. It was globalisation and the increased prosperity of society that made fashion goods cheap, fast and fleeting. Thriving competition reinforced this trend as the entry level of the fashion industry strove to compete aggressively on price and volume. At the same time, it must be noted that TCLF is considered a *low-technology industry*[62] and an *intermediate goods industry* as well as forming part of the *experience economy*[63] and *a mix of creative and cultural industries.* This places the sector at the intersection between social, business and cultural norms, a far more complex situation than legal thinkers have anticipated when drafting intellectual property laws. However, there is a general view that *innovation in services* should be protected by copyright rather than patents.[64]

As rightly pointed out by Sunley et al.,

> as the Work Foundation . . . notes: "Unlike patent law that concentrates upon the relationship between the invention and information in the public domain, the originality test in copyright is concerned with the relationship between the creator and the work; that is, the expressive input that brings idiosyncrasies and serendipities of skill, labour and judgement to bear on the resulting output." In many creative spheres enforcing intellectual property rights through copyright is problematic and innovation specialists have therefore tended to focus on technological innovations in the form of patents and on manufacturing outputs. But given the aesthetisation of products and consumption . . ., it is vain

61 P. Sunley, S. Pinch, S. Reimer, J. Macmillen, *Innovation in a Creative Production System: The Case of Design*, "Journal of Economic Geography", 2008, vol. 8, p. 678.

62 Among high-technology industries, mid-technology industries and low-technology industries, TCLF is placed at the bottom of the competitive edge. This distinction was offered by the Organisation for Economic Cooperation and Development (OECD) that differentiated between industries in terms of R&D intensities. Those spending more than 4% of turnover (such as information and communications technology or pharmaceuticals) were classified as high-technology industries, those spending between 4% and 1% (such as vehicles and chemicals) as medium-technology industries and those spending less than 1% (such as textiles and food) as low-technology industries. Cf. OECD, *ISIC Rev. 3 Technology Intensity Definition*, www.oecd.org/sti/ind/48350231.pdf (accessed: 12.01.2023).

63 The term 'experience economy' has been coned by Pine and Gilmore, and it means an economy of goods, which receive customers' desire to pay more not for the product or service itself but for the experience, feeling that they get by buying/using it. It goes far beyond the tangible good. J. Pine, J. Gilmore, 1999, cf. De Voldere, Jans, Durinck, Plaisier, Smakman, Mirza, Szalavetz, *Study on the Competitiveness* . . ., p. 12.

64 Sunley, Pinch, Reimer, Macmillen, *Innovation* . . ., p. 677.

to try to separate innovation from the effects of creative inputs. Innovation and successful design are inseparable, but compared with manufacturing, we have a relatively poor understanding of what constitutes innovation in design.[65]

The long history of French fashion ateliers reveals a great deal about their creativity, inventiveness and the distinctiveness of fashion designs. First, it shows that most distinguished fashion designers were the apprentices of their masters. Second, it proves that entrants must acquire pre-entry experience (organisational routine, genealogical linkage, ateliers' signature designs), which is impossible to gain from afar. This is also why the fashion business is more approachable by spin-offs than by start-ups. It was noted by Stinchcombe in 1965[66] that new designers are overburdened with the 'liability of newness', which can be overcome only by the experience of an apprentice.[67] According to an interesting premise by Rik Wenting, imitation can be defined as "routine replication between firms without genealogical linkage".[68] This idea does not negate imitation as long as it serves the acquisition of knowledge and skills and takes place with a certain sensitivity. Fashion is a cultural product. It must be acknowledged that the first *haute couture* designers were rich with ideas they brought from other époques, cultures and societies (Paquin, Poiret). Imitation without the deeper understanding of tacit knowledge, resulting from designers' interaction with each other, is not effective. The knowledge acquired by imitation will sustain success only if applied and recombined in a new environment.[69]

3.1.7.4 Craftsmanly quality setting the tone?

A deep dive into the statistics of fashion reveals a few facts about the sector as a creative business. By 2025, a significant change is anticipated that is related to the employment ratio, especially to the skills of the fashion workers. It is believed that the industry's eagerness to hire more highly qualified staff into new roles will create a boom in opportunities for such candidates. However, the same cannot be said for those with medium or lower-level qualifications, given that the roles for such employees are expected to stagnate.[70]

65 Sunley, Pinch, Reimer, Macmillen, *Innovation* . . ., p. 677.
66 A.L. Stinchcombe, *Social Structure and Organizations*, 1965, [in:] J.G. March (ed.), *Handbook of Organizations*, Rand McNally & Company, pp. 142–193.
67 Wenting, *Spinoff* . . . , p. 594.
68 Wenting, *Spinoff* . . . , p. 594.
69 Wenting, *Spinoff* . . . , p. 600.
70 *European Sector* . . ., p. 32. The shift towards better skilled and competitive employees in EU is secured also through legal documents, cf. Pact for Skills for the EU TCLF Industries as of 16 December 2021, https://euratex.eu/wp-content/uploads/TCLF-Pact-for-Skills-FINAL-v1.pdf (accessed: 22.01.2023).

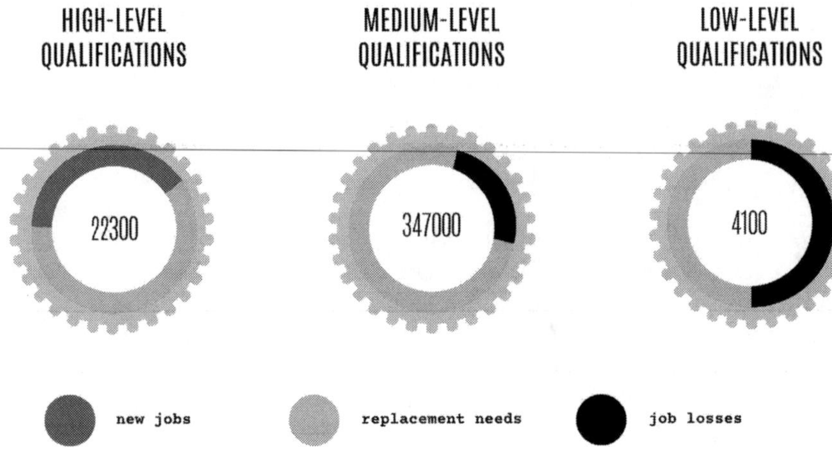

Explanatory item no. 3.3 Expected job opening in the TCLF sectors by 2025
Source: CEDEFOP, EU Skills Panorama 2014, *European Sector . . .*, p. 32

Also, according to the forecast, there will be a further decline in jobs in the coming years, continuing a trend that started a few decades ago. Interestingly, despite shrinking employment, the TCLF business continues to grow annually (Explanatory item no. 3.3). In economics, there is drawn a clear-cut distinction between ***supply-driven*** and ***demand-driven markets.***[71] The first is based on the targeting of consumers by entrepreneurs by offering standard products and lower added value. The latter requires companies to follow clients and their urge for customised production and higher added value.[72] The general conclusion about the decline of TCLF employment refers mostly to the former market. Qualifications and skills will become part of key strategic processes (Explanatory item no. 3.4).[73] This is a vital change in the TCLF business, which has traditionally mostly been based on lower-level skills.[74]

It was outlined by the European Skills Council that

> As much of the European TCLF production was off-shored due to the lower costs of manufacturing overseas, many manufacturers rose to this

71 B.Z. Hull, *Are Supply (Driven) Chains Forgotten?*, "The International Journal of Logistics Management", 2005, vol. 16, no. 2, p. 219; N. Arora, D. Ensslen, L. Fiedler, W.W. Liu, K. Robinson, E. Stein, G. Schüler, *The Value of Getting Personalization Right – Or Wrong – Is Multiplying*, www.mckinsey.com/business-functions/marketing-and-sales/our-insights/the-value-of-getting-personalization-right-or-wrong-is-multiplying (accessed: 22.01.2023).

72 *European Sector . . .*, p. 34; Arora, Ensslen, Fiedler, Liu, Robinson, Stein, Schüler, *The Value . . .*

73 *European Sector . . .*, p. 35.

74 OECD, *ISIC Rev. 3 . . .*

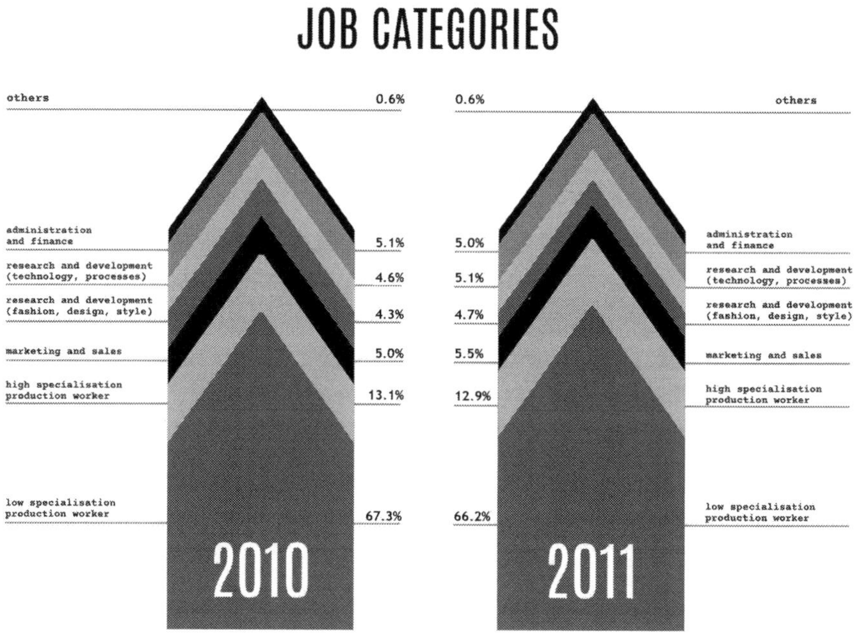

Explanatory item no. 3.4 Job categories by example of the leather tanning industry

Source: COTANCE – INDUSTRIALL 2012, *European Sector* . . . , p. 46

challenge by diversifying and concentrated on high quality and niche manufacture. For example, in many textile producers' cases, this meant diversifying into high added value technical textiles production, textiles made not for aesthetics but for their properties in a variety of applications and sold in many different markets from aeronautics to agriculture, from cars to construction and health. European manufacturers are now among the world leaders in technical textile development. An example of this is the Belgian textile sector which in 2013 saw interior textiles account for 42 per cent and technical textiles 38 per cent of industry turnover and is a trend that is increasingly annually.[75]

European producers pursue the expectation of bringing to market niche value-added activity and working towards product development with regard to

- high-quality fashion and textile goods,
- better service,
- innovative TCLF materials.[76]

75 *European Sector* . . ., p. 70.
76 *European Sector* . . ., p. 70.

3.2 'Be quick to catch the trains'. Fashion as a fast-paced industry

3.2.1 Need for speed in technology-neutral legal surroundings?

3.2.1.1 Product design process

To quote a fashion industry insider, "you have to be quick to catch the trains".[77] The scope of activities related to the production of clothes is very large. In addition are all the necessary processes related to the provision of semi-finished products and raw materials. In the literature, it is noted that the most important stages of the process of creating clothes, which is heavily dependent on the functioning of the supply chain, should be the following:

1 Designing: the phase of making key decisions that reflect the expectations of the market and the willingness to create demand for new products. Market research and trend tracking play an important role in gathering the necessary information on customer requirements. At the time of designing, the type of material and the cut are selected. These are crucial for future business relationships, as the choice of materials is directly related to the choice of suppliers and the process of sourcing resources. This determines the selection criteria and the terms of future cooperation.
2 Sampling (Sample development): the stage of preparing the first pieces to be tested. This is the moment to make decisions about the shape of the future collection, introducing any necessary corrections and setting prices.
3 Selection: introducing corrections to the collection, presentation at trade fairs, demonstrations for customers and distributors and further product development, if necessary.
4 Production, taking into account the data obtained in the previous stages. An important factor – from the perspective of the functioning of the clothing industry – is the place of production (local, global production, i.e. offshoring) and the method of commissioning (own production, outsourcing).
5 Distribution: the process of selecting channels through which products will be delivered to the customer.

3.2.1.2 Time to market and time to money

Product development, design, fabric testing, sample making, brand building, advertising, buying and sourcing – these are only some of the tasks undertaken concurrently in the fashion industry. *Fast pace* is the factor that distinguishes this sector, but to gain a better understanding of its processes, let us reflect on some general business concepts. To paraphrase the general observation

77 Aspers, *Using Design . . .*, p. 202.

by Benjamin N. Roin, as products' time-to-market increases, those products become less profitable.[78] Furthermore,

> as time-to-market increases, firms have higher R&D costs that they must recoup through sales revenue from their inventions (innovations [added by this author – MJ]), and therefore they are more likely to develop highly differentiated product to reduce price competition.[79]

The *time-to-market* for a product is the time it takes to move from the initial idea to its sale as a commercialised product.[80] There is a general understanding that to remain competitive and recoup investment on R&D, private industry has to move quickly. However, not every sector and product follows the same logic, so the imperative for a fast time-to-market cannot be considered universal.[81] This construct has led to many economic theories allowing risk assessment of product development.[82] The concept of time-to-market is closely connected with other concepts, such as time-to-money, product development, product life cycle, market life cycle and customer life cycle.[83] Assessment

78 B.N. Roin, *The Case for Tailoring Patent Awards Based on Time-to-Market*, "UCLA Law Review", 2014, vol. 61, no. 3, p. 685.

79 Roin, *The Case for Tailoring . . .*, p. 686.

80 P.G. Smith, *Accelerated Product Development: Techniques and Traps* [in:] K.B. Kahn (ed.), *The PDMA Handbook of the New Product Development*, 2nd Edition, Wiley, 2005, p. 173; M.A. Cohen, E. Eliashberg, T.-H. Ho, *New Product Development: The Performance and Time-to-Market Tradeoff*, "Management Science", 1996, vol. 42, no. 2, p. 173; TCGen, *Time to Market: What It Is, Why It's Important, and Five Ways to Reduce it*, www.tcgen.com/time-to-market/ (access: 6.01.2023).

81 P.G. Smith, D.G. Reinertsen, *Developing Products in Half the Time: New Rules, New Tools*, 2nd Edition, Wiley, 1997, p. 25.

82 Professors Suzanne de Treville and Norman Schürhoff of OpLab at the University of Lausanne's Faculty of Business and Economics (HEC) developed a time-to-market measure that would be applicable to each sector (Cost Differential Frontier Calculator, available at: http://cdf-oplab.unil.ch/) (access: 6.01.2023). This concept was developed later: S. de Treville, I. Bicer, V. Chavez-Demoulin, V. Hagspiel, N. Schürhoff, C. Tasserit, S. Wager, *Valuing Lead Time*, "Journal of Operations Management", 2013, 32 (2014) 337–346.

83 J. Praxnikar, T. Skerlj, *New Product Development Process and Time-to-Market in the Generic Pharmaceutical Industry*, "Industrial Marketing Management", 2006, vol. 35, no. 6, p. 690; H.S. Hoon, *Time-Based Competition: Some Empirical Data from Singapore*, "Asia Pacific Journal of Manage", 1995, vol. 12, no. 2, p. 123; R.C. Bennett, R.G. Cooper, *The Product Life Cycle Trap*, "Business Horizons", 1984, vol. 27, no. 5, https://doi.org/10.1016/0007-6813(84)90035-1 (accessed: 06.01.2023); G.S. Day, *The Product Life Cycle: Analysis and Applications Issues*, "Journal of Marketing", 1981, vol. 45, no. 4, p. 60; S. Thomke, D. Reinertsen, *Six Myths of Product Development*, "Harvard Business Review", https://hbr.org/*2012/05/six-myths-of-product-development (accessed: 03.04.2022); M.T. Cunningham, The Application of Product Life Cycles to Corporate Strategy: Some Research Findings*, "European Journal of Marketing", 1969, vol. 3, no. 1, p. 39; K.T. Ulrich, S.D. Eppinger, *Product Design and Development*, Sixth Edition, McGraw-Hill Education 2005, p. 2; Loch Ch. H., Kavadias S., *Managing New Product Development: An Evolutionary Framework* [in:] C.H. Loch, S. Kavadias (eds.), *Handbook of New Product Development Management*, Butterworth-Heinemann 2007, p. 3.

of these elements can have a useful impact on planning the launch of new products, pricing policies, marketing mix and financial investment appraisal.[84] Ulrich and Eppinger, in considering the factors that make a product successful, include development time, ***product quality*** (emphasis mine – MJ), product cost, development cost and development capability.[85]

For fashion, fast pace is its most obvious element; however, it has other characteristics that make the general time-to-market concepts less suitable. As pointed out earlier in this chapter (Chapter 3, 3.4.6.), the fashion industry is optimistically believed to be a knowledge-based industry embracing technological change, but in reality, it belongs to the low-technology category of industries for many reasons. Innovation and high-quality products are characteristics of only one part (high fashion) of the large realm of fashion. They are by no means major features of the industry as a whole.

Fashion brand owners are bound to watch the ***market life cycle*** and the ***customer life cycle*** much more closely than the ***product life cycle***.[86] From the investment angle, what matters is the time spent on conceptualising the product, which is the ***innovation process***, that brings together: idea development, idea screening, concept development and testing, business analysis, prototype development and testing, test marketing, and commercialisation.[87] Kotler points out that an innovative firm needs to foster three interrelated areas: idea market, capital market and talent market. In other words, it needs to support and stimulate ideas inside the company, secure its financing and reward the talents.[88] This is demonstrated using an ***innovation index***. Whereas traditional business needs at least a 20% innovation index to outdo the competition, Kotler hints that for a high-fashion clothing business, at least 100% is required.[89]

84 Cunningham, *The Application . . .*, p. 39.

85 K.T. Ulrich, S.D. Eppinger, *Product Design . . .*, p. 3.

86 P. Kotler, *Marketing Insights from A to Z: 80 Concerns Every Manager Needs to Know*, Wiley, 2003, p. 37. G. Stalk, T.M. Hout, *Competing against Time: How Time-Based Competition Is Reshaping Global Markets*, Business & Economics – Management & Leadership, p. 8; B.L. Bayus, *Speed-to-Market and New Product Performance Trade-offs*, "Journal of Product Innovation Management", 1997, vol. 14, no. 6, p. 489; R.G. Cooper, *The Performance Impact of Product Innovation Strategies*, "European Journal of Marketing", 1984/05, vol. 18, no. 5, pp. 13–17; K. Atuahene-Gima, *An Exploratory Analysis of the Impact of Market Orientation on New Product Performance a Contingency Approach*, "Journal of Product Innovation Management", 1995, vol. 12, no. 4, pp. 283–284; C. Chou, K.-P. Yang, *The Interaction Effect of Strategic Orientations on New Product Performance in the High-Tech Industry: A Nonlinear Model,* "Technological Forecasting & Social Change", 2011, vol. 78, pp. 70–73; D. Shim, J.G. Kim, J. Altmann, *Strategic Management of R&D and Marketing Integration for Multi-Dimensional Success of New Product Developments: An Empirical Investigation in the Korean ICT Industry,* "Asian Journal of Technology Innovation", 2016/09, Obj. 24, no. 3, pp. 13–17.

87 Kotler, *Marketing Insights . . .*, p. 83; E.M. Rasiel, P.N. Friga, *The McKinsey Mind: Understanding and Implementing the Problem-Solving Tools and Management Techniques of the World's Top Strategic Consulting Firm*, McGraw-Hill, 2001, pp. xv, 31–32.

88 Kotler, *Marketing Insights . . .*, p. 84.

89 Kotler, *Marketing Insights . . .*, p. 85.

As noted by George Stalk Jr., "the best competitors, the most successful ones, know-how to keep moving and always stay on the cutting edge" (so called 'time-based competitors').[90]

A major part of the clothing industry seems to follow the pattern 'risk abuse for a fast buck' or 'make the money before the pirates catch up'.[91] Inevitably, products that are introduced to the market at a fast pace are of lower quality, a fact which has been proven analytically and empirically.[92] Fashion is one of the sectors that strongly relies on the premise "give customers what they want when they want it".[93] However, there are extra factors that make such a product attractive, such as its market performance and responsiveness.[94] These are two important elements with regard to fashion, given that the industry is based on the seasonality of trends.[95] Given the imitational character of fashion, it is sometimes hard to pinpoint who was the *trend or style innovator* (Chapter 3, section titled "Parties to the business relationship – La Grippe. The target").[96] There is also a substantial difference between a pioneer and a leader. Research conducted in the 1990s, encompassing nearly one hundred years, 500 brands and 50 product categories, showed that 47% of pioneers' new products were failures. At the same time, the failure rate of early leaders was only 8%.[97] This proves that a strategy based on following and accommodating trends and existing products is much safer than going all in on innovation. One of the risks involved is whether the pioneer will recoup its R&D investment.[98]

90 G. Stalk Jr., *Time – The Next Source of Competitive Advantage*, "Harvard Business Review", 1988, https://hbr.org/1988/07/time-the-next-source-of-competitive-advantage (accessed: 06.01.2023).

91 S. Rodwell, P. Van Eeckhout, A. Reid, J. Walendowski, *Study "Effects of Counterfeiting on EU SMEs and a Review of Various Public and Private IPR Enforcement Initiatives and Resources", Framework Contract B3/ENTR/04/093-FC-Lot 6 Specific Agreement n°SI2.448309, Final Report to the Enterprise and Industry Directorate-General Directorate B1 – Development of Industrial Policy*, 2007, p. 14.

92 Bayus, *Speed-to-Market . . .*, p. 489.

93 Stalk, *Time . . .*, p. 10.

94 Cooper, *The Performance . . .*, p. 15.

95 A Van de Peer, *So Last Season: The Production of the Fashion Present in the Politics of Time*, "Fashion Theory the Journal of Dress Body & Culture", 2014/06, vol. 18, no. 3, pp. 334–335; A. Venkatesh, A. Joy, J. F. Sherry Jr., J. Deschenes, *The Aesthetics of Luxury Fashion, Body and Identify Formation*, "Journal of Consumer Psychology", 2010, vol. 20, no. 4, p. 464; T.-M. Choi, C.-L. Hui, Y. Yu (eds.), *Intelligent Fashion Forecasting Systems: Models and Applications*, Springer-Verlag, 2014, p. V.

96 Lieberman, Montgomery, *First-Mover . . .*, pp. 50–51; Urban, Carter, Gaskin, Mucha, *Market . . .*, p. 645 et seq.; Linden, *An Analysis . . .* ; Golder, Tellis, *Pioneer Advantage . . .*, pp. 159–160.

97 Golder, Tellis, *Pioneer Advantage . . .*, pp. 166–167.

98 S. Rodwell, P. Van Eeckhout, A. Reid, J. Walendowski, *Study "Effects of Counterfeiting on EU SMEs and a Review of Various Public and Private IPR Enforcement Initiatives and Resources"*, Framework contract B3/ENTR/04/093-FC-Lot 6 Specific agreement n°SI2.448309, Final Report to the Enterprise and Industry Directorate-General Directorate B1 – Development of Industrial Policy, 2007, p. 14.

Fashion works around micro-trends that usually last three to five years and macro-trends that typically endure for five to ten years. It generally takes 50 weeks to create a design, or in the case of ultra-fast fashion, a much faster 40 days.[99]

Item of note no. 3.4 ZARA success formula

Zara is a Spanish clothing chain that was founded in 1963. It is considered one of the most successful fashion brands for many reasons[100]:

- *vertically integrated business model* – Zara uses a mix of design, just-in-time production (including basic fabric dyeing), marketing and sales. *designers in touch with store managers* – There is quick response from the creative level. *real-time sales data from all stores* – This provide the possibility to supply stores with sought-after goods.
- *super-fast time to money, quick response (QR)* – Zara commits only 15% of its production at the start of the season when the figure for the average EU retailer is as high as 60%. This allows Zara to reorient or cease its production at any time.
- *super-fast time to market* – Zara needs only three weeks to make a new line from scratch, whereas the industry average is nine months.
- *budget interpretations of catwalk styles.*[101]

3.2.1.3 Technology-neutral copyright law?

3.2.2 Many shades of copying. Plagiarism versus piracy, counterfeits, knock-offs, replicas, copycats and imitations

There is a subtle difference between the various words describing imitations and their legal use. There are also no legal definitions to serve as a point of departure for further analysis. Some nuances must be borne in mind,

99 V. Bhardwaj, A. Fairhurst, *Fast Fashion: Response to Change in the Fashion Industry*, "The International Review of Retail, Distribution and Consumer Research", 2010, vol. 20, no. 1, p. 165 et seq.; M. Christopher, R. Lowson, H. Peck, *Creating Agile Supply Chain in the Fashion Industry*, "International Journal of Retail and Distribution Management", 2004, vol. 32, no. 8, p. 367 et seq.; G.F. Iribarren, *Time, the Ultimate Resource of Fashion*, https://gabrielfariasiribarren.com/en/time-the-ultimate-resource-of-fashion/ (accessed: 12.01.2023); M. Cagan, *INSPIRED: How to Create Tech Products Customers Love*, 2nd Edition, Wiley, 2018, p. 112; J. Blau, *Shorter Time to Money Drives Philips R&D*, "Research: Technology Management", 1994, vol. 37, no. 2, pp. 5–6; A. Gustafson, Lit Ng Sz, A. von Schmiesing-Korff, *A Time Efficient Supply Chain Model for an Apparel Company*, Kristianstad University Sweden – Business Administration Project 2004, pp. 9–51; Fernandez-Stark, Frederick, Gereffi, *The Apparel Global . . .*, pp. 82–85.

100 Stengg, *The Textile . . .*, p. 9.

101 Tungate, *Fashion Brands . . .*, p. 50.

especially the fact that both the EU and US approaches are based on different terminology. In the EU, the term 'plagiarism' is generally used for any form of copyright infringement. In the information technology sector, there is also the term 'piracy'. Therefore, these concepts will also be used in this book with those meanings.[102] However, it should be noted that in the US, the term 'plagiarism' would be reserved for works of literature. Also 'infringement' would not be the most obvious term to describe copying of a fashion product. In turn, the US favours the terms 'counterfeits', 'knock-offs' and 'copycats'. These terms should not be used interchangeably and therefore need explanation.

A counterfeit is a product that is identical or nearly identical to another product and thereby infringes upon the product's trademark or on another industrial property right.[103] There is a differentiation between deceptive and non-deceptive counterfeiting that boils down to the consumer's awareness that they are acquiring a copy.[104]

A knock-off is a product that resembles another but is not identical (also referred to as a 'parasitic' or 'look-alike' product. It is "generally understood as a cheap copy intended to evoke the original product by having a similar appearance, but without the identical or nearly identical use of a registered trademark".[105] In other words, this is a copy with a variation in price point.[106] This good is intended to be legal, borrowing only some elements from the original.[107]

There is also a less obvious term, 'replica', technically a morally looking better word. This category falls roughly in between counterfeits and knock-offs.

There are also other concepts, such as 1) rub-offs (referring to a copy of a sewing pattern), 2) near-brands, 3) copycats (used broadly to refer to imitations in general) and 4) fakes.

Berman offered a four-tier qualification of counterfeits:

1 Knock-off, a copy where consumers are aware they are buying a cheaper imitation.
2 Tear-down – a product created through reverse engineering, often involving acquisition of the original product. Berman claimed that tear-downs were

102 L. Palandri, *Fashion as Art: Rights and Remedies in the Age of Social Media*, Laws, 2020, 9, 9, p. 5.

103 Nia and Zaichowsky 2000, Chuen and Phau, McDonald and Roberts p. 52.

104 P. 52; Keith Wilcox, Hyeong Min Kim, Sankar Sen, *Why Do Consumers Buy Counterfeit Luxury Brands?*, "Journal of Marketing Research", 2009, vol. XLVI, p. 249.

105 Elizabeth Kurpis [in:] A. Zaczkiewicz (ed.), *Counterfeits, Knockoffs, Replicas: Parsing the Legal Implications*, WWD, 2.06.2016, https://wwd.com/business-news/retail/counterfeit-knockoff-replica-legal-10437109/ (accessed: 12.01.2023).

106 P.P. Quesenberry, *Apparel Industry Definitions: Copying, Knocking-off, Counterfeiting*, Ph.D. thesis at the Virginia Polytechnic Institute and State University, p iii; https://vtechworks.lib.vt.edu/bitstream/handle/10919/64982/Quesenberry_PP_D_2014.pdf (accessed: 12.01.2023).

107 P. Brown, J. Rice, *Ready-to-Wear Apparel Analysis*, Prentice Hall, 2001; E. Stone, *The Dynamics of Fashion*, Fairchild Publications Inc., 1999, pp. 15, 49 and ff.

intended to deceive consumers; however, this argument can be disputed by example of the practice that is widespread in many countries where replica products are widely available and consumers willingly and knowingly buy copies, happy to be receiving a nearly identical product of similar quality but at a lower price.

3 Ghost-shift manufacturing – third-shift work; can occur in outsourced or contract situations, especially in Asia; the goods are manufactured using original materials during an extra shift or after the contract ends.
4 Seconds – a lower-quality good sold as first quality; happens when outsourced contractors do not return all goods marked as less than perfect and do not destroy them as directed but retain these goods and sell them as firsts.[108]

Legally speaking, the concept of 'counterfeit' in US and EU laws is complicated and can apply to many different kinds of IP goods. From a local Polish perspective, there is no legal definition in the national regulations. It is mostly used to refer to infringement of trademark or design law, but with regard to copyright, the terms 'copy' and 'piracy' are used. This usage resembles the concepts set out in Agreement on Trade-Related Aspects of Intellectual Property Rights (TRIPS). According to Article 51 of TRIPS,

> 'counterfeit trademark goods' shall mean any goods, including packaging, bearing without authorization a trademark which is identical to the trademark validly registered in respect of such goods, or which cannot be distinguished in its essential aspects from such a trademark, and which thereby infringes the rights of the owner of the trademark in question under the law of the country of importation.

This definition contains at least two important limitations: 1) it does not apply to other categories of IPRs, such as patents; 2) it only applies to special cases of trademark infringement, i.e. where an unauthorised party uses a sign identical to the protected sign or at least so similar that it cannot be distinguished from it. With regard to copyright infringements, a term "pirated copyright goods" is used that means

> any goods which are copies without the consent of the right holder or person duly authorized by the right holder in the country of production and which are made directly from an article where making of that copy would have constituted an infringement of a copyright or a related right under the law of the country of importation.

In the US, there are several approaches to use of the term, which has broader effect than in the strictly TRIPS sense, at least with regard to IP rights other

108 P. 51.; B. Berman, *Strategies to Detect and Reduce Counterfeiting Activity*, "Business Horizons", 2008, vol. 51, pp. 191 and ff.

than trademarks. Under US usage, counterfeit is a notion that is used to refer to trademarks, trade dress and counterfeit labels.[109] In the context of copyright law, 'fakes' may be referred to as a "counterfeit" good, but the word is not a statutory definition under the primary Copyright Act but is used only in the ordinary sense of the word. But there are copyright cases where 'counterfeit' is used in what is intended as a specifically legal sense. Later in this chapter, this term will be used in the broadest possible meaning.

3.2.3 Fighting counterfeits and knock-offs in T/C sectors. GTRIC-p

In 2007, there was a report based on a survey answered by 143 respondents (representants of the T/C sector – 45, mechanical engineering – 40, other sectors – 37, toys – 9 and automotive parts – 6), mostly from small and medium-sized businesses and mostly based in Austria, France, Italy, Germany and the UK. According to the survey, 83% were concerned about IPR infringements, as 74% of the respondents had been personally affected by such abuse. When asked about the nature of the infringement of their IPRs, the majority of the abuses related to 'look-alike products', 'parasitic copies' and 'design' (Explanatory item no. 3.5).[110]

According to this survey, 33% of the T/C sector was affected by this problem. As to prosecution, 20% of those in the T/C sector took no action at all, which, compared to the other sectors surveyed, represented the highest level of intervention. In addition, the T/C sector filed the highest number of criminal cases (22%). According to the survey, registration of IPRs in the T/C sector was estimated at 18%, compared with 67% for the toy sector and 33% for automotive parts. It was revealed that the registration of designs and utility models and the use of confidentiality agreements in China is particularly low, at, respectively, 10%, 8% and 3%. It was established that the T/C sector finds the protection of design too costly. It is mostly big enterprises that find registration essential. SMEs are often not aware of the risk of counterfeiting or of the need to register their designs.[111] The protection of IPRs *is seen as a cost, not an investment*. As noted in the report,

> The costs of registration are felt to be objectively very high and in this sector it is hard to predict whether a particular product or a trade mark will be a success. When it is successful it is often too late to register it, so the counterfeiter already has the advantage. Many SMEs appreciate the damage caused by the violation of their IPRs only when they have become directly involved in a case – and by then it is usually too late for anything but a defensive posture.[112]

109 15 U.S. Code § 1127; 18 US. Code § 2320; 18 U.S. Code § 2318.
110 Rodwell, Van Eeckhout, Reid, Walendowski, *Study "Effects . . . "*, p. 61.
111 R. Kiebooms, *An IP Plan for SMEs*, "Managing Intellectual Property", 2008, vol. 70, pp. 70–73.
112 S. Rodwell, P. Van Eeckhout, A. Reid, J. Walendowski, *Study "Effects . . . "*, p. 69.

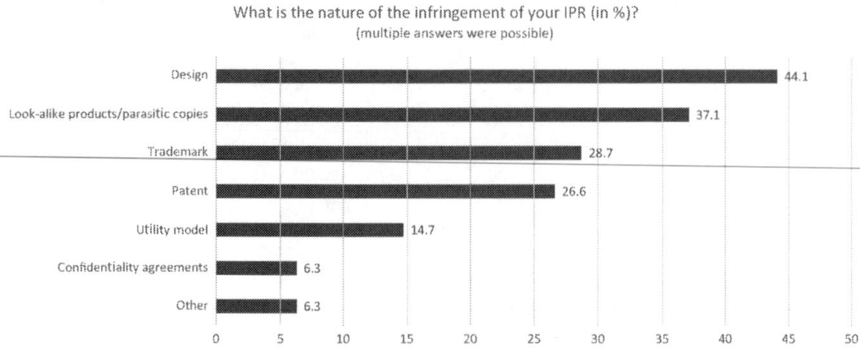

Explanatory item no. 3.5 A breakdown of the legal nature of the IPR infringement

Source: S. Rodwell, P. Van Eeckhout, A. Reid, J. Walendowski, *Study* "*Effects . . .* ", p. 61

In the T/C sector, the success or failure of a product hinges in large part on the design. According to available reports, the investment in creation and innovation for these designs accounts for 10% of the turnover of a business. Because 10% of the turnover is consumed for design and promotion of the trademark, the burden for SMEs is already high. Reportedly, the cost of implementing anti-counterfeiting policies represents a further 2% of turnover.[113]

Many bodies keep formal records of data related to counterfeits.[114] One of these is the Organisation for Economic Cooperation and Development (OECD), which, in addition to the actual numbers of actions taken by customs officers, also measures the severity of infringements, that is, as indices of counterfeiting. One of these is the *GTRIC-p* (General Trade-Related Index of Counterfeiting for products) score, a weighted index having two subcomponents: the values of counterfeit and pirated products in absolute terms in a given product category, and the share of trade held by counterfeit and pirated products in that product category.[115]

From the OECD/European Union Intellectual Property Office (EUIPO) studies, it can be seen that footwear as well as knitted or crocheted clothing have very high GTRIC-p indices, of 0.96 and 0.89, respectively.[116] This places the affected business at high risk of being undermined by counterfeiters. A high GTRIC-p score implies either that a given product category contains

113 Rodwell, Van Eeckhout, Reid, Walendowski, *Study "Effects . . .* ", p. 74, Euratex, 2006a.

114 C. Fink, K.E. Maskus, Y. Qian, *The Economic Effects of Counterfeiting and Piracy. A Review and Implications for Developing Countries*, Policy Research Working Paper 7586, 2016, p. 17.

115 OECD/EUIPO, *Trends in Trade in Counterfeit and Pirated Goods, Illicit Trade*, OECD Publishing, 2019, https://doi.org/10.1787/g2g9f533-en (accessed: 15.01.2023).

116 OECD/EUIPO, *Trade in Counterfeit and Pirated Goods, Mapping the Economic Impact*, 2016, p. 65, https://doi.org/10.1787/g2g9f533-en (accessed: 15.01.2023).

high levels of counterfeit and pirated products in absolute terms (e.g. monetary) or that a large share of imports from that product category are counterfeit and pirated products.[117]

There is also an annual EU report that reveals details of IP enforcement by customs. In 2018, clothing (8.6%) held a proud fifth place, beaten only by cigarettes (15.6%), toys (14.2%), packaging material (9.4%) and the combined category of labels, tags and stickers (8.9%).[118] In terms of interventions by customs, the top five categories are clothes, shoes, bags, toys and watches.[119] Based on the value of the infringed goods, the top five are bags, watches, clothing, sunglasses and sport shoes.[120]

In 2018 and 2019, among EU member states, the top six based on the number of infringement enforcements were Germany, Belgium, Italy, Spain, Austria and Portugal. Those involving the highest number of articles were Germany, Greece, Malta, France, Croatia and Romania. Poland ranked 9th and 18th, respectively.

In summary, in 2019, the four most common subcategories of detained products based on the number of items detained were toys, cigarettes, clothing accessories and clothing (accounting together for 41% of the whole number). When assessed by value (based on original goods), the top four subcategories were clothing accessories, clothing, watches and non-sport shoes, together making up 61% of the entire value.[121]

3.2.3.1 IPRs secured by customs

The EU statistics make clear that, in 2018, a majority of the articles detained by customs were suspected of infringing trademarks, specifically, 88% based on number of articles and 95% based on value (respectively, 76% and 95% in 2019). By contrast, interceptions on the basis of copyright alone accounted for only 0.63% and 0.51%, respectively. Copyright infringements in the period from 2012 to 2019 were mostly noted in connection with such products as toys, furniture, clothing as a whole, of which a notable portion was clothing featuring images of famous cartoon figures. Other products detained for copyright infringement included those that had packaging material containing copyright-protected images or names. Copyright was also a basis for protection of bags including wallets, purses and other similar goods.[122] For packag-

117 OECD/EUIPO, *Trade in Counterfeit . . .*, pp. 63–64.

118 *Report on the EU Customs Enforcement of Intellectual Property Rights: Results at the EU Border, 2018*, Luxembourg 2019, p. 6, cf. *Report on the EU Customs Enforcement of Intellectual Property Rights: Results at the EU Border, 2019*, Luxembourg 2020, p. 6.

119 *Report on the EU Customs . . . (2018)*, p. 13.

120 *Report on the EU Customs . . . (2018)*, p. 14.

121 *EU Enforcement of Intellectual Property Rights: Overall Results of Detentions, 2019*, EUIPO 2021, p. 7.

122 *Report on the EU Customs Enforcement of Intellectual Property Rights: Results at the EU Border, 2016*, Luxembourg, 2017, p. 16; *Report on the EU Customs Enforcement of Intellectual*

Table 3.1 Breakdown per product sector of number of procedures, articles and the retail value of equivalent original goods

Product sector	*Number of procedures, 2018*	*Number of procedures, 2019*	*Number of articles, 2018*	*Number of articles, 2019*	*Retail value of original goods in EUR, 2018*	*Retail value of original goods in EUR, 2019*
Clothing (ready-to-wear)	22,282	22,881	2,305,803	1,601,413	114,482,016	128,459,523
Clothing accessories (belts, ties, shawls, caps, gloves, etc.)	3,337	4,960	346,407	243,030	29,793,085	17,513,720
Sports shoes	13,920	21,596	480,839	601,564	44,236,332	60,588,293
Non-sport shoes	9,680	8,605	275,760	449,799	18,433,750	41,888,818
Bags, including wallets, purses, cigarette cases and other similar goods that can be carried in a person's pocket/bag	8,277	9,791	340,261	412,884	135,467,057	76,033,915
Watches	4,922	6,976	91,271	116,220	117,156,752	162,828,353
Jewellery and other accessories	793	1,519	99,035	155,722	10,289,084	11,385,616
Perfumes and cosmetics	3,933	1,727	1,001,106	1,052,627	17,930,522	39,540,008
Other body care items (razor blades, shampoo, deodorant, toothbrushes, soap, etc.)	197	263	520,329	1,127,837	4,831,761	12,537,342
Labels, tags, stickers,	497	505	2,380,535	1,030,163	6,601,528	1,651,582
Textiles (towels, linen, carpet, mattresses, etc.)	217	464	100,278	171,409	460,528	4,405,155
Packaging materials	1,340	577	1,069,962	5,557,620	10,202,350	4,851,343
For comparison						
Recorded (music, films, software, game software)	34	50	3,806	29,129	274,923	766,251
Games (including electronic game consoles)	1,106	1,983	190,219	40,182	1,956,216	1,801,637
Total for product sectors: food and beverages, cosmetics, clothing, shoes and personal accessories, electronic and computer equipment, recordings, toys, medical products and other goods	89,873	117,343	26,720,827	40,968,254	738,125,867	759,198,194

Source: Report on the EU customs . . . (*2018*), p. 20–21; *Report on the EU customs . . .* (*2019*), p. 20–21.

Table 3.2 The evolution of enforcement cases and numbers of articles detained per member state – period 2017–2019

Member state	*Number of cases*					*Number of articles*				
	2017	*2018*	*Percentage (%)*	*2019*	*Percentage (%)*	*2017*	*2018*	*Percentage (%)*	*2019*	*Percentage (%)*
Germany	18,888	33,421	77	30,923	– 7	2,959,079	4,704,079	59	3,416,121	– 27
Belgium	13,786	12,076	–12	28,393	135	966,155	1,307,944	35	595,705	–54
Italy	3,907	3,230	16	4,402	34	593,487	1,077,920	82	1,881,712	75
Spain	3,740	3,934	5	3,928	0	776,405	1,305,972	–26	563,145	57
Portugal	182	2,275	1,150	1,495	–34	126,594	246,251	95	309,299	26
Greece	108	107	–1	92	–14	2,517,133	2,646,850	5	1,388,284	–48
France	1,050	825	21	727	–12	4,265,443	2,087,423	–51	1,643,560	–21
Romania	327	276	–16	240	–13	3,035,707	1,945,016	–36	9,895,418	409
Hungary	443	422	–5	603	43	68,283	1,460,425	2,039	530,114	–64
Bulgaria	704	407	–42	647	59	1,109,979	1,531,696	38	2,924,055	91
Austria	1,498	759	–49	2,026	167	235,725	38,513	84	370,240	861
Poland	1,425	960	–33	1,415	47	1,193,057	204,829	–83	670,822	228

Source: Own work based on *Report on the EU customs . . .* (*2018*), p. 19 and *Report on the EU customs . . .* (*2019*), p. 19.

Table 3.3 IPRs secured by customs – a general overview 2018–2019

IPRs	*IPRs as a percentage of articles (%)*		*IPRs as a percentage of value (%)*	
	2018	*2019*	*2018*	*2019*
National copyright NCPR	0.63	3.09	0.51	0.89
Patents NPT	0.52	0.04	0.02	0.02
Registered community design and model rights CDR	9.72	17.54	2.59	4.46
International community design and model rights ICD	0.80	0.02	0.53	0.06
Unregistered community design CDU	0.01	0.01	0.01	n/a
EU trademark EUTM	64.13	61.91	55.39	68.47
International trademark ITM	12.63	2.29	32.62	16.63
National trademark NTM	11.37	12.09	7.24	9.35
National Trade Names NTN	0.06	2.17	n/a	0.02
Geographical indications for listed products (in agreements with third countries) CGIL	0.09	n/a	0.01	n/a
Geographical indications for wine CGIW	0.02	0.29	0.01	0.01
Plant protection products SPCP	0.01	0.01	n/a	0.01

Source: Own work based on *Report on the EU customs . . .* (2018), p. 17; *Report on the EU customs . . .* (2019), p. 17.

Property Rights: Results at the EU Border, 2017, Luxembourg, 2018, p. 17; *Report on the EU Customs Enforcement of Intellectual Property Rights: Results at the EU Border, 2014*, Luxembourg, 2015, p. 22; *Report on the EU Customs Enforcement of Intellectual Property Rights: Results at the EU Border, 2014*, Luxembourg, 2015, p. 21; *Report on the EU Customs Enforcement of Intellectual Property Rights: Results at the EU Border, 2012*, Luxembourg, 2013, p. 21; *Report on the EU Customs Enforcement of Intellectual Property Rights: Results at the EU Border, 2013*, Luxembourg, 2014, p. 21; *Report on the EU Customs Enforcement of Intellectual Property Rights: Results at the EU Border, 2011*, Luxembourg, 2012, p. 18; *Report on the EU Customs Enforcement of Intellectual Property Rights: Results at the EU Border, 2010*, Luxembourg, 2011, p. 20.

Table 3.4 Percentage of copyright infringement based on article count – a general overview 2010–2019

	Copyright in percentage of articles (%)								
Year	*2010*	*2011*	*2012*	*2013*	*2014*	*2016*	*2017*	*2018*	*2019*
Percentage with regard to total amount of infringement of all IPRs	2.98	1.12	1.17	0.94	0.29	0.22	0.36	0.63	3.09

Source: Own work based on *Report on the EU customs . . . (2016)*, p. 16; *Report on the EU customs . . . (2017)*, p. 17; *Report on the EU customs . . . (2014)*, p. 22; *Report on the EU customs . . . (2013)*, p. 21; *Report on the EU customs . . . (2012)*, p. 20; *Report on the EU customs . . . (2011)*, p. 18; *Report on the EU customs . . . (2010)*, p. 20.

Table 3.5 Percentage of copyright infringement based on percentage of articles – a general overview 2010–2019

	Copyright based on percentage of articles (%)					*Copyright based on percentage of value (%)*			
Year	*2010*	*2011*	*2012*	*2013*	*2014*	*2016*	*2017*	*2018*	*2019*
Percentage with regard to total amount of infringement of all IPRs	1.49	1.09	0.36	0.37	0.13	0.20	0.51	0.51	0.89

ing materials, glass tableware, body care items, sunglasses, toys and shoes, the most common basis for protection was design and model rights.

The EU statistics hint that copyright is not a frequent basis for IPR infringement claims and actions.

Table 3.5 allows the conclusion that copyright might not be a common basis for protection, but its significance fluctuates from year to year, as does the value of the goods that it protects. According to one of the EU's reports, among the IPRs cited in national market detention records, 72% are trademarks, 16% are copyrights, 10% are designs and 2% patents. To wit, copyright was often the only basis for claimed IP protection for clothing.[123]

123 *Report on the EU Enforcement of Intellectual Property Rights: Results at EU Borders and in Member States, 2013–2017*, 2019, p. 67.

3.2.3.2 Burdens in applying for customs action

The most significant burden for the T/C sector in applying for customs action are the financial costs that can be especially prohibitive for SMEs.

There are several costs that the IPR holder will have to endure in order to even start proceedings:

- Translating the application forms into all languages used by EU customs.
- The obligation, in practical terms, to maintain a company representative in every EU member state; this is necessary if a company wishes to pursue cases and lodge appropriate complaints.
- The expense of the storage and destruction of infringing goods.
- The costs of the judicial procedure, which often cannot be pinned on an infringer within EU territory (e.g. in respect of goods in transit or trans-shipment).[124]

These costs can be cut to a point if a simplified procedure is applied, under which goods suspected of infringing an IPR can be destroyed without there being any need to determine whether an IPR has been infringed under national law (Article 11 of EC Regulation 1383/2003). However, sector representatives note with regret that this provision is only an option for member states, which can decide individually whether or not to include it in national legislation.[125]

3.3 Local fashion players by example of the Polish TCLF industry

3.3.1 Polish TCLF landscape

The T/C industry is also an important sector of the Polish economy. It encompasses over 17,000 companies and is responsible for 5% of Polish gross domestic product. According to experts, this industry has a chance of becoming one of the most important export sectors. Due to its deep restructuring and modernisation, it is well placed to become one of the key branches of the Polish economy. In Poland, research undertaken by Agata Rudnicka and Małgorzata Kostrzewska provided statistics proving that Poland is one of the top ten European countries in the TCLF sector.[126] In 2017, Poland

124 Rodwell, Van Eeckhout, Reid, Walendowski, *Study "Effects . . . "*, p. 75.

125 Rodwell, Van Eeckhout, Reid, Walendowski, *Study "Effects . . . "*, p. 75;
In 84.7% of the detention procedures started by customs, the goods were destroyed under the standard or small consignment procedure after the owner of the goods and the right-holder agreed on their destruction. In 3.6% of the detentions, a court case was initiated to determine the infringement and, in 2.8% of the detentions, the goods were dealt with as part of criminal proceedings. A total of 75% of the detained articles were destroyed or were subject to court proceedings. However, 22% of the detained articles were released because the right-holder did not respond to the notification sent to them by customs (12%), or the articles were eventually found to be original goods (10%), or there was no infringement situation (0.2%).
Report on the EU customs . . . (2019), p. 6

126 Rudnicka, Koszewska, *Uszyte z klasą . . .*, pp. 17–19.

Table 3.6 Economic entities by ownership sectors, sector and divisions

Sector	*Total*		*Public sector*		*Private sector*	
	2005	*2019*	*2005*	*2019*	*2005*	*2019*
Manufacture of textiles	3,506	6,415	16	4	3,490	6,411
Manufacture of apparel	20,336	13,580	16	4	20,320	13,576
Manufacture of leather and related products	4,696	2,644	8	3	4,688	2,641

Source: SYI – P, p. 34.

Table 3.7 Output of industry in millions of PLN

Sector	*2005*	*2010*	*2015*	*2018*	*2019*
Manufacture of textiles	8,022.1	8,852.1	13,433.5	15,858.5	16,539.0
Manufacture of apparel	9,687.1	9,144.0	10,256.7	10,898.6	11,177.6
Manufacture of leather and related products	3,062.0	3,422.9	5,081.6	5,613.5	5,511.3

Source: SYI – P, p. 71.

was seventh among EU countries in terms of the volume of turnover of the textile and clothing industry (with a 3.6% share), after such countries as: Italy (34.7%), Germany (14.5%), France (8.7%), UK (7.4%), Spain (7%) and Portugal (5.1%). A large part of the Polish T/C sector are home textiles, representing one-quarter of overall production. As for the number of businesses in the sector, Poland was second in the EU with a share of 10%.

However, it is worth emphasising the systematic increase in the number of textile enterprises, with the simultaneous decline in the number of those producing clothing.[127]

From 2005 to 2017, the number of textile businesses increased from 3,506 to 5,813, and, in the same period, the number of clothing operators decreased from 20,336 to 13,485. The majority of T/C firms are SMEs, with only a few having more than 500 employees. Also, just a few belong to the public sector.

There is a noticeable diversified distribution of investments between the textile and clothing industries. In the case of textile production, investments were made to a greater extent in machinery and technical equipment.[128]

127 Statistical Yearbook of Industry – Poland, Warsaw 2020, hereinafter: SYI – P.
128 A. Rudnicka, M. Koszewska, *Uszyte z klasą . . .*, p. 22.

Table 3.8 Total revenues in millions of PLN

Sector	*2005*	*2010*	*2015*	*2018*	*2019*
A – total B – SMEs C – SMEs as percentage of all industry					
Manufacture of textiles	A – 6,973.1 B – n/a C – n/a	7,231.7 4,301.6 59.5%	10,427.1 4,976.0 47.7%	12,854.5 5,437.7 42.3%	13,237.4 5,601.4 42.3%
Manufacture of apparel	A – 5,628.8 B – n/a C – n/a	5,059.7 3,353.2 66.3%	4,894.1 3,753.9 76.7%	4,964.9 3,529.3 71.1%	4,702.6 3,518.8 74.8%
Manufacture of leather and related products	A – 2,020.0 B – n/a C – n/a	2,371.0 n/a n/a	3,907.6 1791.3 45.8%	3,899.0 1758.3 45.1%	3,847.3 1707.8 44.4%

Source: SYI-P, pp. 137–140.

Table 3.9 Basic data regarding economic entities in industry by number of paid employees, sector and divisions in 2019 (Data concern entities with ten or more persons employed)

Sectors	*Total*	*Entities with the following number of paid employees*					
A – number of entities B – sales in millions of PLN		49 and less	50–99	100–249	250–499	500–999	1,000 and more
Manufacture of textiles	A – 786	604	82	70	25	2	3
	100%	76.8%	10.4%	8.9%	3.2%	0.3%	0.4%
	B – 14,229.9	2,966.4	1,413.2	2,718.9	2,891.6	–	–
	100%	20.8%	9.9%	19.1%	20.3%	–	–
Manufacture of apparel	A – 1,781	1,522	151	92	13	2	1
	100%	85.5%	8.5%	5.2%	0.7%	0.1%	0.1%
	B – 7,293.2	3,325.0	1,088.8	1,746.3	600.6	–	–
	100%	45.6%	14.9%	23.9%	8.2%	–	–
Manufacture of leather and related products	A – 427	358	36	24	4	4	1
	100%	83.8%	8.4%	5.6%	0.9%	0.9%	0.2%
	B – 4,394.2	1,214.3	373.6	969.5	–	458.4	–
	100%	27.6%	8.5%	22.1%	–	10.4%	–

Source: SYI – P, pp. 47–48.

Table 3.10 Industry output

Sector	*2005*	*2010*	*2015*	*2018*	*2019*
Manufacture of textiles	8,022.1	8,852.1	13,433.5	15,858.5	16,539.0
Manufacture of apparel	9,687.1	9,144.0	10,256.7	10,898.6	11,177.6
Manufacture of leather and related products	3,062.0	3,422.9	5,081.6	5,613.5	5,511.3

Source: SYI – P, p. 71.

Table 3.11 Employees in thousands

Sector	*2010*	*2015*	*2018*	*2019*
A – total B – SMEs C – SMEs as percentage of all industry				
Manufacture of textiles	A – 53.2 B – 38.8 C – 72.9%	53.8 37.5 69.7%	57.3 39.6 69.1%	57.0 23.2 40.7%
Manufacture of apparel	A – 122.4 B – 109.4 C – 89.4%	94.5 85.1 90.1%	87.7 79.2 90.3%	86.5 79.4 91.7%
Manufacture of leather and related products	A – 27.5 B – 22.9 C – 83%	25.2 19.5 77.4%	25.6 19.2 75.2%	23.8 17.8 74.7%

Source: SYI – P, pp. 202, 205.

Table 3.12 Investment outlay in industry in millions of PLN

Sector	*2005*	*2010*	*2015*	*2018*	*2019*
Manufacture of textiles	397.2	257.8	501.9	671.4	762.1
Manufacture of apparel	376.4	171.0	148.0	201.7	182.4
Manufacture of leather and related products	108.0	142.6	157.2	177.5	180.7

Source: SYI – P, p. 311.

Table 3.13 Expenditure on innovation activity for product and business process innovation in industry by type of innovation activity, ownership sector, sections and divisions in 2019 (Data concern entities with 50 or more persons employed), in millions of PLN

Sector	*Total*	*Research and development*	*Capital on tangible and intangible assets (fixed assets [groups 0–8 according to Classification of Fixed Assets], software, intellectual property rights and acquisition of external knowledge)*	*Own personnel working on innovation*	*Services, materials and supplies for innovation*
Manufacture of textiles	268.4	175.1	91.2	1.3	0.4
Manufacture of apparel	–	–	–	1.3	3.5
Manufacture of leather and related products	–	–	–	–	–

Source: SYI – P, p. 415.

Table 3.14 Expenditure on innovation activity for product and business process innovation in industry (Data concern entities with 50 or more persons employed)

Sector	*Sources of funds in millions of PLN*			
	Own	*From abroad in non-refundable form*	*Credit, loans and other financial liabilities from financial institutions*	*Domestic from institutions allocating public funds*
Manufacture of textiles	193.5	14.5	–	–
Manufacture of apparel	24.6	–	–	–
Manufacture of leather and related products	n/a	n/a	n/a	n/a

Source: SYI – P, p. 420.

Table 3.15 Production of major products

Products	*2000*	*2005*	*2010*	*2015*	*2018*	*2019*
Textiles						
Flax yarn (single, multiple or cabled) (in tonnes) (not packed for retail sale)	4,681	5,303	4,382	5,616	4,714	4,727
Synthetic fibre sewing thread (in tonnes)	883	1,517	876	713	849	802
Woven fabrics from carded wool or carded fine animal hair (in km^2)	5.6	6.4	4.0	0.9	0.4	0.2
Woven fabrics from flax (in km^2)	8.2	11.9	0.6	0.9	1.9	2.7
Woven cotton fabrics excluding gauze, medical gauze (in km^2)	298	184	61.0	21.5	18.7	19.1
Woven fabrics from synthetic filament yarns and artificial filament yarn (in km^2)	215	226	133	121	104	88.4
Pile fabrics, terry towelling and other special fabrics (in km^2)	25.4	58.0	24.4	16.2	23.0	21.6
Bed linen (in millions of units)	16.9	21.4	24.8	25.9	26.8	22.6
Sacks and bags for the packing of goods (in tonnes)	7,046	6,413	5,461	7,736	8,111	8,477
Carpets (in thousands of m^2)						
Rugs (in thousands of m^2)	3,536	2,551	9,211	11,352	11,716	12,190
Floor coverings (in thousands of m^2)	3,650	1,226	1,049	1,465	1,286	1,265
Clothes and garments (in thousands of units)						
Men's or boys' overcoats, various types of wind-cheater and other similar articles	3,282	2,004	827	544	446	363
Men's or boys' suits and ensembles	2,638	2,892	1,736	1,450	1,435	1,085
Men's or boys' jackets and blazers	3,098	1,762	839	936	746	619

(*Continued*)

Table 3.15 (Continued)

Products	*2000*	*2005*	*2010*	*2015*	*2018*	*2019*
Men's or boys' trousers, overalls, breeches and shorts	23,327	18,607	8,651	5,725	4,111	3,314
Women's or girls' overcoats, various types of wind-cheater and other similar articles	3,025	2,096	913	545	520	400
Women's or girls' suits and ensembles	3,284	4,025	1,058	588	568	367
Women's or girls' jackets	6,583	5,970	2,110	1,340	919	741
Women's or girls' dresses, skirts and culottes	13,759	8,399	5,719	4,934	3,802	3,243
Women's or girls' trousers, overalls, breeches and shorts	18,373	15,950	4,964	2,645	2,501	2,474
Textile clothing (in thousands of units)						
Men's or boys' textile shirts	13,714	9,355	4,283	3,827	4,015	3,639
Women's or girls' textile blouses and shirt-blouses	18,986	12,476	5,979	2,697	2,453	1,999
Hosiery (in million of pairs)						
Pantyhose and tights (in millions of units)	111	123	155	124	94.5	76.0
Socks (in millions of pairs)	45.2	71.0	63.9	80.8	63.0	63.4
Leather and leather products						
Leather of bovine or equine animals, without hair (in thousands of tonnes)	23.3	16.1	15.0	14.3	20.3	12.6
Of which un-split bovine leather for shoes	12.7	6.0	6.5	6.2	12.0	4.4
Footwear (including rubber) (in millions of pairs)	48.7	45.5	36.4	42.5	43.4	36.9
Of which footwear with leather uppers	19.6	14.9	11.8	12.4	11.5	9.8

Source: SYI-P, pp. 114–116.

From the statistics, it is clear that in 2019, out of 6,411 companies in textiles, 4,839 (75%) had fewer than ten employees. For apparel, the figure was 10,014 (73%) and 1,787 (68%) for leather.[129] At the same time, 42.3% of revenues in textiles, 74.8% in apparel and 44.4% in the leather sector are made by SMEs (from 30 to 250 employees). The largest share of the revenues derive from companies having up to 50 employees. In terms of employment, 40.7% of employees in textiles, 91.7% in apparel and 74.7% in leather work for SMEs. What is striking, however, is that companies in the textile sector, of which there are only half the number as in the apparel sector, make one-third more in income. One of the reasons for this may be that they conduct their own R&D and invest in intellectual property assets. Interestingly, according to the Statistical Yearbook of Industry – Poland (SYI-P), the apparel and leather sectors in Poland do not invest at all in R&D or intellectual capital. Furthermore, it shows that all three sectors find it very hard to access financial support, either in the form of loans or of public funding.

3.3.2 Polish petite couturiers *– survey*

In 2020, this author conducted a survey among Polish fashion designers running small ateliers to understand the nuances of how they operate their businesses. The survey was sent to 32 fashion ateliers having no more than 50 employees. The intention was to identify and target the most active fashion designers on the Polish scene and to establish contact through their ateliers or existing contacts.[130] Out of 32, 14 responded, one of which is a business operating with over ten employees.

These Polish fashion designers also shared their angles on the dichotomy between form and idea, or, in other words, offered their expert, but non-legal, opinion about the boundary between a knock-off and a mere inspired work. As one Polish designer put it,

> One can talk about one hundred percent plagiarism if the model has the same construction and finish. A slight deviation, introducing minimal changes in proportions, frees you from liability for plagiarism. This fact makes it very difficult to prove someone's abuse. The matter is much easier with prints, when it comes to graphics. But even in this case, only an identical print ensures that it has been copied. If one item seems similar, then there is a chance it happened randomly. But there are whole collections "inspired" by someone else's work. I once had a situation when someone spoke openly about being inspired by my style. Back then, it

129 SYI – P, p. 46.

130 Given that the circle of artisan fashion designers is small, the rate of return measured at 43.75% is remarkably high. The small amount of the treatment group did not allow for the use of statistical quantitative methods.

was not about an identical, but only a similar structure, the use of details that build the atmosphere of the collection. In that case, nothing is one-to-one, and it's hard to accuse someone of plagiarism, and the problem is deeper than a copy of one model itself.

There is an opinion that even suing over the copying of a textile pattern is an extremely hard thing to do, something that costs more energy than it can bring satisfaction.

One Polish fashion designer said during her interview that "It is plain to see who reigns supreme in the fashion world. It can be felt through the sense of fashion. Who is chasing after whom". She also expressed disappointment that there is no fashion chamber of which fashion designers need to be members. As a result, she considers, there are too many designers who have no idea about sewing or construction and they offer goods of low quality.

Table 3.16 Summary of survey responses

Q 1: For how many years have you been designing fashion?	
A) less than 1 year	0
B) 1–5 years	3
C) 6–10 years	4
D) 11–19 years	3
E) 20 years or more	4

Q 2: How big is the city in which you operate your fashion business? [by inhabitants]	
A) less than 100,000	4
B) 110,000–200,000	0
C) 210,000–500,000	2
D) 510,000–1,000,000	2
E) 1,000,000 or more	6

Q 3: What is your education?	
A) secondary related to fashion	4
B) secondary not related to fashion	1
C) higher related to fashion	5
D) higher not related to fashion	4
E) other	0

Q 4: have you ever encountered a knock-off of your work?*	
A) yes, very often	2
B) yes, often	3
C) yes, at times	6
D) once	0
E) no	2
F) hard to tell whether it was a copy, or inspiration	3
G) I am not sure	0

Q 5: In relation to Q4, if you have answered yes, please indicate whether it was*:	
A) a verbatim knock-off	5
B) inspiration	5
C) I am not sure	3

Q 6: Do you use legal services?	
A) yes, on a constant basis	0
B) yes, occasionally	5
C) yes, but on issues other than IP	4
D) no, had no need	5

Q 7: Do you create your projects yourself or use outsourced services (e.g. sewing company)?	
A) myself	1
B) yes, sewing company	3
C) half and half	8
D) other (please specify)	2: dressmaker

Q 8: Are there NDA clauses in your contracts with the sewing service you use?	
A) yes	5
B) no	1
C) at times	2
D) I do not make contracts in writing	5

Q 9: Do you believe your fashion design was copied by a sewing service?	
A) yes	2
B) no	3
C) hard to tell	7

Q 10: If your work has been copied, at which stage do you think that happened?	
A) creation stage	2
B) production stage	2
C) first fashion show/dissemination (e.g. Internet)	8

Q 11: Have you heard of IPR?*	
A) yes, own court experience	0
B) yes, I attended a course	4
C) yes, I own a trademark	4
D) yes, from hearsay	8
E) no	0

Q 12: What did you feel about seeing a knock-off of your work?*	
A) pride	3
B) appreciation	2
C) indifference	0
D) anger	6

(*Continued*)

Table 3.16 (Continued)

E) disappointment	8
F) other:	3
• fraud	
• esteem	
• sadness	

Note: * – multiple answers are possible given that a fashion designer may have had more than just one experience.

To summarise the survey, only 5 out of 14 fashion designers had obtained higher education related to fashion. A majority, nine, sew the clothes themselves (eight with the help of sewing services). Interestingly only two have not encountered a knock-off of their work or a work inspired by it. The votes were split *ex equo* between verbatim copies and inspired works, with a few answers betraying uncertainty as to whether the borrowing was one or the other. Despite this wide experience of copying, my respondents had not undertaken any legal action. When asked about the possibility of legal suit, ten designers them rejected the idea on a few grounds:

- lack of trust for law,
- no time or resources for long legal battles,
- the need to engage with lawyers and to delve into copyright law,
- damage to relationship with collaborators due to accusation of copying.

As for familiarity with law, only four have a registered trademark, even though all run a business that is, in many cases, the basis of their financial existence. Their understanding of copyright law is gained from discussions, conferences and friends. Nevertheless, they do not make copyright and its implications the centre point of their creative work. That the designers had not been involved in any legal action also has a positive context for them, namely that they themselves had not been sued for copying anyone else's designs. The answers given show that the copyright protection of fashion is a malleable construct, meaning that any legal action founded on that protection faces an uncertain outcome, leaving designers reluctant to pursue this course.

These were the responses when the designers were asked where inspiration comes from (anonymised):

- "Impulse, something that life brings along"
- "From the inner self"
- "Enchantment, spark, impulse to create something exquisite, entirely individual and new"
- "Inspiration comes from music, architecture, nature and people"
- "I am inspired by colour or colour combination, texture, one or more traits coming from nature, the arts or historical costumes that bring new value to my mind"
- "It comes from people, travels and textiles"

- "I am inspired by textile, its structure and print. I am also inspired by top-notch fashion designers, like Alexander McQueen"

Asked about what originality means to them, they answered (anonymised):

- "Originality is a sum of elements, manners of expression that build the atmosphere, that in turn bring the style and its originality. If independently of a collection we can credit the author, it means that we can read the aesthetic language he communicated to his audience"
- "The overall expression"
- "Originality should be based on creative and innovative thinking. It can take many forms and it is hard to narrow down the concept of originality in fashion"
- "It is the overall image, construction and embellishments"
- "Creating one's own prints and textiles, artisan embroidery as well as buttons, lace, logos, elements, in one's own style. It is the construction and finishing touch"
- "It is about combining different structures, patterns and colours and creating non-banal forms"
- "It is that something that makes a fashion design stand out. But it does not have to be flamboyant at the same time. It may be the design, one of the elements of pattern or print"

Is there a place in fashion for new design (anonymised)?

- "There is always a place for that. It is a matter of impulses and of the courage to go against standards. Precursors pay a heavy price, as they receive a rap on the knuckles"
- "Always"
- "There always is. Humankind lives to create newness, to develop, to reach out further, if not for form then also for material"
- "Yes, but nobody will invent fashion anew. One can believe in fairytales, but most things have already been seen before in fashion. They are either interpreted or merged"
- "If not in construction, then in embellishments"
- "Fashion is just like any other kind of art. Human imagination allows for the creation of new concepts and modification to old forms"
- "They say that fashion comes back over time. This is true but not quite. The old patterns become new with an inch of adjustment"
- "As long as there is gravity on earth, and homo sapiens is symmetrical, we will not overcome certain constraints. A shirt cannot have four sleeves. The world defines us. But technology is at the forefront of creating beautiful textiles and new materials to experiment with"

What does plagiarism personally mean for you (anonymised)?

- "Copying a fashion design 1:1 along with all its elements, such as construction, manner of sewing, embellishment, use of the same fabrics. Mere similarity may be a matter of chance"
- "Illegitimate copying"
- "That is copying, not necessarily 1:1, because it is hard to copy quality"
- "Slavish copying. Re-making of another's design as yours"
- "Every person has different sensitivities, but people too often confuse inspiration with copying"
- "Plagiarism, in contrast to interpretation, is a verbatim repetition of one's work or its many traits such that a client cannot differentiate the origin of the work/its author. That can mean an identical pattern with a characteristic cut – even if made of different textile, the same print, same embellishment. At the same time, one has to be wary of labelling something as 'plagiarism' since fashion is very trend-sensitive and it is possible for a number of ateliers to become inspired by a *haute couture* fashion design in the same way"
- "Appropriation of the fashion design elements I came up with"

3.4 Looking for a business model of IPR protection under current economic and legal conditions

3.4.1 Competition in TCLF. Quality of products in a design-intensive business

Competition plays out in TCLF at many levels. There are many rich countries heavily engaged with the textile and clothing sectors, but there are also developing and underdeveloped countries that strive to be competitive. They try to engage by combining low wage costs, high-quality textile equipment and know-how imported from industrialised countries.[131] The T/C sector is changing from 'industry driven' to 'customer driven'.[132] There is no doubt that, the more T/C enterprises aim to become competitive on international markets, the more challenges and shortcomings they have to deal with.[133] Here are a few examples:

- keeping their R&D up to date by developing production technology and distribution methods and *designing new innovative products* (investment in R&D is estimated at 3% to 5% of turnover for the average T/C enterprise;
- developing information and communication technologies that would address, among other things, the lack of information on supply and demand aspects, long procurement times, supply chain processes and quick response (QR);

131 Stengg, *The Textile* . . ., p. 1.
132 Stengg, *The Textile* . . ., p. 11; J. Fitzpatrick, *Why Textile and Clothing Industries Are Shifting to the Third World*, "Long Range Planning", 1983, vol. 16, no. 6, https://doi.org/10.1016/0024-6301(83)90006-7 (accessed: 15.01.2023).
133 Stengg, *The Textile* . . ., p. 31.

- addressing the need for computer-aided design and other multimedia systems offering realistic simulations of fabrics, their shapes, cuts, colours etc.;
- recruiting highly qualified personnel (not only tech-savvy, but sew-savvy); overcoming the lack of a skilled workforce[134];
- monitoring the shrinking employment share of textiles and clothing between 1980 and 2001; in Europe, as much as a 47% drop in textiles and 40% in clothing[135];
- reviewing the evolution of production costs, low-labour costs in developing countries, giving them a competitive edge;
- exploring external and international markets to make the enterprise grow[136];
- complying with international obligations, including the World Trade Organization, with regard to dumping, export subsidies, technical barriers to trade;
- monitoring difficulties for fashion SMEs in accessing finance.[137]

It was noted in the literature by Werner Stengg that "given that fashion and design are key competitive advantages of European industry, infringements of intellectual property rights may erode those advantages and reduce the return on investment in those areas".[138] The same author argued that "Europe's competitive strength lies precisely in the higher quality of the products" and substantiates this claim with statistics.[139] In many European Commission documents, including EC Communication COM/2003/0649, it was stressed that the competitive advantages of the T/C sector in the EU should be grounded on quality, design, innovation, technology and highly value-added products.[140] It was suggested that the fight against counterfeits should be enabled through "strengthening existing measures and adoption of new measures to protect

134 EC, Press Memo, A new action plan for the fashion and high-end industries endorsed in London, 3 December 2013; MEMP/13/1079.

135 D. Audet, *Structural Adjustment in Textiles and Clothing in the Post-ATC Trading Environment*, OECD Trade Policy Working Paper no. 4, s. 129; www.oecd.org/officialdocuments/publicdisplaydocumentpdf/?doclanguage=en&cote=td/tc/wp(2004)23/FINAL.

136 M.K. Witek-Hajduk, *Strategie internacjonalizacji polskich przedsiębiorstw w warunkach akcesji Polski do Unii Europejskiej*, Szkoła Główna Handlowa – Oficyna Wydawnicza, 2010, p. 103.

137 EC, Press MEMO, VP Tajani: Fashion industry deserves our full support, Brussels, 12 February 2013, MEMO/13/88; EC, Press MEMO, VP Tajani: we need an action plan for the fashion and high-end industries, Brussels, 6 November 2013, MEMO/13/961; Commission Staff Working Document, Policy Options for the Competitiveness of the European Fashion Industries "Where Manufacturing Meets Creativity", Brussels 26 September 2012, SWD (2012) 284 final.

138 Stengg, *The Textile . . .*, p. 31.

139 Stengg, *The Textile . . .*, p. 38.

140 Communication from the Commission to the Council, the European Parliament, the European Economic and Social Committee and the Committee of the Regions – The future of the textiles and clothing sector in the enlarged European Union, 29 October 2003, COM/2003/0649 final.

industrial and intellectual property".[141] Furthermore, the EC mentioned areas in which industrial policy measures should be more effective:

- research, development and innovation;
- new materials and intelligent materials;
- nanotechnology;
- new production processes and cleaner technology;
- focusing on fashion and promoting creativity.[142]

Speaking of creativity, in MEMO/13/1079 it was emphasised that "adding new functionalities, design or other creative content allows companies to move towards more innovative, high-added value products and *new business models*, securing their long-term competitiveness" [emphasis mine – MJ].

Today, in 2021, the EC admits that "companies have improved their competitiveness by reducing or ceasing the mass production of simple products, and concentrating instead on a wider variety of products with higher value-added".[143]

According to Denis Audet's research for the OECD,

> strong enforcement of intellectual property laws and private codes of conduct are considered as assets for countries that aspire to maintain an export-led strategy in the upper market segment of clothing products. It also means that *non-cost factors are becoming increasingly important within* the supply chain, and buying decisions are not based exclusively on price competitiveness, particularly *for brand name* and eco-labelled products[144] [emphasis mine – MJ].

Therefore, it is not low price that makes a brand particularly competitive. It is cachet, renown and distinctiveness as well as sustained brand name recognition and the enduring quality of products. For fashion goods, 'quality' relates not only to the 'technical' aspects (like durability or reliability) but also to *better design*, *better marketing* and *higher fashion content*.[145] As we discuss these issues, there is also the *price effect* to be considered, which is determined by a

141 Opinion of the European Economic and Social Committee on the 'Communication from the Commission to the Council, the European Parliament, the European Economic and Social Committee and the Committee of the Regions: The future of the textiles and clothing sector in the enlarged European Union', 7 December 2004, (COM (2003) 649 final), OJ C 302, 7.12.2004, p. 90–100. Cf. Communication from the Commission to the Council, the European Parliament, the European Economic and Social committee and the Committee of the Regions – Textiles and clothing after 2005 – Recommendations of the High Level Group for textiles and clothing {SEC (2004) 1240}, COM/2004/0668 final.

142 Opinion COM (2003) 649 final.

143 Textiles and clothing in the EU, https://ec.europa.eu/growth/sectors/fashion/textiles-clothing/eu_en, cf. Okonkwo, *Luxury Fashion* . . ., p. 4.

144 Audet, *Structural Adjustment* . . ., s. 19, 34.

145 Stengg, *The Textile* . . ., p. 38, fn. 62.

fusion of the time spent developing the design, investment expenditure, legal costs (including IP) and profit.

The price element can be factored into the decision about an IP protection strategy for a segment of goods. As there are at least three pricing strategies for the apparel industry: ***luxury pricing strategy, budget pricing strategy*** and ***value pricing strategy***,[146] there are also at least as many price-related IP strategies.

For luxury goods, "if you really are an exclusive brand, you can't grow beyond a certain point. Nobody knows where that point is, but there is a limit to the number of handbags you can sell for $1,000. That's the bottom line".[147] As it is common that the selling price of products from the luxury brands far exceed their production costs, and as there is no one systematic justification of this discrepancy, a number of biased opinions are found in the literature claiming that this amounts to consumer deception. But such a view is overly utilitarian, indeed, one-dimensional thinking. I support the view of Uche Okonkwo, who hints that "when people purchase a luxury fashion item, they don't just buy the product but a complete parcel that comprises the product and a set of intangible benefits that appeal to the emotional, social and psychological levels of their being".[148]

3.4.2 Organic memorability, desirability and scarcity

Absence makes the heart grow fonder. This psychological rule is also applied in retail.[149] An example is the Hermès Birkin bag. Although its price ranges from $9,000 up to $400,000, it has become the most sought-after fashion item globally, with a waiting list of up to six years. Hermès reinforces the bag's exclusivity by artificial scarcity, limiting production and scaling down retail to a handful of stores.[150] Targeting a specific group of loyal clients, the brand does not have to bludgeon potential clients into buying their goods, let alone apply other familiar pricing policies (e.g. sales, discounts) or artificial intelligence.[151]

146 Pricing Strategies for the Apparel Industry,

147 Domenico De Sole, CEO for Gucci Group. Gucci Case Study, Harvard Business School 9-701-037 Rev. 10 May 2001 Gucci Group N. V. (A) Historically, fashion was viewed like movies. We made it a business, https://webgamesday.com/gucci case study 1093.

148 Okonkwo, *Luxury Fashion . . .*, p. 2.

149 D. Ott, *How Consumers Relate to Luxury Brands in the 21st Century: The Changing Concept of Sacredness and Its Importance*, Business Administration. Université Paris sciences et lettres, 2018, pp. 110–111; J.-N. Kapferer, P. Valette-Florence, *The Impact of Brand Penetration and Awareness on Luxury Brand Desirability: A Cross Country Analysis of the Relevance of the Rarity Principle*, "Journal of Business Research", 2018, vol. 83, https://doi.org/10.1016/j.jbusres.2017.09.025 (accessed: 16.01.2023).

150 S. Dennis, *Remarkable Retail: How to Win & Keep Customers in the Age of Digital Disruption*, LifeTree Media, 2020, AppleBooks, pp. 34–35.

151 Dennis, *Remarkable* . . . p. 390, with this approach brand meets the consumer halfway offering him the whole gamut of products he was gasping for (often unwittingly). It also gives the retailers the chance to lock in a recurring revenue stream.

A product is the result of a multifaceted creative process that takes much more effort that meets the eye. As demonstrated later in this book, it is not easy to make a clear-cut qualification of a product in terms of IPRs and the protection thereof. This author strongly believes that the available IPR regimes are not suited for fashion goods. On the one hand, it takes a lot of effort and investment to secure the protection of industrial goods; on the other hand, the copyrightability of fashion goods is ephemeral and very uncertain. Therefore, one of the conclusions from my research is that, in many cases the price should be chosen to ensure the recouping of the costs for the creative process as though there was no protection available for the design (see Chapter 5). The price should combine the attractive attributes of being a good deal for the quality while being competitive at the same time. The fashion industry must be careful in achieving the correct balance: although IPR protection should be pursued, there is much evidence to show that it cannot always be relied on. Therefore, fashion goods should often be gauged from a perspective of material goods value, which cost is envisaged in a price tag. Recouping the cost through long-term copyright strategy is risky and may prove ineffective.

3.4.3 Design-related TCLF segments. Imitation strategies' effect on pricing models. Intelligent shopping

The TCLF sector can be divided into three segments:

design oriented,
price/design oriented,
price oriented.

This pyramid needs explanation. It does not propose a clear-cut three-tier segmentation but rather a sliding scale showing how pricing strategy can position a product in the market. It was noted that

> (A)s prices have shown a continuous downward trend and competition from non-EU low-cost suppliers has increased, fashion companies have focused more on customers expecting higher fashion content, thus trying to move up the pyramid. By increasing fashion content (and thus focusing more on symbolic value), EU fashion companies try to move away from the "red ocean" and create their own "blue ocean", where competition is less fierce.[152]

It is important to realise that head-to-head competition opens a variety of *imitation strategies*. At the same time, to become a blue ocean player takes much

152 De Voldere, Jans, Durinck, Plaisier, Smakman, Mirza, Szalavetz, *Study on the Competitiveness . . .*, p. 11. The 'red ocean strategy' means a highly competitive approach to client with many players, products and policy based on price. However, the 'blue ocean strategy' creates an uncontested market space, makes the competition irrelevant, creates and captures new demand, breaks the value–cost trade-off.

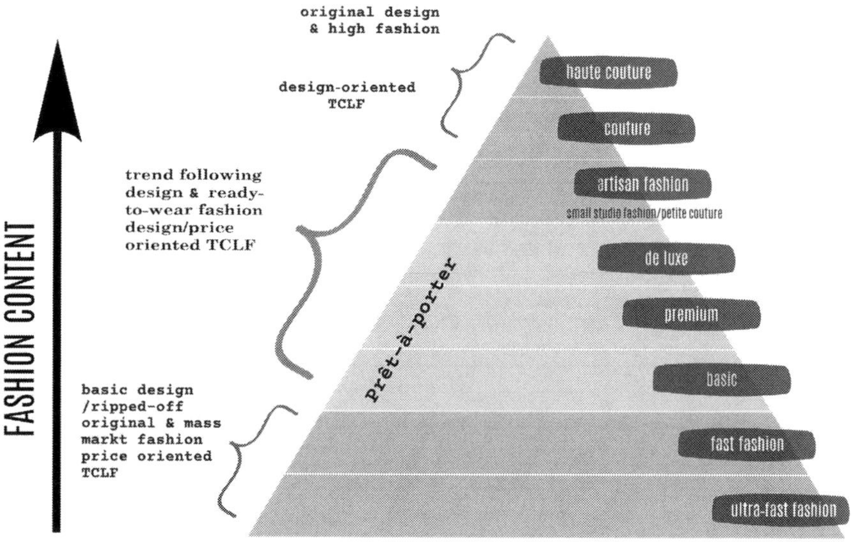

Explanatory item no. 3.6 Market segments in the TCLF industry

Source: Own reinterpretation

Source: Tran (2008), cf. I. De Voldere, G. Jans, E. Durinck, N. Plaisier, F. Smakman, D., Mirza, A. Szalavetz, *Study on the Competitiveness . . .*, p. 11.

more than just an idea, product or service. Creating a new market is one thing, but carving out the profitable growth for oneself is another. Some succeed in attaining temporary renown or fail despite bringing a unique product to the market. By way of example, if we consider who developed the first personal computer (not IBM or Apple, but rather MITS) or who first brought the video recorder to market (not SONY or JVC, but Ampex), we see the same unexpected outcomes in fashion. An idea and a prototype are not enough without the appropriate publicity and without imprinting a fashion design on the public consciousness as a signature model. But in fashion, strategic success need not be entwined with creativity[153] or high fashion quality (Explanatory item no. 3.6).[154]

Item of note no. 3.5 Polo Ralph Lauren: high fashion with no fashion – business strategy

Polo Ralph Lauren is credited with having devised a new and paradoxical fashion business strategy that capitalised on simple design with high prices. The lack of design made the brand prosperous and became its biggest asset. In the beginning, the business idea was criticised by the

(*Continued*)

153 W.C. Kim, R. Mauborgne, *Blue Ocean Strategy Reader*, 2017, p. 164.
154 Tungate, *Fashion Brands . . .*, Harvard Business Review Press, p. 39.

Item of note 3.5 (Continued)

experts, but the formula was demonstrated to sell the brand worldwide. Indeed, Ralph Lauren became the first American design house to achieve this global reach. The core of the business plan was to make a mix of high-end clothing in keeping with classic lines already offered by competitors such as Burberry or Brooks but at a lower price point.[155] The client was happy to pay more for the luxurious feel of the materials, the fine craftsmanship of the garment and the emotional value of wearing it. The brand captured the gap between two buyer segments, those that value *haute couture* and those who also try to get the best design at the best price.

It was interestingly noted by W. Chan Kim and Renée Mauborgne that

> [T]he trendy designs the fashion houses work so hard to create are, ironically, the major drawback of haute couture for most high-end customers. . . . Conversely, customers who trade down for classic lines over haute couture want to buy garments of lasting quality that justify its high prices.[156]

One can also observe that fashion customers are a diverse and elaborate target, meaning that they deploy their own sense of thinking, mix ideas and mix brands, drawing from all points on the luxury spectrum, including the non-luxurious end.

Item of note no. 3.6 Intelligent shopping

Jean-Jacques Picard, fashion guru, once said,

> It's not enough to look fashionable – one wishes to appear intelligent as well. At the same time, we are seeing a complementary reaction, which is that a consumer may accept paying for the latest Dior bag, very trendy, that she's seen in all the magazines and advertisements; but she'll see no shame in going to Zara and buying a T-shirt for 10 euros, because it's pretty and it's a fair quality for the price. Then she may go to another store, a bit more expensive but not as well known, perhaps run by a young designer, where she'll buy a skirt. And these items, when brought together, reassure her and send a message to others that she's an intelligent consumer, not dazzled by marketing, in charge of her own image.[157]

155 W.C. Kim, R. Mauborgne, *Blue Ocean* . . ., p. 54, cf. L. Vincent, *Legendary Brands* . . ., p. 29.
156 Kim, Mauborgne, *Blue Ocean* . . ., p. 54.
157 M. Tungate, *Fashion Brands. Branding Style from Armani to Zara*, Sterling, 2005, p. 40.

Item of note no. 3.7 Karl Lagerfeld: low-priced luxury – business strategy

Karl Lagerfeld was one of the first designers to spot and seize the opportunity, as he did in 2004, to address the crossing point of high and mass fashion. Continuing this strategy, some high fashion brands enter strategic alliances with low-end suppliers in order to capture potential consumers from all walks of life. The trend is referred to as 'massluxe' or 'masstige'.

For any given company in the C/T industry, an examination of their pricing strategy can help gauge where that company sits on the spectrum from mass market to luxury.

This starts with the very working arrangement. A designer may work:

- for retailers,
- for producers,
- for specialised design/fashion houses (as in-house designers),
- independently (as an individual atelier).

To understand a variety of IP policy strategies, it can be helpful to introduce the distinction between three types of design(er)[158]:

- original or trend-setting designs, by designers who anticipate and, to a certain extent, shape trends;
- trend-following designs, for which designers may use information from fashion fairs, catwalk shows, local street fashion, films, music videos and other media or trend analysts;
- basic design, which could be provided by, e.g. manufacturers' designers, who may tailor such designs more specifically according to the collections of specific retailers (often in collaboration with designers from those retailers).

3.4.4 T/C sectors as capital-/labour-intensive sunset industries

Investments made in a business bear better fruit when legally secured. The more capital- or labour-intensive the resulting goods, the greater is the need for legal protection.[159] The textile industry is considered to be *capital intensive*,

158 De Voldere, Jans, Durinck, Plaisier, Smakman, Mirza, Szalavetz, *Study on the Competitiveness . . .*, p. 10.

159 P. Nogal-Meger, *The Quality of Business Legal Environment and Its Relation with Business Freedom*, "International Journal of Contemporary Management", 2018, vol. 17, no. 2,

whereas the clothing industry is *labour intensive*. The latter is considered less reliant on technical innovation and can be operated with minimal capital requirements. The clothing industry has suffered in recent decades from competitive anxiety mostly caused by developing, newly industrialised, countries that challenged the traditional fashion-producing countries which would not compete with them on price.[160]

In the T/C industries, it is not only the fashion design itself but also the category of so-called other textiles, that are the most capital-intensive in the EU. These include carpets, rugs, rope, cordage and netting. In the US, this also includes the finishing and coating segment. It was observed that "textile finishing operations are one of the most important operational steps for product differentiation and specific application are often copyrighted thereby conferring a competitive edge to innovating firms".[161] According to European Commission reports,

> European producers are world leaders in markets for technical/industrial textiles and non-wovens (industrial filters, hygiene products, products for the automotive and medical sectors, etc.), as well as for high-quality garments with a high design content. The trend towards higher value-added products needs to be continued in order to strengthen the competitiveness of the textile and clothing sector.[162]

To wit, it was analysed and argued that the clothing industry, despite being labour intensive, proved resilient to competition by embracing new ideas and techniques. Although this was counter-intuitive, understanding this gives a greater insight into the clothing sector.[163] To return to *quality* (e.g. labour force quality), this is the *special factor* that made countries such as Hungary, Poland and Romania flourish in the T/C industry.[164] By example of Italian

---

p. 115; A. Toukan, *Why Do Some Countries Produce More Capital Intensive Output Than Others?*, "The Journal of Developing Areas", 2016, vol. 50, no. 3, p. 322; The Hindu Business Line, *Credit Rating and Textile Industries*, www.thehindubusinessline.com/opinion/Credit-rating-and-textile-industries/article20407374.ece (accessed: 15.01.2023); K. Wie Thee, *The Development of Labour-intensive Garment Manufacturing in Indonesia*, "Journal of Contemporary Asia", 2009, vol. 39, no. 4, p. 562; OECD, *A New World Map in Textiles and Clothing Adjusting to Change: Adjusting to Change*, OECD Publishing, 2004, p. 39.

160 I. Taplin, *Restructuring and Reconfiguration: The EU Textile and Clothing Industry Adapts to Change*, "European Business Review", 2006, vol. 18, no. 3, p. 173.

161 Audet, *Structural Adjustment . . .*, s. 27.

162 Textiles and clothing in the EU . . .

163 Taplin, *Restructuring . . .*, p. 175; A. Smith, J. Pickles, R. Begg, P. Roukova, M. Buček, *Outward Processing, EU Enlargement and Regional Relocation in the European Textiles and Clothing Industry: Reflections on the European Commission's Communication on 'The Future of the Textiles and Clothing Sector in the Enlarged European Union'*, "European Urban and Regional Studies", 2015, 12(1), p. 86.

164 Taplin, *Restructuring . . .*, p. 180. Also Romania, Bulgaria and especially Ukraine, cf. Smith, Pickles, Begg, Roukova, Buček, *Outward Processing . . .*, p. 85; cf. A. Smith, J. Pickles, M. Bucek, R. Begg, R. Roukova, *Reconfiguring ?Post-socialist? Regions: Cross-Border Networks*

SMEs, the entrepreneurs embraced the competition by engaging on the basis of *design, quality, creativity and fashionability*, thereby managing to bring their products to the level of the highly value-added market segment and commanding a premium price for their products.[165] Many factors, such as the decline of employment in the clothing sector, would prompt the conclusion that the more labour-intensive clothing industry would suffer from the ongoing changes and become a sunset industry. Whereas employment goes down, the productivity and competitive edge can increase by addressing specific business niches, such as fast turnaround, but also quality and small batch production. At the same time, interestingly, the capital-intensive textile industry has not embraced the opportunity to improve their circumstances by putting up a fence of innovative high-tech solutions.[166]

The aforementioned changes factored into the clothing industry shift it towards more *design-intensive activity*, marketing, retailing, product and production chain management. The textile industry also started working towards developing more design-intensive fabrics and technical textiles.[167]

3.4.5 Democratisation of Luxury. Demise of couture?

One other factor that influences the TCLF sector heavily is the changing perception of luxury, which is no longer limited to high-end and highly priced products. As consumers' expectations rise, they expect better quality at a better price.[168] These expectations can be served by so-called neo-luxury.[169] Beautiful design and high quality are slowly becoming affordable to all, which means that profit margins are sinking.[170] But is this necessarily true? As noted in the literature,

> In the apparel industry, traditional luxury brands have introduced secondary lines with lower prices aimed at neo-luxury consumers: *Miu Miu* from Prada, *Just Cavalli* from Roberto Cavalli, *D&G* from Dolce & Gabbana, V*ERSUS* from Versace and *McQ* from Alexander McQueen lines. Thus, a neo-luxury good may be defined as one that has been

and Regional Competition in the Slovak and Ukrainian Clothing Industry, "Global Networks", 2008, 8(3), p. 281.

165 Taplin, *Restructuring* . . ., p. 180, Guercini.

166 Taplin, *Restructuring* . . ., p. 183.

167 Smith, Pickles, Begg, Roukova, Buček, *Outward Processing* . . ., p. 83.

168 A. Cabigiosu, *An Overview of the Luxury Fashion Industry, Digitalization in the Luxury Fashion Industry: Strategic Branding for Millennial Consumers*, 2020, https://doi.org/10.1007/978-3-030-48810-9_2 (accessed: 15.01.2023); M.J. Silverstein, N. Fiske, J. Butman, *Trading Up. Why Consumers Want New Luxury Goods – and How Companies Create Them*, Penguin Group USA, 2008, p. 1.

169 A. Cabigiosu, *An Overview* . . ., B. Canziani, K. Watchravesringkan, J. Yurchisin, *A Model for Managing Service Encounters for Neo-Luxury Consumers*, "Worldwide Hospitality and Tourism Themes", 2016, https://doi.org/10.1108/WHATT-10-2015-0036, p. 43.

170 *European Sector* . . ., p. 80.

systematically created to fill the gap between the traditional luxury good and a mass good, allowing consumers to perceive sufficient evidence of upgrades in product design and material quality to feel satisfied that they are purchasing upscale products.[171]

By targeting new groups of consumers with new products to form new segments of clients, these brands also expand their market position. They make it possible to recoup their investments from groups of consumer that their products never originally addressed. The question is whether these new groups of client would have opted for the previous 'old luxury' product had there been no cheaper substitute. The answer is most likely 'no'.

To many, especially those not in a close relationship with fashion and trends, creative fashion may appear to be confined mostly to *haute couture*. It is believed that there are only a few *haute couture* houses in the true sense and between 300 and 1,000 *couture* houses. It is also estimated that there are around 1,000 *haute couture* customers around the world (Chapter 1, "Shades of fashion").[172] It is through high fashion that TCLF aspires to be perceived as a part of art. However, the sumptuousness and lavishness of *haute couture* raise questions as to whether it truly recoups its investment. Again and again, there is speculation about its inevitable demise.

From the joint business–legal perspective, the key to brand identity lies in originality, even though, in business, originality arises in many different ways. A luxury brand's positioning is based on many elements, but the major ones are *design, style* and *quality*. The more *fanciful, original and innovative the design, style, tradition and heritage*, the better and stronger the *brand positioning*. As noted by Uche Okonkwo, 1) the products must be in alignment with the desired positioning, 2) the positioning must be credible (the brand must have a *raison d'être*, 3) the positioning must be distinctive and cannot be shared by competitors, 4) the positioning must justify a luxury association, 5) the positioning must be relevant to the moment but also have the capacity to be extended with time, and 6) the positioning must have a contingency positioning plan.[173]

3.4.6 *Legal horizon for a low-technology industry*

3.4.6.1 *State of play*

It has been argued that C/T players have traditionally been 'technology users' much more than 'technology generators', however this situation is slowly changing. The TCLF business is evolving based on new materials and improved textile processing technologies and offers new highly value-added

171 Canziani, Watchravesringkan, Yurchisin, *A Model* . . ., p. 43.
172 Tungate, *Fashion Brands* . . ., p. 139.
173 Okonkwo, *Luxury Fashion* . . ., pp. 117–118.

products on the market.[174] This is not the first time in history to witness the emergence of new competitive players in textiles and clothing. During the mid-19th century, England, France and the US were the driving forces behind the race for innovative production and selling techniques. The industrial revolution brought significant adjustment in the T/C industries, while at the same time paving the way for worldwide growth and broader trade opportunities.[175]

Awareness of IP rights allows T/C firms to license their brand. Licensees may manufacture part or all of the product line; in some cases, they might acquire the rights to design and distribute products under an entrepreneur's name. A brand can create sub-brands and make an alluring *fashion environment*.[176] This is a very effective way to expand and extend a brand,[177] via *line extension*, *brand extension* or even *brand stretch*.[178] For Armani alone, we see *Giorgio Armani, Armani Collezioni, Emporio Armani, Armani Jeans, A/X Armani Exchange, Armani Dolce,* and *Armani Casa*. Ralph Lauren is also known for its range of clothing and home furnishings.

The legal landscape in Europe shows that SMEs' reliance on the IP system is minimal. An overwhelming 99% of SMEs do not own any patents, 91% do not own any registered marks and only 0.7% own a registered design. In general, nine out of ten SMEs do not own any industrial property rights.[179]

According to the recent joint study by economists from the European Patent Office and the European Union Intellectual Property Office (EUIPO), SMEs that own at least one IPR increase their chances of subsequent growth by 21% and are 10% more likely to become a high-growth firm (HGF). In general, the likelihood of experiencing a high-growth period is 9% higher for those SMEs that have filed at least one patent, 13% higher for those that have filed at least one trademark[180] and 17% higher for SMEs that have filed at least one European IPR. Most interesting is the observation that as much as the predictive power of a European patent is quite high in high-tech industries (110%), it is particularly high for low-tech industries (172%). This figure is so

174 Stengg, *The Textile* . . ., p. 31.
175 Audet, *Structural Adjustment* . . . , pp. 39–40.
176 Tungate, *Fashion Brands* . . ., p. 144.
177 Gucci Case Study . . .
178 P. Kotler, *Marketing Insights from A to Z: 80 Concerns Every Manager Needs to Know*, Wiley, 2003, pp. 11–12.
179 Annex to the Commission Implementing Decision on amending the Commission Implementing Decision C(2016) 7033 concerning the adoption of the work programme 2017 and the financing decision for the implementation of the Programme for the Competitiveness of Enterprises and small and medium-sized enterprises, European Commission, Brussels 17.2.2017, C(2017) 1042 final, Annex 1, E, https://plataformapyme.es/es-es/Internacional/PoliticaEuropeaPyme/Documents/Work-Programme-2017.pdf.
180 N. Wajsman, M. Kazimierczak, Y. Ménière, I. Rudyk, *High-Growth Firms and Intellectual Property Rights, IPT Profile of High-Potential SMEs in Europe, May 2019*, https://euipo.europa.eu/tunnel-web/secure/webdav/guest/document_library/observatory/documents/reports/2019_High-growth_firms_and_intellectual_property_rights/2019_High-growth_firms_and_intellectual_property_rights.pdf, p. 5.

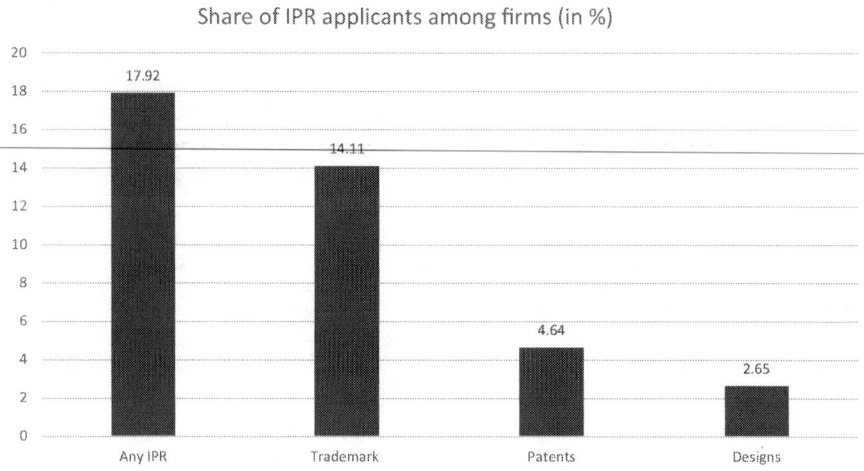

Explanatory item no. 3.7 Frequency of IPR use by European SMEs in a sample limited to manufacturing industries (2015–2016)

Source: N. Wajsman, M. Kazimierczak, Y. Ménière, I. Rudyk, *High-growth firms . . .* , p. 29.

high mainly because, in the low-tech sector, filing a patent is a relatively rare event.[181] That is to say that future HGFs rely more often on IPRs than other SMEs. The study argues that the type of IPR and industry segment of the SME together indicate whether an SME will become a HGF.[182]

In general, only 14% of SMEs own a trademark and, at the same time, ***designs*** (most often associated with the TCLF sector) ***seem to be the least registered category of IPR*** (Explanatory item no. 3.7). One important factor escaped the attention of the report's authors. To wit, the clothing industry is a labour-intensive industry, meaning that its competitive success has traditionally been managed through ***cost minimisation***.[183] To build a bank of expensive IPRs that can be cashed in later is a luxury, available only to the biggest players in the sector.

3.4.6.2 Stepping up efforts for the improvement of IPR protection. Concept of CLO

The European Commission issued a Communication COM/2003/0649 as of 29 October 2003 making clear that the EU's C/T industry is based on a mix of innovation, branding, fashion and design and that it is necessary to step up efforts for the improvement of IPR protection and enforcement, including in non-EU countries. Among other conclusions, the EU should make the fight against trade in counterfeited goods more efficient. IPR protection at the international level relies on multilateral (e.g. TRIPS) and bilateral

181 Wajsman, Kazimierczak, Ménière, Rudyk, *High-Growth Firms . . .*, p. 6.
182 Wajsman, Kazimierczak, Ménière, Rudyk, *High-Growth Firms . . .*, p. 59.
183 Taplin, *Restructuring . . .*, p. 173.

agreements[184] and on devised enforcement mechanisms. It was also noted that the *IP awareness of EU right-holders itself should be improved*, especially with regard to the comprehension of the benefits of IPR registration. Following are a few areas of awareness:

- risk associated with IP-problematic countries, in which right-holders do business,
- registration as a condition for IPR protection,
- IPR enforcement possible only after appropriate registration in the countries where the infringement takes place,
- impact of counterfeiting, including loss of foreign investment and technology transfer, links with organised crime,
- importance of public–private partnerships in fighting counterfeits.

In the EC's Staff Working Document, it was highlighted that TCLF should become a competitive industry with a clear strategy.[185] This is not an easy task as

> [T]he efforts European fashion companies make in creativity and innovation may be hampered by illegal activities, such as intellectual property rights infringements. In the current economic situation, access to finance, which is a key determinant for the start-up, development and growth of businesses in the fashion industry, remains a major difficulty.[186]

With this in mind, it is crucial to provide for a detailed analysis of the challenges and opportunities given by IPRs. It is especially important that the EU press home the importance of investing in knowledge, skills, creativity and innovation. An understanding of IPRs should be at the forefront of securing every business model. It should be borne in mind that

> (e)ntrepreneurial and managerial skills as well as hybrid ones, combining effective leadership with creativity, innovation and understanding of technologies are necessary to understand changing consumer needs and new opportunities, and translating them into *profitable business models*. However, for the EU fashion industries to remain competitive, these modern skills have to go together with technical and traditional skills and know-how, which are the core of the European manufacturing tradition.[187]

184 E.g., The Italian Federation of the textile and fashion industry (SMI-ATI) and the China National Textile and Apparel Council (CNTAC) signed a bilateral agreement aimed at improving the protection of IPR during a mission of the Italian Government to China, in September 2006 The Economic Impact of Counterfeiting and Piracy, OECD, 2008, cf. p. 240.

185 SWD(2012) 284 final, p. 3.

186 SWD(2012) 284 final, p. 3.

187 SWD(2012) 284 final, p. 4.

In the TCLF industry, companies engage in a mixture of creative and knowledge-based business, generating intangible goods that contribute to the intellectual capital of the company. Asserting rights should go hand in hand with an understanding that fashion is trend-sensitive and seasonal. These characteristics require and stimulate the creative efforts taken throughout the value chain (e.g. between designers and manufacturers, manufacturers and suppliers) while heavily influencing the sector's organisation and logistics.

For many years, IPR has been a serious concern for the EU economy with regard to the TCLF industry. In 2011, fashion goods accounted for the largest proportion of IPR-infringing goods, making up a total of over 60% of the cases registered by customs. It was noted at the European level that European entrepreneurs, especially SMEs, lack the essential knowledge, information, but also financial means to adequately protect their rights or to act in the event of an infringement.[188]

It was observed that a great number of violations happen in non-EU countries that do not offer essential IP protection and that are unlikely to become important markets for European entrepreneurs. The EC highlighted in 2012 that bilateral trade agreements were the best path to adequate protection, an approach that also needs to address necessary technical issues and to implement concrete measures for fighting infringements. It advocated cooperation between market surveillance authorities, juridical bodies and other authorities about the specificities of fashion products to counter the illegal practices, including illicit trade, counterfeiting, piracy and parallel import of fashion goods.

In 2012, the EC began work on COPIS: an anticounterfeit and antipiracy information system for all customs actions related to IPR enforcement.[189] Bearing in mind the specific needs of the fashion industry, plans included an IPR SME Helpdesk, an IPR SME China Helpdesk and an EU Observatory on Infringements of Intellectual Property Rights.[190]

According to a recent study on counterfeits, a great many 'self-help measures' can strengthen an entrepreneur's standing against counterfeiters:

- conducting regular audits of IPR registration for the company's current commercial markets and sources (focus on registrations related to the

188 SWD(2012) 284 final, p. 8.

189 SWD(2012) 284 final, p. 9.

190 Regulation (EU) No 386/2012 of the European Parliament and of the Council of 19 April 2012 on entrusting the Office for Harmonization in the Internal Market (Trade Marks and Designs) with tasks related to the enforcement of intellectual property rights, including the assembling of public and private-sector representatives as a European Observatory on Infringements of Intellectual Property Rights Text with EEA relevance, OJEU L 129/1 as of 16 May 2012; Opinion of the European Economic and Social Committee on the 'Proposal for a Regulation of the European Parliament and of the Council on entrusting the Office for harmonisation in the Internal Market (Trade Marks and Designs) with certain tasks related to the protection of intellectual property rights, including the assembling of public and private sector representatives as a European Observatory on Counterfeiting and Piracy' COM(2011) 288 final – 2011/0135 (COD), 2011/C 376/11.

company's existing IPR portfolio, including consideration of the whole supply chain);

- demonstrating use, self-worth and protection of registered IPRs by placing appropriate '©', '®' and '™' marks on goods; manifesting one's IPR portfolio is proven to have a strong deterrent effect;
- performing IPR risk assessment of markets and sources (including likelihood of IPR abuse), especially when introducing a product to a new market; strong brand holders make IPR management plans for cases of infringement to safeguard business continuity (risk management);
- designing products or services to minimise the risk of abuse (e.g., use of sophisticated technologies or techniques that are difficult to replicate);
- combating reverse engineering through technological advances and techniques, e.g. by making the product too sophisticated to be decomposed easily into simple parts;
- using in-house legal team or hiring lawyers, IPR auditors and investigators;
- conducting staff education and training, involving staff in policing of IPR;
- including IPR-related clauses in employee contracts (e.g., non-compete clauses) as there is a general belief among experts that it is mostly employees and other in-house sources that should be held responsible for infringements;
- using 'political influence' with local commercial and non-judicial authorities;
- maintaining background relationships with IPR-related authorities;
- deliberately avoiding risky markets;
- withholding IPR-sensitive technologies from risky markets despite the fact that this may be taken as insulting or patronising in that market;
- trialling risky markets with older technology;
- performing due diligence checks on contractors and partners (including local representatives, suppliers, shipping agents, distributors and customers);
- including IPR protection clauses in commercial contracts;
- retaining critical design activities in the home country;
- retaining critical elements of production in the home country;
- using contract manufacturing service companies as sourcing intermediaries;
- distributing the manufacture/sourcing of components parts of product across multiple territories;
- offering a (high quality) service in addition to the basic product;
- making regular changes to key elements of products and packaging, making it uneconomical for infringers to keep pace with the original;
- maintaining tight control of drawings, tooling and other key elements of production;
- incorporating tracers or fingerprinting into product/packaging designs;
- monitoring direct contact/visits with production sources and distributors (since such supply chain partners are entrusted with IPR, specifications and trade secrets);
- policing production and packaging overruns.[191]

191 Rodwell, Van Eeckhout, Reid, Walendowski, *Study "Effects of Counterfeiting . . . "*, pp. 30–38.

This listing of supralegal or non-processual measures provides an overview of IPR protection indicators. Notwithstanding their great value, these actions also come at great cost. But one must bear in mind the very modest head-count of an average T/C enterprise. Many of the actions listed are unfeasible for a small TCLF business for reasons of cost and capacity. It is beyond the influence of many small businesses to force their partners into signing such contracts (e.g. with sewing workshops), even assuming they had the resources to negotiate them.

The authors of the report also recommend retaining an expert on IPR issues: "(E)ach company, of whatever size, should nominate a person as its 'IPR manager'". They go on to say that

> This person need not be an expert or legally trained but should have the task of understanding the challenges to the company's intellectual property and gathering, and disseminating internally, information about the various forms of assistance available to the company from its own and external resources.[192]

I have advocated many times the introduction of the position of a Legal Officer at the C-level (CLO). Such a role perfectly complements the other common positions in a senior team (including Chief Executive Officer, Chief Financial Officer, Chief Design Officer, Chief Information Officer, Chief Technology Officer and many others). It seemed obvious to me that, where the capacity of an enterprise permits it, top strategic decisions should be informed by a person armed with IPR&S[193] knowledge. However, I challenge the blanket assumption that every company, regardless of size, can even sustain an IPR&S Counsellor, let alone the assertion that this person's background may be in an arbitrary field. Here are several reasons why:

1 I reject the idea that an IPR manager does not need to be an expert nor legally trained. From my practice I can assert that this level of business scrutiny is not within the capabilities of the average legal practitioner but requires the know-how of seasoned professionals or people with a knack for both law and business.
2 Given that an IPR manager lacking legal training has the duty to manage the business from a legal perspective, it is unfeasible to expect to address the legal and business issues without this role being filled by a legal counsellor or other expert, if possible.
3 The T/C business consists mostly of SMEs, most with only a few staff, meaning that the IPR manager's role would have to be undertaken by the owner.

192 Rodwell, Van Eeckhout, Reid, Walendowski, *Study "Effects of Counterfeiting . . . "*, p. 55.
193 Intellectual Property Rights and Strategy.

From the foregoing arguments, it is plain to see that for a 'IPR manager' or 'CLO', one size definitely does not fit all.

3.4.6.3 Drawbacks of industrial property rights

Securing protection based on the concept of industrial property rights is subject to a number of difficulties and challenges. An entrepreneur trying to assert his rights in cases of infringement may encounter rough weather for which he is not prepared. First, there is the principle of territoriality, which makes protection overseas possible only after registering the IPR in the country where the infringement originates, unless the entrepreneur had filed a costly application for IPR at the international level.[194] Given that many counterfeits originate in China, he would require a counsel with local expertise. With regard to design rights, it has been noted that the T/C sector produces goods whose life spans are too short to gain effective protection. In other words, the long time taken to grant design rights (notably in China) makes it impractical to register fashion designs.[195]

It should be also pointed out that there is a subtle difference between the concepts of *counterfeits* and *knock-offs*, which are *'parasitic' or 'look-alike' products*, which may look similar to the originals but might not infringe upon IPR.

Inventions in the labour-intense T/C industry can be very effective and can keep infringers at bay, especially if the originator is highly innovative and has secured the weighty budget necessary to register their IPR. However, the best way to outdo competitors is to keep one's innovation far ahead of the curve, which, again, comes at a price.[196]

The study on counterfeiting produced an interesting observation, in which it was pointed out that

> Well-resourced companies may find it possible to overcome the impacts of IPR abuse such as those mentioned above. They may be in a position to make good preparations, take excellent advice, enact text-book enforcement measures and use influence in the marketplace. For example bringing *high-profile cases against infringers* will probably have a deterrent effect, while companies with multiple product lines may be able to select less vulnerable products to introduce into risky markets. However the problem of these potential impacts is far greater for SMEs, which are invariably less well resourced. Barriers for SMEs are not confined to the difficult conditions to be found in remote markets. A number of EU regulations concerning IPR enforcement measures set high

194 M. Świerczyński, *Zasada terytorializmu praw własności intelektualnej* [in:] J. Kępiński, K. Klafkowska-Waśniowska, R. Sikorski (eds.), *Własność intelektualna w obrocie elektronicznym*, vol. V, C.H. Beck, 2015, p. 3–7.

195 Rodwell, Van Eeckhout, Reid, Walendowski, *Study "Effects of Counterfeiting . . . "*, p. 16.

196 Rodwell, Van Eeckhout, Reid, Walendowski, *Study "Effects of Counterfeiting . . . "*, p. 14.

financial barriers for smaller companies, for instance the requirement for applications for customs action to be translated into all the EU customs languages. It is important to note that some EU customs accept to have the application filed in English, while France and Greece request the submission of this application in their own language.[197]

3.4.7 *Ultimate solution. Brand love*

Without doubt, the scale of the counterfeiting problem is financially substantial.[198] But the magnitude of this abuse does not have to directly translate to actual damage to fashion brands for a number of reasons.[199] In the literature, there is a huge disconnect as to whether IP protection in fashion is either effective or required. As noted by P. P. Quesenberry,

> counterfeiting may slow product development, as well as increase exponentially the cost of IP protection, new products, and loss of potential profits. This slowdown in turn leads to another part of the circle of product development to production to consumer and back to product development and to fewer dollars available to direct towards research and development.[200]

On the other side, there is a body of opinion that knock-offs increase awareness of brands, thereby contributing to growth of the original product.[201] Apart from the *Piracy Paradox* theory,[202] a number of independent studies question the need for strong IP protection for fashion goods.[203] Yi Qian has proven that counterfeits hurt low-end products while serving as advertising for high-end ones. Counterfeits can also have a positive effect on high-quality goods offered by brands that are still building their position. The same author argues in a number of papers that there is no IPR protection that fits all sizes of business. The optimum level of protection may vary depending on a country, sector, brand and even product (based on its type and quality level).[204]

197 Rodwell, Van Eeckhout, Reid, Walendowski, *Study "Effects of Counterfeiting . . . "*, p. 14.
198 Quesenberry, *Apparel Industry . . .*, p. 4.
199 J.M. Wilson, C. Grammich, F. Chan, *Organizing for Brand Protection and Responding to Product Counterfeit Risk: An Analysis of Global Firms*, "Journal of Brand Management", 2016, vol. 23, pp. 345–361, https://doi.org/10.1057/bm.2016.12.
200 Quesenberry, *Apparel Industry . . .*, p. 53.
201 M. Jankowska, *Copyright – an Ally for Fashion in the Intellectual Property Rights System?*, "CC&EEL", 2019, no. 1 (133), pp. 64 and ff.
202 K. Raustiala, C.J. Sprigman, *The Piracy Paradox: Innovation and Intellectual Property in Fashion Design*, "Virginia Law Review", 2006, vol. 92, no. 8, p. 1721; K. Raustiala, C.J. Sprigman, *The Piracy Paradox Revisited*, "Stanford Law Review", 2009, vol. 61, no. 5, p. 1201.
203 A. Nia, J. Lynne Zaichkowsky, *Do Counterfeits Devalue the Ownership of Luxury Brands?*, "Journal of Product & Brand Management", 2000, vol. 9, no. 7, pp. 485–497; cf. K. Wilcox, H. Min Kim, S. Sen, *Why Do Consumers . . .* p. 249.
204 Y. Qian, *Counterfeiters: Foes or Friends? How Counterfeits Affect Sales by Product Quality Tier*, "Managements Science", 2014, vol. 60, no. 10, p. 2398.

There is a view that fashion designers, or especially design houses, should adopt their own methods of fighting counterfeiting, such as 1) altering product presentation; 2) technology to create special inks used in barcodes; 3) holograms on the package, the label, or within the barcode; 4) heat transfer labels; 5) invisible inks; 6) unique thread; 7) merchandise-tracking technology; 8) hard-to-copy trademarks[205]; 9) radio-frequency identification; and 10) blockchain and blockchain-enabled non-fungible token.[206] At first appearance these measures may seem helpful, but any of these – very costly – practices would misfire if not applied in connection with IP policy, since any measure that will not help obtain court enforcement is of questionable value. With regard to copyright law, these measures resemble the so called "copyright traps" used in other creativity-sensitive sectors (such as geoinformation), an approach that failed despite the high hopes of its proponents. The core issue is that copyright protection can be claimed through originality and individuality only, and not through mere slavish copying.

Research published in 2020 addressed the potential tactics and strategies that could reduce counterfeiting. The author examined 32 papers published between 1985 and 2015 to find that only ten were concerned, even tangentially, with the effectiveness of various legal remedies. The author noted that

> the review reveals that major discrepancies within and between nations in both IP and criminal law significantly limit effectiveness of legal action. Inconsistent application of laws and reluctance to enact additional demand- and supply-side penalties are also limited by cultural perceptions about the negative societal impacts of luxury counterfeits.[207]

Civil court proceedings to recoup damages prove to have limited effect, as the legal action rarely succeeds and the damages, where granted, are usually very low.[208] Some of the supply-side strategies deemed potentially effective were 1) corporate investigation and surveillance activities, 2) assistance from taxation authorities and 3) lobbying legislators and law enforcement officials to enforce and strengthen anti-counterfeiting measures.[209] Interestingly, one of the demand-side strategies that was found potentially effective was the *increasing of investment in brand equity*. Companies can create brand equity for their products by making them *memorable, easily recognisable and superior in quality and reliability*. Such investment could encourage higher loyalty towards

205 R. Bush, P. Bloch, S. Dawson, *Remedies for Product Counterfeiting*, "Business Horizons", 1989, vol. 1, no. 32, pp. 59 and ff.; Quesenberry, *Apparel Industry . . .*, p. 57.

206 L. Meraviglia, *Technology and Counterfeiting in the Fashion Industry: Friends or Foes?*, "Business Horizons", 2018, vol. 61, no. 3, pp. 355–356.

207 N.B. Amaral, *What Can Be Done to Address Luxury Counterfeiting? An Integrative Review of Tactics and Strategies*, "Journal of Brand Management", 2020, vol. 27, no. 6, pp. 1–19.

208 M. Lambkin, Y. Tyndall. *Brand Counterfeiting: A Marketing Problem That Won't Go Away*, "Irish Marketing Review", 2009, vol. 20, no. 1, p. 35.

209 Amaral, *What . . .*.

genuine luxury products.[210] However, none of these measures are realistic for micro- or small enterprises. In any case, though, if copyright law was supposed to be the legal basis for protection, simple to grasp and unified prerequisites of protection would be needed.

As for IP protection strategies, this author advocates four: 1) landlords taking action against tenants in case of counterfeit production or sales, 2) IP (mostly trademark) protection, 3) criminal prosecution and 4) lobbying and education of law enforcement and government agencies. All these options are of limited effectiveness.[211]

Other studies examine the purchasing environment and the rationale for buying either a counterfeit or an original product. Interestingly, the inclination towards counterfeits is not only related to the social status of the buyer or the price tag of the product but also to the social and cultural norms of the society.[212] Some of the consumers who take part in the cultural and social aspects of stimulating the counterfeit market are people who see themselves as *'anti-big business'* or have the *'Robin Hood'* syndrome.[213] In such cases, top-tier price tags become the moral and social justification for these practices.[214] Since buying branded products triggers emotions, a number of commentators have advocated that one of the measures a brand should reconsider is to communicate about the emotional drawbacks resulting from an illegal purchase or social disapprobation about buying counterfeits.[215] This finding is related to theories of social hierarchy and social identity.[216] Furthermore, there is a view that luxury brands should encourage consumers to view the brand itself

210 D. Yang, G.E. Fryxell, A.K.Y. Sie, *Anti-Piracy Effectiveness and Managerial Confidence: Insights from Multinationals in China*, "Journal of World Business", 2008, vol. 43, no. 3, pp. 321–339. A.E. Wilcock, K.A. Boy. *Reduce Product Counterfeiting: An Integrated Approach*, "Business Horizons", 2014, vol. 57, no. 2, pp. 279–288; H.R. Kaufmann, S.M.C. Loureiro, A. Manarioti, *Exploring Behavioural Branding, Brand Love and Brand Co-Creation*, "Journal of Product and Brand Management", 2016, vol. 25, no. 6, pp. 516–526; cf. J.M. Wilson, C.A. Grammich, *Protecting Brands from Counterfeiting Risks: Tactics of a Total Business Solution*, "Journal of Risk Research", https://doi.org/10.1080/13669877.2020.1806908, p. 14.

211 Amaral, *What* . . ., p.

212 Kay Ka-Yuk Lai, Judith Lynne Zaichkowsky, *Brand Imitation: Do the Chinese Have Different Views?*, "Asia Pacific Journal of Management", 1999, vol. 16, no. 2, pp. 179–192.

213 K.K. Kwong, O.H.M. Yau, J.S.Y. Lee, L.Y.M. Sin, A.C.B. Tse, *The Effects of Attitudinal and Demographic Factors on Intention to Buy Pirated CDs: The Case of Chinese Consumers.* "Journal of Business Ethics", 2003, vol. 47, no. 33, pp. 223–235; A. Nill, C.J. Shultz, II, *The Scourge of Global Counter-Feiting*, "Business Horizons", 1996, vol. 39, no. 6, pp. 37–42.

214 Meraviglia, *Technology and Counterfeiting in the Fashion Industry* . . ., pp. 355–356.

215 Qian, *Counterfeiters* . . ., p. 2398. E. Penz, B. Stöttinger, *A Comparison of the Emotional and Motivational Aspects in the Purchase of Luxury Products Versus Counterfeits*, "Journal of Brand Management", 2012, 19, pp. 581 and ff.; Nia, Lynne Zaichkowsky, *Do Counterfeits* . . ., p. 495.

216 "When females from a higher social class viewed or imagined another woman using a counterfeit luxury brand, they rated the genuine luxury brand more negatively when the counterfeit user was from a different (i.e., lower) social class", N.M. Amaral, B. Loken, *Viewing Usage of Counterfeit Luxury Goods: Social Identity and Social Hierarchy Effects on Dilution*

as a hedonic experience.[217] The '*brand love*' strategy builds on a strong brand image that would suffer from disaggregation if undermined by the purchasing of counterfeits.[218]

3.5 Conclusions

This chapter revealed that the *fashion industry* does not have one single accepted definition. Rather, the concept is vague and malleable. This author proves that its broadest meaning covers a range of TCLF industries, including furniture, gems and jewellery and beauty as well as everything that touches attractive looks and lifestyle. It extends to a multitude of processes, from R&D and design, through production, retail and marketing up to waste and recycling. In its *less broad meaning*, fashion could be confined to textiles, clothing, shoes, bags and accessories, with elements of jewellery and fragrances. In searching for definitions, the idea of a 'fashion good' can be helpful. This is defined by five criteria: 1) consumer goods; 2) relating to personal dress and personal image; 3) a mix of functionality and 'symbolic value'; 4) creative, often a product of artisan work; and 5) highly trend sensitive. As much as the idea of a 'fashion good' is worth incorporating into the discussion, it should be kept in mind that defining the 'fashion industry' based on the notion of a 'fashion good' is one of the major legal, *idem per idem*, failures.

Fashion goods extend far beyond tangible goods. The fashion industry is perceived as a 'knowledge-based industry' and an 'experience industry', meaning that fashion goods trigger customers' desires to pay more not for the product or service itself but for the feeling of having them. At the same time, although highly creative process is involved in production, with less than 1% of the sector's income being spent on R&D, fashion is considered to be a 'low-technology industry'. It is important to note that the fashion business is nowadays changing from a supply-driven to a demand-driven market. In order to flourish, it has to embrace change based on niche production, employees qualified in R&D and sales. That change can also be a factor triggering greater copyrightability.

By example of Italian SMEs, these entrepreneurs engage the competition by competing on the basis of *design*, *quality*, *creativity* and *fashionability*, and therefore managed to bring their products to the level of the highly value-added market segment and to demand premium prices for their products.

One of the major takeaways from my research is that, in many cases the price should be chosen to ensure the recouping of the costs for the creative

---

and Enhancement of Genuine Luxury Brands, "Journal of Consumer Psychology", 2016, vol. 26, no. 4, pp. 483–495.

217 E. Triandewi, F. Tjiptono, Consumer Intention to Buy Original Brands Versus Counterfeits, "International Journal of Marketing Studies", 2013, vol. 5, no. 2, pp. 23–32; Kaufmann, Loureiro, Manarioti, *Exploring . . .*, pp. 516 and ff.

218 G.M. Grossman, C. Shapiro, *Foreign Counterfeiting of Status Goods*, "The Quarterly Journal of Economics", 1988, vol. 103, no. 1, pp. 79–100.

process as though there was no protection available for the design. A product's price should be informed by the quality and by the need to be competitive in the market. Where a company can avail of strong IPR protection, they may feel stronger in their market position. Nonetheless, because of remaining uncertainties around IPR protection in the fashion sector, companies need capable staff to manage this area.

This research proved that the creative process often does not begin with an idea for a product itself, but with the *brand identity*, the crafting of a clear brand personality or brand concept that permits the consumer to spot the brand and its products and not only feel at ease with the purchase but long for it and make it part of their own self-image. Clients allocate space in their minds (so-called *brand share*) for the brands to which they stay loyal. Surprisingly, as noted by Miuccia Prada and Patrizio Bertelli, this makes a place for *fashionless fashion*. The brand effect is so strong that it easily extends to every product regardless of its degree of creativity or product segment. At the same time, top-tier fashion brands successfully capitalise on their earned position by *artification* of their product.

From the research it can be seen that the protection of fashion IPRs *is a cost, not an investment*. The survey conducted among Polish fashion designers demonstrated that only four of them had a registered trademark, but none had any IP court experience despite most of them (12 out of 14 designers) having encountered a knock-off of their works. In summary, in 2019, the four most common subcategories of seized products based on the number of items seized were toys, cigarettes, clothing accessories and clothing (accounting together for 41% of the total number). The strongest protection through customs was secured for EU trademarks. Copyright ranked very low but still above patents, international community design and model rights and unregistered community designs.

In many European Commission documents, including EC Communication COM/2003/0649, it was stressed that the competitive advantages of the T/C sector in the EU should be grounded on quality, design, innovation, technology and highly value-added products. It was suggested that the fight against counterfeits should be enabled through "strengthening existing measures and adoption of new measures to protect industrial and intellectual property". It is hard to share this perspective. When asked about the nature of the IPRs infringement, the majority of abuses referred to 'look-alike products', 'parasitic copies' and 'design'. It should also be stressed that there is a subtle difference between the concepts of *counterfeits* versus *knock-offs, 'parasitic' or 'look-alike' products*, which may look similar to the originals but might not infringe upon IPRs. There is also a different way of gauging these matters legally. In terms of copyright law, what in the US angle would be considered a knock-off or just a copy would in the EU count as plagiarism. The European approach to plagiarism is somewhat wider than in the US, where this term is mostly used for literature infringement.

The fashion industry is a mix of both creative and cultural industries with all the attendant consequences. One cannot discuss the issue of plagiarism of fashion goods without accepting that fashion is a live social phenomenon with consumers willing to play a major part. The textile industry is considered to be *capital intensive*, whereas the clothing industry is *labour intensive*. The latter is considered less reliant on technical innovation and can be operated with minimal capital requirements. The clothing industry has suffered in recent decades from competitive anxiety mostly caused by newly industrialised developing countries that have begun to out-compete the traditional fashion-producing countries. The takeaway, however, is that emotion pervades fashion, whether during design or purchase, but that this emotion is not accommodated by the existing copyrightability criteria.

There are many IP policies that concern the protection of IP goods, however they need not be based solely on legal solutions. The data resulting from many studies show that the relationship between original works of fashion and their clones is quite delicate. Many consumers choose to purchase imitations due to a lack of financial resources. For customers who can afford to buy originals, brands need to find ways of keeping them mesmerised in ways that have nothing to do with legal constraints. Brand love would be the answer. However, this IP policy can only be based on the special qualities a product can offer.

4 Copyrightability of fashion design in US and EU law

In search of a copynorm

4.1 Overview: general angle

Historically, concepts of intellectual property and fashion as we know them today are both of European origin.[1] If we dive into historical study and take a broad socio-legal-political perspective, it is easy to connect the dots that reveal patterns of reasoning behind certain decisions, in this case the *niveau* of creativity that is protectable. It is unquestionable that French *couturiers* opened the floodgates of stylish apparel, but fashion was an already indispensable daily companion in the Roman Empire. The Romans elevated fashion and arts, because in their empire's glory days there was a constant hunger for fine and resplendent goods.[2] The idea of seasonal fashion and the distinction between women's and men's fashion goes back to that time. On a side note, it can be observed that the Roman Empire style was largely influenced by British, German and Hispanic style, proving that the adoption of style, trends and intricate ornaments is a genetically embedded feature of fashion. Fast-forwarding to the Renaissance, its heart beat strongest in Italy. France came to the forefront of artistic taste only in the Baroque era. The French government became known for incentivising the textile and fashion sectors and for implementing strong supporting policies. In the 20th century Italy reasserted its position in the world of fashion, thanks largely to the emergence of fashion houses such as Fendi in 1897, Prada in 1913, Gucci in 1921, Ermenegildo Zegna in 1912 and Salvatore Ferragamo in 1927.[3] Compared to France, which views fashion as a form of art, Italy's outlook on fashion considers it more as a lifestyle and a traditional business developed during a lifetime and passed down through generations.

The American approach to fashion was somewhat different. The earliest encounters involved imported French fashions which became available in

1 It is beyond argument that early fashion was a concept also heavily developed in Egyptian, Persian and Etruscan civilizations. Between the 5th and 12th centuries, the most fashionable point on the map was Constantinople, which set trends and imprinted itself on lifestyles of many across Europe. Okonkwo, *Luxury Fashion* . . ., pp. 18–26.

2 This led to the adoption of sumptuary laws and demonstrates that, even at that time, there was a strong public urge to copy prestigious looks.

3 Okonkwo, *Luxury Fashion* . . ., pp. 29, 39, 45–47.

DOI: 10.4324/9781003376033-4

the early 20th century in retailing and distribution and were sold in department stores. Clearly, this buying experience in no way resembled French chic nor did it provide the cachet of shopping at Parisian ateliers. Furthermore, the French designs being sold in New York and Chicago at that time were bulk production allowed through licensing but also included a large portion based on copying. Only in the 1940s and 1950s did the US start to make an impact on fashion through Hollywood movies. But a characteristic of the American market is that American consumers demand simplicity in fashion design, which is sometimes referred to as an 'understated fashion style'.[4] This simple, classy, but casual style was adopted by such American brands as Ralph Lauren, Calvin Klein and Tommy Hilfiger. Styles in Europe were more elaborate, and it is therefore perhaps no surprise that Europe introduced the concept of intellectual property (IP) and has strongly supported it to this day. The US was very resistant to the idea and implemented IP concepts only gradually. Just as France and Germany embraced the personality-based philosophy of creativity in their intellectual property rights (IPR) regulations, the US supported a utilitarian approach. The US always represented a pragmatic and functional approach. Nowadays, by the same token, if we look more closely at the attitude towards fashion, it comes as no surprise that legal protection of fashion differs significantly between both sides of the Atlantic.

This chapter offers a deep dive into the *niveau* of copyrightability of fashion design that is comparative and illustrated with a rich pictorial representation whenever possible. This author wants to establish an understanding of where the level of originality for fashion goods lies. For this reason, analysis of specific cases and a look behind the pure legal curtains are provided. Nearly 300 judgements and decisions were examined, regarding clothing, shoes and jewellery: 102 in the US, 32 in Italy, 109, in France, 33 in the Netherlands and 23 in Germany. This chapter starts with an analysis of the US legal ground against the backdrop of the well-known 'useful article' doctrine that is responsible for setting the copyright bar noticeably higher for fashion goods than for others. As the heart of fashion in Europe has always been Italy and France, both countries are considered next in the analysis. The research is supplemented with examples drawn from Dutch copyright law, which has a reputation for a regime that is distinctively liberal with the bar for protection set very low. Given that the continental European tradition of law reduces to the Roman and German systems that heavily influenced the other national regimes, the research does not seem complete without providing a German angle on the protection of fashion goods. This book also reflects on Polish law, in order to give this author's national home-turf perspective. It shall be noted that being a lawyer trained at a Polish university in the Polish legal system, this author is not allowed to comment on any other law than Polish.

4 Okonkwo, *Luxury Fashion . . .*, p. 32.

4.1.1 Copynorm

It is generally believed that copyright law, similarly to other areas of law, works only if the majority of society finds it plausible and is willing to follow it without compulsion.[5] Mark F. Schultz, by example of the digital environment (blogs, the sharing of content like MP3s etc.), demonstrates how a social norm works. Regarding copyright, L. Solum uses the term "copynorm". It is advocated that applying sanctions to enforce legal norms is not the best approach to law-making. It should be exactly the other way around. A legal norm should follow the pre-existing social norm, meaning that society would generally obey the law as the only morally justifiable behaviour. It is noted that "copynorms matter because social norms matter".[6]

But ultimately not every situation is black and white. It needs a careful blending of social, cultural, religious and moral norms. Fashion, as a specific area of life, is the best example of how the current copyright law is in conflict with customers' expectations to keep pace with the cycle of fashion. Whereas copyright law is designed to provide long-term protection to enduring works, fashion is recognised by its consumers as transient.

In fact, even the origins of copyright regulations go back to a time when there was no general social understanding of authors' rights. Today's copyright laws can easily be seen to have been created by and for writers, philosophers and lawyers to address their specific needs.

The emergence and potential of new technologies demonstrate how society's expectations substantially change. Resources available online are widely believed to be part of the public domain, for which reason users expect free access and take sharing for granted. This phenomenon easily shows the pure clash of interests that arise at the intersection of social norms on the one hand and legal norms on the other. Fashion is another, somewhat neglected, area showing that strict norms of copyright law do not fit seamlessly without an understanding of fashion as a social phenomenon, something that is inherent to a person, specifically, a social being. This book offers an angle on cultural and social norms, historical constraints and economic environment, all of which combine to define the idea of fashion.

Specifics to consider about fashion:

- there are many myths that it does not benefit from copyright protection – which are totally incorrect;
- the axiom of the idea and expression dichotomy is a poor fit for this area;
- the cycle of fashion is much shorter compared to any other area of creativity, such as design or fine arts;

5 M.F. Schultz, *Copynorms: Copyright Law and Social Norms* [w:] P.K. Yu (red.). *Intellectual Propery and Information Wealth, Issues and Practices in the Digital Age*, t. I, Copyright and Related Rights, 2007, ss. 207, 216–218.

6 Schultz, *Copynorms* . . ., s. 207.

- it is of utilitarian purpose with less emphasis on capitalising on single works of authorship (or works of art) and having a totally different pace (much faster) of work;
- social acceptance of the copying of works that are *à la mode*.

These factors combine to question the premises of contemporary copyright law. Without a change in lawmakers' sociological approach to copycats, copyright protection will remain vague, and proposals for improvement will continue to be *de lege ferenda*. This chapter sheds light on the copyrightability of fashion goods under existing law.

4.2 Copyrightability of fashion goods in the US

4.2.1 Overview: theories of separability

Clothing, in particular shirts, dresses, pants, coats, shoes or outerwear, *as such* are not considered to be eligible for copyright.[7] This is because, as they provide utilitarian functions, they fall under the 'useful article' doctrine. This means that neither clothing nor clothing design can constitute a work of authorship of itself, however, anything that can be classified as a pictorial, graphic or sculptural work can be considered copyrightable. The same rule is followed for costumes, decorative masks,[8] fabrics, watches, furniture and furnishings, but not for jewellery. In this context, it is sometimes noted that "jewellery is not useful".[9] In general, a product design is reduced to its individual components in order to decide on its status. This approach is consistent with the theories of separability. In the case *Blue Fish Clothing, Inc. v. Kat Prints*, it was noted that "protection has, however, been extended to the designs affixed or applied to a dress or other clothing".[10]

As for fabric and textile, as much they have useful functions, it is asserted that the designs printed in or on fabric are conceptually separable from the utilitarian aspects of garments, linens, furniture or other products.

4.2.2 Copyright Office line of reasoning

4.2.2.1 General

Each year, the US Copyright Office receives over half a million applications for copyright registration, of which at least 10% are declined.[11] Once a work

7 Compendium § 924.3 (ed. 2014).

8 There was a case where a mask was not considered a useful article because it did not perform a utilitarian function and was eligible for registration as sufficiently creative, cf. *Masquerade Novelty, Inc.* v. *Unique Industries, Inc.*, 912 F.2d 663, 671 (3d Cir. 1993).

9 Opinion of Professor Guillermo Jimenez. Private consultation.

10 no. 91–1511, 1991 U.S. Dist. LEXIS 5720, at *4 (E.D. Pa. Apr. 29, 1991).

11 *Ellen Solovsky* v. *Delta Galil USA and Sock Drawer*, LLC, 14 Civ. 7289 (GHW), Statement of Interest on Behalf of the U.S. Copyright Office, as of 5 July 2016, p. 5, www.copyright.

is registered in the US Register of Copyrights, there is a statutory presumption that the copyright is valid (17 U.S.C. § 410 (c)). An opposing party bears the burden of proving the invalidity of a registered copyright. Moreover, as observed by the Copyright Office,

> In making a *de novo* determination of copyrightability as permitted under 17 U.S.C. § 411(a), it is nonetheless proper for the Court to consider and give weight to the Copyright Office's interpretations of the copyright law and its determinations on copyrightability in light of the Office's expertise in this area.[12]

The Copyright Office registration specialists, as well as the Board of the US Copyright Office, are not in a position to make aesthetic judgements in evaluating the copyrightability of particular works. It was noted that

> the attractiveness of a design, the espoused intentions of the author, the design's visual effect or its symbolism, the time and effort it took to create, or the design's commercial success in the market places are not factors in determining whether a design is copyrightable. . . . Though the Supreme Court in *Feist* established a low threshold for copyrightability, there is indeed a threshold. There are a wide variety of protectable works, including innumerable protectable jewelry designs, many of which include combinations of common shapes and other public domain elements.[13]

Therefore, every work is checked from the angle of whether it qualifies as an "original work . . . of authorship fixed in any tangible medium of expression" (17 U.S.C. § 102(a)). The term "original" consist of two elements: being an independent creation and being the result of sufficient creativity.

US Copyright Law prohibits registration of "words and short phrases such as names, titles, and slogans; familiar symbols or designs; mere variations of typographic ornamentation, lettering or coloring; mere listing of ingredients or contents" (37 C.F.R. § 202.1 (a)). It goes on to say that "in order to be acceptable as a pictorial, graphic, or sculptural work, the work must embody some creative authorship in its delineation or form" (37 C.F.R. § 202.10 (a)).

4.2.2.2 *Jewellery*

Just to give a detailed example of one decision, the Review Board of the US Copyright Office denied Richemont International S.A. and Piaget's request

gov/rulings-filings/411/solovsky-v-delta-galil-usa-no-14-cv-7289--sdny-july-5-2016.pdf (accessed: 30.01.2023).

12 Op. cit., p. 7.

13 Second Request for Reconsideration for Refusal to Register POSSESSION TOI & MOI BRACELET 1; POSSESSION TOI & MOI BRACELET 2; Correspondence ID: 1–248JI9S, SR# 1–2406151726, 21 May 2018, www.copyright.gov/rulings-filings/review-board/docs/possession-toi-and-moi-bracelet.pdf (accessed: 28.11.2021).

to register two bracelets "POSSESSION TOI & MOI BRACELET 1" and "POSSESSION TOI & MOI BRACELET 2" on the grounds that they lacked the authorship necessary to support a copyright registration.[14]

Item of note no. 4.1 Possession Toi & Moi Bracelets – uncopyrightable

Possession Toi & Moi Bracelet 1 is a bracelet made of rose gold. The bracelet consists of two interlocking rings of different sizes, attached to a thin gold chain. The larger ring is smooth gold; the smaller ring is white gold set with small diamonds. A "P" charm dangles from the bracelet's clasp.

Possession Toi & Moi Bracelet 2 is also made of rose gold. The bracelet consists of a curved gold bar, set with brilliant-cut diamonds, attached to a circular band engraved with the word "POSSESSION" with a cuff-type mechanism. These elements are attached to a thin gold chain on either side. A diamond charm dangles from the bracelet's clasp.

The board agreed that only a modicum of creativity is necessary but concluded that "[a] mere simplistic arrangement of non-protectable elements does not demonstrate the level of creativity necessary to warrant protection" and that "[a] combination of unprotectable elements is eligible for copyright protection only if those elements are numerous enough". In the case of *geometric shapes*, a work must be *sufficiently creative* or *expressive*. The board wrote,

> Possession Toi & Moi Bracelet 1 consists of two rings of different sizes, linked together, attached to a thin chain, with a small charm dangling from the clasp. That combination of elements is commonplace and expected in jewelry designs; many bracelets and necklace have a nearly identical design with similar elements. Similarly, Possession Toi & Moi Bracelet 2 consists of only a few elements: a bar with diamonds arranged in an ordinary pattern, a ring with a word embossed on it, and a basic chain. Those elements are individually uncreative and are combined in a commonplace way.[15]

14 Second Request for Reconsideration for Refusal to Register POSSESSION TOI & MOI BRACELET 1; POSSESSION TOI & MOI BRACELET 2; Correspondence ID: 1–248JI9S, SR# 1–2406151726, 21 May 2018, www.copyright.gov/rulings-filings/review-board/docs/possession-toi-and-moi-bracelet.pdf (accessed: 28.01.2023). Jankowska, Meghaichi, Pawełczyk, *Illustrated Fashion Law*.

15 Second Request for Reconsideration for Refusal to Register POSSESSION TOI & MOI BRACELET 1; POSSESSION TOI & MOI BRACELET 2 . . . , p. 5.

There are a good many examples of denials of copyright protection regarding jewellery, as "standard industry designs" cannot be the basis for a copyright claim.[16] The Review Board rejected the qualification as original 'artistic craftsmanship',[17] and therefore protection, of the "Manchettes Cannage" bracelet employing a repeating pattern of diamonds and triangles along the bracelet as well as the "Manchettes Tresse" with a repeating trapezoid pattern. The Review Board observed that common geometric shapes do not support registration ("Bague Ruban"),[18] unless they fulfil some additional originality criteria, as in this case where the shapes were seen to "evoke the elegant and interlocking geometric patterns on a giraffe's fur" ("Bague Girafe"). Altesse also argued that the use of the "•G•" logo or the embossed "Made in France" text inside the ring could have supported registration. But the Review Board noted that "those elements are part of the 'Bague Girafe' registration, and previously registered material cannot be the basis for a new copyright registration".[19]

Item of note no. 4.2 Garden-variety elements doctrine

With regard to the "Bangle Collection", it observed that spheres, hexagons and a c-shaped cuff are merely minor variations on common shapes, that fall under the so-called *garden-variety elements* doctrine and therefore fail to attain the originality threshold. On another note, being a combination of commonplace tropes it constitutes *scènes à faire* in the jewellery industry.[20] Similarly, for the "Laurel Leaf Bracelet" the Review Board rejected registration of "an inverted laurel leaf closure", and a circular charm engraved with SNC's brand name, 'Kinsley Armelle' because the design was commonplace, expected in jewellery design and because its geometric shape constituted a so called *trivial variation*. Only an unusual pattern would be eligible for protection.[21]

16 COMPENDIUM (THIRD) § 313.4(J).

17 Copyright protects works of artistic craftsmanship as pictorial, graphic, or sculptural works "insofar as their form but not their mechanical or utilitarian aspects are concerned." 17 U.S.C. § 101; see 37 C.F.R. § 202.10(a).

18 Second Request for Reconsideration for Refusal to Register Bague Ruban, Manchettes Cannage, and Manchettes Tresse (Correspondence IDs 1–3MJ8ZMM, 1–3MJHD3S, 1–3MJ8G1WA; SR # 1–6990592562, 1–6990592702, 1–6990592802), 29 June 2021, p. 1, 7–8, www.copyright.gov/rulings-filings/review-board/docs/manchettes-et-al.pdf (accessed: 04.01.2023).

19 Op. cit., p. 7, fn. 2. Jankowska, Meghaichi, Pawełczyk, *Illustrated Fashion Law*.

20 Second Request for Reconsideration for Refusal to Register Bangle Collection Bracelet (Correspondence ID: 1–3YQGXCU; SR # 1–7026393061), 28 June 2021, p. 4, www.copyright.gov/rulings-filings/review-board/docs/bangle-collection.pdf (accessed: 10.01.2023).

21 Second Request for Reconsideration for Refusal to Register Laurel Leaf Bracelet (Correspondence ID: 1–3GFXFNF, SR # 1–6843666234), 6.10.2021, pp. 1, 4, www.copyright.gov/rulings-filings/review-board/docs/laurel-leaf-bracelet.pdf (accessed: 10.01.2023).

The Review Board also denied copyright protection for "Cirque square stud with pave diamond, Style PE55" on the ground that round-cut diamonds and square-cut topaz are merely minor variations on common shapes arranged in an unoriginal manner.[22] Regarding the design of "The Explorer", it was noted that "the fact that the gold strands separate and connect in a symmetrical pattern does not imbue The Explorer with sufficient creativity to merit copyright protection".[23] On the other hand, the "Forget Me Not" design was granted copyright protection because it featured "numerous elements, including plain and textured gold strands, gold beads, pearls, and several strands woven together in a distinct manner".[24] There were also several decisions finding that some pieces of jewellery were close to the line but still eligible for registration by containing a sufficient amount of original authorship based on the low standard for copyrightability established in *Feist*. It was found that these designs combined more than a few elements in a creative way: RERGY001 (convex shapes and diamond encrusting), REEGY005 (asymmetrically laid out diamonds, pear-shaped jewel at the end of each strand), REEGY004 (shape of the eye encrusted in round-cut diamonds), REEGY001/002/003 (outer oval shape of the eye, single pear-shaped diamond dangles from the end).[25] Protection was denied for a ring in the shape of a simple 12-petal gold flower (ENRGY002), a ring with a round diamond, surrounded by a gold band with evenly spaced baguette diamonds (RERGY002), and the "chandelier" design of a necklace (RERGY003).[26] Interestingly, a gold link bracelet resembling "back-to-back anthropomorphized crescent moons similar to those found in children's books" was registered, as the Review Board found the shape to have

22 Second Request for Reconsideration for Refusal to Register "Cirque square stud with pave diamonds, Style # PE55"; Correspondence ID: 1–3FRDC16; SR # 1–6127581819, 23 December 2019, p. 4, www.copyright.gov/rulings-filings/review-board/docs/cirque-square-stud.pdf (accessed: 17.01.2023).

23 Re: Second Request for Reconsideration for Refusal to Register The Explorer and Forget Me Not; Correspondence IDs: 1–2UQNX9Q, 1–2V2KYPR; SR 1–4000614358, SR 1–4440340247, 8 May 2019, p. 6, www.copyright.gov/rulings-filings/review-board/docs/the-explorer-and-forget-me-not.pdf (accessed: 17.01.2023); see *Jane Envy, LLC v. Infinite Classic Inc.*, 2016 U.S. Dist. LEXIS 23621, at *22,*24 (W.D. Tex. Feb. 26, 2016) (stating that chains and "textured gold links" are not copyrightable).

24 Op. cit.

25 Re: Second Request for Reconsideration for Refusal to Register Endless Engagement Ring (ENRGY002), Reflections TU Engagement Ring (RERGY002), Reflections Cocktail Ring (RERGY001), Reflections Hero Earrings (REEGY005), Reflections Hero Necklace (RENGY003), Reflections Hero Earrings (REEEGY004), and Reflections Hoop Earrings (REEGY001/002/003); 1 Correspondence IDs: 1–20QG984, 1–20QDVFL, and 1–20QG984; SR Numbers 1–3401927454, 1–3402136367, 1–3402136282, 1–3401928073, 1–3402136217, 1–3401927207, and 1–3401927778, 24 January 2019, pp. 8–9, www.copyright.gov/rulings-filings/review-board/docs/endless-engagement.pdf (accessed: 17.01.2023).

26 Op. cit., p. 9–11; cf. *Jane Envy, LLC v. Infinite Classic Inc.*, 2016 WL 797612 (W.D. Tex. 26 February 2016).

an ambiguous connotation: handcuffs, or a decorative figure-eight ("Gemini Link Bracelet").[27]

Many decisions deny copyright registration based on the assumption that merely minor variations on common shapes arranged in an unoriginal manner do not reach the low burden established in *Feist*.[28] These include circles[29] ("Tu Sole Engagement Ring"; "Prime, Solo and Sole Stacking Rings"; "Unity Earrings"[30]; "Nexus"[31]), rectangles, thorny branches,[32] a polygon plate with diamonds arranged in a "caviar" setting,[33] curlicue configuration accented with a small gold heart on the bottom curve of the inner loop ("Arms of Love"),[34] dragon or animal scales ("Naga Jewelry"),[35] a modified cross,[36] metal bands and wires ("Grandma Waverly Bracelet"),[37] gemstone in a loop ("Promise Bracelet")[38] and two circular intersecting

27 Re: Second Request for Reconsideration for Refusal to Register TBPF16 1(3d); Correspondence ID: 1-lTDGOUS; SR #1–2748391622, 11.07.2017, p. 1, www.copyright.gov/rulings-filings/review-board/docs/tbpf16-1.pdf (accessed: 17.01.2023). Jankowska, Meghaichi, Pawełczyk, *Illustrated Fashion Law*.

28 *Hoberman Designs, Inc. v. Gloworks Imports, Inc.*, 2015 WL 10015261 at *4 (C.D. Ca. 2015) (holding that the use of "geometric shapes like squares, triangles, and trapezoids . . . does not preclude copyright protection").

29 Re: Second Request for Reconsideration for Refusal to Register JAIPUR LINK necklace; Correspondence ID: 1–2OW1TE; Service Request: 1–4933166111, 19 April 2018, www.copyright.gov/rulings-filings/review-board/docs/jaipur-link.pdf (accessed: 17.01.2023).

30 Re: Second Request for Reconsideration for Refusal to Register THE LIGHT COLLECTION; Correspondence ID: 1–1MUXUYM, SR# 1–2520268001, 23 May 2018, p. 6, www.copyright.gov/rulings-filings/review-board/docs/the-light-collection.pdf (accessed: 17.01.2023).

31 Re: Second Request for Reconsideration for Refusal to Register Nexus; Correspondence ID: 1–1IV50Q3; SR# l-2500688671, pp. 3–4, www.copyright.gov/rulings-filings/review-board/docs/nexus.pdf (accessed: 18.01.2023).

32 Re: Second Request for Reconsideration for Refusal to Register Plain Thorn Bracelet with Logo, Plain Thorn Ring with Logo, Pave Thorn Bracelet with Logo, and Pave Thorn Ring with Logo; Correspondence ID: 1–18RFMF5, 18 January 2017, p. 4, www.copyright.gov/rulings-filings/review-board/docs/plain-thorn-bracelet.pdf (accessed: 18.01.2023).

33 Re: Second Request for Reconsideration for Refusal to Register Ten Table Thorn Link ID Bracelet; Correspondence ID: 1–185 VNWS, 13 January 2017, p. 4, www.copyright.gov/rulings-filings/review-board/docs/ten-table-thorn-bracelet.pdf (accessed: 18.01.2023).

34 Re: Second Request for Reconsideration for Refusal to Register Arms of Love – LAR08–08C3–1, Arms of Love – LAR08–08C3–3, Arms of Love – LAR08–08C3–4, and Arms of Love – LAR08–08C3-S; Correspondence ID t -108JOER, 20.10.2016, www.copyright.gov/rulings-filings/review-board/docs/arms-of-love.pdf (accessed: 19.01.2023).

35 Re: Second Request for Reconsideration for Refusal to Register Naga Gold & Silver (Season XX); Correspondence ID: l-1EY2QAE, 3 October 2016, p. 5, www.copyright.gov/rulings-filings/review-board/docs/naga-gold-and-silver.pdf (accessed: 19.01.2023).

36 Re: Second Request for Reconsideration for Refusal to Register Grace Bracelet; Correspondence ID: 1V3XJDJ, 23 September 2016, www.copyright.gov/rulings-filings/review-board/docs/grace-bracelet.pdf (accessed: 19.01.2023).

37 Re: Second Request for Reconsideration for Refusal to Register Grandma Waverly Bracelet, Correspondence ID: 1–119ISG8, 23 September 2016, p. 5, www.copyright.gov/rulings-filings/review-board/docs/grandma-waverly-bracelet.pdf (accessed: 19.01.2023).

38 Re: Second Request for Reconsideration for Refusal to Register Promise Bracelet; Correspondence ID: 1–143DTHF, 30 June 2016, www.copyright.gov/rulings-filings/review-board/docs/promise-bracelet.pdf (accessed: 19.01.2023).

metal bands decorated with channels of diamonds forming a standard symmetrical "X" ("Eva Fehren X Ring").[39] Elements that are combined in a way that does not differentiate them from their basic shape and design components or are arranged in ***garden-variety configurations*** do not contain a sufficient amount of originality.[40] In other words, "the separate elements must be ***physically*** bundled together for distribution to the public as a single, integrated unit".[41]

In addition, it was noted that collections of jewellery are not registrable as "units of publications".[42] That means that each work needs to be examined separately.[43]

Neither would simple words or phrases add to the creativity of a work, as established by a range of rejections[44]: "Work 431386", "Work 433516", "Naga Jewelry" (initials "J" and "H" in an interlocking logo in a circle or the name "John Hardy" printed on the underside), "Linx Bracelets" (with the phrase "What is in your Heart" around the ring).[45]

As the copyright law does not extend to procedures, processes and methods, it was noted that "faceting" of a gemstone is a mechanical process, a technique that falls out of protection. If the gem's originality was to be assessed as the result of this process, it would be lacking creative authorship.[46] Even if the work was to be examined for its shape, selection, coordination and arrangement, the originality test would still most probably fail.[47]

39 Re: Second Request for Reconsideration for Refusal to Register Eva Fehren X Ring and Eva Fehreo X Ring-Black Gold, Correspondence ID: 1-IW1A44, 25 April 2016, p. 4, www.copyright.gov/rulings-filings/review-board/docs/eva-fehren-x-ring.pdf (accessed: 19.01.2023).

40 Re: Second Request for Reconsideration for Refusal to Register "Solcin & Atelier 2015 Collection"; Correspondence ID: 1–1HR3ZRY; SR# 1–3114944301, 1–3134585300, 3 August 2017, p. 2, www.copyright.gov/rulings-filings/review-board/docs/solcin-atelier.pdf (accessed: 17.01.2023).

41 Op. cit., p. 2.

42 COMPENDIUM (THIRD)§ 1107.1.

43 Cf. "Solcin Collection" containing 66 and "Atelier 2015 Collection" consisting of 106 pieces of jewelry, including bracelets, necklaces, earrings and rings, op. cit. 4.

44 Re: Second Request for Reconsideration for Refusal to Register L.A. Rocks Footnotes; Correspondence IDs: 1–1C3ME75, 1–1QR79X5, 1–1E8Z24T, 1–1RCJ51Q; SR #s: 1–2270636230, 1–2345733369, 1–2034893168, 1–2345733, 27 June 2017, pp. 2, 3, 8, www.copyright.gov/rulings-filings/review-board/docs/la-rocks.pdf (accessed: 17.01.2023)

45 Re: Second Request for Reconsideration for Refusal to Register What is in Your Soul-Round Locket, What is in Your Heart Linx Lockets -Round Watch, and What is in Your Heart Linx Lockets -Round Locket with Bail; Correspondence ID: 1-WIFQCV, 27 September 2016, www.copyright.gov/rulings-filings/review-board/docs/what-is-in-your-soul.pdf (accessed: 19.01.2023); however the "What is in Your Heart?"(R) Jewelry Designs, Registration Number V A 1–908–855 was granted a certificate of registration.

46 Re: Second Request for Reconsideration for Refusal to Register Star Brilliant Cut 57 Facet Diamond, Correspondence ID: I-YX6QVV; SR# 1–1069429181, 20 March 2017, p. 4, www.copyright.gov/rulings-filings/review-board/docs/star-brilliant-cut-diamond.pdf (accessed: 18.01.2023); see V. MacCarthy, *Beading with Gemstones: Beautiful Jewelry, Simple Techniques*, Lark Books, 2007; D. Clark, *Lapidary Fundamentals: Gemstone Faceting*, International Gem Society, www.gemsociety.org/article/lapidary-fundamentals-gemstone-faceting/ (accessed: 18.01.2023).

47 Jankowska, Meghaichi, Pawełczyk, *Illustrated Fashion Law*.

Yet, a work may be copyrightable even though it is entirely a compilation of unprotectable elements.[48] Yurman's four copyrighted bracelets and earrings consisted of "silver, gold, cable twist, and cabochon cut colored stones". Yurman succeeded in acquiring copyright protection for the "artistic combination and integration of these common elements" because of the way they "are placed, balanced and harmonized".[49]

There is a record of the US cases where copyright protection was refused to diamond rings,[50] barbed wire jewellery,[51] mere interpretations of "ancient inspired" trends[52] or a strand of pearlized beads.[53] There are, however, cases that proved that jewellery can be copyrightable: "Swirled Hoop Earring",[54] pin designs (composed of two-dimensional silhouettes of natural or symbolic subjects cut from polished chrome and embellished with copper wire and beading. These are simplistic designs of subjects taken from nature, such as frogs, turtles, and hummingbirds, mythical subjects like cupids, knights, and mermaids, and Southwestern Indian fetishes like firebirds),[55] "Kobi Katz ring number BW 2798)".[56]

In the Wolstenholme case ("Charmed" series of bracelets and necklaces), the New York District Court decided on 25 September 2017 about a set of silver and/or gold replicas of various pharmaceutical pills (the "Pill Charms"). Wolstenholme had shown that she held copyrights for the designs in Canada. The designs were submitted to the US Copyright Office for copyright registration, but the protection was denied. Yet the court assumed that "the creative

48 See *Yurman Design, Inc. v. PAJ, Inc.*, 262 F.3d 101, 109 (2d Cir. 2001); *Knitwaves, Inc. v. Lollytogs Ltd. (Inc.)*, 71 F.3d 996, 1003–04 (2d Cir. 1995).

49 The designs are designated as "Yurman B4973" (Copyrt. Reg. no. VA 643–194) "Yurman B4977" (Copyrt. Reg. no. VA 785–335) "Yurman E4973" (Copyrt. Reg. no. VA 785–334), and "Yurman B4809" (Copyrt. Reg. no. VAu 254–365); *Yurman Design, Inc. v. PAJ, Inc.*

50 On the ground they are "on the whole, not exceptional, original, or unique" *DBC of New York, Inc. v. Merit Diamond Corp.*, 768 F. Supp. 414, 416 (S.D.N.Y. 1991); cf. *Vogue Ring Creations, Inc. v. Hardman*, 410 F. Supp. 609, 612 (D.R.I. 1976) (finding the ring design not protectable because it was "utterly devoid of any 'original creativity.' ".

51 On the ground that "aesthetic choices, the final arrangement of the elements in her jewelry still corresponds to the arrangement of public domain barbed-wire" *Todd v. Montana Silversmiths, Inc.*, 379 F. Supp. 2d 1110 (D. Colo. 2005).

52 The jewelry falls within a genre known as "ancient inspired" . . ., which has been in vogue since at least 1988. . . . incorporate common elements of the ancient inspired genre, including the use of 18 karat green colored gold, matte finishes, beading, granulation, rope twists, fluting, cabochon stones, columnar designs, pyramid designs and art deco design. . . . These elements have been used by designers for a long time.

Judith Ripka Designs, Ltd. v. Preville, 935 F

53 See *Jane Envy, LLC v. Infinite Classic Inc.*, 2016 WL 797612 (W.D. Tex. 26 February 2016) (noting that a strand of pearlized beads is not copyrightable, and the addition of two beads which hang from the top of a cross represents only a "trivial amount of authorship").

54 *Charles Garnier, Paris v. Andin Intern., Inc.*, 844 F. Supp. 89 (D.R.I. 1994).

55 *Maggio v. Liztech Jewelry*, 912 F. Supp. 216 (E.D. La. 1996).

56 *Weindling International, Crop. v. Kobi Katz, Inc.*, 00 Civ. 2022 (JSR) (S.D.N.Y. 29 September 2000) (Weindling rings numbers SA 3000 and SA 3068 infringed Kobi Katz's copyright in Kobi Katz ring number BW 2798).

selection, arrangement and combination of the pills in Charmed and Hail Mary is sufficient to meet the low bar of originality".[57] The substantial similarity test as applied did not allow for protection against infringement.[58]

On 4 October 2008, the New York District Court decided in the *Van Cleef Arpels* case that the copyright for its well-known *Vintage Alhambra* necklace design was valid despite the fact that the clover design on the jewellery piece was similar to a prior clover-shaped military insignia. The court did not decide on substantial similarity in this case as the parties settled the case.[59]

By contrast, the District Court in Colorado decided in the *Todd* case on 19 July 2005 that the barbed wire jewellery under consideration did not pass muster under the court's scrutiny,[60] because it was not recast or arranged in an original way but instead stuck with the "elemental arrangement" of barbed wire.[61]

Item of note no. 4.3 Barbed wire jewellery – individual versus holistic approach

This case proved to be noteworthy. The dispute arose around two approaches to originality. The defendant argued that each element of the jewellery should be ***examined separately***, alleging that each constituent element fell into one of the unprotected categories.[62] The plaintiff asserted that emphasis on the individual elements was misplaced and that the copyright rested on the "overall design of the pieces". The

(*Continued*)

57 *Colleen Wolstenholme v. Damien Hirst, et al.*, 271 F. Supp. 3d 625 (S.D.N.Y. 2017).

58 M. Whyte, *Canadian Artist Sues Damien Hirst, Alleging Copyright Infringement,* 20 June 2016, "Toronto Star", www.thestar.com/entertainment/visualarts/2016/06/17/canadian-artist-sues-damien-hirst-alleging-copyright-infringement.html (accessed: 15.01.2023); cf. *Damien Hirst Plagiarised My Pill Bracelet Says Canadian Artist Colleen Wolstenholme,* 6 August 2016, "Artlyst", www.artlyst.com/news/damien-hirst-plagiarised-my-pill-bracelet-says-canadian-artist-colleen-wolstenholme/ (accessed: 15.01.2023).

59 *Van Cleef Arpels Logistics, S.A. v. Jewelry*, 547 F. Supp. 2d 356 (S.D.N.Y. 2008). K. Martens, *The Crown Jewels: How to Protect Your Jewelry Design*, 18 January 2019, www.jdsupra.com/legalnews/the-crown-jewels-how-to-protect-your-46967/ (accessed: 15.01.2023).

60 K. Martens, *The Crown . . .*

61 *Todd v. Mont. Silversmiths*, 379 F. Supp. 2d 1110 (D. Colo. 2005).

62 Examining each element in turn, Defendants assert[ed] that:

> The wire twist, shape of the barbs, end caps, ear posts, and earring clasps are unprotectable because they are based on functional or utilitarian considerations.
>
> The placement of the barbs and the spacing between them is dictated by elemental symmetry and is unprotectable as expression inherent in the idea of barbed-wire jewelry.
>
> The size and shape of Plaintiff's jewelry are based on common 'cuff-style' and 'hoop-style' designs which exist in the public domain.
>
> The use of silver wire rather than steel is unprotectable because a change of medium does not qualify for copyright protection.
>
> Todd v. Mont. Silversmiths, 379 F. Supp. 2d 1110, 1112 (D. Colo. 2005)

Item of note 4.3 (Continued)

plaintiff took the *holistic approach (gestalt theory)*,[63] meaning that "copyright can reside in a work's 'creative gestalt' – a certain ineffable quality which is incapable of objective description".[64] The court reconciled these two theories adhering to the *Yurman Design* approach.

The District Court in California gave a decision on 5 April 2004 on the "Plumeria Lei Series" noting that, in this case, the design was eligible for protection. Regardless of prior copyright registration,[65] the court noted that the designer was the first to apply this combination of finishes (e.g. sand-blasted finish on the petals with petal's curl having a highly polished raised edge). The plaintiff submitted a botanist expert's academic opinion advocating for originality of the Plumeria blossom interpretation and pointed to a list of 11 features that were considered copied.

4.2.2.3 Letters and logos

A mere simplistic arrangement of non-protectable elements does not demonstrate the level of creativity necessary to warrant protection.[66] For example, the US District Court for the Southern District of New York upheld the Copyright Office's refusal to register simple designs consisting of two linked letter "C" shapes "facing each other in a mirrored relationship" and two unlinked letter "C" shapes "in a mirrored relationship and positioned perpendicular to the linked elements".[67]

In the US law, it is assumed that a mere simplistic arrangement of non-protectable elements does not demonstrate the level of creativity necessary to warrant protection, especially when neither the work's individual elements nor the work as a whole exhibit copyrightable authorship. Registration was denied to the Thomas Burberry monogram ("TB Diamond Logo"),[68] the "Tommy Hilfiger Flag",[69] and the "Adidas 3-Bars logo".[70]

63 This theory was also rejected in *DBC of New York, Inc. v. Merit Diamond Corp.*, 768 F. Supp. 414 (S.D.N.Y. 1991).

64 *Todd v. Montana Silversmiths, Inc.*, 379 F. Supp. 2d 1110, 1112 (D. Colo. 2005).

65 Plaintiff obtained Copyright Registration Number VA 804–690 for the Plumeria Lei Series, effective 14 October 1997, and Supplemental Copyright Registration no. VA 1–006–840, for the Plumeria Lei Series, effective 1 June 2000.

66 Jankowska, Meghaichi, Pawełczyk, *Illustrated Fashion Law*.

67 *Coach, Inc. v. Peters*, 386 F. Supp. 2d 495, 496 (S.D.N.Y. 2005).

68 Re: Second Request for Reconsideration for Refusal to Register TB Diamond Logo (Correspondence ID: 1–42UMH5I; SR # 1–8313812653), 16 June 2021, p. 4, www.copyright.gov/rulings-filings/review-board/docs/tb-diamond-logo.pdf (accessed: 19.01.2023).

69 Re: Second Request for Reconsideration for Refusal to Register "Tommy Hilfiger Flag"; Correspondence ID: 1–33DWZTC; SR 1–4413364221, 15.03.2019, p. 5, www.copyright.gov/rulings-filings/review-board/docs/tommy-hilfiger-flag.pdf (accessed: 19.01.2023).

70 Re: Second Request for Reconsideration for Refusal to Register Adidas 3-Bars logo Correspondence ID: 1 -KN3QOX, 20.04.2016, pp. 3–4, www.copyright.gov/rulings-filings/review-board/docs/adidas-3-bars.pdf (accessed: 20.01.2023).

Graphical elements appearing on clothing have occasionally been granted copyright protection.[71] There was an interesting case, *I.C. ex rel. Solovsky v. Delta Galil USA*, regarding a hand-drawn design consisting of "Hi" with a smiley face on the front of a T-shirt and "Bye" with a frowning face on the back. The Copyright Office denied the registration of the "Hi/Bye" design pointing out that "the amount of creative input by the author required to meet the originality standard is low, it is not negligible".[72]

4.2.2.4 Textiles

The Copyright Office's regulations bar the registration of ***familiar designs*** (including common patterns), simple combinations of ***basic geometric shapes***, and ***mere variations of colouration***.[73] The Compendium offers a clear-cut explanation "in all cases, a visual art work must contain a sufficient amount of creative expression. Merely bringing together only a few standards forms or shapes with minor linear or spatial variations does not satisfy this requirement".[74]

In the "Pendry Plaid Pattern" case, the Copyright Office noted that

> the Work's individual elements consist of straight lines, which are common, familiar shapes, combined in a repeating pattern with predictable, repetitive spacing to form a standard, garden-variety plaid pattern, which is a basic fabric design configuration. As such, the Work falls squarely into the category of works lacking sufficient creativity to support a claim of copyright. The combination of black, white, and gray colors do not raise the design into copyrightability.[75]

The Copyright Office juxtaposed it with the *Covington*[76] pattern that

> consists of lines in at least five different colors, including several that are arranged at 45 degree angles, which are themselves made up of small intersecting segments, creating a "basket weave." Nor is the spacing

71 Including uniforms, see *Knitwaves, Inc. v. Lollytogs Ltd.*, 71 F.3d 996, 1004 (2d Cir. 1995); *Silvertop Assocs. v. Kangaroo Mfg.*, no. l:17-cv-7919, 2018 U.S. Dist. LEXIS 89532, *16 (D.N.J. May 29, 2018); *MPD Accessories B. V. v. Urban Outfitters*, 111 U.S.P.Q. 2d 1211, 1217 (S.D.N.Y. 2014); *In Design v. Lynch Knitting Mills, Inc.*, 689 F. Supp. 176, 178–79 (S.D.N.Y. 1998), aff'd, 863 F.2d 45 (2d Cir. 1988).

72 *Ellen Solovsky* v. *Delta Galil USA and Sock Drawer*, LLC, 14 Civ. 7289 (GHW), Statement of Interest on Behalf of the U.S. Copyright Office, as of 5 July 2016, www.copyright.gov/rulings-filings/411/solovsky-v-delta-galil-usa-no-14-cv-7289--sdny-july-5-2016.pdf (accessed: 30.01.2023).

73 Jankowska, Meghaichi, Pawełczyk, *Illustrated Fashion Law*.

74 COMPENDIUM (THIRD) §§ 313.4(J), p. 905.

75 Second Request for Reconsideration for Refusal to Register Pendry Plaid Pattern (Black and White) (Correspondence ID: 1-3ZD84RU; SR # 1-8337057171), 21 July 2021, p. 4, www.copyright.gov/rulings-filings/review-board/docs/pendry-plaid.pdf (accessed: 28.01.2023).

76 *Covington Indus., v. Nichols*, Case no. 02 Civ. 8037, 2004 U.S. Dist. LEXIS 6210, at *7–11 (S.D.N.Y, 5 April 2004).

> between each segment of the design entirely uniform . . .. Thus, because the *Covington* fabric design incorporates different colors and utilizes varied spacing and a basket weave effect that is not expected in a common plaid design, it is distinct from the Work, which merely consists of seven overlapping horizontal and vertical lines, arranged in a mirror image configuration with a black, white, and grey color scheme.[77]

While the court did find that particular design to be protectable, it noted the particular "use and arrangement" of stripes, colours, and basket weave (in particular the basket weave effect, which the court observed "has not previously been incorporated into a plaid") along with an unusual 17-inch repeat and specific "choices as to the width and spacing of the various stripes as well as the manner in which to incorporate color".[78]

For the "Bowtie Pattern" work, the Review Board denied copyright registration as a "2-D artwork" on the ground that "every bowtie is in the same size, color, and orientation".[79] As for the "Server Uniform" (consisting of a top, a skort and a shield patch), the Review Board noted that it constituted "a useful article that does not contain any copyrightable authorship needed to sustain a claim to copyright".[80] The "Tartan Fabric Design" was denied protection as it is a "common plaid pattern, similar in composition to the well-known Royal Stewart tartan. The red, blue, yellow, white, and black colors do not raise the design into copyrightability".[81] The outcome was similar for "Hastens Sangar AB Fabric Pattern", which, in the Copyright Office's view, was "a simple combination of basic geometric shapes and mere variations of coloration".[82] The "Yampa" pattern, a configuration of pyramid structures and diagonal columns of flowers, was deemed copyrightable. The board noted that "although pyramids are common and familiar geometric shapes not themselves copyrightable . . . Yampa's specific combination of elements, including its spacing variations and interior stitching" demonstrates

77 Second Request for Reconsideration for Refusal to Register Pendry Plaid Pattern, p. 5.

78 *Covington Indus., v. Nichols*, at *9–11.

79 Second Request for Reconsideration for Refusal to Register Bowtie Pattern; Correspondence ID: 1-GLPNWV, 24 August 2016, www.copyright.gov/rulings-filings/review-board/docs/bowtie-pattern.pdf (accessed: 03.01.2023).

80 Second Request for Reconsideration for Refusal to Register Tilted Kilt Server Uniform Applied Artwork (SR 1–4798347915) and Tartan Fabric Design (1–4798347471); Correspondence IDs: 1–2TVWFAG, 1–3B324D9, 2 January 2020, p. 3, www.copyright.gov/rulings-filings/review-board/docs/tilted-kilt-server-uniform.pdf (as of 3.1.2023).

81 Op. cit., p. 6.

82 Second Request for Reconsideration for Refusal to Register Hastens Sangar AB Fabric Pattern (repeating two-dimensional fabric pattern); Correspondence ID: 1–2BDGRHF; SR 1–4268431251, 5 October 2018, p. 4, www.copyright.gov/rulings-filings/review-board/docs/hastens-sangar-fabric-pattern.pdf (accessed: 03.01.2023).

the modicum of copyrightable authorship.[83] The "Updraft" design, however, was denied protection on the ground of being a derivative work not containing a sufficient amount of original expression, as it does not add any copyrightable elements to the prior product.[84]

The Review Board granted copyright protection to the "Staggered Carbon" pattern as it agreed the work was original; however, it made clear that "that registration covers only the original and creative features displayed in the Work, and not standard designs or other unoriginal elements".[85] Therefore, the copyright protection does not cover the woven patterns and carbon fibre appearance, nor does it extend to processes, systems, or methods embodied in the work. "Gold Wood" was denied protection as it was "made up of only a very few elements (monochromatic lines in a few shades of gold) arranged in an unoriginal manner (densely and with only minor and repeating variations throughout the pattern)".[86]

Based on the assumption that copyrighted shapes cannot be too simplistic, the Review Board denied the registration of a placemat consisting of rows of "U"-shaped holes ("Bellagio Pressed Vinyl Placemat").[87] An exemplary level of creativity regarding geometric shapes is set out by the Copyright Office in its compendium by making reference to a wrapping paper consisting of multiple geometric shapes whose display is not preordained or obvious.[88]

83 Second Request for Reconsideration for Refusal to Register ZX2 Yampa/Light Beam, Correspondence ID 1–25KFE2N, SR 1–3815608161; and Updraft Ecotread X2/Yellow Beams, Correspondence ID 1–25KFE2N, SR 1–3775632401, 31 January 2018, p. 5, www.copyright.gov/rulings-filings/review-board/docs/zx2-yampa-light-beam-and-ecotred-x2-yellow-beams.pdf (accessed: 03.01.2023).

84 Op. cit., p. 4, "Special caution is appropriate when analyzing originality in derivative works, 'since too low a threshold will give the first derivative work creator a considerable power to interfere with the creation of subsequent derivative works from the same underlying work.' " ' *We Shall Overcome Found. v. The Richmond Org., Inc.*, 16-cv-2725, 2017 WL 3981311, at *13 (S.D.N.Y. Sept. 8, 2017). Cf. *Diamond Direct, LLC v. Star Diamond Group*, 116 F.Supp.2d 525, 529 (S.D.N.Y. 2000) (considering the originality of diamond ring designs as a derivative work of authorship).

85 Second Request for Reconsideration for Refusal to Register "Gold Wood"; Correspondence ID: 1–26ELC75, SR# 1–3400883831; and "Staggered Carbon"; Correspondence ID: 1–1USZPC3, SR# 1–3391838351, 25 October 2017, p. 3, 6, www.copyright.gov/rulings-filings/review-board/docs/gold-wood-and-staggered-carbon.pdf (accessed: 04.01.2023).

86 Op. cit., p. 6.

87 Re: Second Request for Reconsideration of Refusal to Register "Bellagio Pressed Vinyl Placemat"; Correspondence ID: 1–2S415K5; SR 1–5296636621, 4 December 2018, pp. 5–6, www.copyright.gov/rulings-filings/review-board/docs/bellagio-pressed-vinyl-placemat.pdf (accessed: 27.01.2023).

88 COMPENDIUM (THIRD) § 906.1, www.copyright.gov/comp3/chap900/ch900-visual-art.pdf (accessed: 27.12.2021).

Several other cases found patterns eligible for copyright protection, including *Primcot*,[89] *MPD Accessories B.V.*,[90] *Nicholls*,[91] *Sunham Home Fashions*,[92] *L.A. Printex*,[93] *Mannington Mills*,[94] *Odegard*,[95] *Malibu Textiles*[96] and *Textile Innovations*.[97] Even though copyright law does not protect common shapes, they can be protected for their unique representation: *Star Fabrics*.[98]

4.2.2.5 Gloves and shoes

The Review Board declined to grant protection for "Overlay for Glove" on the ground it was a 'useful article' that does not contain any separable features that are copyrightable and that it does not cross the threshold of protection.[99]

89 *Primcot Fabrics, Dep't of Prismatic Fabrics, Inc. v. Kleinfab Corp.*, 368 F. Supp. 482, 484–85 (S.D.N.Y. 1974) (protecting a fabric pattern that consisted of "eight squares, each square containing a distinctive design in a different color with a background of varying colors").

90 *MPD Accessories B.V. v. Urban Outfitters*, no. 12 Civ. 6501, 2014 U.S. Dist. LEXIS 74935, at *15 (S.D.N.Y. May 30, 2014) (protecting a fabric design that consisted of numerous unevenly spaced lines of varying widths and colors laid out in varying angles).

91 *Nicholls v. Tufenkian Import/Export Ventures, Inc.*, no. 04 Civ. 2110 WHP, 2004 WL 1399187 (S.D.. Y. June 23, 2004) (the court observed that the circles arranged on a grid had unique shading, and were not arranged in a repeating pattern, but rather "four and three quarter rows" of four circles each).

92 *Sunham Home Fashions v. Pem-America, Inc.*, 2002 U.S. Dist. LEXIS 24185 (S.D.N.Y. Dec. 17, 2002) (the court found plaid and floral quilts copyrightable due to the "careful thought [that] went into the colors used, the size of the shapes in the designs and the spacing of the designs' patterns", at p. 19).

93 *L.A. Printex Industries, Inc. v. Aeropostale, Inc.*, 676 F.3d 841, 850 (9th Cir. 2012) (concluding that the plaintiff's selection, coordination and arrangement of a "repeating pattern of bouquets of flowers and three-leaf branches" was "original").

94 *Home Legend, LLC v. Mannington Mills, Inc.*, 784 F.3d 1404 (11th Cir. 2015) ("The copyright at issue in this case covers Mannington's décor paper design called 'Glazed Maple,' which is a huge digital photograph depicting fifteen stained and apparently time-worn maple planks").

95 *Odegard, Inc. v. Costikyan Classic Carpets, Inc.*, 963 F.Supp. 1328, 1335 (S.D.N.Y. 1997) (holding that the "plaintiffs' arrangement of [eight-pointed] motifs [on the carpet] . . . would be sufficiently original to be copyrightable" even if the motifs themselves were not protectable.

96 *Malibu Textiles, Inc. v. Carol Anderson, Inc.*, no. 07Civ. 4780, 2008 WL 2676236 (S.D.N.Y. 8 July 2008) (granting partial summary judgement as to liability for copyright infringement of a "floral lace design").

97 *Textile Innovations, Ltd. v. Original Textile Collections, Ltd.* no. 90 Civ. 6570, 1992 WL 125525. at *5 (S.D.N.Y. May 26, 1992) (finding that plaintiff has valid and enforceable copyright in a floral pattern).

98 *Star Fabrics, Inc. v. DKJY, Inc.*, no. 2:13-cv-07293-ODW(VBKx), 2014 U.S. Dist. LEXIS 2775, at *15 (C.D. Cal. Jan. 9, 2014) (noting that the copyright owner did not own a copyright in the chevron design itself, just in the way the pattern was uniquely represented with "purple, violet, and black undulating lines in a distorted chevron pattern. White, purple, and salmon dots are nestled within the waves").

99 Second Request for Reconsideration for Refusal to Register Overlay for Glove; Correspondence ID: 1-2V1EUOL; SR 1-4260743051, 27 February 2019, p. 2, www.copyright.gov/rulings-filings/review-board/docs/glove-overlay.pdf (accessed: 03.01.2023).

The Review Board considered Snickers eligible for copyright protection as '2-D artwork' and 'sculpture'. It observed that the works, as a whole, contain a sufficient amount of original and creative authorship. The decision did not extend to any specific features, such as lines, stripes or swirl designs.[100]

Yeezy Boost 350 Version 1's design consists of irregular black lines of various lengths and shapes on a grey fabric with a black semi-circle in the arch and an orange dotted stripe on an off-white heel loop. Yeezy Boost 350 Version 2's design includes several grey lines in a wave pattern with a thick orange stripe on the outsole that fades toward the heel of the sneaker. Underneath Yeezy Boost 350 Version 2's outer cloth layer is an inner orange layer that adds intermittent orange colouring.[101]

4.2.3 Originality and substantial similarity test

In the US, like in any other legal system, it must initially be demonstrated that a work is sufficiently original to warrant copyright protection. This requisite level of creativity is very low, to the extent that a work may be entirely a compilation of unprotectable elements and still acquire the protection.[102]

The test used in the courts in cases regarding plagiarism or copying is the substantial similarity test, that consists of two steps of proving that:

1 The defendant has actually copied the plaintiff's work or had access to the copyrighted work,
2 The copying is illegal because a substantial similarity exists between the defendant's work and the protectable elements of the plaintiff's work.

In most cases, the test for substantial similarity is the *ordinary observer test*, which gauges whether the average lay observer would find that the defendant appropriated the copy at issue from the copyrighted work. Importantly, when a work comprises both protectable and unprotectable elements, a court should apply the *more discerning ordinary observer test* by attempting to eliminate the unprotectable elements from gauging and comparing only the protectable elements for substantial similarity. In the *Wolstenholme* case, the Court of Appeals decided that

> the plaintiff must show that the defendant appropriated the plaintiff's particular means of expressing an idea, not merely that he expressed the same idea. The means of expression are the 'artistic' aspects of a

100 Second Request for Reconsideration for Refusal to Register Yeezy Boost 350 Version 1, Yeezy Boost 350 Version 2; Correspondence ID: 1–390ELT5; SR #s 1–4601414311, 1–4600937107, 8 May 2019, p. 2, www.copyright.gov/rulings-filings/review-board/docs/yeezy-boost.pdf (accessed: 13.01.2023).

101 Jankowska, Meghaichi, Pawełczyk, *Illustrated Fashion Law*.

102 See *Yurman Design, Inc. v. PAJ, Inc.*, 262 F.3d 101, 109 (2d Cir. 2001); *Knitwaves, Inc. v. Lollytogs Ltd. (Inc.)*, 71 F.3d 996, 1003–04 (2d Cir. 1995).

> work; the 'mechanical' or 'utilitarian' features are not protect[a]ble . . .. Where, as here, we compare products that have both protect[a]ble and unprotect[a]ble elements, we must exclude comparison of the unprotect[a]ble elements from our application of the ordinary observer test.[103]

This more discerning ordinary observer test does not change the degree of similarity required, only what elements of the works are being compared.[104] Like the ordinary observer test, the more discerning ordinary observer test still considers the work's *'total concept and feel'*. It was observed that "through *Knitwaves*, the Second Circuit has recently reconfirmed that the more discerning ordinary observer test is not an invitation to dissect a work into its constituent elements or features. The works as a whole must be compared to each other".[105]

There was a valid discussion as to whether issues of *access* and *substantial similarity* are findings of fact or questions of law, which concluded that they are the former.[106]

4.2.4 Two-part test: extrinsic and intrinsic

The US courts apply a two-part test, an extrinsic test and an intrinsic test, to compare the similarities of ideas and expression in two works. This is part of the "filtration" process established by the Ninth Circuit to determine or assess "substantial similarity". This process of deduction was well explained in the *Idema* case: the "extrinsic" test "objectively considers whether there are substantial similarities in *both* ideas and expression".[107] This is then followed by the second step of this analysis: the "intrinsic," or "subjective" test, which measures substantial similarity in the "total feel and concept of the works".[108] Under the "extrinsic" test, generally a court will maintain the so-called analytic dissection, which is a process wherein each of the "constituent elements" of the copyrighted work(s) are isolated, to the exclusion of other elements, combinations of elements or types of expression therein.[109] In other words, "analytic dissection" requires breaking each work covered by copyright down into its constituent elements, and comparing only those "elements" for proof

103 *Wolstenholme v. Hirst*, 271 F. Supp. 3d 625, 637 (S.D.N.Y. 2017).

104 *Wolstenholme v. Hirst*, 271 F. Supp. 3d 625, 637 (S.D.N.Y. 2017).

105 *Wolstenholme v. Hirst*, 271 F. Supp. 3d 625, 637 (S.D.N.Y. 2017).

106 *Kepner-Tregoe, Inc. v. Leadership Software*, 12 F.3d 527 (5th Cir. 1994).

107 *Apple Computer, Inc. v. Microsoft Corp.*, 35 F.3d 1435 (9th Cir. 1994) (emphasis in original); see *Smart Inventions, Inc. v. Allied Communications Corp.*, 94 F. Supp. 2d 1060, 1065 (C.D. Cal. 2000).

108 *Data East USA, Inc. v. Epyx, Inc.*, 862 F. 2d 204, 207 (9th Cir. 1988); It asks "whether the ordinary, reasonable person would find the total concept and feel of the works to be substantially similar".

109 *Dr. Seuss Enterprises, L.P. v. Penguin Books USA, Inc.*, 109 F.3d 1394, 1398 (9th Cir. 1997), n. 3.

of copying as measured by "substantial similarity." It is the copyright plaintiff's burden to identify the "elements" for the purposes of this comparison. The court is obliged then to apply the relevant limiting doctrines in the context of the particular medium involved, through the eyes of the "ordinary consumer of that product".[110] Finally, having dissected the alleged similarities and considered the range of possible expression, the court must define the scope of the plaintiff's copyright – that is, decide whether the work is entitled to 'broad' or 'thin' protection. The "scope of protection" sets the appropriate standard for a subjective comparison of the works "as a whole" to determine whether they are sufficiently similar. Where a copyrighted work is composed largely of "unprotectable" elements, or elements "limited" by "merger," "*scènes à faire*," and/or other limiting doctrines, it receives a "thin" rather than a "broad" scope of protection.

The extrinsic test is an objective test based on specific expressive elements: the test focuses on "articulable similarities between the plot, themes, dialogue, mood, setting, pace, characters, and sequence of events" in two works. The intrinsic test is a subjective test that focuses on "whether the ordinary, reasonable audience would recognize the defendant's work as a 'dramatization' or 'picturization' of the plaintiff's work".[111] Summary judgements are issued based on extrinsic test only.

4.2.5 "Useful articles and separability" doctrine

4.2.5.1 After Star Athletica

Copyright protection does not extend to 'useful articles' as such, which are defined since 1976 in the US Copyright Act as "article[s] having an intrinsic utilitarian function that is not merely to portray the appearance of the article or to convey information" (17 U.S.C. § 101). Interestingly, however, artistic features applied to or incorporated into a useful article may be capable of copyright protection if they constitute pictorial, graphic, or sculptural works under sections 101 and 102(a)(5) of the Copyright Act. This protection is limited to the " 'pictorial, graphic, or sculptural features' [that] 'can be identified separately from, and are capable of existing independently of, the utilitarian aspects of the article' ". In order to draw the line between "works of applied art" and "industrial design not subject to copyright protection", a number of approaches were developed in order to interpret the test, including 1) the separability test: physical and conceptual[112]; 2) subjective concept by

110 These "limiting doctrines" include the "merger" and "*scènes à faire*" doctrines.

111 *Kouf v. Walt Disney Pictures & Television*, 16 F.3d 1042 (9th Cir. 1994).

112 J. Mencken, *A Design for the Copyright of Fashion*, "Boston College Intellectual Property & Technology Forum" 1997, 121210, p. 6; D. Nimmer [in:] M.A. Leaffer (ed.), *Understanding Copyright Law*, 7th ed., Carolina Academic, 2019, p. 241; *Fashion v. Cinderella Divine, Inc.*, 808 F. Supp. 2d 542, 2011 Copr. L. Dec. P. 30104, 100 U.S.P.Q.2d 1381 (S.D.N.Y. 2011), M. Chatterjee, *Conceptual Separability as Conceivability: A Philosophical Analysis*

Robert C. Denicola[113]; 3) temporal displacement by Jon O. Newman[114]; and 4) conception by Raymond M. Polakovic.[115] However, the flagship judgement regarding fashion design and the "useful article doctrine" was made in the *Star Athletica* case[116] that offered a "separability regularity test" often referred to in case law and in US Copyright Office decisions.

Trying to delineate both the utilitarian and artistic features of a work, the court examines whether the feature

> (1) can be perceived as a two- or three-dimensional work of art separate from the useful article and (2) would qualify as a protectable pictorial, graphic, or sculptural work – either on its own or fixed in some other tangible medium of expression – if it were imagined separately from the useful article into which it is incorporated.[117]

In the case *Star Athletica*, it was observed that, while useful articles as such are not copyrightable, if an artistic feature "would have been copyrightable as a standalone pictorial, graphic, or sculptural work, it is copyrightable if created first as part of a useful article".[118]

Based on this, there is a two-step test that requires to check whether the elements

1 meet the "separate identification" requirement, in other words, it is possible to spot "some two- or three-dimensional element that appears to have pictorial, graphic, or sculptural qualifies"[119];
2 have "the capacity to exist apart from the utilitarian aspects of the article", in other words, if the asserted features represent "an article that is normally a part of a useful article" then they are unprotectable by copyright.

---

of the Useful Articles Doctrine, "New York University Law Review", 2018, vol. 93, no. 3, pp. 559, 564; R.M. Polakovic, *Should the Bauhaus Be in the Copyright Doghouse – Rethinking Conceptual Separability*, "University of Colorado Law Review", 1993, vol. 64, no. 3, p. 875.

113 R.C. Denicola, *Applied Art and Industrial Design: A Suggested Approach to Copyright in Useful Articles*, "Minnesota Law Review", 1983, vol. 67, no. 4, p. 709; R.S. Brown, *Design Protection: An Overview*, "UCLA Law Review", 1987, vol. 34, no. 1341, p. 1350; this concept was applied in *Pivot Point v. Charlene Products, Inc.*, 372 F.3d 913 (7th Cir. 2004).

114 *Carol Barnhart Inc. v. Econ. Cover Corp.* – 773 F.2d 411 (2d Cir. 1985); Mencken, *A Design* . . ., p. 6.

115 M. Barrett, *Intellectual Property*, 2nd ed., The Emanuel Law Outlines Series, Wolters Kluwer Law & Business, 2008, p. 119; Raymond M. Polakovic, *Should the Bauhaus be in the Copyright Doghouse? Rethinking Conceptual Separability*, "University of Colorado Law Review", 1993, no. 64, pp. 871–73.

116 *Star Athletica, LLC v. Varsity Brands, Inc.*, 137 S. Ct. 1002, 1007 (2017). See also *Mazer v. Stein*, 347 U.S. 201 (1954) (holding ballet-dancer-shaped lamp base to be copyrightable).

117 COMPENDIUM OF U.S. COPYRIGHT OFFICE PRACTICES § 924 (3d ed. 2017), p. 1007.

118 *Star Athletica*, 137 S. Ct. at 1011.

119 *Star Athletica*, 137 S. Ct. at 1010.

Item of note no. 4.4 Useful article test by example of "Overlay for Glove"

The 'Work' was a three-dimensional sculptural work consisting of black moulded pieces that were an overlay on the palm of work gloves. The claim related to the overlay, not to the overall glove, or to other parts of the glove. Specifically, the Work consisted of six individual black pieces that were applied to the digit and hand areas of the back of the glove.

For the first step of the test, the Review Board examined the overall shape of the overlay panels, as well as the horizontal and diagonal cuts in the overlay (that is, both the two- and three-dimensional qualities of the Work). It also considered whether the three-dimensional qualities of the horizontal and diagonal cuts in the overlay's rubber contained copyrightable aspects. As for the second step, the board noted that the overlay lacks the capacity to exist independently of the utilitarian function of the work. It noted that "even when viewed separate from the glove, the shape of the overlay is dictated and constrained by its functional purpose; it is not possible to remove the shape of the overlay panels and leave any part of the overlay behind".[120]

The US Copyright Office is prolific at making furniture decisions based on the *Star Athletica* case. In the "Violet" decision, it was asserted that this work "displays sufficient separable and creative authorship" because 1) "the drawer and headboard designs can be perceived as two- or three-dimensional works of art separate from the useful article. The designs themselves are not useful but instead serve as pure ornamentation",[121] 2) "the separable portions of the design display creative authorship. They involve, as a whole, a host of elements in the headboard and drawers created from several different materials that are combined in a distinctive manner indicating some ingenuity".[122] But the protection is not warranted if the considered elements cannot be separated from the work without eliminating core utilitarian functions of the useful article itself. On the other hand, if the shape was separable, it would have to prove sufficiently creative in order to support a claim to copyright. On

120 Second Request for Reconsideration for Refusal to Register Overlay for Glove . . . , p. 7; *Star Athletica*, 137 S. Ct. at 1013–14.

121 Re: Second Request for Reconsideration for Refusal to Register Violet (Correspondence ID: 1-480TQEL; SR 1-7948240619), 26 July 2021, p. 2, www.copyright.gov/rulings-filings/review-board/docs/violet.pdf (accessed: 20.01.2023); COMPENDIUM OF U.S. COPYRIGHT OFFICE PRACTICES § 924.3(A) (3d ed. 2021) (noting that "an artistic pattern woven into a rug" and "an artistic print on wrapping paper or a paper bag" are examples of features that are typically separable).

122 Op. cit., p. 3.

these grounds the registration was denied for the bevelled wooden top of a television stand ("Walker Edison Furniture"),[123] the decorative contours and carvings on a locker ("Sculpture of Locker"),[124] the "Kitchen Helper Children's Stool",[125] a chandelier in a typical basic Flemish or Dutch style candelabrum shape ("Socorro Chandelier"),[126] a rectangular-shaped lamp ("TRIO Wall Sconce")[127] and Samsonite's bag in a raised scallop shell or clamshell-like design ("Cosmolite Design 3D").[128] In some cases the work did not even pass the first prong of the test, as the geometric elements were not separable from the useful work: "Celine Jewelry Armoire" ("Celine"), "Cabby Jewelry Armoire" ("Cabby"), "Landry Jewelry Armoire" ("Landry") and "Hillary Jewelry Armoire" ("Hillary").[129]

Taking the example of the "Crosshatch Band", it can be seen that the band's pattern was separable from the useful article but did not pass the originality test.[130]

As for fashion, there is a simple example of the application of these criteria for the "Air Mesh Tank Designs", a collection of six different-coloured tank

123 Re: Second Request for Reconsideration for Refusal to Register Walker Edison; Correspondence ID: 1–3VNFHPU; SR # 1–7896666711, 26.07.2021, p. 5, www.copyright.gov/rulings-filings/review-board/docs/walker-edison.pdf (accessed: 20.01.2023).

124 Re: Second Request for Reconsideration for Refusal to Register Sculpture of Locker (Correspondence ID: 1–3XNOMTF; SR # 1–8073830571), 19 July 2021, p. 6, www.copyright.gov/rulings-filings/review-board/docs/sculpture-of-locker.pdf (accessed: 20.01.2023).

125 Re: Second Request for Reconsideration for Refusal to Register Kitchen Helper Children's Stool (Correspondence ID: 1–30JN911, SR # 1–6843395721), 27 October 2021, p. 4, www.copyright.gov/rulings-filings/review-board/docs/kitchen-helper-childrens-stool.pdf (accessed: 20.01.2023).

126 Re: Second Request for Reconsideration for Refusal to Register Socorro Chandelier; Correspondence ID: 1–3S94EJ8; SR # 1–7777005741, 7 August 2020, p. 5, www.copyright.gov/rulings-filings/review-board/docs/socorro-chandelier.pdf (accessed: 25.01.2023). As it was made in a typical "rustic" or "industrial" style, its elements fell under the *scènes à faire* doctrine; cf. *Zalewski v. Cicero Builder Dev., Inc.*, 754 F.3d 95, 106 (2d Cir. 2014) (denying copyright protection for elements that are "features of all colonial homes, or houses generally").

127 Re: Second Request for Reconsideration for Refusal to Register TRIO Wall Sconce; Correspondence ID: 1–3HMG4FJ; SR # 1–6278787931, 25 June 2020, p. 5, www.copyright.gov/rulings-filings/review-board/docs/trio-wall-sconce.pdf (25.1.2023).

128 Re: Second Request for Reconsideration for Refusal to Register Cosmolite Design 3D, Correspondence ID: 1–3DW2EKU; SR 1–4444510923, 24 September 2019 p. 5, www.copyright.gov/rulings-filings/review-board/docs/cosmolite-design-3d.pdf (accessed: 25.01.2023).

129 Re: Second Request for Reconsideration for Refusal to Register "Celine Jewelry Armoire" (SR 1–4060952433), "Cabby Jewelry Armoire" (SR 1–4060952366), "Landry Jewelry Armoire" (SR 1–4060952319), and "Hillary Jewelry Armoire" (SR 1–4060952272); Correspondence ID 1–2VUCORF, 11 March 2019, p. 5, www.copyright.gov/rulings-filings/review-board/docs/celine-jewelry-armoire.pdf (accessed: 25.01.2023).

130 Re: Second Request for Reconsideration for Refusal to Register Garmin Switzerland GmbH – Watch Bands; Correspondence IDs: 1–32PXY25, 1–32QDQNC; SR 1–6171893851, SR 1–6077016811, 22 January 2019, p. 5, www.copyright.gov/rulings-filings/review-board/docs/garmin-switzerland-watch-bands.pdf (accessed: 27.01.2023).

tops with stacked curved lines outlining the collar and sleeve holes and stacked straight lines on the bottom of the garment.[131] The Review Board, applying both prongs of the test, concluded that 1) the features of the work that are blocks of colour and stripes "are separable graphic design elements applied to the surface of the Works", thus meeting the first condition and that 2) these blocks "are common and familiar geometric shapes, individually lacking the necessary creative authorship" to claim copyright registration.

By the example of "Clothing with a Stylized 'C' ",[132] it can be seen that a yellow and black sleeveless romper with a "C" shape over the left leg does not possess the requisite separable authorship to sustain a claim to copyright.[133] Though the colour blocks and the "stylized C" shape were separable elements applied to the surface of garments and had graphic qualities, they were not copyrightable. Neither was the curvilinear shape.

There are, however, records of cases in the US law that proved that combinations of shapes and lines are eligible for copyright protection.[134]

4.2.5.2 Before Star Athletica

Before the flagship *Star Athletica* judgement, the Copyright Office used to employ two tests to assess separability:

1 a test for physical separability – to satisfy this test, a useful article had to contain pictorial, graphic or sculptural features that could be "physically separated from the article by ordinary means while leaving the utilitarian aspect of the article completely intact"; the copyrightable elements had to

131 Re: Second Requests for Reconsideration for Refusal to Register Air Mesh Tank Designs; Correspondence IDs: 1–3REUKJ8; 1–3OI9MCY; 1–3PQMG23; 1–3S8DPIT SR Numbers: 1–6797687431; 1–6959663675; 1–6822495962; 1–6822496154; 1–6959663482; 1–6959663579, 20 October 2020, p. 5, www.copyright.gov/rulings-filings/review-board/docs/air-mesh-tanks.pdf (accessed: 25.01.2023).

132 Jankowska, Meghaichi, Pawełczyk, *Illustrated Fashion Law*.

133 Re: Second Request for Reconsideration for Refusal to Register *Clothing with a Stylized C* (SR # 1–5860747051; Corr. ID 1–38NLKUR); *Button Top Clothing with a Stylized "C"* (SR # 1–5885676411; Corr. ID 1–38NFXA4), 3 June 2019, p. 5, www.copyright.gov/rulings-filings/review-board/docs/clothing-with-a-styled-c.pdf (accessed: 27.01.2023).

134 *Silvertop Assocs. v. Kangaroo Mfg.*, 931 F.3d 215 (3d Cir. 2019); *Soptra Fabrics Corp. v. Stafford Knitting Mills, Inc.*, 490 F.2d 1092, 1094 (2d Cir. 1974); *Tennessee Fabricating Co. v. Moultrie Mfg. Co.*, 421 F.2d 279, 282 (5th Cir. 1970); *Concord Fabrics, Inc. v. Marcus Bros. Textile Corp.*, 409 F.2d 1315, 1316 (2d Cir. 1969); *In Design v. Lynch Knitting Mills, Inc.*, 689 F. Supp. 176, 178–79 (S.D.N.Y. 1988), cf. *Olem Shoe Corp. v. Wash. Shoe Co.*, no. 09–23494-CIV, 2011 U.S. Dist. LEXIS 138285 (S.D. Fl. 1 December 2011), *aff'd*, 591 F. App'x 873 (11th Cir. 2015) ("particular arrangement of different sized dots at varying distances along vertical and horizontal planes . . . it is not merely a uniform change in dimension, size, or proximity from some specifically identifiable polka-dot pattern that separately exists"); *Prince Group, Inc. v. MTS Prods.*, 967 F. Supp. 121 (S.D.N.Y. 1997) (irregularly shaped and shaded polka dots in several different colors); *Klauber Bros., Inc. v. Target Group*, no. 14 Civ. 2125 (S.D.N.Y. 16 July 2015) (lace textile design).

be able to be physically removed without altering the useful aspect of the article (e.g., a decorative hood ornament on an automobile – Copyright Office's example)[135];

2 a test for conceptual separability – to satisfy this test, a useful article had to contain pictorial, graphic or sculptural features that could be visualised, on paper or as a freestanding sculpture, as a work of authorship separate from the utilitarian aspect of the article (e.g. artwork printed on a t-shirt, beach towel, or carpet; a drawing on the surface of wallpaper; a floral relief decorating the handle of a spoon – Copyright Office's examples).[136]

The idea of conceptual separability was applied whenever physical separability was impossible. There is a good record of Copyright Office decisions in court cases where the test was applied.[137] In the decision regarding the "Experia Sock Design",[138] it was noted that

> while the design printed on the sock clearly lacks physical separable design elements, it is clear that the imprinted design is conceptually separable. . . . The geometric elements in the imprinted design are able to be visualized separately and independently from the clothing without destroying the basic shape of the sock or impairing its utilitarian features.

That the elements in this instance did not prove to be creative is a different matter.

4.2.6 US copyright doctrine's approach to fashion

The copyrightability of fashion is not a new topic. Protection specifically tailored for fashion design was discussed in the US Congress at least as early as 1914, when one Congressman noted,

> the trouble with this bill is that it is for the benefit of two parties; that is, the enormously rich who want to display their splendid apparel that they can wear in this country that the ordinary riff-raff ought not to be allowed to wear, and those rich concerns who have these extra and selected designers to design these special patterns for those elite.[139]

135 Compendium 924.2(A) (ed. 2014), www.copyright.gov/comp3/docs/compendium-12-22-14.pdf (accessed: 27.01.2023).

136 Compendium 924.2(B) (ed. 2014), op. cit.

137 *Inhale, Inc. v. Starbuzz Tobacco, Inc.*, 755 F.3d 1038, 1041 n.2 (9th Cir. 2014); *Custom Chrome, Inc. v. Ringer*, 35 U.S.P.Q.2d 1714 (D.D.C. 1995).

138 Re: Second Request for Reconsideration for Refusal to Register Experia Sock Design; Correspondence ID: 1–18TE4KP, 13 January 2017, p. 5, www.copyright.gov/rulings-filings/review-board/docs/experia-sock-design.pdf (accessed: 27.01.2023).

139 Hearings on H.R. 11321, 63d Cong. (1914); Ch. Cox, J. Jenkins, *Between the Seams, A Fertile Commons: An Overview of the Relationship Between Fashion and Intellectual Property,*

The main concern was that an overly protective model of copyright protection would create monopolies, hinder competition and therefore stifle the creativity of new fashion designers, while stimulating higher prices for apparel.[140] Therefore, the Congress and the Supreme Court, "have answered in favor of commerce and the masses rather than the artists, designers and the well-to-do".[141] In 1930, the House of Representatives passed the Design Copyright Bill (House Bill 11852), that could have covered fashion designers; however, the Senate limited its application to certain industries, which did not include fashion.[142]

Apparel designers have tried to obtain copyright protection arguing that apparel, similarly to jewellery, is a sculptural work. US law, despite protecting "applied art", has refused this protection based on the "useful article" argument, extending protection only to artistic elements that go beyond functionality.[143] It has therefore been emphatically noted by the Fashion Originators' Guild of America that

> It may be unfortunate – it may indeed be unjust – that the law should not thereafter distinguish between "originals" and copies; but until the copyright law is changed, or until the Copyright Office can be induced to register such designs, . . . they both fall into the public demesne without reserve.[144]

---

https://learcenter.org/pdf/Fashion&IP.pdf (accessed: 25.01.2023); Industrial Design Protection: Hearings Before the Subcomm. on Courts, Intellectual Property, and the Administration of Justice of the H. Comm. on the Judiciary, 101st Cong. 445–46 (1990).

140 Ch. Cox, J. Jenkins, *Between . . .*, cf. T.T. Ochoa, *What Is a "Useful Article" in Copyright Law after Star Athletica?*, "University of Pennsylvania Law Review", 2017, p. 110; L. Chickl, *Protection of Industrial Design in the United States and [in:] EU: Different Concepts or Different Labels?*, "The Journal of World Intellectual Property", 2013; J. Stronski, P. Chakrabarti, J. Parker, *The New Standard for Copyright Protection of Useful Articles: Star Athletica and Its Impact on the 3-D Printing Industry*, "BNA's Patent, Trademark & Copyright Journal", 2017, p. 3; G. Ghidini, *Sequential Cumulation of Copyright with Protection of Products of Industrial Design. A Critique, and an Alternative Proposal*, "Stockholm Intellectual Property Law Review", 2 February 2019, 6, www.stockholmiplawreview.com/wp-content/uploads/2019/12/Online_IP_nr-2_2019_A4.pdf (accessed: 25.01.2023).

141 Kieselstein-Cord v. Accessories by Pearl, 632 F.2d 989, 998 (Weinstein, J., dissenting) (2d Cir. 1980). 7 17 U.S.C. § 102(a) (2001); Ch. Cox, J. Jenkins, *Between . . .*

142 L.J. Hedrick, *Tearing Fashion Design Protection Apart at the Seams*, "Washington and Lee Law Review", 2008, no. 65, pp. 234–235; *The Vestal Bill for the Copyright Registration of Designs*, "Columbia Law Review", 1931, vol. 31, p. 477 no. 3–4.

143 Unless the shape of an automobile, airplane, ladies' dress, food processor, television set, or any other industrial product contains some element that, physically or conceptually, can be identified as separable from the utilitarian aspects of that article, the design would not be copyrighted under the bill.

H.R. REP. NO. 94–1476 at 55

144 Fashion Originators' Guild of Am., Inc., 114 F.2d, p. 84; cf. Millinery Creators' Guild, Inc., 109 F.2d at 177 (citing *Cheney Bros. v. Doris Silk Corp.*, 35 F.2d 279 (2d Cir. 1929)); *Cheney Bros. v. Doris Silk Corp.*, 35 F.2d 279 (2d Cir. 1929).

The need for creators to have an incentive to create was successfully used to obtain stronger protection in the music and film industries. For the fashion business it has been demonstrated that this reasoning does not hold. It is argued that, in fashion, the lack of protection can actually feed the creative process. As rightly noted by Ch. Cox and J. Jenkins,

> Fashion designers are free to borrow, imitate, revive, recombine, transform, and share design elements without paying royalties or worrying about infringing intellectual property rights . . .. With fashion, the constant frenzy of creation and imitation may actually drive rather than destroy the market for original goods. Perhaps the ubiquity of a design makes owning the original more desirable and prestigious. Perhaps designers recoup costs by marketing to high-end consumers who want the brand name and quality of the original, while knock-off goods serve those who would not buy couture anyway.[145]

This approach can, however, be juxtaposed with the stance that knock-offs of poor quality not only steal the designer's profits but also cause damage to their reputation. This strict approach led Congress in 2006 to consider an extra three years of copyright-like protection for original fashion designs. The bill (House Bill 5055),[146] along with others from 2007 (House Bill 2033[147] and Senate Bill 1957[148]), collectively referred to as "Design Piracy Bills", failed in Congress.[149]

4.3 Copyrightability of fashion DESIGN in the EU

4.3.1 Overview: AOIC mantra. EU – back door harmonisation

The issue of originality tests has been scarcely addressed by the EU directly[150] but has been subject to many debates before the Court of Justice of the EU (CJEU) (so-called back door harmonisation). The CJEU has established that

145 Cox, Jenkins, *Between* . . . ; cf. K. Raustiala, Ch. Sprigman, *The Piracy Paradox: Innovation and Intellectual Property in Fashion Design*, Virginia Law Review, 2006, vol. 92, 1687, 1691.

146 A Bill to Provide Protection for Fashion Design: Hearing on H.R. 5055 Before the Subcomm. on Courts, the Internet, and Intellectual Property of the H. Comm. on the Judiciary, 109th Cong. 2 (2006) (opening statement of Rep. Howard L. Berman, Ranking Member, Subcomm. on Courts, the Internet, and Intellectual Property), http://judiciary.house.gov/media/pdfs/printers/109th/28908.pdf (accessed: 25.01.2023); L.J. Hedrick, *Tearing Fashion* . . ., p. 218.

147 H.R. 2033, 110th Cong. (2007). The only difference between House Bill 2033 and House Bill 5055 is that House Bill 2033 names the proposed legislation the "Design Piracy Prohibition Act."

148 S. 1957, 110th Cong. (2007); "Design Piracy Prohibition Act".

149 For a complete list of bills submitted before 1979, *see* Rocky Schmidt, *Designer Law: Fashioning a Remedy for Design Piracy*, "UCLA Law Review", 1983, vol. 30, p. 861.

150 The EU undertook quite some effort to harmonize the concepts of originality relating to only three categories of work: computer software, databases and photographs. Cf. Ramón Casas Vallés, *The Requirement of Originality*, [in:] E. Derclaye (ed.), *Research Handbook on the Future of EU Copyright*, Edward Elgar, 2009, p. 130.

to be copyrightable, a work should bear its author's personal stamp, something that is achieved through free and creative choices.[151] CJEU has addressed this topic many times,[152] though only once, and indirectly, with regard to fashion works of authorship.[153] Steadily, but successfully, the CJEU is achieving a policy of European harmonisation of copyright premises.[154]

Item of note no. 4.5 AOIC mantra

The European approach to originality, which is based on an 'author's own intellectual creation', playfully but scintillatingly abbreviated by Karnell as the *'AOIC mantra'*, leaves room for co-existence with traditional national standards. Ramón Casas Vallés offers the more fully rounded perspective that it would be reasonable to harmonise the concept of originality. Given that this very concept is a touchstone of copyright protection, this should serve as a *symbol* that copyright law, in the opinion of that author, is currently lacking.[155] But does the stamp of personality or the 'AOIC mantra' not serve this purpose already? Consider that each of these core premises already allow for different interpretations from each other, and these differences can additionally vary across jurisdictions. Lawyers' desire to have a strong guiding principle can cause these core premises to become a kind of legal juju. But like any charm, this comes with the danger that the principles can be applied mindlessly with potentially arbitrary outcomes. So any attempt to further codify this matter is at risk of exchanging one juju for another, providing scope for yet more subjective interpretation.

As noted by A. Lucas, the urge to accommodate many genres of work has led to a shifting in the club's membership criteria, but to admit different concepts of originality would be like demagnetising a compass that is relied upon to provide

151 Mireille Van Eechoud, *Adapting the Work* [in:] M. Van Eechoud (ed.), *The Work of Authorship*, Amsterdam University Press, 2014, p. 162; cf. T. Dreier, G. Karnell, *Orginality of the Copyrighted Work*, ALAI, Congress of the Aegean Sea II, 19–26 April 1991, pp. 153–166.

152 The judgements include newspaper articles (Infopaq I), user interfaces (BSA (Case C-393/09 Bezpeˇcnostn ı softwarova ´ asociace – Svaz soft- warov ́e ochrany v Ministerstvo kultury [2010] ECR I-13971)), photos (Painer (Case C-145/10 *Eva-Maria Painer v Standard VerlagsGmbH and others*, 7 March 2013)), databases (Football Dataco (Case C-604/10 *Football Dataco Ltd and others v Yahoo! UK Ltd and others*, 1 March 2012)) and sporting events (Premier League (Cases C-403/08 and C-429/08 Football Association Premier League and others [2011] ECR I- 09083)).

153 GStar.

154 Cf. *Commission Staff Working Paper on the Review of the EC Legal Framework in the Field of Copyright and Related Rights*, Brussels, 19 July 2004, SEC (2004), p. 995.

155 Ramón Casas Vallés, *The Requirement . . .*, pp. 131–132.

guidance.[156] This vacuum, however, provides the incentive to look for new protection criteria. From the point of view of Ramón Casas Vallés, the introduction of new criteria would only prove that originality is a concept of variable geometry. It would also expose the vulnerability, which spends much of its existence buried behind courtroom doors, of the subject matter of copyright protection. Artistic works would "remain subject to a high standard of personal imprint", whereas factual or functional works would become subject to the criterion of " 'personalized intellectual effort' (that is not a copy with a reasonable quantum of creativity)".[157] As noted by Per Jonas Nordell, the "notion of originality is a fiction. It is a way to describe a very complex set of facts and considerations".[158] The notion has become redundant over the years since a philosophical understanding of it was offered in 1900. As Per Jonas Nordell puts it, 'originality' is "mainly just a matter of definition – a game of words. Originality is not static".[159] Therefore, the highly sought-after *juju* is the term 'originality'.

Fashion and industrial design have stirred some debate in the European literature, as D. W. F. Verkade, P. G. Hugenholtz and S. van Gompel undertook a deeper dive in this area of applied arts and exposed the problem from the perspective of Dutch law.[160] The last-named author has also rightly observed that these areas of creativity come perilously close to what we would consider a 'style'. This is especially true with regard to fashion, but the problem is too multifaceted to be addressed with a 'one-size-fits-all' solution. Here, we shed light on the practice of such European countries as UK, Italy, France, Germany, the Netherlands and Poland in order to gain a better understanding of the myriad of aspects that must be considered when deciding on the copyright protection of fashion design (and design as a whole) based on originality. It seems agreeable to note after Antoon Quaedvlieg that originality serves at least two functions: internal and external.[161] It is a delineator within the subject matter of copyright to choose which works from each category are granted protection. It allows also delineation of the copyright domain from other considerations. As for fashion and design, the question arises as to the overlapping natures of the copyright and industrial design regime and the ***doctrine of hyperfunctional design*** (fr. ***multiplicité des formes***).[162]

156 A. Lucas, Debate, ALAI Congress of the Aegean Sea II, p. 250.

157 Ramón Casas Vallés, *The Requirement . . .*, p. 131.

158 Per Jonas Nordell, *The Notion of Originality – Redundant or Not?*, NIR, 2001 p. 110.

159 P. 110; cf. Gunnar W.G. Karnell, *European Originality: A Copyright Chimera* [in:] *Intellectual Property and Information Law: Essays in Honour of Herman Cohen Jehoram*, Kluwer Law International, 1999, p. 206.

160 D.W.F. Verkade, *Annotation of Hoge Raad 29 December 1995 (Decaux v. Mediamax)* (in Dutch). NJ, 1996, p. 546; P.G. Hugenholtz, *Annotation of Hoge Raad 16 April 1999 (Biggott v. Doucal)*. NJ, 1999, p. 697, Stef van Gompel, *Creativity, Autonomy and Personal Touch. A Critical Appraisal of the CJEU's Originality Test for Copyright* [in:] M. Van Eechoud (ed.), *The Work of Authorship*, Amsterdam University Press, 2014, p. 112.

161 Antoon Quaedvlieg, *Overlap/Relationships between Copyright and Other Intellectual Property Rights* [in:] E. Derclaye (ed.), *Research Handbook on the Future of EU Copyright*, Edward Elgar, 2009, p. 483.

162 Quaedvlieg, *Overlap/Relationships . . .*, p. 494 et seq.

Interestingly, the Dutch copyright system proves to be one of the least restrictive. Not only is there no separate regulation for applied art (as there is in Italy), but there is also a very lenient understanding of the premises of creativity.[163] The only fashion design case decided by CJEU thus far was one referred by the Dutch jurisdiction.

4.3.2 *Italy*

4.3.2.1 *Overview: from severability to institutional theory. Italian reform*

According to Article 2, point 10 of the Italian Copyright Law (ICL),[164] copyright protection is granted to industrial design only if the work has inherent artistic value (it. le opere del disegno industriale che presentino di *per sé carattere creativo e valore artistico*). This feature is assessed using an objective test, in other words, leaving its functional aspect aside, as to whether the work receives recognition as a work of art in the cultural sector.

Item of note no. 4.6 Institutional theory

The institutional theory of art is applied in this regard. In other words, its artistic value is proven in the event of high opinions by art critics and based on exposure in museums and galleries. The name or reputation of the author, as well as the author's intention, is of no legal relevance. The work must possess not only creative quality but also artistic value. A reform to Italian law was made in 2001 by deleting from Article 2, point 4 the reference to works of art applied to industry and the criterion of separation on the one hand (more precisely "severability criterion", requirement of "scindibilità"), and, on the other hand, by introducing point 10.[165] The reform is related to the Italian approach

(*Continued*)

163 Cf. Antoon Quaedvlieg, *The Copyright/Design Interface in the Netherlands* [in:] E. Derclaye (ed.), *The Copyright/Design Interface: Past, Present, and Future*, Cambridge University Press, 2018, p. 49.

164 Law no. 633/1941.

165 Cf. Article 22 of Legislative Decree 95/2001 as of 2.02.2001; D.lgs. 95/2001 Gazzetta Ufficiale della Repubblica as of 4.04.2001, the so called: Design Directive; M. Panucci, *La nuova disciplina italiana dell'"industrial design"*, in Dir. Ind., 2001, pp. 313; O.F. Afori, *Reconceptualizing Property in Designs*, in "Cardozo Arts & Entertainment Law Journal", 2008, pp. 1133–1151; Margherita Rudian, *Il disegno industriale e la moda tra disciplina dei disegni e modelli e normativa sul diritto d'autore*, The Trento Law and Technology Research Group Student Papers Series Index, 2021, no. 63, https://iris.unitn.it/retrieve/handle/11572/300393/435817/LTSP_n._63.pdf (as of 27.01.2023); Roberto Caso, Giulia Dore, *Opere di disegno industrial tra creatività, neutralità e valore artistico: esercizi (e acrobazie) sulla quadrature del cerchio*, The Trento Law and Technology Research Group Student Papers Series Index, 2021, no. 40, https://zenodo.org/record/4518812#.Yhw-b7i1Q3UK (as od 27.01.2023); A. Vanzetti, V. Di Cataldo, Manuale di diritto industriale, VII edizione, 2012, p. 531; E. Varese, S. Barabino, *La tutela delle forme delle creazioni di moda: problematiche e prospettive* [in:] B. Pozzo, V. Jacometti (eds.), *Fashion law. Le*

Item of note 4.6 (Continued)

to cumulative copyright/industrial design protection, which, before Directive 98/71/EC, was excluded. After the reform, a work of applied art benefits from cumulative protection, but on different premises.[166] This approach was in line with Article 17 of Directive 98/71/EC that allowed the countries to designate "the extent to which, and the condition under which, such a protection is conferred, including a level of originality required". The *quid pluris* requirement avoided a complete overlapping of copyright protection with industrial design protection.

Before the reform, the Italian approach was very similar to the US one, as it afforded copyright protection only to those industrial design works whose artistic value could be appreciated *separately* from the industrial nature of the product to which it pertained. A product itself was excluded from the copyright protection unless the ornamentation on the product was creative and could be separated from the piece of work. In the Italian literature, it is noted that the separability test posed problems due to the necessity to interpret separation in the abstract. There was an ongoing debate over whether the divisibility between the artistic value and usefulness had to be material and achievable in practice, or could be only potential.[167] Vanzetti and Di Cataldo offered the approach that the premise of separability is fulfilled if the aesthetic aspect of a work could be appreciated in a context separate from the usefulness of the work, in which case the same aesthetic element could readily be applied to different products.[168] The separation theory refused protection to three-dimensional works, allowing only two-dimensional works to benefit. Moreover, whenever a work could not be "detached" from the industrial object, it was excluded from copyright protection.[169] The separation test did not prove

problematiche giuridiche della filiera della moda, Milano, 2016, p. 93 et seq.; A. Fittante, Lezioni di diritto industriale. Marchi, disegni e modelli, contraffazione e Made in Italy, Torino, 2020.

166 B. Ferraro, *Il controverso riconoscimento della tutela autorale all'opera di industrial design: il requisito del valore artistico*, master thesis, Università Degli Studi Di Trento, 2018/2019, www.studiotorta.com/wp-content/uploads/2019/12/beatrice-ferraro-il-controverso-riconoscimento-della-tutela-autorale-allopera-di-industrial-design-il-requisito-del-valore-artistico.pdf (accessed: 12.01.2023), p. 38.

167 B. Pasa, *Industrial Design and Artistic Expression: The Challenge of Legal Protection*, p. 100; S. Magelli, *Moda e diritti IP nella giurisprudenza italiana* [in:] Il Diritto Industriale, 2013, IV, p. 385; M. Bogni, *Moda e proprietà intellettuale, tra estetica e comunicazione* [in:] Il Diritto Industriale, 2013, IV, p. 329.

168 Pasa, *Industrial Design* . . ., p. 1001; cf. Vanzetti, Di Cataldo, *Manuale di diritto industriale*, Milan 012, p. 479.

169 B. Ferraro, *Il controverso riconoscimento della tutela autorale all'opera di industrial design: il requisito del valore artistico*, master thesis, Università Degli Studi Di Trento, 2018/2019, www.studiotorta.com/wp-content/uploads/2019/12/beatrice-ferraro-il-controverso-

helpful where *corpus mysticum* and *corpus mechanicum* merged, leaving the work without protection.

The "scindibile" theory seems to be an outcome of the Art Nouveau or Art Deco style (19th and 20th centuries) in furniture, which allowed for separate acknowledgement of an industrial object and the piece of art it incorporated. The modern design trend has proven that these two spheres blend on the one hand, but on the other hand, the separability test left many works of applied art lacking protection.[170] The wording of the Italian legal act was the result of the influence of Benedetto Croce's philosophy of art, according to which copyright was meant to cover intellectual works of 'pure arts' only.[171]

The introduction of Article 2, point 10 of the ICL triggered a question as to whether works of industrial design are really subject to a higher copyright tier that is the sum of "creative character" and "artistic value".[172] It has aroused a bewildered debate throughout Italy, which was aggravated by the fact that copyright protection has instead ended up granted to works with a much more modest (and in some cases almost non-existent) degree of creativity, such as a collection of jurisprudence maxims or culinary recipes.[173] The legal doctrine on the topic has, in fact, taken a variety of standpoints. Some scholars emphasised that the requirement of artistic value is too limiting, not substantiated, discriminatory and detrimental for the category of works of industrial design. This approach is based on the ground that the amendment lacks a well-founded motivation as to why specific categories of works and creators should be differentiated and enjoy copyright protection based on different thresholds of creativity.[174] The other standpoint accepts the specificity of design, where a piece of work might be intellectually loaded but not creative. This account is represented by Pellegrino, who points to the distinction between a "photographic work" and "simple photography"[175] as an example of varied protec-

---

riconoscimento-della-tutela-autorale-allopera-di-industrial-design-il-requisito-del-valore-artistico.pdf (accessed: 12.02.2022), p. 80.

170 Ferraro, *Il controverso riconoscimento . . .*, p. 79; M. Bosshard, *La tutela dell'aspetto del prodotto industriale*, G. Giappichelli Editore, 2015, p. 61.

171 B. Pasa, *Industrial Design and Artistic Expression: The Challenge of Legal Protection*, Koninklijke Brill NV, 2019, pp. 99–100.

172 Bosshard, *La tutela dell'aspetto . . .*, p. 64.

173 Ferraro, *Il controverso . . .*, p. 80; cf.

> In the past, I have always been struck by the singularity . . . inherent in the fact of seeing regularly exhibited in numerous and important museums . . . the most famous and appreciated works of industrial design, on one hand; on the other, of having to note that, despite this kind of consecration resulting from being housed in art temples, such works were, at least in Italy, excluded from the protection of copyright.
>
> G. Bonelli, Industrial design e tutela del diritto d'autore [in:] Dir. Aut., 2003, p. 497–498; trans. Sara Ricetti

174 M. Panucci, *La nuova disciplina . . .*, p. 313.

175 R. Pellegrino, *La nuova disciplina delle opere del disegno industriale* [in:] Giur. Comm., 2005, p. 82.

tion. Whereas the first category enjoys full copyright protection, the latter is instead subject to neighbouring[176] and minor rights.[177] This reasoning follows the idea that copyright protection should be confined to the works of design that are most deserving.[178]

B. Ferraro points out that there is a general anxiety that an extension of copyright scope such that it becomes less discriminatory, specifically, allowing for additional categories of product to be granted protection, would affect market competition and allow for monopolies of big companies that can afford to collaborate with the most respected and distinguished designers and would likely often choose to buy out the copyright. This would make market entry difficult for new and small competitors, who would not be able to survive in such circumstances. The industrial design sector, on the other hand, needs constant creative contributions and cannot risk the stagnation that could be caused by huge portfolios of potentially ancient copyright protections covering many everyday product categories.[179] As interestingly noted by Fabbio,

> an interest in the inclusion into the public domain also exists for design creations . . . ; and it regards economic, cultural and social interests, linked to the specific dynamics of entrepreneurial innovation and the evolution of taste in this sector.[180]

Ferraro claims that

> this assumption is supported by a number of observations. First, not all companies focus on design: many of them, in fact, are limited to pick up (and, therefore, imitate) forms and styles already present on the market, without altering them much. Yet, even these companies contribute to the economic system, responding to the demand of those consumers who show ordinary taste in their choices, preferring conventional and aesthetically not too innovative products. Therefore, to demand a continuous competition between companies, with an incessant experimentation of highly innovative design, would be unrealistic.[181]

176 Cf. Article 87 of ICL.

177 Cf. Article 92 of ICL.

178 FABBIO, Contro una tutela autoriale "facile" del design. Considerazioni a margine di una recente pronuncia della Cassazione tedesca (Bundesgerichtshof, sent. 13 novembre 2013 – "Geburtstagszug") e brevi note sul diritto italiano vigente, in Riv. Dir. Ind., 2015, LXIV, p. 45 et seq.

179 Ferraro, *Il controverso riconoscimento* . . ., p. 82; FITTANTE, Carattere creativo e valore artistico, nota a Trib. Monza, 16 July 2002, Ord., in Dir. Ind., 2003, pp. 58 et seq.; FABBIO, *Contro una tutela* . . . , p. 45.

180 FABBIO, *Contro una tutela* . . . , p. 45.

181 Ferraro, *Il controverso riconoscimento* . . ., p. 83.

Finally, allowing for copyrightability of design with a low bar to entry would negate the usefulness of industrial property protection.[182] The other argument for an elevated threshold of protection is the fact of rapidly changing trends that make a long period of copyright protection pointless and not tailored to the needs of the creator. The inclusion of the premise of 'artistic value' in the copyright debate will surely trigger the question of how it complies with the recent *Cofemel* and *Brompton* cases decided by CJEU[183].

4.3.2.2 Creative character and artistic value per se. Le Corbusier *case and the array of copyright theories*

Italian literature and jurisprudence have a good deal to tell about the premise of 'creative character', however without the benefit of a uniform angle. The analysis mostly builds on the ideas of the author's personality and originality juxtaposed to objective novelty.[184]

The aforementioned change to Italian law has challenged many distinguished Italian minds as to how the premise of "intrinsic artistic value" should be interpreted. The doctrine relies on the expression "in itself," explicitly mentioned in point 10 of Article 2 ICL.: 'the work of design, in order to be protected, must have an artistic value in itself', which is independent from the utilitarian value of the product and its industrial quality.[185] As for Italian jurisprudence, two consecutive verdicts of the Tribunale di Monza, from 23 April 2002[186] and 16 July 2002, offered two different angles on the criterion of separation. Interestingly, both concerned the famous Le Corbusier *chaise-longue* that had already been denied protection in 1994.[187] The Verdict of 23 April 2002 is particularly relevant, as it was the very first on the recognition of copyright protection to industrial design after the issuance of the legislative decree 95/2001. The court employed an argument that could be called syllogistic: the furniture designed by Le Corbusier and his co-authors, while it certainly presents originality and creative character, cannot be considered to

182 V. Di Cataldo, D. Sarti, M.S. Spolidoro, *Riflessioni critiche sul Libro Verde della Commissione della Comunità europea sulla tutela giuridica dei disegni industriali*, "Rivista di diritto industriale", 1993, pp. 55–56.

183 The *Cofemel* decision of 12 September 2019, C 683/17 and the *Brompton* decision of 11 June 2020, C 833/18; Carlo Sala, *Italy: Copyrightable Designs Under Italian Law*, 24 March 2021, www.mondaq.com/italy/copyright/1049974/copyrightable-designs-under-italian-law (accessed: 25.01.2023).

184 G. Sena, *Industrial Design*, Giuffrè, Milan, 1977, p. 30; G. Sena, *La diversa funzione ed I diversi modelli do tutela della funzione del prodotto* [in:] *Rivista di diritto industriale*, Wolters Kluwer, 2002, I, p. 577.

185 SPADA, Industrial design e opere d'arte applicate all'industria, (vol. II). Rivista di diritto civile, 2002; p. 267 et seq.

186 Verdict no. 200229; Trib. Monza, 23.04.2002, Ord., A. Fittante, Quale legittimità per il concetto di scindibilità in materia di tutela dell'industrial design?, in Dir. Aut., p. 433 et seq.

187 Pasa, *Industrial Design* . . ., p. 100, Cass. Civ. Sez 1, 10516/1994, Foro It., 1995, I, 810; AIDA 1995, 3014.

possess artistic value in itself and, therefore, does not merit copyright protection. The judge, in fact, admitted to having serious doubts about the possibility of ascribing artistic value to the previously mentioned products: he reiterated that it is not enough for an object to be original and aesthetically creative in order to be considered a work of figurative art comparable to works of art, rather it is necessary that its creative character totally transcend its practical function making it enjoyable in a manner independent from its material form. The works of design deserving copyright protection, therefore, are those that possess such high artistic and creative value as to appear enjoyable beyond their ordinary use and to draw them together with works of pure art.[188]

With the second verdict, issued on 16 July 2002, the Collegio di Monza ruled again at the request of the company Cassina Ltd. to obtain copyright protection for a series of furniture accessories based on Le Corbusier's original design. The court presented an angle that copyright protection cannot be assigned to any industrial design work that is simply original and aesthetically pleasing. It surely cannot be extended to works whose form can be easily mass produced and copied on a vast scale. The court put emphasis on the quality and mass production that detach the functional aspect from the aesthetic.[189]

Apart from the criterion of mass production, there are some other approaches. One relies on the idea of a 'superior aesthetic level' that can 'arouse aesthetic emotions'. This means that a work of applied art should be invested with a deeper meaning to obtain copyright protection. This approach is criticised for its subjectivity.[190] Another equates 'artistic value' with 'high-end products' or 'top-tier design' (it. *fascia alta del design*, whose quality can be perceived from recognition in artistic circles.[191] B. Farro points out that the Italian literature and courts have a good deal to say about the concept of

188 Ferraro, *Il controverso riconoscimento . . .*, p. 87. At that time, cumulative protection was denied in Italian law; therefore, the court made it clear that this type of work should be registered as an industrial design, which regime is more suitable for this category. Also, the shorter duration of protection is more valid. F. Cozzolino, *The Protection of Industrial Designs as Works of Applied Art in Italy and China. The Case of Ikea Systems B.V. v. Taizhou Zhongtian Plastic Co., Ltd.*, master's degree thesis, 2017/2018, pp. 39–40, http://dspace.unive.it/bitstream/handle/10579/13780/865808-1221351.pdf?sequence=2 (accessed: 13.01.2023).

189 Ferraro, *Il controverso riconoscimento . . .*, p. 88; Trib. Monza, 16 July 2002, Ord., A. Fittante, *Carattere creativo e valore artistico* [in:] Dir. Ind., 2003, p. 55 et seq. The bulk production was also addressed by the Court of Bari, that noted: "the mass- and large-scale production of a model excludes the artistic value . . . required by law for the extension of copyright protection to industrial design" Trib. Bari, 27 October 2003, Ord., in Sez. Spec. P. I., 2004, p. 2, "la produzione in serie e su vasta scala di un modello ne esclude il valore artistico . . . richiesto dalla legge per l'estensione al disegno industriale della tutela accordata dal diritto d'autore"; Ferraro, *Il controverso riconoscimento . . .*, p. 88.

190 M. Fabiani, *La protezione dell'opera d'arte applicata nella nuova disciplina del disegno industriale*, "Il diritti d'autore", 2002, vol. 73, p. 206, cf. Cozzolino, *The Protection of Industrial Designs . . .*, p. 41.

191 Trib. of Bologna judgement of 2 July 2008 [in:] *Rivista di diritto industriale*, 2009, II, p. 225.

recognition, and she proposes to put these approaches into two main streams. The first touches on the idea that an industrial design possesses artistic value only if it boasts an independent value within the art market. Massimo Montanari's view on "artistic value" is not merely based on reference to the principles of aesthetics but by perceiving the object as having its own commercial value on the art market.[192] He offers the angle that commercial value exists where the object has been made as a single piece or as part of a limited series of numbered creations; this, therefore, excludes from copyright protection so-called popular art, which consists of objects created by famous designers and architects but reproduced on an industrial scale. It is rarity, together with function and shape, that bestows the works with commercial value. *A contrario*, commercial accessibility deprives the work of this feature and excludes it from copyright protection. Based on this theory, the Panton Chair and Chaise Longue LC4 would not prove copyrightable.[193] There has been a series of verdicts (Bologna, Venice, Florence) based on this copyright concept supporting the view that a work of design must be a "unique piece of its kind" with its own commercial value (*aesthetic concept of art*) – recognition given by museums or trade fairs is not enough (cf. *institutional concept of art*).[194] The second approach offers to gauge "artistic value" through the lens of probability of forgery. It allows protection of design as a work of authorship in the event that a forged work is offered for sale in art circles. This approach does not extend to counterfeiting as such, which remains the domain of industrial property law.[195] It has been criticised on many grounds, mostly for the reason that a work should not be discriminated against based on the purpose of the work.[196] Also, it runs contrary to the principle of minimum harmonisation in EC law, as it excludes cumulation of protection in an even more radical way than the criterion of separation, in contrast with Directive 98/71/EC. Article 17 of the Directive, which allows for cumulative protection.[197]

The "creative character" of a work is the basic prerequisite for protection, but it represents a relatively low threshold of creativity. There are accounts that discuss the need to fulfil the additional premise of "artistic value" in order to obtain protection for designs under Italian law. In these accounts, it is noted that qualifying under this more elevated standard is more difficult.

192 M. Montanari, *L'industrial Design tra Modelli, Marchi di Forma, e Diritto d'Autore*, Rivista di Diritto Industriale, 2010, vol. LIX, pp. 7–25.

193 Ferraro, *Il controverso riconoscimento* . . ., p. 91.

194 Trib. Bologna, 08.09.2005, Ord., in Giur. Ann. Dir., 2006, 4983; Trib. Bologna, 30.03.2009, Ord., in Giur. Ann. Dir. Ind., 2009, 5416; Trib. Venezia, 15.12.2010, Ord., in Riv. Dir. Ind., 2011, p. 308; Trib. Firenze, 04.04.2011, Ord., in Riv. Dir. Ind., 2011, p. 308; see Ferraro, *Il controverso riconoscimento* . . ., pp. 91–92.

195 G. Ghidini, Spada, Industrial design e opere d'arte applicate all'industria, cit. p. 267 ss.; Ferraro, *Il controverso riconoscimento* . . ., p. 92.

196 SANNA, *Il messaggio estetico del prodotto*, cit., p. 81.

197 AUTERI, *Industrial design e opere d'arte applicate all'industria*, cit., p. 267 et seq.; Ferraro, *Il controverso riconoscimento* . . ., p. 93.

Item of note no. 4.7 Institutional, aesthetic and historical-cultural concept of art

There are at least three approaches that provide a deeper understanding of the premise: the *institutional concept of art*, the *aesthetic concept of art* and the *historical-cultural concept of art*. In other words, it is not about "typical creativity" but *quid pluris*, which means going beyond socio-cultural trends and putting some innovation into the process of creating.[198] As noted by Beatrice Ferraro, it is not enough for the work to be of a different shape or to be whimsical compared to others offered on the market, but it should introduce a new point of reference in design up to the point of constituting a new paradigm and triggering inspiration among future designers.[199] According to Morri's view, the work is expected to deviate from the known state of the art and to break with the existing cultural landscape.[200]

Bosshard offers an account that links the premise of 'artistic value' to the more general concept of culture, the fundamental manifestation of a given society; however, in order to be art, it is not enough that a work is a generic product of culture, it is necessary for it to be "historicized", that is, it has to become a testimony of civilisation and, therefore, a paradigm and a source of inspiration.[201] This interpretation of 'artistic value' lines up with the definition of 'cultural good' coined by the Hague Convention of 1954.[202] Bosshard takes an angle that only most successful works, arousing the interest of museums, public opinion and magazines, should enjoy copyright protection. There is a series of judgements in Milan and Bologna that follow this approach.[203]

4.3.2.3 *Iconic design cases: the Bauhaus lamp, FLOS, Panton Chair, Chase-longue LC4, Vespa*

On 18 June 2003, the Tribunale di Firenze adjudicated an interesting case concerning the table lamp designed by Wilhelm Wagner and Carl Jakob Kucker in 1924 (the work known as the *Bauhaus lamp*).[204] The lamp was held to be sufficiently creative and artistic to render copyright protection.

198 Ferraro, *Il controverso riconoscimento* . . ., p. 94; M. Fabiani, Rivoluzione nella protezione dell'arte applicata e del disegno industriale, in. Riv. Dir. Aut., 2001, cit., p. 189; cf. the *species ad genus* theory authored by Dalle Vedore, Dal modello ornamentale all'industrial design, cit., p. 342.

199 Ferraro, *Il controverso riconoscimento* . . ., p. 95.

200 F. Morri, *Le opere dell'industrial design tra diritto d'autore e tutela come modelli industriali: deve cambiare tutto perché (quasi) nulla cambi?*, "Riv. Dir. Ind", 2013, p. 177.

201 M. Bosshard, La tutela dell'aspetto del prodotto industriale, cit., pp. 72–73.

202 Ferraro, *Il controverso riconoscimento* . . ., p. 98.

203 Trib. Milano, 22 April 2010 (Soc. Antica Murrina Veneziana c. Soc. Cose Belle Cose Rare) [in:] Giur. Ann. Dir. Ind., 2011, p. 313 et seq.; Trib. Bologna, 30 August 2011 (Bisazza S.p.A. c. F.P. S.R.L.), [in:] Giur. Ann. Dir. Ind., 2012, pp. 463 et seq.; Ferraro, *Il controverso riconoscimento* . . ., p. 98.

204 *Bauhaus lamp* by Wilhelm Wagner and Carl Jakob Kucker designed 1923–1924, www.moma.org/collection/works/4056.

In the famous FLOS case regarding the Arco floor lamp, the Milan District Court decided in the judgement of 12 September 2012 that the design at issue was copyrightable as a 'high-end' work of art. In doing so, the court gave protection against a copycat lamp called 'Fluida' imported from China and marketed in Italy by Semeraro Casa e Famiglia SpA. The court, in order to assess the work's copyrightability, applied an objective test relying on the institutional theory of art.[205] The fact that the Arco lamp had been exhibited in the Museum of Modern Art collection, among other internationally renowned collections, was not of minor significance. It proved that a 'mere elegance and pleasantries of the form' were not adequate thresholds of protection.[206] All in all, the Milan Court pointed out that, based on the premise of 'artistic value', a work retains copyright protection only if it is of "consolidated and permanent representative and evocative character".[207]

Other objects granted the copyright protection in Italy were Arco floor lamp designed by Achille and Pier Giacomo Castiglioni in 1962; Panton Chair by Vitra designed in 1960, Chase-longue LC4 designed by Le Corbusier in 1928, and Vespa designed by Piaggio 1945–60.[208]

Similarly, copyright protection was granted to the Panton Chair by Vitra,[209] Chase-longue LC4 by Le Corbusier[210] and Vespa by Piaggio.[211]

4.3.2.4 *Threshold of 'artistic value' revisited:* Metalco *case and* Castiglioni Brothers *case (after* Cofemel*)*

In the recent *Metalco* judgement of the Italian Supreme Court as of 13 November 2015,[212] it was found that the concept of artistic value requires of a work to be endowed with a ***quid pluris***, an attribute which "enriches the

205 The case also triggered a debate as to whether the institutional recognition should be measured *ex ante* or *a posteriori*.

206 G. Spedicato, *Italy: Copyright Protection Only for 'High Level' Industrial Design*, Kluwer Copyright Blog, 11 October 2012, http://copyrightblog.kluweriplaw.com/2012/10/11/italy-copyright-protection-only-for-high-level-industrial-design/ (accessed: 18.01.2023). Cf. Judgement of the Court of Milan as of 8 February 2007, Riv. Dir. Ind. 2007, 11, p. 42.

207 Martino case, judgement as of 19 October 2007, pp. 6–7.

208 https://usa.flos.com/modern-floor-lamps, www.vitra.com/en-us/product/panton-chair?gclid=Cj0KCQiApL2QBhC8ARIsAGMm-KGw48PyKFsXjt7NQKy5PgNx-8uK9uaPwate4noN0OZUxCW2hy7qETMaAq-0EALw_wcB; www.architonic.com/en/product/cassina-lc4/1001968; www.vespa.com/pl_PL/ (accessed: 18.01.2023).

209 Judgement of the Court of Milan as of 18 January 2007, Riv. Dir. Ind., 2007, 11, p. 56 and Judgement of the Court of Milan as of 28 November 2006, Riv. Dir. Ind., 2006, p. 49.

210 Judgement of the Court of Milan as of 9 January 2004, no. 2311/2014; cf. judgement of the Court of Monza as of 15 July 2008.

211 Judgement of the Court of Torino as of 6 April 2017, no. 1900/2017; M. Bellia, *Comment on the Italian Supreme Court Decision "Vespa"*, International Review of Industrial Property and Copyright Law, 2018, no .49, pp. 373 and ff.

212 *Metalco* case. Decision of the Supreme Court of Cassation, I Civil Division (Suprema Corte di Cassazione, Sezione I Civile) 13 November 2015 – Case no. 23292/2015 *Metalco S.p.A. et al. v. City Design S.p.A.*; IIC 2016, 47:859–862; cf. M. Bellia, *Comment on "Metalco" – "Top Tier design", Copyright Protection, and the Assessment of the "Artistic Value" Requirement Under Italian Law. Decision of the Supreme Court of Cassation, I Civil Division 13*

functionality and mere aesthetic elegance of the object".[213] It also acknowledged the importance of an expert, in other words a technical consultant. The court assumed that Metalco's *Libre* product line of benches was insufficiently artistic to merit copyright protection. The court pointed out that the assessment of the "artistic value" should be made with reference to objective and subjective factors and listed these in a non-exhaustive manner.

The subjective factors imply that the premise of artistic value is met when

the industrial design is apt to raise aesthetic emotions,
the degree of creativity is higher,
the design transcends the functionality of the product but also gains separate and autonomous significance.

These factors do not stand alone because of judges' subjective sense of aesthetic, cultural background, artistic sensibility, taste perceptions, etc.

The court's guideline mentions objective parameters such as

(a) the recognition the design has received in the relevant cultural and institutional circles, revealed inter alia by exposure of the work in museums and exhibitions, its publication in non-commercial dedicated journals, participation in artistic events, awards received, reviews by experts in the relevant field, etc.;
(b) the commercialisation of the design in the art market and not just in purely commercial markets, or higher value gained by the design in the purely commercial market;
(c) creation of the design by a famous artist.

In the judgement of 15 February 2021 made by the Milan District Court, known as the *Castiglioni Brothers* case, the court did not reflect on the *Cofemel* case findings. It acknowledged the Castiglionis' lamp's artistic value instead and found the work at issue copyrightable[214] on the premise that

> the lamp . . . should be counted among the most relevant expressions of the design concepts, whose interest and aesthetic value still remains intact decades after its creation with confirmation of the specification

November 2015 – Case no. *23292/2015*, International Review of Industrial Property and Copyright Law, 2016, p. 875.

213 Cozzolino, *The Protection of Industrial Designs* . . ., p. 42.

214 Judgement of the District Court of Milan as of 15 February 2021, no. 1320/2021, RG no. 49527/2017; Report. no. 1052/2021; Riccardo Perotti, *The Court of Milan on the Impact of Cofemel on the Copyright Protection of Industrial Designs in Italy. A New CJEU Referral on the Horizon?*, 22 June 2021, https://iplens.org/2021/06/22/the-court-of-milan-on-the-impact-of-cofemel-on-the-copyright-protection-of-industrial-designs-in-italy-a-new-cjeu-referral-on-the-horizon/ (accessed: 25.01.2023).

representative capacity of an artistic taste that is able to differentiate this product from the congeries of design productions of ephemeral and ordinary conception.[215]

4.3.2.5 Jewellery: Martino *case*

The Tribunale di Venezia made a relevant judgement in the *Martino* case on 2 February 2004 regarding three pendants that were made inspired by works of Mirò, Picasso and Modigliani (collection "Linea Artisti").[216] The court found Martino's designs copyrightable and Gioielli & Magie's copies of these to be copycats infringing the plaintiff's rights. The court interestingly noted that the premise of 'artistic value' should be gauged in relation to the 'creative nature of the work', but insightfully added that the emotions the work is able to arouse should also be included in copyright assessment.[217] The case continued in the judgement of the Venice District Court on 19 October 2007.[218]

The court assumed that

> Indeed, Martino succeeds not in transferring particular pendants of historically existing works of art to her own, but rather in identifying fundamental lines in the work of each artist cited (or of a particular artistic period of theirs) and in proposing it again in a personal way in her jewels, making evident the artistic references to the past even in the innovative forms of a modern production: thus – in a nutshell – 'Homage to Picasso' proposes the typical elements of the artist's cubist production, 'Homage to Mirò' the combination of colours bright and curved and closed lines while 'Homage to Modigliani' the elongated shape of the female face, elongated (the nose) or stylized (the mouth, the eyes) even in the individual details of the physiognomy.

In this case the court applied the institutional theory of art pointing out that the evaluation of the artistic character should include the opinion of critics and that the work should exhibit a greater aesthetic standard.[219]

215 Ibidem, p. 10.

216 Jankowska, Meghaichi, Pawełczyk, *Illustrated Fashion Law*.

217 Trib. Venezia, 02.02.2004, SPI 2004, n. 163 (*Martino v. Gioielli & Magie*); Ferraro, *Il controverso riconoscimento . . .*, p. 95; By the same token a Court in Milan denied copyright protection to a watch; Trib. Milano, 29 March 2005, [in:] Annali It. Dir. Aut., 2005, p. 640.

218 Judgement of the District Court of Venice as of 19 October 2007, *Martino e Menegatti F.lli S.p.A. v. Gioielli & Magie S.R.L.*, no. 2274/2204.

219 Exemplary works by F.lli Menegatti and Tiziana Martino; indicative of one of the disputed pendants: *Picasso Modernist Face Pendant Necklace*; modernist ring inspired by Pablo Picasso's works and a ring dedicated to Andy Warhol, cf. www.worthpoint.com/worthopedia/flli-menegatti-sterling-silver-1473096816, www.catawiki.com/en/l/49044983-f-lli-menegatti-tiziana-q-martino-925-silver-ring; www.barnebys.com/auctions/lot/menegatti-925-silver-ring-colored-nail-polish-j23llxfvgo (accessed: 18.01.2023).

4.3.2.6 *Cases involving clothes and shoes: MaxMara and Moon Boots (before and after* Cofemel*)*

When it comes to the protection of fashion design, there are a few significant, but controversial, judgements in Italy. On 5 May 2017, the Court of Appeals in Milan decided on the *Max Mara* case, that sued Liu.Jo for copying its collection *The Cube*.[220] The defendant launched a collection *Les Plumes* 2012/2013, which supposedly led to the copyright infringement. The court, however, did not support the plaintiff's view that its collection was copyrightable. It was recognisable for its 'modularity', the possibility of accessorising the jackets with detachable buttons, buckles, belts and cuffs. The court found that the specific idea of modularity does not meet the premise of artistic value.[221]

Based on expertise in Italian law, Barbara Pasa made an observation that this "explains why all the most important fashion houses, including Prada, Louis Vuitton and Gucci, pursue a "usealization" policy, showing an increasingly widespread tendency to exhibit their fashion products in museum spaces, or in their foundations, often together with works of art".[222] There is a remarkable case of *Moon Boots* that were held copyrightable by the District Court in Milan in the verdict of 12 July 2016.[223] The court asserted that the Moon Boots design is endowed with artistic value as "its appearance on the market it has profoundly changed the aesthetic concept of the after-ski boot and became a true icon of Italian design". It influenced taste and affected an entire historical period of style. The court took into consideration that the shoe model was the subject of many national and international awards, publications on contemporary art, and in 2000, was selected as one of the 100 most significant symbols of 20th-century design exhibited in the Louvre Museum.

This judgement was made in the aftermath of applying the institutional theory of art in the Italian copyright jurisprudence and is fully compliant with the verdicts granting copyright protection to designs such as the Pantom Chair, Arco Lamp or Le Corbusier. Therefore, copyright law stimulates "art, that is understood as a creative and innovative interpretation of the world, into the context of everyday life".[224]

220 Judgement of the Court of Appeals of Milan as of 5 May 2017, no. 1893, *Max Mara Fashion Group S.R.L. v. Liu.Jo S.p.A.*

221 Max Mara, *The Cube* collection and Liu. Jo *Les Plumes* collection, https://twitter.com/maxmara/status/1216374271917817857/photo/2; www.the-spin-off.com/news/stories/LIU-JO-WITH-FIRST-DOWN-JACKET-COLLECTION-4893 (accessed: 22.01.2023).

222 B. Pasa, *Industrial Design* . . ., p. 109.

223 Trib. Milano Sez. spec. Impresa, 12 luglio 2016, in dirittodautore.it; no. 70313/2013 R.G.

224 Cf. Moon Boots design by Tecnica Group S.p.A. versus Anouk design by Gruppo Aniel SNC Di Simeoni Anna & C. and Chiara Ferragni; Elena Martini, Copyright on industrial design: the IP Court of Milan grants protection to the Moon Boots, 27 July 2016, https://martinimanna.com/copyright-on-industrial-design-the-ip-court-of-milan-grants-protection-to-the-moon-boots/ (as of 25.01.2023). www.pinterest.ie/pin/773422935980377914/?amp_client_id=amp-qMgyEzoji9AmthGWPk_2mQ&mweb_unauth_id=89990000887f47239c966843aecdffa7&simplified=true&amp_url=https%3A%2F%2Fwww.pinterest.ie%2Famp%2Fpin%2F773422935980377914%2F (accessed: 25.01.2023).

Item of note no. 4.8 Moon Boots – copyrightability

An expert in this case found that the fashion design of the Moon Boots was creative based on its features:

Therefore, it seems to this Court that the Moon Boots should be granted the copyright protection that covers all the creative characteristics that make up their essence. According to the same consultant of the defendant, with respect to products that incorporate the same massive (functional) shapes, the Moon Boots model is substantially characterized by an ambidextrous sole to which an upper is connected, without visible seams, that has a high band enveloping the toe area and the lateral one of the foot up to approximately in correspondence with the area in front of the malleolus, in this area there is a connection with a buttress that develops more in height to wrap part of the rear end of the foot. There are also laces turned up on three pairs of associated eyelets, two at the upper edge of the fascia and one at the buttress; below the sole has an ambidextrous shape.

The Anouk model of the defendants Anniel has all the aforementioned characteristics, except that the height of the leg is reduced and the pairs of eyelets are two instead of three (with an almost imperceptible aesthetic effect, see doc. 21 att.).[225]

The artistic value of the Moon Boots model was recognised by exhibitions held at the Triennale Design Museum in Milan (2016) and the Metropolitan Museum of Modern Art (2018). Between these events, its copyrightable character based on artistic value was confirmed by the Court of Cassation in 2017 as well as District and Appellate Courts in Venice in 2019.[226]

It will be interesting to observe whether the recent decisions made by the CJEU in *Cofemel* and *Brompton*, regarding works of applied art, will in any

225 https://dirittodautore.it/wp-content/uploads/2016/07/SentTribMilano8628_2016_ok.pdf (accessed: 25.01.2023). Pertanto, pare a questo Tribunale che ai Moon Boots debba essere riconosciuta la tutela autorale che copre tutte le caratteristiche creative che ne costituiscono l'essenza. Secondo lo stesso consulente di parte convenuta, rispetto a prodotti che ne riprendano le analoghe forme (funzionali) massicce, il modello Moon Boots è contraddistinto sostanzialmente da una suola ambidestra a cui è raccordata, senza cuciture a vista, una tomaia che presenta un fascione di elevata altezza avvolgente la zona della punta e quella laterale del piede sino circa in corrispondenza della zona antistante i malleoli, in tale zona essendovi un raccordo con un contrafforte che si sviluppa maggiormente in altezza ad avvolgere parte dell'estremità posteriore del piede. Sono inoltre presenti dei lacci risvoltati su tre coppie di occhielli associate, due in corrispondenza del bordo superiore del fascione ed una del contrafforte; inferiormente la suola presenta una forma ambidestra. Il modello Anouk delle convenute Anniel presenta tutte le predette caratteristiche, salvo che l'altezza del gambale è ridotta e le coppie di occhielli sono due anziché tre (con effetto estetico pressochè impercepibile, cfr. doc. 21 att.).

226 Court of Cassation judgement no. 7477/2017; Court of Venice judgement as of 15 March 2019; Court of Appeal Venice judgement of 7 March 2019.

way affect the series of copyright judgements that make copyright protection conditional upon the premise of 'artistic value'[227] with regard to fashion. Interestingly, in the judgement of 25 January 2021, the IP Court of Milan confirmed its copyright protection based on the same premises as before *Cofemel* (Moon Boots II case[228]). It provided an elaborate expertise on the idea of 'artistic value' and confirmed the existing angle on this matter.[229]

4.3.2.7 Buccellati *case (after* Cofemel*)*

This case, adjudicated by the District Court of Milan on 19 April 2021,[230] is one of the most interesting cases for several reasons.[231] First, the court explicitly asserted that it has to comply with EU law and the *Cofemel* findings, meaning that member states are no longer allowed to 'filter' copyright protection through the requirement of 'artistic value'.[232] This is a far-reaching conclusion that calls into question the rich Italian scholarship and jurisprudence conclusions made since 2 February 2001.

This case concerned two renowned Italian jewellers,[233] Buccellati (established in 1919) and Meini (established in 1971) that were fighting over copyright protection for the excellence of the goldsmith technique inspired by Florentine renaissance style, but the court did a great deal of work that interestingly reflects intellectual property bedrocks.

Item of note no. 4.9 'Buccellati style' – uncopyrightability

The plaintiff claimed exclusive ownership of the 'Buccellati style' that had supposedly been honed and personalized through a variety of choices that resulted in the creation of jewellery masterpieces. The style's features were as follows:

- specific jewellery assortment and its types, such as band for the ring and the cuff for the bracelet, choices repeated and continued over time;

227 Carlo Sala, *Italy: Copyrightable Designs* . . .
228 *Tecnica v. Chiara Ferragini*, case no. 493/21 (*Tecnica Group S.p.A. v. Diana S.R.L.*, no. 30937/2018); www.thelegalmatch.it/data/uploads/docs/69A1DB9E-7045-11EB-A797-6B244E5F79CB.pdf (as of 25.01.2023); Emidia Di Sabatino, *Chiara Ferragni "strizza l'occhio" alla forma dei Moon Boots*, 16 February 2021, www.thelegalmatch.it/it/pagine/92B1228A-0B7C-11EA-AC01-C9B840F04A91,11881546-939A-11EA-BCFB-E7B20A3C62A3,3283AAF2-7045-11EB-82C1-5D244E5F79CB/ (as of 25.01.2023).
229 *Tecnica v. Chiara Ferragini*, judgement pp. 18–19.
230 *Buccellati Holding Italia S.p.A. v. Meini Gioielli S.N.C.*, RG no. 39048/2018; no. 3204/2021; Repert. no. 2946/2021; cf. Riccardo Perotti, *The Court of Milan* . . .
231 Jankowska, Meghaichi, Pawełczyk, *Illustrated Fashion Law*.
232 Riccardo Perotti, *The Court of Milan* . . .
233 www.buccellati.com/en/timeline; www.gioielleria-meini.com/la-storia/ (as of 26.01.2023).

- the *gold's surface treated as a textile texture* of rich quality, a concept first introduced by Mario Buccellati and accomplished using numerous techniques, such as:
  - telato (with texture obtained through thin crossed hatches),
  - segrinato (with incisions in all directions as an overlap of textures),
  - rigato (with parallel lines cut on the surface of the material to obtain a satin effect),
  - modellato (decoration method to achieve the effect of a shiny and silky surface),
  - traforo (engraving technique devised in the art of the Byzantine Empire that involves the removal of metal and cutting the surface to obtain a 'honeycomb' or 'tulle' effect;
- personal interpretation of ancient goldsmith techniques such as smoothing (it. l'ageminatura), niello (it. il niello), chiselling (la cesellatura), engraving (l'incisione), chaining (l'incatenatura) and fretwork (il traforo), inspired by the elegant and complex weaves of Venetian tulle and devised by Mario Buccellati;
- edges with chiselled designs in three dimensions on a minuscule scale;
- prevalence of gold over single gems;
- modular repetition of small decorations such as stars, rosettes, flowers framed by diamonds;
- use of mixed metals to obtain a chromatic white and yellow effect (silver and gold, platinum and gold, yellow gold and white gold).

The court ruled that particular processing and engraving techniques, like those mentioned, may be the subject of patent or trade secret protection as long as they are eligible.[234] A specific method may be protected and even monopolised by copyright law not of itself but with regard to the peculiarity with which the technique is applied to obtain an aesthetic effect. The author should apply these techniques with the addition of their own artistic flair – they can include the decision to use a particular method, the choice of materials and any geometric, floral or other designs.

Assessing the originality of the disputed works, the court reiterated CJEU's angle that the work should reflect the personality of the author and be a manifestation of the author's free and creative choices.[235] There must be an 'autonomo elemento' that provides a way to inject one's interpretation and

234 Cf. District Court of Milano verdict as of 8.06.2017 regarding denial of protection for Louis Vuitton technique of processing leather alla "granapaglia" and "cuir epi".

235 Cf. Painer case, C-145/10, as of 1 December 2011, EU:C:2011:798 points 88, 89 and 94; Renckhoff case, C-161/17, as of 7 August 2018, EU:C:2018:634, point 14.

contribution that is so significant that it justifies copyright protection.[236] In this regard, it rested on the Milanese Court's stand taken in the famous *Kiki v. Wjcon* case regarding beauty concept store:

> this requirement is not eliminated by inspiration or the reference to other historical periods or to other artists, since a choice, however small, that attributes the work to the personal and individual expression of the author, is enough, even when the work consists of simple ideas and notions, included in the intellectual knowledge of experts in the field.[237]

This reference is remarkable, because the *Koko* case regarded an architectural work (Article 2, point 5 of ICL) and not a work of applied art (Article 2, point 10 of ICL). It allows the conclusion, based on the judgement *in pleno* (point 4.3.3. of the verdict), that the court let go of the 'artistic value' criterion and equated the protection of applied art with the works of other categories. Notably, the *Koko* case does not set a high originality threshold for copyright.

In essence, the court admitted that the author should not copy but create a work having a personal touch according to the author's own flair and imagination.

The court observed that the Buccellati 'Broche Tulle', consisting of a star-shaped brooch-pendant

> is made of white gold and diamonds, with a tulle perforated design with cells in white gold and a central rose window with a diamond. . . . the composition is accentuated by the recessed edges in diamonds. The emptiness of the extremes diamonds emphasizes lightness and brightness.

The defendant's piece has differently shaped contour lines, more rounded with a "curvilinear and sweet effect". Its geometric interior design does not reproduce the Buccellati's play of emptiness. These differences make the jewellery pieces at issue quite distinct with no evidence that the latter was copied. The Meini design looks like the result of autonomous work.

The court also noted:

> the "Eternelle Sagome Quadre" ring, made by Buccellati in white and yellow gold, twelve diamonds are set in the central row and the perforated decoration of the structure gives lightness and harmony to the whole. The use of two golds is accompanied by the use of diamonds presented in a square design. It is characterized by a workmanship on a surface that gives a sense of compactness.

236 Cf. District Court of Milano verdict as of 4 February 2015.

237 District Court of Milano verdict as of 13 October 2015, verdict no. 11416/2015, RG no. 80647/2013, Repert. no. 9771/2015.

Again, however, the court concluded that the visual effect is too distant to prove infringement.

The plaintiff's design, Buccellati 'Bracciale Cuff con Rosoni', was made "in yellow and white gold and striped decoration with five diamond rosettes, punctuated by diamond points of light on the four corners. The rosettes have two rows of concentric petals". The central flower is accompanied with punctiform on the sides. In the defendant's design,

> the triangular ornaments placed on the edge of the defendant's piece fill the space of the surface, ideally recalling the same design on the opposite edge and creating an almost seamless geometric reference with the central rose window. The rose window also has a different shape on the contour, more circular and less airy.

The visual impressions are distinct.

The court asserted that Buccellati's design were copyrightable but did not grant injunction based on the opinion that the solutions adopted by Meini were the result of autonomous creative choices. The court punctiliously weighted the parties' arguments through the prism of the expert's opinion and concluded that "minimal details and differences can lead to different evaluations" (point 6.3. of the verdict).

4.3.3 *France*

4.3.3.1 *Overview: 'unity of art' theory*

It can safely be claimed that France is the cradle of modern copyright law.[238] The historical roots of French copyright law go back to two revolutionary acts, one from 13 January 1791 (also referred to as *Loi Le Chapelier*) and the other from 19 July 1793 (referred to as the *Declaration of genius*).[239] Protection of design had been introduced earlier still.[240] The second of the two acts survived with few changes until 1957, laying the foundations of French copyright law

238 L. Pfister, *La Propriété Littéraire Est-elle Une Propriété? Controverses Sur La Nature Du Droit D'auteur Au XIXe Siècle*, "The Legal History Review", 2004, vol. 72, no. 1, pp. 103 and ff. E. Pouillet, *Traité de la propriété littéraire & artistique et du droit de représentation*, Marchal et Billard, 1908, p. 29.

239 Loi des 19–24 Juillet 1793; Cf.R. Birn, *The Profit of Ideas: 'Privilèges en librairie' in Eighteenth-Century France*, "Eighteenth-Century Studies 1970–1971", no. 4/2, p. 160; D. Bécourt, *The French Revolution and Authors' Rights: Toward a New Universalism*, "Copyright Bulettin", 1990, no. 4/23, pp. 4–5; D. Burkitt, *Copyrighting Culture – the History and Cultural Specificity of the Western Model of Copyright*, IPQ 2001, nr 2, p. 159; M. Jankowska, *Autor i prawo do autorstwa*, Wolters Kluwer, 2011, pp. 72–73.

240 The so-called *Lettres Patentes* enacted in 1737 and 1744 for creations of the silk industries of Lyon (*Manufactures de Lyon*).

(amended on 11 March 1902; legal act as of 11 March 1957),[241] also known in general as the *droit d'auteur*.

Item of note no. 4.10 Doctrine of unity of art

The principle of the *unity of art* recognised in France made the country renowned for enabling total cumulation of the copyright and industrial design regimes.[242] This principle was allowed by the copyright law of 1902 that extended copyright protection to *applied art*, that is, the works of architects, sculptors and ornamental designers, "whatever the artistic merit and the designation of the work".[243] This was a remarkable amendment, as the 'Declaration of Genius' mentioned only protection for *pure art*. Applied art was later acknowledged in the act for designs and models on 14 July 1909, which, in Article 1, established industrial property law protection "without prejudice to the rights they may hold under other provisions and in particular the law of July 19–24, 1793, amended by the law of March 11, 1902".[244] With this change of law, the most reputed French *couturiers* could effectively sue the *maisons de belles copies* merely based on the legal protection the copyright law had secured for design, including fashion design.[245]

The unification of protection remains until this day a subject of detailed analysis and is not accepted without reservations.[246] It is the fruit of a long-lasting and zealous discussion of the scope of protection for applied art that still applies under the regime of the act for industrial design from 18 March 1806.[247] In the aftermath of these legal discussions, a few criteria were

241 Loi no. 57–298 du 11 mars 1957 sur la propriété littéraire et artistique.

242 Cf. Y. Gaubiac, *La théorie de l'unité de l'art*, "RIDA", 1982, no. 111, pp. 3 and ff.

243 A.-E. Kahn, *The Copyright/Design Interface in France* [in:] E. Derclaye (ed.), *The Copyright/Design Interface. Past, Present and Future*, Cambridge Univeristy Press, 2018, p. 13; A. Françon, *The Development of Law in the Field of Copyright as a Result of the Interaction of the Berne Convention and French Legislation*, "Copyright", 1986, no. 6, p. 204.

244 Loi du 14 Juillet 1909 sur les dessins et modèles; https://wipolex.wipo.int/en/text/214529 (accessed: 10.01.2023).

245 J. Vinagre e Lima, *Intellectual Property and Fashion: The Rise of Fashion Law*, 8/08/2016, Institute for Research on Internet and Society, https://irisbh.com.br/en/intellectual-property-and-fashion-the-rise-of-fashion-law/ (accessed: 10.04.2022).

246 More cf. Kahn, *The Copyright/Design* . . ., pp. 11 and ff.

247 This act introduced the *conseil des prud'hommes*, where projects of fashion designs were deposed in order to claim design protection. Cf. *Société Paquin limited v. Beer*, Court of Paris judgement of 26 October 1905 (Pataille, 06.7).

put forward[248] and discussed as candidates for a premise delineating works deserving copyright protection from those that did not:

- the mechanical method with which the design in question was reproduced,
- the ancillary nature of the factory design,
- qualities of the author,
- future industrial or artistic use ("theory of destination"),
- artistic character of the work ("theory of the artistic nature of the creation").

The last criterion prevailed with the strict interpretation that only works devoid of artistic character were denied copyright protection.[249] Over time, courts and literature found it unfeasible to draw an explicit line between the artistic and industrial, hence the line became blurry with copyright protection granted quite liberally. The eagerness to differentiate between these categories was abandoned by courts and legislation following Eugène Pouillet's argument that law should not judge the works.[250]

It was also Eugène Pouillet who questioned whether *creations du couturier et de la modiste* in fact benefited from the legal extension of 1902, since these could easily have qualified as artistic works under the act of 1793. He argued that

> not only because the admiration of the clientele qualifies these creations as works of art and because intended to highlight feminine beauty, they flatter the aesthetic feeling of connoisseurs and are for them the source of artistic pleasures, but because they are based on a work of graphic or plastic arts and are the realization, by various materials, of a drawing, a sketch, a design of lines, shapes and colours, as the work built by the contractors is the realization of the plans and drawings of the architect.[251]

He also opposed the courts' use of the law of 1902 to demonstrate the qualification of fashion design as copyrighted works. Poillet takes the view that this qualification was already established back in 1793.[252]

4.3.3.2 Threshold of originality. Overall impression doctrine

At the heart of the French approach was the belief by scholars and philosophers that a person of 'genius' should be protected based on personality

248 For in-depth discussion cf. A.-E. Kahn, *The Copyright/Design . . .*, p. 11–12.

249 Kahn, *The Copyright/Design . . .*, p. 12.

250 Kahn, *The Copyright/Design . . .*, p. 12, cf. Pouillet, *Traité théorique et pratique des dessins et des modèles*, 1884, p. 28.

251 Pouillet, *Traité de la propriété . . .*, p. 110.

252 Pouillet, *Traité de la propriété . . .*, p. 112.

theory.[253] Le Chapelier, in the report of 1791, mentioned that the fruit of a writer's thought is the most personal property.[254] A poet, Lamartine, wrote in 1842 that a work of authorship is a personal property, united with the thought of its author.[255] This approach, based on personality, is clearly visible in the wording of French copyright law, which, in place of 'work of authorship' puts 'work of mind' (Fr. *œuvre de l'esprit*). The legal literature and jurisprudence work based on the criterion of "the imprint of the personality of the author". The French concept of work is based on the premise of *originalité* that is encapsulated in Article L111–1 of FCL.[256] It is also referred to as *effort créatif* (*travail créatif*[257]), "intellectual effort" or "aesthetical bias" (Fr. *parti-pris esthétique*).[258] It is significant that French copyright law protects fashion design without deep consideration of the differentiation between fine and applied arts (cf. 2.3.1.).[259] Moreover, French law does not impose a minimum artistic threshold for qualification of a work as original.[260]

Both design and fashion are included in the listing of Article L112–2 of the FCL that includes the categories of copyrightable works:

10° works of applied art,
14° creations of the seasonal industries of dress and articles of fashion.

Industries which, by reason of the demands of fashion, frequently renew the form of their products, particularly the making of dresses, furs, underwear, embroidery, fashion, shoes, gloves, leather goods, the manufacture of fabrics of striking novelty or of special use in *haute couture* dressmaking, the products of manufacturers of articles of fashion and of footwear and the manufacture of fabrics for upholstery shall be deemed to be seasonal industries.

Exceptional as it may seem to include fashion design in Article L112–2 of the FCL, it makes perfect sense if we put this phenomenon into historical, social and economic perspective. Point 14° did not arise of the blue but is an obvious consequence of French *haute couture* traditions. As explained

253 As Lakanal, the official rapporteur for the decree of 19 July 1793 said: "Of all forms of property, the least debatable is that of a genius",

254 Report of Le Chapeliera of 15 January 1791, *7 Réimpression de l'ancien Moniteur 113*, 116–18 (1860) [after:] J.L. Piotraut, *An Authors' Rights-based Copyright Law: The Fairness and Morality of French and American Law Compared*, "Cardozo Arts & Entertainment Law Journal", 2006, no. 24, p. 565; Jankowska, *Autor* p. 257.

255 A. de Lamartine, *On Literary Property, Report to the Chamber of Deputies* [in:] *Œuvres Complètes*, 1842, no. 8, p. 394, 405 [after:] J.L. Piotraut, *An Authors'*. . ., p. 566; A. le Tarnec, *Manuel de la propriété littéraire et artistique*, Dalloz, 1966, p. 1.

256 p. 122.

257 p. 120.

258 Kahn, *The Copyright/Design* . . ., p. 17.

259 Palandri, *Fashion as Art* . . ., pp. 5, 129.

260 Kahn, *The Copyright/Design* . . ., p. 16.

by Berenika Sorokowska, "to get a better understanding of this, one should take into account the hard, time-consuming work done not only by tailors, but also specialists whose professions do not have a translation into" other languages

> because of the peculiar nature of the art of craftsmanship, deep rooted in French fashion. There are specialists such as *brodeur* (an embroiderer applying pearls, feathers, crystals, sequins by weaving them and matching the rest of the creation), *boutonnier* (specialist in hand-made buttons) or *formier*, also known as *chapelier-modiste* (profession registered with INMA [Institut National des Métiers dArt] under the UNESCO [UN Educational, Scientific and Cultural Organization] Convention for the Safeguarding of the Intangible Cultural Heritage; a specialist in wood making hat and accessory forms for hair).[261]

These professions are registered with the *Institut National de Métiers d'art* and are subject to ministerial scrutiny. The special status of the French sewing tradition is echoed in the names of many sewing and embroidery techniques, such as French knots, *tambour* (Lunéville, early 19th century),[262] baby French binding,[263] French seams,[264] as well as in the couture secrets applied in order to perfect the finishing touch. There are also a good many French textiles, some of them even named after Frenchmen, e.g. batiste (named after the French weaver, Jean Batiste)[265] and toile (translates to English as 'linen cloth', in the US known as 'muslin').[266]

The wording of Article L112–2 points 10 and 14 of the FCL seems to be obvious and to allow for trouble-free interpretation. In fact, its wording has caused a lot of interpretational issues, such as whether only seasonal fashion should be included in point 14. Given that the listing in Article L112–2 is only explanatory, the debate is mostly theoretical, but it is still important to understand which legal basis would apply to each kind of fashion (seasonal/classic).[267]

261 Berenika Sorokowska, *Ochrona fashion designu w prawie Unii Europejskiej*, Wolters Kluwer, 2022, p. 34; Claire B. Shaeffer, *Couture Sewing Techniques*, Newtown, 2011, p. 11 et seq.; Jessica Jane Pile, *Fashion Embroidery: Embroidery Techniques and Inspiration for Haute Couture Clothing*, Batsford, 2021, p. 169 et seq.; Andrea Hirsch-Cianciarulo, *Perles de Rocaille Haute Couture. Bijoux et accessoires tissés à l'aiguille*, 2006.

262 Jessica Jane Pile, *Fashion* . . ., pp. 169, 261.

263 Lynda Maynard, *The Dressmaker's Handbook of Couture Sewing Techniques. Essential step-by-Step Techniques for Professional Results*, Interweave Press, 2010, p. 44.

264 Maynard, *The Dressmaker's* . . ., p. 118.

265 Maynard, *The Dressmaker's* . . ., p. 121.

266 Maynard, *The Dressmaker's* . . ., p. 124.

267 A. Lucas, H.-J. Lucas, A. Lucas-Schloetter, *Traité de la propriété littéraire et artistique*, 4 éd., Lexis-Nexis, 1975; A. Bertrand, *Le droit d'auteur et les droits voisins*, 2 éd., Dalloz, 2013, p. 804.

A work is granted copyright protection based on the premise of the "personality of the author".[268] In the French jurisprudence there are flagship judgements that paint a full picture of how widely the premise is used: *cafetière Bodum*,[269] *Chaise LC4* by Le Corbusier[270] and stainless-steel nail clipper by Vitry Frères Paris.[271]

The premise of originality in French law does not distinguish itself with a high threshold of originality that a work should meet in order to merit copyright protection. As for fashion design, there are a number of cases regarding many different garments that prove that the French concept of originality is very capacious and rather predictable. The cases outlined in this section will give an insight into the French understanding of originality with regard to fashion. The Court of Appeal in Paris in its judgement on 11 September 1996, *Antik Batik v. Monoprix*, adjudicated on a 'cloche' hat, which it found ineligible for protection. The court noted that

> it must . . . constitute a creation, that . . . presents an original, decorative or ornamental character, testifying to the personal effort or individual interpretation of its author. However, the elements from the public domain as grouped and assembled in this case do not have a particular configuration that would distinguish the model invoked from other models that may belong to the same style.[272]

There are hundreds, if not thousands, of cases that have been disputed in French courts, many of them resulting in the granting of protection to many different garments; however, a diligent classification of these works goes far beyond the capacity of this book.[273]

268 Jankowska, Meghaichi, Pawełczyk, *Illustrated* . . . .
269 CA Paris, 8.3.2000.
270 CA Paris 7.10.1993.
271 TGI Paris, 11.02.2011.
272 CA Paris, 4e ch., 11 sept. 1996, Antik Batik c/ Monoprix, RDPI 1996, n° 69, p. 22.
273 Cour d'appel de Paris, Pôle 5, Chambre 2, Arrêt du 26 février 2021, Répertoire général n° 19/15130 (wedding dresses, Cymbeline, models Ironie, Indulgence, Belle, Byzance and Idylle); Tribunal de Grande Instance de PARIS 3ème Chambre 1ère Section, 8 March 2011, RG n° 10/00121; Court of Appeals of Paris, 16 March 2012, RG no. 11/08414 (children dress, SAS MAJOR, model Adrienne); CA Paris, pôle 5, ch. 2, 6 Déc. 2013, n° 2/17382, S A Minelli c/ SA La Redoute; CA Paris, pôle 5, ch. 1, 11 Sept. 2013, n° 11/22046, Sté Repetto c/ Sté Karine; CA Paris, pôle 5, ch. 1, 6 nov. 2013, n° 12/12518, Sté Christian Dior c/ Sté Brandalley et a.; Cour d'appel de Paris, Pôle 5, Chambre 2, Arrêt du 19 octobre 2018, Répertoire général n° 17/00906; Tribunal de grande instance, Paris, Jugement du 20 octobre 2016, Répertoire général n° 14/06769; Tribunal de grande instance, Paris, Jugement du 11 mars 2016, Répertoire général n° 14/11357; Cour d'appel de Paris, Pôle 5, Chambre 2, Arrêt du 22 mars 2019, Répertoire général n° 17/21767; Cour d'appel de Bordeaux, 1ère Chambre, Section A, Arrêt du 29 février 2016, Répertoire général n° 14/00841; Cour d'appel de Paris, Pôle 5, Chambre 1, Arrêt du 25 avril 2017, Répertoire général n° 15/19367; Cour d'appel de Paris, Pôle 5, Chambre 1, Arrêt du 25 avril

2017, Répertoire général n° 15/23772; Cour d'appel d'Aix-en-Provence, 2ème Chambre, Arrêt du 11 mai 2017, Répertoire général n° 14/12788; Tribunal de grande instance, Paris, Jugement du 27 septembre 2012, Répertoire général n° 09/19175; Tribunal de grande instance, Paris, Jugement du 17 janvier 2012, Répertoire général n° 10/09343; Tribunal de grande instance, Paris, Jugement du 17 janvier 2012, Répertoire général n° 10/08663; Cour d'appel de Paris, 4ème Chambre, Section B, Arrêt du 17 octobre 2008, Répertoire général n° 07/12475; Cour d'appel de Versailles, 12ème Chambre, Section 1, Arrêt du 10 décembre 2009, Répertoire général n° 08/08262; Cour d'appel de Paris, 4ème Chambre, Section B, Arrêt du 17 octobre 2008, Répertoire général n° 07/10131; Tribunal de grande instance, Paris, Jugement du 23 juin 2011, Répertoire général n° 10/11506; Cour d'appel de Versailles, 12ème Chambre, Section 1, Arrêt du 28 mai 2009, Répertoire général n° 08/01705; Cour d'appel de Paris, 4ème Chambre, Section A, Arrêt du 7 février 2007, Répertoire général n° 06/16707; Cour d'appel de Paris, 4ème Chambre, Section A, Arrêt du 7 mai 2008, Répertoire général n° 07/01418; Cour d'appel de Paris, 4ème Chambre, Section A, Arrêt du 24 septembre 2008, Répertoire général n° 07/11740; Tribunal de grande instance, Paris, Jugement du 2 mars 2012, Répertoire général n° 10/11977; Cour d'appel de Paris, 5ème Chambre, Section B, Arrêt du 19 février 2009, Répertoire général n° 08/10103; Cour d'appel de Paris, 4ème Chambre, Section B, Arrêt du 23 mars 2007, Répertoire général n° 05/22013; CA Paris, pôle 5, ch. 2, 17 janv. 2014, n° 13/02955, Sté Pourquoi pas nous c/ Sté La Redoute; Cass. com., 6 mai 2014, n° 11–22.108 (Sté Louis Vuitton Malletier vs. Sté H&M); Cour d'appel de Paris, 4ème Chambre, Section B, Arrêt du 26 septembre 2008, Répertoire général n° 07/08593; Cour d'appel de Paris, Pôle 5, Chambre 2, Arrêt du 4 juin 2021, Répertoire général n° 18/23947; Cour d'appel de Paris, Pôle 5, Chambre 1, Arrêt du 12 avril 2016, Répertoire général n° 14/23137; Cour d'appel de Paris, Pôle 5, Chambre 2, Arrêt du 16 décembre 2016, Répertoire général n° 16/02794; Cour d'appel de Paris, Pôle 5, Chambre 1, Arrêt du 28 septembre 2021, Répertoire général n° 18/20106; Tribunal de grande instance, Paris, Jugement du 14 novembre 2014, Répertoire général n° 13/17041; Tribunal de grande instance, Paris, Jugement du 17 décembre 2010, Répertoire général n° 09/16372; Cour d'appel de Toulouse, 2ème Chambre, Section 1, Arrêt du 1 février 2007, Répertoire général n° 05/02223; Cour d'appel de Douai, 2ème Chambre, Section 1, Arrêt du 3 avril 2008, Répertoire général n° 04/07615; Cour d'appel de Paris, Pôle 5, Chambre 2, Arrêt du 29 avril 2011, Répertoire général n° 10/05763; Cour d'appel de Paris, Pôle 5, Chambre 2, Arrêt du 20 novembre 2020, Répertoire général n° 19/06739; Cour d'appel de Paris, Pôle 5, Chambre 1, Arrêt du 11 mai 2011, Répertoire général n° 09/06212; Cour d'appel de Paris, Pôle 5, Chambre 2, Arrêt du 12 novembre 2010, Répertoire général n° 09/13664; CA Paris, pôle 5, ch. 1, 27 févr. 2013, n° 11/11787, Sté My Pant's c/ Sté Mango France et a.; Cour d'appel de Paris, Pôle 1, Chambre 4, Arrêt du 29 avril 2011, Répertoire général n° 10/16263; Cour d'appel de Lyon, 1ère Chambre civile A, Arrêt du 4 juin 2020, Répertoire général n° 18/00480; Cour d'appel de Paris, 4ème Chambre, Section B, Arrêt du 16 février 2007, Répertoire général n° 05/00208; Cour d'appel de Paris, Pôle 5, Chambre 1, Arrêt du 14 décembre 2021, Répertoire général n° 20/05805; Cour de cassation, Première Chambre civile, Arrêt n° 107 du 25 janvier 2017, Pourvoi n° 15–25.210; Cour d'appel de Paris, Pôle 5, Chambre 1, Arrêt du 25 avril 2017, Répertoire général n° 15/23772; Cour d'appel de Paris, Arrêt du 10 mars 2006, Répertoire général n° 04/24570; Cour d'appel de Paris, 4ème Chambre, Section B, Arrêt du 30 mars 2007, Répertoire général n° 05/12257; Cour d'appel de Paris, 4ème Chambre, Section B, Arrêt du 8 septembre 2006, Répertoire général n° 05/00208; Cour d'appel de Versailles, 12ème Chambre, Section 1, Arrêt du 15 octobre 2009, Répertoire général n° 08/05170; Cour d'appel de Versailles, 12ème Chambre, Section 1, Arrêt du 28 mai 2009, Répertoire général n° 08/01705; Cour d'appel de Paris, 4ème Chambre, Section B, Arrêt du 7 mars 2008, Répertoire général n° 07/00704; Cour d'appel de Douai, 1ère Chambre, Section 2, Arrêt du 15 septembre 2009, Répertoire général n° 07/04157; Tribunal

On the other hand, as listed by Andre Bertrand, the French courts refused copyright protection for[274]

- shortening or lengthening a skirt or sleeves[275];
- the use of traditional sewing elements such as the neckline of a collar[276];
- the use of a particular colour[277];
- a change of fabric that does not affect the shape, such as the use of a non-woven fabric instead of a traditional fabric[278];
- the adorning of a fabric by tracing parallel stripes of brighter colours[279];
- the adding of pockets[280] or a zip[281] to trousers or a jacket;
- adding a ruffle to a ruffled skirt[282];
- putting a zip centrally down the front of a jacket and buttons on its wrists[283];
- replacing a large button on a sleeve with two small buttons or adding a button under the collar of a blouse[284];

de grande instance, Paris, Jugement du 28 avril 2011, Répertoire général n° 10/07942; Tribunal de grande instance, 3ème Chambre civile, Paris, Jugement du 12 février 2008, Répertoire général n° 06/02833; Cour d'appel de Douai, 1ère Chambre, Section 2, Arrêt du 30 août 2018, Répertoire général n° 17/03581; Cour d'appel de Paris, Pôle 5, Chambre 1, Arrêt du 23 mai 2017, Répertoire général n° 16/02857; Cour d'appel d'Aix-en-Provence, 2ème Chambre, Arrêt du 29 avril 2010, Répertoire général n° 09/07058; Cour d'appel de Paris, 4ème Chambre, Arrêt du 21 mai 2008, Répertoire général n° 07/3611; Cour d'appel de Paris, 4ème Chambre, Section A, Arrêt du 10 septembre 2008, Répertoire général n° 07/06408; Cour d'appel de Paris, Pôle 5, Chambre 2, Arrêt du 29 avril 2011, Répertoire général n° 10/05466; Cour d'appel de Paris, 4ème Chambre, Section A, Arrêt du 15 janvier 1997, Répertoire général n° 95/012188; Cour d'appel de Paris, Pôle 5, Chambre 2, Arrêt du 19 octobre 2018, Répertoire général n° 17/00906; Cour d'appel de Paris, Pôle 5, Chambre 1, Arrêt du 25 janvier 2022, Répertoire général n° 19/18139; Cour d'appel de Paris, Pôle 5, Chambre 1, Arrêt du 15 octobre 2019, Répertoire général n° 18/00134; Cour d'appel de Paris, Pôle 5, Chambre 1, Arrêt du 23 mai 2017, Répertoire général n° 16/02857; Cour d'appel de Paris, Pôle 5, Chambre 1, Arrêt du 9 mars 2011, Répertoire général n° 08/23705.

274 Andre Bertrand, *Droit d'auteur*, Dalloz Action 2010, electronic database; cf. P. et F. Greffe; *Les dessins et modèles*, Litec 1974, p. 190.

275 CA Paris, 4 ch., 7 juin 1995, PIBD 1995, III, 434. Changing the size of garment, CA Paris, 4 ch., 26 janv. 1960, Chabaud c/ Bonnichon, Ann. 1969, 89.

276 TGI Paris, 3 ch., 13 juill. 1988, Pierlot c/ Turquoise, PIBD 1989, III, 126.

277 TGI Paris, Bobigny 5 ch., 15 déc. 1992, Reverchon c/ Diester, PIBD 1993, III, 274, pour une couleur « fluo »; Com. 21 janv. 1973, D. 1973. 52.

278 CA Paris, 4 ch., 4 oct. 1995, Matfer c/ Pal, PIBD 1996, III, 27; CA Paris, 4 ch., 24 nov. 1993, Brajntich c/ SARL, PIBD 1994, III, 164 – Dans le même sens TGI Paris, 3 ch., 29 janv. 2003, Sunyoung, Prop. ind. 2003. n 11, obs. P. Greffe.

279 CA Paris, 4 ch., 11 mai 1987, Mamou c/ Micosancho, D. 1988. somm. 393, obs. J.-J. Burst.

280 CA Paris, 4 ch., 11 janv. 1990, Deguy c/ Snoboy, PIBD 1990, III, 311.

281 T. com. Seine, 13 janv. 1931, Sem. Jur. 1931, 239.

282 T. com. Paris, 15 ch., 13 déc. 1996, Pit'choun c/ P'tit môme, RDPI 1997, n 79, p. 50.

283 CA Paris, 4 ch., 20 mars 1996, Tucker c/ Galerie Lafayette, PIBD 1996, III, 419.

284 CA Paris, 4 ch., 7 juin 1995, PIBD 1995, III, 434.

- using as a belt a ribbon corset only reduced in length at the top[285];
- bringing up to date an old model that had fallen into the public domain, in particular a pattern of fabric reproduced identically.[286]

But copyright protection is not granted to any garment that is just a result of choice and selection.[287] As noted in some of the following cases, courts judge originality based on the "overall impression" (Fr. *impression d'ensemble*). Unfortunately, pictorial representations for French cases are not as widely available as for the Italian or Dutch cases and will be mostly provided using representative images accessible online.

4.3.3.3 Christian Dior Sneakers B 18

This case was adjudicated by the Court of Appeals in Paris on 6 November 2013.[288] It concerned the men's sport shoe Dior Sneaker B 18, of which a knock-off (tennis shoe Leoss) was offered at the Internet website www.brandalley.fr.

In the first place, the court had to judge whether the Dior shoe design was copyrightable. The appeal judges acknowledged the originality of the shoe based on its characteristic general tapered shape, specific for this model and distinguishing it from other models of the same type. The defendant contested originality based on the argument that the

> affixing of side stripes on the side of a tennis-type sports shoe is known, while the other elements such as the presence of eyelets for inserting the laces, buttresses to reinforce the shoe and protect the foot, are also in the public domain, as a result of the search not for an aesthetic result but for a functional result.

Item of note no. 4.11 Dior Sneaker B 18 – copyrightability

The court made clear that Société Christian Dior had acquired copyright protection based on the association of the separate elements and the arrangement thereof. The original character of the shoe was obtained through

(*Continued*)

285 T. corr. Paris, 25 avr. 1895, Monin c/ Lanclair, Ann. 1895, 152.

286 CA Nîmes, 2 ch., 21 janv. 1993, Les Olivades c/ Hello, RDPI 1992, n 52, p. 42.

287 Cour d'appel de paris, pôle 5, chambre 1, arrêt du 11 septembre 2013, répertoire général n° 12/08392 (dress model by Comptoir du Labe, "Bal").

288 CA Paris, pôle 5, ch. 1, 6 nov. 2013, n° 12/12518, Sté Christian Dior c/ Sté Brandalley et a., www.lamyline.fr.

Item of note 4.11 (Continued)

- a series of straight stitch topstitching,
- a small quadrilateral within which fine perforations were arranged in three parallel horizontal lines,
- an upside-down triangle framed by double straight stitch topstitching,
- a buttress framed by double topstitching in a straight stitch.

Putting the concept of *overall impression* into action, the court asserted:

> assessment of originality must be made globally, according to the overall appearance produced by the arrangement of the various elements specific to the model in question and not by examining each of them, viewed individually, gives this model its own physiognomy, which distinguishes it from other models of the same genre and reflects a creative effort through which arbitrary choices and aesthetic biases of the author.

4.3.3.4 Spartan and gladiator sandals

In 2013, K.Jacques sought protection for their shoe model based on the idea that it bore the imprint of its creator.[289]

K.Jacques claimed that its design merited copyright protection through

- "balanced mixture between the traditional component of the Spartan, namely the flat sole, the crisscrossing of the straps and the thick and robust leather and a modern component allowing it 'to reach a young audience' ";
- "adornment of the ankle bracelet with a mosaic of rivets in the shape of pyramids, which gives the whole a studded and a 'rock' character completely opposite to that of the spartan which rather recalls a natural and simple way of life";
- establishing a visual contrast between "the imposing ankle bracelet" and the "lightness of the structure which dresses the foot"; that was claimed to be the fruit of artistic research and a real aesthetic bias.

The court denied protection for this design, pointing out that the Spartan model has existed for thousands of years and has inspired many shoe manufacturers, including K.Jacques themselves, that have created Caravelle, Pirate, Gina, and Kenya designs.

In the other case, SA Minelli c/SA La Redoute, it was disputed whether gladiator sandals fall short of originality just because the idea of such shoes goes

289 Cour d'appel de Paris, Pôle 5, Chambre 4, Arrêt du 23 octobre 2013, Répertoire général n° 11/19941.

back to the ancient times.[290] The Court of Appeal noted, however, that "the choice of proportion and shapes and the combination of elements according to a particular arrangement, which give the whole its own physiognomy and reflect an aesthetic bias reflecting the imprint of the personality of its author". The court also emphasised that copyright infringement is established by the visual comparison and on the basis of the overall impression.

4.3.3.5 Women's footwear

In 2013, a very interesting case regarding women's high heels was disputed before the Court of Appeal in Paris.[291] The case concerned five designs offered by Sté Repetto that were allegedly copied: Baya, Gitane, Garbo, Kurt and Judith.[292]

The plaintiff claimed that each design was a combination of characteristic elements and described the models as follows:

- BAYA: the strap with a very particular arrangement of yokes at the front (overlay of yokes) and at the back of the shoe (rounded yoke),
- GITANE: the strap system and a system for superimposing the two main inserts on the side of the shoe,
- GARBO: characteristic shoe with a short and rounded boot shape with a particular yoke system,
- KURT: characteristic shoe with a high boot shape and presenting a particular yoke system,
- JUDITH: particular characteristics, combining the representative shape of REPETTO ballet flats (grosgrain border, lace, deep cutout on the front of the foot), with a yoke at the front of the foot contrasting with the rest of the shoe, and a small spool heel.[293]

The defendant contested the originality of these models with a historical argument claiming that these were mere representations of well-known general shoe models:

> the BAYA model would constitute a so-called 'Salomé' model and the GITANE model would correspond to a basic model often called 'CHARLES IX' or 'BABIES', these models having existed for decades

290 CA Paris, pôle 5, ch. 2, 6 déc. 2013, n° 2/17382, SA Minelli c/ SA La Redoute, www.lamyline.fr.

291 CA Paris, pôle 5, ch. 1, 11 sept. 2013, n° 11/22046, Sté Repetto c/ Sté Karine, www.lamyline.fr.

292 Jankowska, Meghaichi, Pawełczyk, *Illustrated* . . . .

293 CA Paris, pôle 5, ch. 1, 11 sept. 2013, n° 11/22046, Sté Repetto c/ Sté Karine, www.lamyline.fr.

in the world of footwear, being defined in the book 'Encyclopédie Les accessoires de A à Z', and available for many years,

- the GARBO and KURT models correspond respectively to a 'Richelieu' model, also existing for decades, and to the definition usually given to the 'LACED BOOT', already disclosed, the pad at the front of the sole, claimed for these two shoes, based on a technique already used by many shoemakers,
- JUDITH is a classic ballerina model with small heels and the yoke on the toe of the shoe is a particularity largely pre-dating the claimed distribution.

Moreover, the defendant argued that its designs did not constitute a slavish copy of the plaintiff's design. Interestingly, the Paris Court of Appeal upheld the first instance court's verdict that made it clear that the applicant company did not explain the imprint of the author's personality for the shoes in question. The plaintiff did not provide an in-depth analysis of how its overall shoe design was individual and not just borrowed from the common realm of shoes. It can be assumed that the Repetto models were too simple and too common to merit copyright protection; however, there was no detailed claim substantiation from the plaintiff.

In a different case in 2014, the Court of Cassation had to decide whether the use of studded soles substantiated a copyright claim.[294] The court denied protection based on the observation that studded soles were part of a fashion trend and that it was insufficient to derive copyright from the "overall appearance" based on that element only. Moreover, the court noted that the Santiago Pons Quintana model was introduced to the market before Tod's Dee Fibbietta model.

4.3.3.6 *"Extrême Dior" high heels and implied licence*

In February 2013, the Paris Court of Appeals decided the case of a Dior model of high-heeled shoe, one in which there was no doubt whatsoever that the design was creative (SA Christian Dior Couture vs. SAS Sodilog).[295] The court acknowledged all of the shoe's features that, according to the suing party, merited copyright protection:

> very high-heeled platform sandals with no reinforcement at the heel, and open on the front of the foot; the body of the shoe is characterized by a set of geometrically shaped leather strips linked together by rounded metal rivets; a first piece covers the front of the upper, uncovering the toes. On each of the lateral ends of this yoke is fixed a small

294 Cass. 1re civ., 20 mars 2014, n° 12-18.518, F-D.
295 Jankowska, Meghaichi, Pawełczyk, *Illustrated* . . . .

> rounded metal rivet; a second large piece in the general shape of a diamond is located on the central part of the upper. On the upper and lower end of this diamond-shaped yoke there are two rounded metal rivets which connect the parts together; a third piece is located at the level of the instep, it has an inverted triangle shape on the front of the upper and continues on the sides with a strap intended to surround the ankle and comprising a metal buckle on the side. The two ends of the small strap are connected to this yoke by a rounded metal rivet; a fourth part consisting of a wide band surrounds the upper end of the heel and is connected to the part previously described by two rounded metal rivets.[296]

The case is important as an exemplary case of how the originality threshold works in practice for fashion design. The court also noted that the case is still valid if the party suing for copying is not the fashion designer themself. According to the court, if the work is exploited under a legal person's name, it is presumed that the legal person has a legal title to the work of authorship. This is a rule made by the French Supreme Court in 1993 in order to ease civil proceedings from strict rules of copyright law that require the author to transfer economic copyright by contract in writing. This rule, the so-called safety valve, requires the company to prove either unequivocal exploitation or public exhibition under its name. It has been noted in the literature that this approach has freed applied art from the rules of copyright.[297]

4.3.3.7 Cocktail dress and skirt: niveau *of creativity*

A general idea of originality with regard to fashion design can be inferred from a good many decisions made by Parisian courts in relation to women's dresses.

In 2019, the Court of Appeals in Paris decided that a, quite simple, dress model ASM 1302C, designed by ASHWI, was creative enough to benefit from copyright protection. The design was described as:

> a short, flared dress made up of a succession of four rows of full-length ruffles arranged in a staggered pattern, giving an impression of fluidity; rounded ruffles on the bias to maintain a light and seductive physiognomy; the neckline highlighted with a band made up of six lines of rhinestones, extending along the straps and ending at the back without

296 Cour d'appel de Paris, Pôle 5, Chambre 2, Arrêt du 8 février 2013, Répertoire général n° 11/02407; Jugement du 27 janvier 2011 – Tribunal de Grande Instance de PARIS 3ème Chambre 4ème Section – RG n° 09/15874.

297 Kahn, *The Copyright/Design* . . ., pp. 30–31.

joining; a flower at the bottom of the left strap, made up of a veil rolled up on itself creating an appearance of volume, the centre of the flower being embellished with three brilliants reminiscent of the rhinestones found along the neckline, two strips of veiling as well as three loops of different sizes hanging from this flower.[298]

Also of note is the decision made by the Court of Appeals in Paris in 2019[299] that considered MAJE's design of a dress and a skirt worthy of copyright protection.[300] The RAYURE dress presents an original combination of the following characteristics:

- This is a dress featuring a fitted top,
- comprising a vertical yoke on the front of the model, stopping at the waist, and composed vertical bands of openwork mesh,
- also comprising, to the right and left of the perforated vertical band, symmetrical yokes, arranged at an angle, tracing a diagonal from the armpits to the waist,
- the bottom of the dress is composed of a flared skirt,
- in openwork knit,
- tightened at the waist,
- comprising a series of darts at the front and at the back of the skirt, arranged symmetrically,
- the entire dress is made up of a series of alternating side strips of fabric,
- with bands of openwork mesh, presenting a geometric pattern made up of interlocking cells presenting a honeycomb effect,
- the dress has an inner lining that is shorter than the dress.[301]

There was also a testimony from the designer of the dress, who testified that it was created on 30 July 2014, as part of her employment contract. The designer attached a dated sketch of the dress and related that she wanted to 'create a dress with a very structured effect for the top of the dress and a flared skirt, of great lightness, revealing the legs in transparency, given the fabric, openwork described above. By choosing to use a light, honeycomb-like material, I wanted to create a dress with both transparency and a chic, structured look. I wanted to surprise customers with the combination of a particular cut

298 TGI Paris, 17 Nov. 2017, RG n° 16/08321; Court of Appeals in Paris, Pôle 5, Ch. 1, arrêt du 24 Sept. 2019, RG no. 18/00814, cf. other ASHWI models 2134, 1313T, 8232 et 2022 Ordonnance du 27 mai 2016 -Président du TGI de PARIS – RG n° 16/04388; Cour d'appel de Paris, Pôle 5, Chambre 1, Arrêt du 29 novembre 2016, Répertoire général n° 16/14008.

299 TGI Paris RG no. 15/10180, judgement as of 10 June 2016, Court of Appeals of Paris, Pôle 5, Ch. 1, arrêt du 11 June 2019, nr no. 16/16167.

300 Jankowska, Meghaichi, Pawełczyk, *Illustrated* . . . .

301 https://www.pinterest.com/pin/477522366731517979/; TGI Paris RG no. 15/10180, judgment as of 10 June 2016, Court of Appeals of Paris, Pôle 5, Ch. 1, arrêt du 11 June 2019, nr no. 16/16167.

and an unexpected fabric. In fact, with this structured top with yokes placed at an angle to slim the waist, I wanted a corset effect that underlined the femininity of the garment design. This top contrasts with the bottom of the dress with a ball effect, which further refines the waist. I wanted to create a very feminine, elegant and surprising dress, thus allowing any use.'

In another decision dated 11 March 2016, the Paris TGI ruled that the companies Mango France, Mango Haussmann, Mango online and Punta FA committed acts of infringement against the company Chloé by reproducing on a dress reference 23035573 the characteristics of the combination of square embroidery patterns on which the plaintiff holds copyright.[302]

It seems important to point out that a design need not be elaborate or rich in ornamentation, details or elements in order to prove copyrightable. There is evidence of a theoretically "simple" dress, where, given the choice of elements, but also the well-knit construction of the dress, the overall impression was considered copyrightable.

The Court of Appeals in Paris noted that L'Onkel's "Boucle L" dress met the criterion of creativity[303] because of the following features:

- long straight strapless dress, split, in a polyester elastane mesh fabric with a cutout on the chest,
- the top is double-layered with a bust dart,
- the dress has a cutout in the front, on the left from which pleats start and a keel of about 80cm which takes up the same folds stitched at 3cm and which makes it possible to partly hide a slit with a height of 80cm,
- the back has a lined bustier like on the front.[304]

As capacious as the French premise of originality may seem, it does not allow for just any *niveau* of choice or selection. A good example is a dress designed by S.A.R.L. Gamara, brand Mamouchka, model Ness,[305] that was found insufficiently creative to invoke any feel of originality.[306] The court went on to stress that

> the originality of a work must be assessed globally so that the combination of elements which characterizes it by virtue of their particular arrangement gives it a physiognomy which demonstrates the creative

302 TGI Paris, jugement du 11 mars 2016 – Tribunal de grande instance de PARIS – 3ème chambre 2ème section – RG n°14/11357 – jugement du 27 mai 2016 – Tribunal de grande instance de PARIS – 3ème chambre 2ème section – RG n°16/08209; Court of Appeals of Paris, Pôle 5, Ch. 2, judgement of 22 September 2017, RG no. 16/14195.

303 Jankowska, Meghaichi, Pawełczyk, *Illustrated* . . . .

304 Jugement du 20 décembre 2007 – Tribunal de Commerce de PARIS, RG n° 2007013934, Court of Appeals of Paris, 4ème Chambre, Section B, Arrêt du 21 novembre 2008, Répertoire général n° 08/01060.

305 Jankowska, Meghaichi, Pawełczyk, *Illustrated* . . . .

306 TGI Paris, RG n°16/06287, judgement of 14 December 2017, Court of Appeals of Paris, Pôle 5, Ch. 2, judgement of 24 May 2019, RG no. 18/02145.

> effort and the aesthetic bias bearing the imprint of the personality of the author.

The court observed that not just any "lines and shapes" are eligible for copyright protection. In this case, the court denied protection based on the observation that the plaintiff did not claim the choice of material in any way, nor that of the material patterns for both the upper and lower part.

4.3.4 *Netherlands*

4.3.4.1 *Overview*

The Dutch Copyright Act of 1912 (Auteurswet, hereinafter: DCA) sets forth in Article 1 that "copyright is the exclusive right of the author of a literary, scientific or artistic work".[307] It expands on this rule by providing a non-enumerative listing of the works included, which, in points 6, 8 and 11 of Article 10, makes clear reference to "drawings, paintings, works of architecture and sculpture", "designs, sketches" as well as to "works of applied art and industrial drawings and models". Dutch copyright does not provide any register for works, nor does it condition protection on the placing of a copyright notice on the work.[308] In the Dutch legal literature, as well as in the jurisprudence, it is observed that a work, in order to merit copyright protection, has to be original (Dutch *oorspronkelijkheid*); that is, it must meet the criteria of individual character and a personal stamp.[309] This level or creativity was also adopted

307 www.vevam.org/wp-content/uploads/2016/09/Dutch-Copyright-Act-2015.pdf (access: 02.01.2023), cf. S. Rothenberg, *Copyright and Public Performance of Music*, Martinus Nijhoff, 1954, p. 92; F.W.J.G. Snijder van Wissenkerke, *Het auteursrecht in Nederland: Auteurswet 1912 en herziene Berner Conventie,* Gouda: Van Goor Zonen, 1913, p. 162; H.L. de Beaufort, *Het auteursrecht in het Nederlandsche en Internationale recht*, P. den Boer, 1909 (Heruitgave in opdracht van Buma) 1993.

308 However, as noted by P. Bernt Hugenholtz, despite the strong tradition of applying copyright and design protection concurrently,

> pursuant to former article 21(3) of the Benelux Act, copyright terminated automatically upon expiry of the shorter term of design protection, unless the rights owner deposited an instrument of copyright reservation with the Benelux Design Registry. In a case concerning imitations of Italian furniture designs, the Hoge Raad held that former article 21(3) of the Benelux Act conflicted with the prohibition on formalities of article 5(2) of the Berne Convention, and therefore did not apply to foreign works subject to the convention.

The article 21(3) of the Benelux Act was revised and the deposit of an instrument of copyright reservation is no longer needed. P. Bernt Hugenholtz, *Chronicle of The Netherlands, Dutch copyright law, 2001–2010*, RIDA 2010; cf. Hoge Raad, 26 May 2000, NJ 2000, 671, GRUR Int. 2002, 1050 (Cassina a.o./Jacobs Meubelen BV a.o.); Hoge Raad 11 May 2001, AMI 2001, p. 97, GRUR Int. 2002, 10 (Vredestein/Ring 65).

309 Lucie Guibault, Kevin van 't Klooster, *The Balance of Copyright. Dutch Report,* www.yumpu.com/en/document/read/23603040/netherlands-balance-of-copyright-report-final-06092011pdf-ivir (accessed: 28.01.2023); M. van Eechoud, S. van Gompel, L. Guibault,

for designs and models in the flagship case *Screenoprints*, that confirmed that applied art does not need to meet any higher standard.[310] There is an opinion that the Dutch Copyright law does not set a high threshold of creativity,[311] and the Dutch Supreme Court is known for a couple of judgements proving its easy-going approach to the principle of originality[312] by granting copyright protection to perfumes,[313] kinetic schemes,[314] simple games,[315] standardised holiday homes[316] or even by attempting to extend protection to food.[317] With

B. van der Sloot, B. Hugenholtz, Questionnaire – boundaries and interfaces: answers by the Dutch ALAI group. In *ALAI Dublin 2011: national reports* Copyright Association of Ireland, 2011, www.alaidublin2011.org/wp-content/uploads/2011/05/Netherlands.pdf (as of 28.01.2023).

310 Screenoprints (Vacuum Formers) Limited vs. Citroën Nederland B.V., HR 29 November 1985, NJ 1987/880; Judgement of Cour de Justice Benelux as of 22 May 1987, case file no. A 85/3/

311 J.H. Spoor, *The Novelty Requirement in Design Protection Law: The Benelux Experience*, "American Intellectual Property Law Association Quarterly Journal", 1996, vol. 24, p. 725, p. 744.

312 The easy-going approach extending to the Benelux IP Office can be spotted also by example of the case *G-Star* v. *Benetton*, in which the claimant obtained two trademarks on the shape, stitching and cuts of its jeans design. It was the ECJ that made a final decision that the jeans shape had not acquired distinctiveness and was not eligible for trademark protection. P. Kuris, K. Schiemann, L. Bay Larsen, *European Court of Justice, 20 September 2007*, IPPT20070920, ECJ, Benetton v G-Star, p. 1; P. Bernt Hugenholtz, *Chronicle* . . .

313 H.C. Jehoram, *The Dutch Supreme Court Recognises "Dilution of Copyright" by Degeneration of a Copyright Design into unprotected Style: The Flying Dutchman: All Sails, No Anchor*, "EIPR", 2007, vol. 29, no. 6, p. 206; Hoge Raad 16 June 2006, NJ 2006, 585 (Kecofa/Lancôme); cf. French Supreme Court [Cour de Cassation] on the contrary in the ruling of 13 June 2006, RIDA October 2006, 210, p. 348 (Bsiri-Barbir/Haarmann & Reimer); L. Calleja, *Why Copyright Law Lacks Taste and Scents*, "Journal of Intellectual Property Law", 2013, vol. 21, no. 1, pp. 16–19, cf. T.G. Field Jr., *Copyright Protection for Perfumes*, "IDEA: The Journal of Law and Technology", vol. 45, no. 1, 2004, p. 19; C. Cronin, *Genius in a Bottle: Perfume, Copyright, and Human Perception*, "Journal of the Copyright Society of the USA", vol. 56, no. 2–3, p. 427; E. Derclaye, *One on the Nose for Bellure: French Appellate Court Confirms That Perfumes Are Copyright Protected*, "Journal of Intellectual Property Law & Practice", 2006, vol. 1, no. 6, p. 377.

314 Hoge Raad Judgement of 24 February 2006, 28 IIC 615 (2007) (Technip Benelux BV/Goossens).

315 Hoge Raad Judgement of 29 June 2001, NJ 2001, 602 (Impag/Hasbro), (LJN AB2391, NJ 2001, 602 m.nt. DWFV, AMI 2001, nr. 15, p. 111).

316 Hoge Raad Judgement of 8 September 2006, NJ 2006, 493 (Timans/Haarsa & Agricola),(LJN AX3171, NJ 2006, 493, AMI 2006, p. 220).

317 E. Coche, *Should Taste Be Subject to Copyright Protection? Heksenkaas Will Tell Us*, Kluwer Copyright Blog, 31.01.2018; http://copyrightblog.kluweriplaw.com/2018/01/31/taste-subject-copyright-protection-heksenkaas-will-tell-us/ (access: 02.01.2023); *Levola Hengelo BV v Smilde Foods BV*, case C-310/17, 13 November 2018, ECLI:EU:C:2018:899; cf. L. Dijkman, *CJEU Rules That Taste of a Food Product Is Not Protectible*, "Journal of Intellectual Property Law & Practice", 2019, vol. 14, no. 2, p. 86; E. Rosati, *Ehy the CJEU Cheese Copyright Case Is Anything But Cheesy*, "Journal of Intellectual Property Law & Practice", 2017, vol. 12, no. 10, p. 813.

this approach to originality, it generally accepted that clothing or furniture[318] contain the requisite authorship necessary to sustain a claim to copyright.[319]

Item of note no. 4.12 Total impression doctrine

In the Dutch case law, there is a lot of emphasis on the *'total impression' approach*,[320] meaning that it is subject to a court's investigation whether a defendant has distanced themself sufficiently from the existing works and expressed themself in an individual way that is protected as an original combination of free elements.[321] This criterion is somehow controversial, because it invites style or technique into the copyright debate, elements that should inherently fall outside protection.[322] Moreover, the concept of 'overall impression' has been borrowed from the Dutch design law and the doctrine of slavish imitation[323] and was adopted into the copyright law since the *Decaux v. Mediamax* case.[324]

4.3.4.2 *Protection of style*

A line between the form of individual expression and style therefore also triggers a lot of attention in the Dutch copyright law.[325] There is a series of European cases that explicitly excludes copyright protection for style. In an old case, *Gelder* v. *Van Rijn*, the Dutch Supreme Court, in its judgement of 1946,

318 Cf. Hoge Raad Judgement of 22 February 2013 (Stokke vs. H3 Products); Hoge Raad Judgement of 12 April 2013 (Hauck vs. Stokke); Hoge Raad Judgement of 12 April 2013 (Stokke vs. Fikszo); H. Koenraad, *Dutch Supreme Court Tripp Trapp Children's Chair Cases*, "Journal of Intellectual Property Law & Practice", 2013, vol. 8, no. 12, p. 909.

319 However, a minimally creative filing cabinet fell short of the originality criteria, cf. *Stealth*, Hoge Raad Judgement of 4 March2003, AMI 2003/11.

320 Antoon A. Quaedvlieg, *De totaalindruk, kern van het bewerkingsrecht*, BIE, November 2015, pp. 240–245; J. Spoor, *Hoezo totaalindrukken?*, Dommeringbundel, 2008, pp. 321–332; C. Gielen, *De totaalindruk in het auteursrecht*, IER, 2004, nr. 55, pp. 255–259.

321 Cf. Supreme Court of the Netherlands, 22 February 2013, Stokke v. H3, LJN BY1529; AMI 2013, 158; NJB 2013/500, RvdW 2013/331, JWB 2013/107, ECLI:NL:HR:2013:BY1529.

322 M.R. de Zwaan, *De totaalindruk: onjuist maar niet onbruikbaar*, AMI 20016, no. 5, p. 113; Mike Landerbarthold, *Minimalistisch ontwerp. Een onderzoek naar de consequenties van de toenemende trend van minimalisering in productontwerp*, master's thesis, 215, p. 35, https://docplayer.nl/19148246-Minimalistisch-ontwerp.html (accessed: 05.01.2023).

323 P.B. Hugenholtz, 'Gezamenlijke noot onder Stokke/H3, Stokke/Fikszo en Hauck/Stokke', Amsterdam: IVIR 2013, NJ 2013, afl. 46, no. 503, p. 5896–5900.

324 HR December 29, 1995, NJ 1996, 546, m.nt. Verkade.

325 Cf. Antoon A. Quaedvlieg, *Ideeën, techniek en stijl als dark matter van de auteursrechtelijke beschermingsomvang*, AMI, 2015/2, pp. 29–37.

asserted that applying burn and steel-brushing techniques does not merit copyright protection. Similarly, in the Dutch cases *Decaux* v. *Mediamax* (1995) and *Broeren v. Duijsens-Kroezen* (2013), it was emphasised that the exclusion of style from copyright law is its rule of thumb that cannot be circumvented by applying other legal regimes, like tort law.[326] In the Netherlands, there is a *theory of slavish imitation* (*slaafse nabootsing*) that was used as a 'safety net', when copyright or other IPR regimes fell short of protection, especially for industrial designs. The Dutch Supreme Court, in the *Broeren* ruling, made clear that style as such is not copyrightable.[327]

4.3.4.3 Artistic value in Dutch copyright protection

As noted in the Dutch literature, the originality threshold for copyright protection is low for two reasons. First, the premise of originality is based on reasonably simple ideas about creativity, and second, there was never any question about 'artistic value'. Instead, this relatively undemanding bar has triggered debates as to whether it may in effect lead to a dilution of the line between protected work, style and trend.[328]

This light-hearted approach has been taken by the Dutch Supreme Court (*Hoge Raad*) for many years, with such notable outcomes as the copyrightability of mattress cloth[329] and eggcups as applied art,[330] but the approach has also been the subject of discussion. From the 1970s to 1987, there was much uncertainty and discussion regarding a higher threshold for works of applied art. The catalyst for this was the mention of the word 'art' in Article 10, section 1, subsection 11 and the formulation of the Uniform Benelux Law on Designs and Models (1975) that required that, in order to be eligible for copyright protection, models and designs must be of a 'clearly artistic

326 Article 6:162 of the Dutch Civil Code; Stef van Gompel, *Creativity, autonomy and personal touch. A critical appraisal of the CJEU's originality test for copyright* [w:] M. van Eechoud, *The Work of Authorship*, Amsterdam University Press, 2014, p. 122. HR 28 juni 1946, NJ 1946, 712 (Van Gelder/Van Rijn); HR 29 December 1995, NJ 1996, 546 (Decaux/Mediamax); HR 29 maart 2013, IEF 12509, LJN BY8661, ECLI:NL:HR:2013:BY8661 (Duijsens/Broeren).

327 Piter de Weerd, *NL: Confusing Slavish Imitation of a Painting Style Is Not Illegitimate*, 4 April 2013, http://copyrightblog.kluweriplaw.com/2013/04/04/nl-confusing-slavish-imitation-of-a-painting-style-is-not-illegitimate/ (accessed. 22.01.2023).

328 Stef van Gompel, *Creativity, Autonomy and Personal Touch. A Critical Appraisal of the CJEU's Originality Test for Copyright* [in:] *The Work . . . , p. 112*; J.L.R.A. Huydecoper, *Originaliteit of inventiviteit? Het technisch effect in het auteursrecht*, BIE, 1987, pp. 106–112.

329 District Court of Amsterdam, 14 October 1929, *Baekers en Raymakers' Textielfabrieken v. Leeuwin*, see Antoon Quaedvlieg, *The Copyright/Design Interface in the Netherlands* [in:] E. Derclaye (ed.), *The Copyright/Design Interface: Past, Present, and Future*, 2018, Cambridge University Press, p. 43.

330 Court of Appeal of Amsterdam, 2 March 1961, *BIE* 1961, no. 77 (*Eierdopjes*), p. 180, cf. Stef van Gompel, Erlend Lavik, *Quality, Merit, Aesthetics and Purpose: An Inquiry into EU Copyright Law's Eschewal of Other Criteria Than Originality*, RIDA 2013, no. 236, p. 16, fn. 99.

character'[331] (Dutch *een duidelijk artistiek karakter*, fr. *un caractère artistique marqué*).[332] The uncertainty was put to an end by the judgements of the Benelux Court of Justice (*Benelux-Gerechthof*, BenGH) of 22 May 1987 and the Dutch Supreme Court in a case from 1985/1988 referred to as *Screenoprints v. Citroën*.[333] The court asserted that copyright protection should rest on the criterion of originality and not on 'artistic value'. At the same time, it observed that there is also another approach to the requirement of 'certain art value', meaning that 'a certain artistic endeavour on the part of the maker' should be expressed. It is generally assumed that the originality-based approach rests on relatively small amounts of artistic value.[334] The protection would be rejected only if the 'original character' concerned only the achievement of a technical effect.[335]

The historical method of legal analysis proves that it was not the Dutch lawmaker's intention to limit the application of the law to artistic works with 'a specific and apparent artistic quality'. In the process of drafting the legal text of 1912, its choices were substantiated this way:

> The question arises whether one is conscious of the particular difficulties that the legislature would impose on the court if the protection of the law was expressly or implicitly limited to works with artistic value. Where would the court have to draw the line? Which particulars should be taken into consideration? Artistic value is a matter of personal appreciation. Art history, especially of later times, gives numerous examples of artworks, which at first were denied any artistic value by very competent critics, but which eventually were praised as masterpieces.[336]

331 Quaedvlieg, *The Copyright/Design Interface . . .*, p. 39; M. Ritscher, R. Landolt, *Shift of Paradigm for Copyright Protection of the Design of Products*, GRUR Int., 2019, p. 125. As.

332 As explained by Antoon Quaedvlieg the clearly artistic character was eventually interpreted as meaning not more than just original, cf. Quaedvlieg, *The Copyright/Design Interface . . .*, p. 39, fn. 13.

333 NJ 1987, 880, AMI 1986, p. 13, BIE 1986, nr. 15, p. 55; note L. Wichers Hoeth, NJ 1987, p. 881; note Steinhauser BIE 1987, no. 49, p. 196; note H. C. Jehoram, Ars Aequi 1987, p. 717–25; note J. H. Spoor, AMI 1987, p. 78–83.

334 Case no. 11/00477; NJB 2013/886, IER 2013/50, JWB 2013/217,

335 D.W.F. Verkade, Comment on *Stokke v. Fikszo* (in Dutch), 5 October 2012, ECLI:NL:PHR:2012:BY1532. Cf. cases regarding rejecting the protection for a draining tile, HR 27 January 1995 (Dreentegel), (NJ 1997, 293), lighting for greenhouse horticulture, HR 29 January 2010 (Gavita/Helle), (LJN BK1599, RvdW 2010, 223) or water treatment machine, BIE 2006, no. 17, p. 100 (Holland Marine Services Amsterdam v. DVZ Services).

336 *Parlementaire geschiedenis van de Auteurswet 1912* (1989), *supra* note 92, I, 10.14 and 10.6 (Memorandum of Reply [*Memorie van Antwoord*] of the Dutch Lower Chamber 1912), L.De Vries (ed).; see Stef van Gompel, Erlend Lavik, *Quality, Merit, Aesthetics . . .*, p. 15, fn. 94–96; cf. Erlend Lavik, Stef van Gompel, *On the Prospects of Raising the Originality Requirement in Copyright Law: Perspectives from the Humanities*, "Journal of the Copyright Society of the USA", 2013, vol. 60, no. 3.

With that in mind, the *Hoge Raad* allowed copyright protection of a piece of delftware and asserted, based on two expert opinions, that the emotions the designer wants to evoke are of relevance and that the observer's impression of beauty is what matters.[337] Thus, in the history of Dutch case law, there is also an account on this very subjective approach.

According to the Dutch standards, a work is denied copyright protection in case of the absence of any creativity, that is, for a work so trivial or banal that it involves no creative labour of any kind. This approach has been subject to extensive criticism.[338] As noted by Michael Ritscher and Robin Landolt, "despite the criticism, the Dutch courts adhere to this indulgent practice, which is currently even strengthened by the emerging harmonization of the level of originality initiated by the CJEU in 2009".[339]

4.3.4.4 *Low threshold for design? Tripp Trapp cases*

In one of the Hoge Raad flagship cases, that of 12 April 2013, *Stokke v. Fikszo*,[340] the Tripp Trapp chair design, produced since 1972, was considered to be original for two separately protected features: 1) the inclined uprights into which all elements of the chair are incorporated and 2) the L-shape of the uprights and beams. The court stressed that a revolutionary design with a high degree of originality and a new vision of the prior concept of a children's chair required a wide scope of protection and that it could not be accepted that adopting just one of these features would entail no copyright infringement.[341] It is relevant to know that the Tripp Trapp chair design had been awarded several prizes and was exhibited in the Vitra Design Museum. This was one of the reasons for the court to acknowledge its revolutionary design and to see the premise of originality in this project. The Hoge Raad pointed out that including public opinion in the legal reasoning process does not constitute an incorrect interpretation of the law and can be supported.[342]

337 Supreme Court of the Netherlands (Hoge Raad), 27 May 1929, 'Objects of delftware', NJ 1929, p .1315–16; Court of Appeal of Arnhem, 30 October 1928, Weekblad van het Recht, no. 11921; see Quaedvlieg, *The Copyright/Design Interface* . . ., p. 44, fn. 33, 34.

338 Quaedvlieg, *The Tripod of Originality and the Concept of Work in Dutch and European Copyright*, GRUR Int. 2014, pp. 1105–1109; cf. Quaedvlieg, *The Copyright/Design Interface* . . ., p. 48.

339 Ritscher, Landolt, *Shift of Paradigm* . . ., p. 129.

340 HR 12 April 2013, ECLI:NL:HR:2013:BY1532, IER 2013/50 m.nt. P.G.F.A. Geerts, NJ 2013/502.

341 Cf. case no. 14/04455; Stokke v. Hauck, Hoge Raad judgement of 1 May 2015 ECLI:NL:HR:2015:1200; A. Hammerstein, Opinion on the Hoge Raad judgement (in Dutch), 20 March 2015, ECLI:NL:PHR:2015:317.

342 Ibidem.
www.stokke.com/USA/en-us/highchairs/TT01.html?dwvar_TT01_color=136&cgid=15134; https://uitspraken.rechtspraak.nl/inziendocument?id=ECLI:NL:PHR:2015:317 (as of 1.01.2023); www.boek9.nl/items/iept20091021-rb-amsterdam-stokke-v-jamak (as of 2.01.2023).

Item of note no. 4.13 Copyrightability of the Scandinavian style

Just on a side note, even Dutch courts exhibit a lack of unanimity in this respect, as the Court of Appeals of Amsterdam on the *Stokke v. Jamak* case (Leander chair)[343] and *Stoke v. H3*[344] contested the Tripp Trapp chair design's copyright protection. In the latter case, the *Scandinavian style's* eligibility for copyright protection was also contested on the grounds that it is too minimalist. This reasoning was supported by the Hoge Raad in 2013.[345] The Supreme Court accentuated that the Tripp Trapp is revolutionary, while concluding that its copyright protection cannot extend to its *purely technical features, style elements, and choices that are largely dictated by technology and usability.*

The Supreme Court concluded that

> the basic shape of the Carlo is not reminiscent of a cursive capital L, but rather of an (unfinished) S. Seen from the front, the Carlo is narrower at the top than at the bottom. The Carlo looks playful and is somewhat reminiscent of a rocking chair; . . . The overall picture of the Carlo deviates so much from the overall picture of the Tripp Trapp.

The Carlo design was found to be an independent design, and not an imitation, reproduction, modification or malformation of any sort. Based on this conflict in Hoge Raad pronouncements related to the Tripp Trapp design, Antoon Quaedvlieg criticises the Dutch jurisprudence for the "great legal uncertainty" created.[346] Having analysed the cases, I would rather say that this multitude of decisions regarding the single Tripp Trapp design gives a broad range of arguments to discuss but is also a great source of knowledge and inspiration. I would not go so far as to criticise the two discrepant lines of reasoning. Rather, they prove how 'delicate' the area of design is and that, even in this very narrow area of copyright, one size does not fit all the issues at

www.boek9.nl/items/iept20090107-rb-haarlem-stokke-v-h3-tripp-trapp-stoel (as oof 2.01. 2023).

343 Court of Appeals of Amsterdam judgement of 17 January 2012, AMI 2012, 81, LJN BV 3404.

344 Court of Appeals of Amsterdam judgement of 15 March 2011, LJN BQ3808.

345 Supreme Court of the Netherlands, 22 February 2013, Stokke v. H3, LJN BY1529; AMI 2013, 158; NJB 2013/500, RvdW 2013/331, JWB 2013/107, ECLI:NL:HR:2013:BY1529. Cf. J. Köklü, S. Nérisson, *How Public Is the Public Domain? The Perpetual Protection of Inventions, Designs and Works by Trademarks*, [in:] H. Ullrich, R.M. Hilty, M. Lamping, J. Drexl (eds.), *TRIPS plus 20 – From Trade Rules to Market Principles*, Springer 2016, p. 561; Pasa, *Industrial Design* . . ., p. 94.

346 Quaedvlieg, *The Copyright/Design Interface* . . ., p. 57.

stake. Fashion is equally 'sensitive' if not more so. From my perspective, these two contradictory decisions give an explicit explanation of how every detail matters. The *boundary line for copyright protection in fashion (design) is not something that can be learned or hammered out, it has to be felt.*

Interestingly, the *Hoge Raad*, in its judgement of 22 February 2013, followed the reasoning it had expressed in the *Decaux v. Mediamax* case of 1995 regarding resemblance of street furniture, specifically billboards.[347]

The court made clear that the personal stamp has to apply to the work within two sets of boundaries: 1) fashion, trend or style and 2) functionality of the work. The key is to express the prevailing style, trend or fashion of the design in a sufficiently individual way that also presents sufficient distance (Dutch *voldoende afstand*) from the other works on the market (see points 4.5 and 4.6. of the judgement). The court applied the *overall impression doctrine* in this case.

The vague application of this doctrine can, however, be observed in the *Fatboy-the-Original* cases, that show how much room is left for interpretation.[348]

The District Court in Antwerp[349] asked in the *Fatboy v. ZET BVBA* case how a beanbag, that is, an enlargement of a classic pillow, bears the stamp of the author's personality. None of the plaintiff's arguments permitted the court to grant copyright protection. These arguments concerned 1) its rectangular shape, 2) the size of the beanbag and 3) choice of the raw nylon finish that is water and stain resistant. The court noted that the beanbag's functional features are excluded from copyright protection and that the arrangement of those features does not make it eligible for protection either. A similar case, *Fatboy v. Sitting Bull*, was pending before the District Court in Hertogenbosch but was dismissed in the first instance.[350] The situation diametrically changed in the court of the second instance, which invoked the overall impression doctrine in order to grant relief to plaintiff's claim. Despite the fact that a floor cushion is an ancient concept, the court, armed with this doctrine, found the Fatboy design original. It held that "the combination of all different elements gives a different impression than that of a classic pillow and therefore copyright can be applied to the whole, despite the fact that the different parts individually are not protected".[351]

347 Supreme Court of the Netherlands, 29 December 1995, Decaux v. Mediamax, NJ 1996, 546, D.W.F.V. en AMI 1996, 195 with a note of A. Quaedvlieg; Bijblad Industriële Eigendom, 16.09.1997, no. 9, pp. 343–354; ECLI:NL:HR:1995:ZC1942, www.ie-forum.nl/backoffice/uploads/file/IE-Forum_klassiekers_modellenrecht_HR29december1995,BIE1997,66(Decaux-Mediamax).pdf (accessed: 03.03.2023).

348 Stefanie Christiaens, *De bescherming van designmeubelen door het intellectueel eigendomsrecht*, master's thesis, 2017/2018, pp. 26–28, https://libstore.ugent.be/fulltxt/RUG01/002/479/295/RUG01-002479295_2018_0001_AC.pdf (accessed: 04.03.2022).

349 Judgement of the District Court in Antwerp as of 31 October 2008, case no. 04/6468/A, cf. Chrisiaens, *De bescherming* . . ., p. 25.

350 Judgement of the District Court in Hertogenbosch as of 17 June 2008, case no. 173431.

351 Judgement of the Court of Appeals in Hertogenbosch as of 16 February 2010, case no. HD 200.011–393. See Chrisiaens, *De bescherming* . . ., pp. 27–28.

4.3.4.5 Shoes, Jansen versus Armani

Jan Jansen, who established his business in Amsterdam in 1963, carved out a reputation as a successful shoe designer. He was nicknamed "godfather of the platform shoe", and was also the designer of the 'High Heeled Sneaker' (1977). In 1994, he designed a shoe 'Tutti Piedi', a design consisting of one folded piece of leather. The shoe has "minimum stitching, three pleats on each side and five on top, and a lace fastening consisting of one long lace, which is threaded along the shoe through small holes applied beside the pleats".[352] In 2005, Jansen noticed that Armani was featuring the same design in his fashion and fragrance advertisement. Jansen asked Armani to cease the alleged infringement, to provide information about its sales and to publish an apology. Armani hedged, mentioning that the design would not appear in the new collection, and rebutted the allegation by arguing that the shoe did not meet the copyright threshold, with Jansen himself having said that "It is almost no shoe".[353] In court, Armani submitted an exhibit of proof that shoes consisting of one piece of leather pulled together by a lace have been known for centuries, e.g. the 'Irish Slipper' and 'Drumacoon Bog Shoe' were worn in Ireland and Scotland (10th century). The Dutch court found that the 'Tutti Piedi' design bore the stamp of personality and was therefore sufficiently creative. It also found the two designs at issue generally similar (the so called overall impression), which lent weight to the claim. Armani, on the other, did not manage to substantiate the counterclaims that 1) this kind of shoe design was known long before 1994 and that 2) disparities between both shoe designs made them independent creations. The court therefore granted Jansen the requested injunction at the national level but did not extend it to other Berne Convention countries, making clear that, in other countries, this design might not prove copyrightable. Since Armani did not offer this particular design for sale in the Netherlands, the court did not order Armani to grant information about his sales. The court also denied rectification on the grounds that the case was already sufficiently exposed to the public gaze such that this remedy would be disproportionate. To recap, as summarised by Maarten Schut in the Netherlands, an object of applied art may benefit from copyright protection even if its design is minimalistic.[354]

4.3.4.6 G-Star v. Benetton

In this case, the Amsterdam Court of Appeals observed that in order to consider the Elwood design eligible for protection, the design would have to be proven to have its own original character and to bear the personal stamp of its author. The court asserted that although the various elements of the Elwood,

352 M. Schut, *Armani found to infringe copyright of Dutch shoe designer*, "Journal of Intellectual Property Law & Practice", 2006, vol. 1, no. 5, p. 308.

353 Schut, *Armani* . . ., p. 308.

354 Schut, *Armani* . . ., p. 309.

such as the stitching, inserts and the contrasting band, could each be found individually in jeans and other items of clothing, the elements in the Elwood had been incorporated in such a combination that it was an original product. Leaving aside the fact that Elwood had registered its design as a trademark, a creative combination can, by itself, be a creative achievement on the part of the designer and can therefore be copyrightable. The court also stressed that the elements of the Elwood design were not yet common in that part of the clothing industry in which G-Star and Benetton operate.

*4.3.4.7 Two-piece parka (*The Sting v. Krakatau*)*

The Dutch Court of Appeal Arnhem-Leeuwarden decided this case on 23 June 2020.[355] The court, heeding the CJEU's *Cofemel* decision,[356] found the defendant's design (The Sting) to be a knock-off.[357]

The courts, establishing whether the copied work was copyrightable, noted that a combination of unprotected elements can merit a copyright claim as long as the combination bears the stamp of personality of the author. In both instances, it was affirmed that the combination of the Krakatau's design features proved that the author made creative choices and therefore made the design recognisable as their own creation. The Court of Appeal further noted that the CJEU's *Cofemel* decision does not impose a stricter test for originality than had previously been applied in the Netherlands.

4.3.4.8 Interchangeable pieces of jewellery, Melano v. Quiges *fashion jewels*

The widely quoted *Melano* case was decided on 29 January 2013 by the Hertogenbosch Court of Appeal. The case concerned pieces of jewellery with interchangeable coloured elements, but this aspect is not relevant for discussion because the court dismissed the claim on the grounds that authorship, the author's personal stamp and the defendant's act of imitation were not found to be substantiated. This case is often juxtaposed with the case *SEVV v. AY Illuminate*, in which the District Court of Amsterdam in 2010 found interchangeable elements for lamps copyrightable.[358]

This case, however, allows for an observation that will be made in greater detail with reference to the Polish jurisprudence, that obtaining copyright protection involves a great deal of argument, proof and the presentation of expert opinions before the court. Ultimately, the outcome of court proceedings is

355 ECLI: NL: GHARL: 2020:4773; https://uitspraken.rechtspraak.nl/inziendocument?id=ECLI:NL:GHARL:2020:4773) (accessed: 03.01.2023).

356 C-683/17, EU: C:2019:721.

357 The Bird and Bird IP Team, *Fashion-Related IP Decisions Round-Up 2020*, "Journal of Intellectual Property Law & Practice", 2021, vol. 16, no. 6, p. 603.

358 Pasa, *Industrial Design* . . ., p. 94; van Gompel, *Creativity, Autonomy* . . ., p. 130; P.G.F.A. Geerts, *Noot onder Hof's-Hertogenbosch 29 januari 2013 (Melano/Quiges Fashion Jewels)*, IER, 2013/25, pp. 222–228.

dependent on many factors, so it is often impossible to make simple assumptions based on different cases adjudicated in different legal regimes.

4.3.4.9 *Kitchen collection* (Bu-Wear Clothing Company B.V. v. Bożena Janina Reinders-Sobieraj, De Culinaire Makelaar B.V.)

This case is of special comparative value, as the same collections have been subjects of court copyright under both the Dutch and Polish legal regimes. The case was first decided by the Dutch district court of Zwolle-Lelystad on 7 May 2010,[359] then 3 August 2011 and later by the Polish district and appellate courts in Poznań. Interestingly, these two decisions were mutually exclusive and proved that legal concepts of originality can vary to a great extent. The court in Zwolle-Lelystad concluded that the defendant infringed on the plaintiff's copyright by introducing a nearly identical kitchen collection to the market (plaintiff's collections: 'Chaud Devant', 'Le Chef Etoilé' and 'Beau Rocher'; defendant's collection: 'Chefs-Fashion'). The defendant's collection was produced by PPHU "Anna" S.C., subsequently the subject of legal proceedings in court in Poznań.

4.3.4.10 *Slavish imitation theory – quirky Dutch way of handling copycats*

The Dutch jurisprudence developed a theory of slavish imitation to handle cases where *look-alikes* are put on the market by competitors.

Slavish imitation is a form of wrongful act of essentially sponging off someone else's distinctive product by offering a virtually identical copy.[360] This institute offers protection for the appearance of products and not their technical functions. Even though the functional aspect is not regulated in a legal act, it is part of the tort law. In order to make use of this theory in the court, it is essential that these premises are met:

- the product has its own, distinctive position on the market;
- the claimant needs to make sufficient efforts to prevent the marketing of imitations;
- there is room for differences in the product that can be made without detrimental effect on the product;
- there is a risk of confusion between the products on the market;

359 Preliminary judgement of Dutch district court in Zwolle-Lelystad, as of 7 May 2010, based on Article 1019 e of Dutch Civil Procedure Code.; Preliminary judgement of Dutch district court in Zwolle-Lelystad, as of 3 August 2011, case file no. 181699, HA ZA-11-168; Case files no. IX Gc 433/10 p. 1349, 1351.

360 Thomas Remmerswaal, *Slavish Imitation: Prohibiting Imiration without Patent or Design Right*, 24 July 2018, www.epc.nl/en/blog/slavish-imitation-prohibiting-imitation-without-patent-or-design-right (accessed: 05.01.2023).

the infringement must be based on fault, that is, the perpetrator has to be aware of the previous design.[361]

What is of interest to this study is that the *premise of confusion* is decided based on the concept of *overall impression* that is also used in Dutch copyright law. There is a delicate similarity between this concept and copyright law, as neither can prevent a third party from using the same style or trend.[362] Besides, the fact that a copying work has to imitate the original work slavishly, not just its main features or style, the original product has to maintain its distinctiveness by maintaining its position on the market in order not to allow for dilution. As noted in the judgement of the Dutch Supreme Court in the *All Round v. Simstars* case of 2017,[363]

> the distinctive character of a product can be liable to reduction, even total phasing-out ('dilution') to the extent that a growing amount of similar products gain access to and maintain their position on the market. As far as slavish imitation of a product is concerned, the producers marketing the original product can, under circumstances, be required to expend considerable effort to inhibit the market entry of unauthorised copies of that product, in order to maintain the distinctive character of their own product.[364]

In other words, the producer of the original product should prove a *strong IP policy*, something that can be obtained through sending summonses and subpoenas and by filing injunction proceedings. This case is of particular importance here as regards protection of jewellery under the slavish imitation theory. One of the courts deciding on the case found the design unprotectable because it had become diluted.[365]

Since 2009, All Round has been marketing a line of jewellery for women on the Dutch market under the name 'Mi Moneda'.[366] The collection consists of a pendant in three different colours (silver, gold and rosé) in three sizes and

361 Cf. Remmerswaal, *Slavish* . . . ; There was a case of a Dutch designer against IKEA that was alleged to have copied its lamp design. IKEA disputed ever having seen the lamp before, on which basis the claim was judged to be unfounded. Europe: Slavish imitation not lightly assumed, Managing IP Correspondent, 23 June 2013, www.managingip.com/article/b1kbplb6hd29s1/europe-slavish-imitation-not-lightly-assumed (accessed: 05.01.2023).

362 Piter de Weerd, *NL: Confusing slavish imitation of a painting style is not illegitimate*, Kluwer Copyright Blog, 4 April 2013, http://copyrightblog.kluweriplaw.com/2013/04/04/nl-confusing-slavish-imitation-of-a-painting-style-is-not-illegitimate/ (accessed: 05.01.2023).

363 Judgement of 19 May 2017, no. 16/01404, ECLI:NL:HR:2017:938.

364 Dirk Visser, *Jewellery can get 'diluted'*, 31 May 2017, https://leidenlawblog.nl/articles/jewellery-can-get-diluted (as of 5.01.2023).

365 Court of Appeals of Arnhem-Leeuwarden, 2012.

366 Mi Moneda design by All Round v. Nikki Lissoni design by Simstar; www.ie-forum.nl/artikelen/hr-eigen-gezicht-van-hangers-kan-afnemen-en-zelfs-verwateren; www.pinterest.ie/vsinead/

of a variety of compatible coins or discs. The Mi Moneda pendant consists of two parts connected by a hinge and can be opened to insert an interchangeable coin or disc. Since February 2012, Simstars has been marketing a line of jewellery for women under the brand name 'Nikki Lissoni', whose collection consists of similar pendants in three different colours (silver, gold and rosé) in three sizes, again with suitable coins or discs. The Nikki Lissoni pendant also consists of two parts connected by a hinge and can also be opened to insert an exchangeable coin or disc.

As for the concept of overall impression, it is used here with a different meaning. Since the prohibition of slavish imitation is intended to protect economic operators against unfair competition, assessing whether the consumer will be able to confuse an imitation with the imitated product depends on the influence of the likeness on the consumer's purchasing decision. The decisive factor here is the overall impression of each product and how it is viewed by an unobservant purchasing public that does not usually see the two products side by side.[367] The judge who must assess whether, in a specific case, in view of the overall impressions of comparable products, there is a risk of needless confusion among the relevant public, must take into account all relevant circumstances of the case. In doing so, the judge need not, as a rule, assume that points of similarity are given more weight in the question of confusion than points of difference. There is also no reason to distinguish according to whether any confusion relates to the products themselves ('direct confusion') or to their origin ('indirect confusion'). After all, both if the public considers the imitation to be the original and if it believes that the products concerned – even if they are not identical but give a similar overall impression – come from the same or economically linked undertaking(s), there is confusion that may influence that public's purchasing decision.[368]

4.3.5 Germany

4.3.5.1 *Overview – from Zwei-Stufen Test to artistic achievement*

German copyright protection is conditioned on the premise of personal spiritual creation (Ger. persönliche geistige Schöpfung), translated also as 'own intellectual creation' (§ 2 Sec. 2 UrhG).[369] According to § 2 Sec. 1 no. 4, copyright law protects 'artistic works, including works of architecture and of applied art and drafts of such works'. It also covers fashion sketches.[370]

---

mi-moneda/; www.bol.com/nl/nl/p/nikki-lissoni-p05rgs-hanger-s/9200000037360342/ (as of 5.01.2023).

367 HR 7 June 1991, ECLI:NL:HR:1991:ZC0273, NJ 1992/392 (Rummikub).

368 Points 3.4.4. and 3.4.5. of the Supreme Court judgement in the *All Round* case.

369 Legal act as of 9 September 1966 (BGBl. I S. 1273; amended as of 23 June 20221, BGBl. I S 1858), referred to as UrhG.

370 I. Kirchner-Freis, A. Kirchner, *Urheberrechtlicher Schutz von Mode* [in:] Handbuch. Moderecht, A. Kirchner, I. Kirchner-Freis (eds.), Erich Schmidt Verlag, 2011, pp. 144–145.

Item of note no. 4.14 Zwei-Stufen Test

The German courts have exerted some influence on interpretation of § 2 Sec. 2 UrhG to interpret this as referring to a creation of an individual character, whose aesthetic content is of such a level that, in the understanding of artistic circles and of people who are reasonably familiar with artistic views, one can speak of an 'artistic' achievement.[371] It is believed that the aesthetic effect of the design can only justify copyright protection if it is based on an artistic achievement and expressed in physical form.[372] However, for copyright protection of works of applied art and fine arts as well as for all other types of work, a design level that is not too low is required.[373]

It is important to note that until the Geburtstagszug case, the level of originality required from works of applied art was higher than for other genres of work (theory of the Zwei-Stufen Test). This was justified by the perception of the intersection of industrial design and copyright protection. These two regimes of protection were believed to be of the same character but pertaining to different levels of creativity. The theory of "kleine Münze" did not apply to works of applied art.[374] It was also noted, by the example of Coco Chanel's women's suits, that copyright protection can be granted to a specific form, meaning that, whereas a particular Coco Chanel suit that fulfils the obligations of originality may be eligible for copyright protection, the generalised concept of a Coco Chanel suit style falls outside of protection.[375] In the BGH case, Modeneuheit, it was generally admitted that protection is usually only possible for the period of the publication season, after which there is generally freedom of imitation, the so called *Nachahmungsfreiheit*.[376] However, if an individual case does not concern a seasonal fashion product that can be clearly assigned to a specific season, protection can exist for more than one season.

371 *BGH, Urteil vom 29.4.2021 – I ZR 193/20, ZUM 2021, 1040, 1047 – Zugangsrecht des Architekten; st. Rspr.; vgl. BGH GRUR 1983, 377, 378, juris Rn. 14 – Brombeer-Muster; GRUR 1987, 903, 904, juris Rn. 28 – Le-Corbusier-Möbel; ZUM-RD 2011, 457, Rn. 31 – Lernspiele; ZUM 2012, 36 Rn. 17 – Seilzirkus; BGHZ 199, 52 = ZUM 2014, 225Rn. 15 – Geburtstagszug.*

372 *BGH ZUM 2012, 36 Rn. 36 – Seilzirkus; BGHZ 199, 52= ZUM 2014, 225 Rn. 41 – Geburtstagszug.*

373 Nordemann [in:] *Urheberrecht*, Fromm/Nordemann, 2008, §2 side note 139; Eschman, *Rechtsschutz von Modedesign*, p. 32; *vgl. BGHZ 199, 52 = ZUM 2014, 225 Rn. 40 – Geburtstagszug; BGH ZUM 2015, 996 Rn. 44 – Goldrapper.*

374 W. May, *Gestaltungsschutz durch Design- und Urheberrecht* [in:] T. Hoeren (ed.), *Moderecht. Handbuch*, C.H. Beck, 2019, p. 71.

375 Kirchner-Freis, Kirchner, *Urheberrechtlicher . . .*, p. 145.

376 BGH GRUR 1973, 478, 480 – Modeneuheit.

For a very long time, the German standpoint on fashion design was that it could, in theory, be qualified as a work of applied art and therefore enjoy copyright protection; however, in practice, it was hard to prove the essential modicum of originality to exercise that protection.[377] There was one exceptional case regarding a dress adjudicated by the District Court in Leipzig in 2002 that was known for actually providing protection for a fashion design.[378] It was noted, however, that the design was outstanding and more than met the originality criterion.[379] For a long time, it was accepted in the German jurisprudence that both *haute couture* as well as *prêt-à-porter* (Ger. *Konfektion*) are eligible for copyright protection. In the *Mantelmodell* case, the court made clear that mass production is not excluded from protection *per se* and that originality can be experienced through so called *individuelle Gestaltung*, that could arise through new cuts of lines or a creative combination of elements that, if they occurred individually, would be in the public domain.[380] It was observed in the Gipürespitze case that

> the prerequisite is that it is a new fashion release that is above average and whose overall impression is characterized by individual aesthetic design features; models with classic elements or classic lines are no exception, because fashion is mainly based on what is already known.[381]

It was observed that "excessive demands are not to be made, so it can be enough [for copyright protection] for a shirt dress if it is a tasteful dress in terms of style and colour that are out of the ordinary".[382]

However, in the *Hemdblusenkleid* case, protection was refused to a shirt dress with a pleated skirt and a large coloured checked pattern (Ger. *Karomuster*) on the grounds that the combination of the elements was not artistic and lacked the sufficient level of individuality.[383] There is a string of German judgements that also refer to fashion design pattern, however protection was not granted to any of them. In the *Gipürespitze* (guipure lace) case, it was observed that

> the design elements used in the models, that is the respective cut of the models, the eyelet embroidery, the guipure lace and its motifs as well as

377 W. May, *Gestaltungsschutz . . .*, pp. 71–72; See BGH as of 10.11.1983, I ZR 158/81, BGH, GRUR 1984, p. 453 – Hemdblusenkleid; BGH, GRUR 1973, pp. 478–479 – Modeneuheit; BGH GRUR 1955, 445 – Mantelmodell; cf. OLG München GRUR 1995, 275 (276) – Parka-Model; OLG Hamburg GRUR 1986, 83 – Übergangsbluse; BGH GRUR 1998, 477 ff. – Trachtenjanke.

378 LG Leipzig; GRUR 2002, pp. 424–425 – Hirschgewand.

379 May, *Gestaltungsschutz . . .*, pp. 71–72.

380 BGH, 14.12.1954 – I ZR 65/53 – GRUR 1955, p. 445 – Mantelmodell, cf. BGH GRUR 1998, 477 ff. – Trachtenjanker; OLG München GRUR 1995, 275 (276) – Parka-Modell.

381 OLG Hamburg as of 24.02.2005, 5 U 66/04 – GRUR-RR 2006, p. 95 and ff – Gipürespitze.

382 OLG Hamburg as of 24.02.2005, 5 U 66/04 – GRUR-RR 2006, pp. 95 and ff – Gipürespitze.

383 BGH as of 10.11.1983, I ZR 158/81, BGH, GRUR 1984, p. 453 – Hemdblusenkleid.

> the textile bows are already known in themselves and widespread in the field of underwear, so that they alone are not able to justify an individual aesthetic effect. The overall effect conveyed by the concrete combination of the designing elements does not reach the level of an artistic-individual creation. It is by no means so original that the special perspective and individual creative power of its creator would be expressed in it.[384]

In another *Brombeermuster* (Blackberry pattern) case of 1983, it was also noted that a so called individuell geprägte Schöpfung (individually stamped creation) comes into existence when it can be proved that the content is of such an aesthetic quality that it can be discussed in terms of artistic effort.[385]

As noted in the German literature, the jurisprudence has changed in the meanwhile, as the reasonably high threshold of originality has been lowered. Works of applied art are subject to the same examination as any other works, such as pure art, literature or music. A case regarding sandals decided in March 2022 gives a general idea of the limits of copyright protection for fashion design in German law. The focus is not primarily on individual design elements, but on the overall impression that the work conveys to the viewer (OLG Hamburg, GRUR 2002, 419, 420).

4.3.5.2 *Case concerning sandals*

The District Court in Cologne, in its decision of 3 March 2022, attempted to draw a bigger picture of how copyright should be applied to works of fashion. In the first place, it referred to the EU jurisprudence to emphasise that the national courts are competent to assess the level of design and the quality of the work, points which are decisive for the copyright protection of works of applied art. In any case, the national courts – even though a uniform, EU-wide definition of a work of authorship is fundamentally recognised – have a comprehensive scope of assessment when fitting the definition of a work of authorship to the individual types of work. It is in line with the autonomous interpretation of the concept of a work of authorship under EU law if the national courts are allowed to exercise discretion. The CJEU leaves it up to the national courts to determine when leeway is used in individual cases.[386]

Barudi noted that the

> existence of a creation, of individuality and originality cannot be deduced solely from the objective properties of the respective work. Rather, these characteristics are to be considered based on their relation to the concrete creative process. The work-creator relationship cannot be adequately

384 OLG Hamburg as of 24.02.2005, 5 U 66/04 – GRUR-RR 2006, pp. 95 and ff – Gipürespitze.

385 BGH, Urteil vom 27.01.1983 – I ZR 177/80 – "Brombeer-Muster" (OLG München); BGHZ 35, 341, 345 [BGH 14.07.1961 – I ZR 44/59] – Buntstreifensatin; BGH as of 4.11.1966, Ib ZR 77/65, Skaicubana.

386 CJEU, GRUR 2020, 736, para. 38 – Brompton.

> grasped either from a one-sided view of the author or from an analysis of his work alone[387] . . . Rather, what is decisive is the rules according to which the author of a certain work worked, whereas it is irrelevant whether he was aware of it. Only when there are no existing rules specifying how the creator of a product has to manufacture it in a specific area – for example using learned processing techniques and design rules – is there no longer any freedom of design, with the result that the development of individuality is then no longer possible, even if a product that has been manufactured to perfection by hand is new and unique and could therefore definitely claim design protection. The purely manual or routine performance does not bear the stamp of individuality, no matter how solid and professional it may be . . .. [388] However, the manufacturer must also fill out the existing scope for design with his own creative decisions in order to become the author . . .. This means that the creative individuality is not a product of rules, but rather a rule for judging other products, i.e. it must happen on case-by-case basis.[389]

> It was observed by the court that

> the creative process must then be analyzed to determine whether the originator only oriented himself to what was given and did not fill the leeway with his own decisions. If it can be ruled out that a designer worked completely according to given rules, it can be concluded that he made his own creative decisions to a certain extent. Then there is an assumption that he actually used the given creative freedom to produce his intellectual product. According to this, the claiming author regularly fulfills his obligation to demonstrate the protectability of his work and to make it credible by submitting a copy of the work and presenting its special features.[390]

Also that

> if the person sued for copyright infringement defends himself with the objection that the work in dispute is not protectable or that the scope of protection is restricted because the author has resorted to previously known designs, the author must explain and prove the existence and appearance of such designs.

387 Barudi, Author and work – a formative relationship? 2013, 32 f; Zech, ZUM 2020, 801, 803.
388 Leistner, in: Schricker/Loewenheim, 6th edition 2020, § 2, marginal note 53.
389 LG Köln 3.03.2022; Cf. Haberstumpf, GRUR 2021, 1249, 1256.
390 Cf. BGH, GRUR 1981, 820, 822 – Stahlrohrstuhl III.

Therefore, the court noted

> In accordance with these principles, the disputed sandal models "B" and "H" are protected by copyright. . . .. LC has experimented with certain materials and design elements and combined them with each other in such a way that the result has a creative character. This applies regardless of the fact that some of these design elements were already known and found in sandal models from other manufacturers. Because the originality of the design devised by LC lies in their uniform combination. In doing so, he distanced himself sufficiently from the forms of representation for sandal models that existed, were customary and well-known in his creative field, and made artistic designs that went beyond the form dictated by the function. The other sandal models raised by the defendant, which are said to oppose the protectability of the models "B" and "H", illustrate that there is a wide range of design leeway in the field of sandals and numerous possibilities for filling them. L C has found its own rules for sandal design and implemented them in its sandal models "B" and "H".

4.3.6 Poland

4.3.6.1 Overview: personal stamp and statistical uniqueness

In the Polish copyright law (PCL), the concept of a 'work of authorship' is formed as a legal term with the help of the legal definition that was introduced in Article 1, section 1 of the PCL and reads, "The subject matter of copyright is each individual creative work, embodied in any form, regardless of its value, designation, or medium of expression (work of authorship)".[391] This definition is supplemented with a representative listing of works that gives an idea of how broad the concept is. Article 1, section 2 of PCL reads:

> In particular, the subject matter of copyright encompasses:
>
> 1) works expressed in words, mathematical symbols or graphics (literary, journalistic, scientific, cartographic and computer programs);
> 2) artistic works;
> 3) photographic works;
> 4) works of string instrument craftsmanship;
> 5) works of industrial design;
> 6) works of architecture, urban architecture, and urban planning;

391 Legal act of 4.02.1994 on Copyright and Related Rights, JoL of 2021 Item no. 1062.

7) musical works as well as musical and lyrical works;
8) dramatic works, dramatic works with music, choreographic works, and pantomimes;
9) audiovisual works (including motion pictures).

Although *fashion design* itself is not a subject matter explicitly listed in this enumeration, it can be advocated that it belongs to the wider category of 'industrial design' (Article 1, section 2, point 5 of PCL). However, it is noteworthy that this listing is introduced by the phrase "in particular", that, in the legal sense, is used to indicate an open catalogue of items. For the way ideas are expressed in the legal act, that is the definition encapsulated by section 1 and its examples in section 2, it is pointed out the concept 'work of authorship' is explained with the reference to the definition that is both synthetic and analytic. This legal approach can also be observed in the previous Polish legal acts on copyright law.[392]

Based on this definition, the copyright doctrine indisputably assumes that a work of authorship is an object that meets the following positive criteria: 1) it is creative, 2) it has an individual character, 3) it comes from a human being and 4) it can be manifested. It should be pointed out that the catalogue set forth in Article 1, section 2, point 5 of PCL is only an open enumeration that gives an idea of what kind of objects can be subject to copyright regulation, but it remains necessary to check the positive premises necessary to recognise that a specific object is a work of authorship.

The premises of *creativity* and *individuality* are subject to many tests, of which the most relevant tend to be the *test of personal stamp* (Pol. *piętno osobiste*); *test of subjective novelty* (Pol. *subiektywnie nowy wytwór intelektu*); *test of selection*, *arrangement*, *layout of a work* (Pol. *selekcja, aranżacja, ułożenie dzieła*); as well as *statistic uniqueness* (Pol. *statystyczna jednorazowość*, also *as statystyczna powtarzalność*).[393] Despite many attempts to define these premises, Max Kummer's theory of statistic uniqueness proves to be of use many times. According to this concept, it is tested whether the result of creative work is sufficiently unique, assuming that the topic would be developed by several artists on their own. As indicated in the judgement of the Supreme Court of 30 June 2005,

> the possibility of obtaining a similar result by different authors does not constitute an independent premise that excludes assigning a given manifestation of creative activity an individual character within the

392 Legal act on copyright law of 10 July 1952 (JoL of 1954 no. 34 Item 234) and legal act on copyright law of 29 March 1926 (JoL of 1935 no. 36 Item 260).

393 Judgement of Court of Appeals in Warsaw of 24.10.2019, case no. I Aca 651/18, LEX no. 2753736; judgement of Court of Appeals in Białystok of 10.03.2019, case no. I Aca 841/18, LEX no. 2722031; judgement of the Supreme Administrative Court of 11.07.2018.

> meaning of Art. 1 Section 1 of PCL. Even if it is possible that different people can achieve the same result, the individual character of the work should not be negated if the individual elements of the creative choice and representation are not the same, especially when the creator used the area of freedom when shaping the content and form of the work, and notwithstanding certain pre-defined requirements, the result of the work was not entirely determined by these requirements.[394]

The greater the scope of creative freedom, the easier the recognition of a given work as a work of authorship. Individuality may come through the *selection*, *arrangement*, *layout of a work*, the shape of which may be determined by the type of creativity or the utilitarian nature of the work.

Apart from the fact that the bar of creativity is not set high in copyright law, it should be noted that a work is not examined qualitatively or quantitatively to determine the characteristics of the creativity. This means that all works, from very high to medium quality, enjoy the same scope of copyright protection.

At the same time, setting the creativity bar at not too high a level means that "protection disappears only where the possibility of individual work ceases to exist, or where the recreation of facts is only a repetition in a form devoid of any independence (multiplication table, announcements)".[395] Katarzyna Jasińska drew attention to the fact that the protection of copyright in an increasingly broader scope of the subject is visible in Poland, Germany, UK and France, and cited railway timetables or machine manuals as examples of questionable works benefitting from copyright protection.[396] She criticised such a broad extension of the limits of copyright, pointing out that it should serve authors who make a greater creative contribution. However, this standpoint is not in line with the views of Polish jurisprudence. For example, the court of appeals in Kraków, in its judgement of 29 October 1997, stated that

> making protection dependent on the presence of an individuality feature in a work does not mean that this feature should be manifested to any specific degree of its intensity. Also, in the case of a minimum degree of individuality, it is permissible to classify a work revealing this feature as an object of copyright.[397]

394 Case file no. IV CK 763/04.
395 Supreme Court judgement of 21.03.1938, case file no. II 2531/37.
396 K. Jasińska, Commentary to the Supreme Court judgement of 27.02.2009, I CSK 337/08, Lex 2009.
397 Case file no. I ACa 477/97, Lex no. 533708.

Item of note no. 4.15 Pure versus applied arts

The Polish copyright law does not differentiate between works of *pure* and *applied arts*. In the judgement of the Supreme Court of 31 March 1953, it was pointed out that protection can apply "even when a work was created for practical purposes, as long as the work, at least in terms of form, exhibited certain creative elements". Similarly, in the justification for the judgement of the Court of Appeal in Poznań of 9 November 2006, it was found that

> the condition for granting copyright protection is, however, that such a study should be characterized by specific, resulting from individual creation author, elements expressed in the method of selecting and presenting data and their interpretation, as well as in the form of a personal and free (at least to some extent) presentation of them.[398]

4.3.6.2 Fashion design cases in Poland

INTRODUCTION

To gain a better understanding of how and whether *fashion design* is protected by the Polish copyright regime, this author undertook the task of investigating how many decisions regarding fashion were enacted in Polish district courts (45) and courts of appeal (11) in between 2000 and 2020. Only seven cases were reported, of which five are described and analysed in this book. The exact number of fashion design copyright cases is not certain, as, during the research, it was determined that the cases are not reported that much by subject matter but rather by the general concept of work of authorship. However, the cases discussed in this book give a general idea of the level of copyright protection and of what to expect in the Polish courts in respect to fashion design and its copyrightability.

TIGHTS AND LEGGINGS

The first case took place in the Court of Sieradz between 2004 and 2006.[399] The plaintiff requested an injunction banning of fixation, reproduction and the placing on the market of artistic works constituting a pattern in use on tights and leggings (the plaintiff's name of the product lane of the design was Veena). The plaintiff filed a motion to accept evidence based on the opinion of an expert, a visual artist, to prove that the defendant had plagiarised

398 Case file no. I ACa 490/06; see the judgement of the Supreme Court of June 30, 2005, file case no. IV CK 763/04, OSNC 2006, issue 5, item 92.

399 Case file no. I C 122/04.

the claimant's works or made obvious borrowings of the concept, layout, and graphics of the plaintiff's designs.

The defendant was one of the most recognisable producers of tights in Poland (Ferax – Iril sp. z o.o. in Zduńska Wola, owner of the brand "Gatta"), whereas the plaintiff was a student. In 2003 Ferax invited young designers to submit their projects, based on the possibility of future cooperation. The projects were created according to the defendant's guidance as to the colours and technology to be used: termoprint and stitching. The plaintiff's design, discussed at the job interview, was very well received. The plaintiff left her drawings at the defendant's office. However, she never was contacted afterwards. After a few months, the defendant put its latest tights collection on the market, which included a few designs that were allegedly modelled on the plaintiff's works, including graphical and colour elements. These are graphical patterns based on the motif of a vertical stripe running along the outer part of the leg (stripe), in a colour contrasting with the background, and jacquard patterns that can be applied using the stitching technology applied by the defendant (lockstitch effect). The colour scheme dominating the youth line of tights produced by the defendant was different from the one used hitherto and similar to that proposed by the claimant in the projects presented to the defendant. The plaintiff submitted a private opinion authored by an expert employed by the Academy of Fine Arts in Łódź, that opined that

> her [the plaintiff's] designs were characterized by a fresh look at such a typical product as tights, new, fashionable colours based on both on new trends and on knowledge of the youth market and the needs of young customers. In her projects, she used new ideas and new, bold colours. Her collection was surely a good complement to the base Gatta collection.

The defendant claimed that he creates his designs in a group of his own designers, taking into account the global trends of the hosiery market.

The argument centred on two questions that had to be answered by the experts from the Institute of Industrial Design in Warsaw:

1 Did the "Veena 10" model of tights and the "Noggi" model of leggings contain original elements that were taken over from the plaintiff's design?
2 Could the defendant's projects have been created independently of the plaintiff's designs?

The experts opined that there was no borrowing of concepts, layout or graphics with regard to the tights model, neither was there any analogy in the models of leggings. Furthermore, it was found that the plaintiff's models were not any source of inspiration to the defendant, which only made use of generally available fashion trends. In greater detail, it was pointed out that

> the designs presented were only preliminary designs. They do not specify the technique of making patterns (lockstitch). It is not clear what is a design,

> what is a variant of a pattern, and what is an element of a pattern, nor is the colour scheme specified exactly (according to the claimant's catalogue or the Pantone catalogue). It is only a basis for further design work after making joint arrangements with the future implementer of ideas. The presented design concept, in the event of further cooperation, would require the designer to precisely specify both the artistic pattern, its colour scheme and the technology of its execution. The presented designs used graphical elements – a continuous line, broken line, dashed line, horizontal stripes, arrangements of diagonal stripes, a stylized flower, double circles. Pattern geometry – vertical, horizontal, continuous and dashed lines were not novel relative to previous projects. Only their use in particular arrangements would become a copyrightable solution. A stripe in the shape of a lightning bolt, a flower with an elongated stem transforming into a stripe, a stripe with circles or horizontal stripes with the number 88 had not been used in any pattern implemented by the company and presented in catalogues.

Interestingly, having received the opinion, the plaintiff changed the argumentation, alleging that the intellectual good that was misused was her *know-how* based on her knowledge and experience regarding specific clothing *fashion trends*, particularly the decorative patterns of tights and leggings. This was based on the contention that the defendant did not make any tights, stockings or leggings using the decorative "stripe" pattern. Allegedly, the defendant made use of the plaintiff's professional knowledge in the fields of fashion and arts without paying any remuneration. Therefore, based on the course of events, the unlawful inspiration, in this case, was evident. The plaintiff requested an injunction based on the concept of "explicit" know-how, that is, empirical knowledge accessible for all experts in the field but not necessarily held by all of them. This kind of expertise, having commercial value, was provided without work, effort or cost.

The court noted that in the legal literature, it was stated beyond any doubt that confidentiality is a constitutive feature of know-how. It is claimed that "extending the definition of the concept of know-how to explicit solutions and experiences should be excluded, as this would lead to the creation of a group of referents of this concept, protected in various ways by law".[400]

The District Court in Sieradz assumed that the claim was not substantiated, as the defendant did not infringe on the plaintiff's copyright. The plaintiff did not prove that the defendant used her knowledge and experience related to particular youth fashion trends for tights and leggings.[401] The Court of Appeals in Łódź upheld the verdict, vaguely addressing the claim based on the "explicit" know-how argument. Moreover, it was noted that the prerequisites of the *ex delicto* liability were not shown to be met.

400 Wojcieszko-Głuszko, *Ochrona prawna know-how w prawie polskim na tle porównawczoprawnym*, pp. 56, 57, 59.

401 Verdict of District Court in Sieradz as of 5 May 2006, case no. I C 122/04.

Discussion The works at issue were not provided in this case, which makes it is impossible to refer specifically to the disputed objects. This case does, however, reveal one of the major linchpins of copyright protection for fashion, which is a strong need to provide clear-cut and detailed expertise on copyrightable elements that might have been appropriated by the defendant. According to Article 278, section 1 of Polish Code of Civil Procedure (CCP),[402] "in the event that some special information is required, the court, having heard the petitions of the parties as to the number and selection of expert witness, may summon one or more expert witnesses to testify". The rules of Polish civil procedure law are tailored to assure the ***principle of contradictory dispute*** (in other words the right for a fair trial or ***audi alteram partem*** principle) as expressed in Article 232 of CCP, stating that "Parties shall be obliged to present evidence in order to establish facts from which they derive legal consequences. The court may admit evidence which has not been presented by a party". In the Polish procedural law, a lot of significance is given to the principle of burden of proof that is gauged from two angles: material (objective) and formal (subjective). The first is derived from Article 6 of the Polish Civil Code. The activities of the parties should be clearly targeted and be intended to make the effort to present the facts from which they derive legal consequences for themselves. Thus, the institution of the burden of proof gains its importance in mobilising the parties to action. Pursuant to Article 232 of CCP, parties are required to provide evidence to establish the facts from which they derive legal effects. The court may admit evidence not presented by a party. In the current legal situation, the activity of the parties in presenting procedural material is of significant importance – the burden of proof in a formal, subjective sense.[403] The court's right pursuant to Article 232 of CCP, second sentence, concerns only the evidence and not a factual allegation. Although the court may admit evidence without a party's request, it has the power to act in this respect only within the limits of the factual basis of the future decision outlined by the parties' statements, cited in accordance with the act, including the ***rules of concentration of procedural material***. In other words, when admitting evidence *ex officio*, the court is not authorised to introduce new facts to the proceedings, either in terms of the claim or the defendant's defence.[404] Therefore, it is important to realise that it is the plaintiff's duty of care to prove the copyrightability of its fashion design.

402 Act of 17 November 1964 Code of Civil Procedure, JoL 2021 item 1805.

403 See the judgement of the Supreme Court of February 15, 2008, I CSK 426/07, LEX no. 46591; H. Dolecki, T. Radkiewicz [in:] T. Wiśniewski (ed.), *Kodeks postępowania cywilnego. Komentarz. Tom I. Artykuły 1–366*, 2021, Art. 232, Wolters Kluwer, lex/el. 2021, side notes 3 and 4.

404 Judgement of the Supreme Court of 8 February 2019, I CSK 803/17, LEX no. 2618429; H. Dolecki, T. Radkiewicz [in:] *Kodeks* . . ., side notes 3 and 4.

SHOES AND BAGS

A case was recently decided with regard to one of the Polish manufacturers of shoes and bags, WOJAS S.A., which was accused of infringing the moral and economic author's rights for some projects of shoes (models no. 6460–51, 6790–24, 679024, 7552–61) and bags (6767–51, 6867–54).[405] The plaintiff argued that the manufacturer should not only cease and desist the production thereof, and pay damages amounting to 528,000 PLN, but should also make a public statement admitting having infringed the copyright. The public statement was asked to be displayed on the defendant's websites and in shop windows along with the copied designs for 90 days.[406] The plaintiff was a well-reputed shoe designer, cooperating with one of the biggest Polish shoe manufacturers, Kazar, and exhibiting her designs at international fashion shows. The plaintiff sent her design projects to the defendant as part of her job application, which concerned the designing of a New Year's Eve 2015/2016 collection. The parties negotiated a cooperation agreement, but presumably the financial expectations of the plaintiff were too high. In January 2016, the plaintiff saw on the WOJAS website ankle shoes and sandals that were produced based on the plaintiff's design. When the plaintiff claimed remuneration for this, she was sent a pair of shoes as a token of gratitude for the cooperation. As the plaintiff did not file a complaint to court, some time later she saw another unauthorised use of her project, this time for tassel-fringed sandals and a tassel-fringed bag (designs 7552–61, 6460–51, 6790–24). The shoe model 7552–61 received commercial exposure at the Miss Poland gala 2016, and the shoe model 679024 was awarded the title of 'best product' of the year 2016 by the women's magazine *Oliwia*. The plaintiff mentioned that at the production stage the defendant had to provide parametric modelling, including technology and construction constraints. Despite the fact that her designs were remodelled in order to include technical changes, the defendant infringed on the manner of expression of her work of authorship, and not just an idea of it.

The defendant argued that the shoe model no. 7552–61 is a classic design that has been created in many variants by a number of shoe designers. It does not stand out with any specific detail, except for a small and contrasting junction on the lower part of the shoe. But this element of the shoe cannot be claimed to be original, and therefore copyrightable. Its presence is determined with the technical constraints and can by no means be alleged to be the outcome of a creative process. As a side note, it was mentioned that in the plaintiff's design, this part does not contrast with the rest of the shoe.[407] It was also argued that this shoe design is not only subjectively, but also objectively new.

405 Judgement of the District Court in Nowy Sącz as of 30 April 2018, case file I C 962/17; judgement of the Court of Appeals in Kraków as of 19 May 2019, case files I Aca 862/18, I ACz 1018/18. Jankowska, Meghaichi, Pawełczyk, *Illustrated* . . . .

406 Case file, p. 3.

407 Case file, p. 115.

As for shoe model 6460–51, it was offered to the defendant by the EBATA, producer from Kalwaria Zebrzydowska, inspired by the fashion trends presented at the 2015 Milan shoe fairs.

Moreover, the defendant argued that the plaintiff's drawings were of illustrative character and, as they did not constitute a project, were of little value. The essential value is in the choice of material and in making a pattern of the shoe model, including blanking dies and forms that comply with technical norms. It was asserted that a drawing may become an inspiration for the shoe project, but that it is not one of itself. The defendant claimed that the plaintiff's drawings were a presentation of a trend, inspiration for proper commercial design.

In case of the shoe model no. 6790–24, the copyright claim was based on the choice of the original ornamentation, that is, tassel fringes. The defendant argued that, apart from this element, the defendant's shoe model differs strongly, and that the tassel fringes are only a trend, one that had been used over a fair number of years. The same explanation was offered in connection with the tassel-fringed bag model.

The defendant also shed some light on the inspiration process that takes place in the fashion industry. Before each selling season, the major manufacturers attend fashion fairs in fashion capitals, such as Milan or Paris, and, based on range of knowledge gained, design their bulk production. Therefore, in each season there is a significant confluence of designs, which are, however, in principle created independently and without consultation. It is especially so, that it is not allowed to take pictures at fairs.[408]

The defendant even went as far as to say that the disputed shoe and bag designs were not copyrighted, as they did not meet the criteria of creativity and individuality. Even if there were about to meet these requirements, the burden of proving a fact lies with the person who asserts legal consequences arising from this fact.[409] It was argued that the disputed design models varied substantially, but that the common elements (tassel fringes) were not original.

Item of note 4.16 Differences between the items at issue – creative freedom

As for the shoe model 7552–61:

> "The differences between the specific items of the first model, which define the area of creative freedom of designers, come down to the proportions of individual elements and additional decorative elements, such as stitching or patterns. The upper line

(*Continued*)

408 Case file, p. 115.
409 Cf. Art. 6 of Polish Civil Code.

Item of note 4.16 (Continued)

of the shoe above the ankle bends at a different angle, the height of the heel is different, the shape of the element connecting both parts of the shoe is different. In the claimant's design, an ornament is attached to the zip on the back of the shoe, which is not present in the shoe offered by defendant. In the plaintiff's design, the outer surface of the shoe was not enriched with any decorative elements, so there was no possibility of copying".[410]

For the shoe model 6790–24:

"The general shape and use of the tassel fringes is not an expression of creative activity. The defendant's model differs from that of the claimant:

1. it has two buckles, while the claimant's design does not have any,
2. the fringed front part of the shoe is wider than the claimant's model,
3. in the defendant's model, there is one row of fringes that end behind the ankle, and in the claimant's model, there are three rows of fringes that extend to the ground, in the defendant's model, the wearer's toes are visible, in the claimant's model they are not,
4. in the defendant's model, there are additional straps that hold the foot and they are placed differently".

For the bag model 6867–54:

"The defendant's bag is designed differently in that:

1. its size and proportions are different,
2. its tassel fringes do not protrude beyond the outline of the bag,
3. it does not have an additional pocket in the upper part,
4. it is not ornamented, whereas the plaintiff's bag has an ornament across the entire width,
5. its lock runs the other way,
6. the bottom line of the fringes is a horizontal line, while the claimant's line slopes downwards".[411]

The stance of the defendant was that, in any case, no appropriation of creative elements took place.

The court of first instance dismissed the case in the ruling of 30 April 2018. It noted that the disputed models of shoe and the bag are not works of authorship as they lack the features of individuality and originality.[412] The disputed

410 Case file, p. 117.
411 Case file, p. 117.
412 Case file, pp. 231–232.

works have a mutual resemblance because they were created in the same period of time and were based on the general trends created at the level of fashion fairs. The burden of proof in that matter lies on the plaintiff, who limited herself only to quoting a few judgements, without referring any of them to her works. She did not even try to prove that her works met the copyright premises. The plaintiff submitted a motion for an expert to estimate whether the defendant's models were based on hers.[413] The court dismissed that motion and stated that the plaintiff should have submitted a motion for an expert to establish whether her projects were copyrightable in the first place, which she did not do. The court noted that it is for the author to prove that he has "created" something that is a "projection of his imagination". It is not contradicted by the use of commonly known or generally available elements given that their "choice, segregation, manner of presentation bears the mark of originality".[414] It agreed that "a work is individual, when there is no other work of a similar character (retrospective approach), but moreover it is statistically unlikely (that is, there is no high probability) that such a work will be created in future".[415] This is not the case when a work follows a pattern[416] or is of a routine or banal character. Therefore, the court italicised a few times that the plaintiff should have started the dispute with a motion for an expert's opinion on whether her work actually met the copyright criteria. This was especially important given that sartorial design is part of the intimate knowledge and skills that the plaintiff and the court do not have.[417]

The court pointed out that as shoes and bags are mostly of utilitarian character, it would therefore be extremely rare for them to fall under copyright protection. These items should, in general, be protected by the industrial law regulations for registered industrial designs.

The court asserted that the plaintiff provided drawings of shoes, which is the starting point of creating a project with the aid of a hoof for modelling shoes. A draft is transformed into a technical description, which is the basis of the shoe model.

413 The motion read:

> allow and conduct the proof of an opinion of an expert in the field of graphic design and industrial design in order to establish whether the shoe models no. 7552–61, 6460–51, 6790–24 and the bag model no. 6867–51 and 6867–54 were created with reference to the plaintiff's projects attached in the case files, to assess the plaintiff's copyright infringements caused by the use of plaintiff's projects for the production of the aforementioned models of shoes and bags.
>
> Case file p. 3

414 Polish Supreme Court Judgement of 25 January 2006, I CK 281/05, OSNC 2006, no11, pos. 286.

415 Polish Supreme Court Judgement of 27 February 2009, case file no. V CSK 337/08, LEX no. 488738.

416 Polish Supreme Court Judgement of 15 November 2002, case file no. II CKN 1289/00, OSNC 2004, no. 3, pos. 44.

417 Case file, p. 233.

On a side note, the court interestingly burdened the winning party with all costs, as it took account of the character of the case and of the proven fact of the defendant's use of some of the plaintiff's projects.[418]

The Court of Appeals in Kraków, in its judgement of 14 May 2019, upheld the verdict *in extenso*.

Discussion This case illustrates the specificity of fashion law cases, especially the vague and blurry border between an idea and a form of expression. One of the major reasons for this is the character of the works, which, most of the time, is purely utilitarian. The Polish Supreme Court noted that

> with regard to works of a utilitarian character, there has been a line of court decisions that the achieved result – that is not determined by the assumed utilitarian functions – must significantly (sufficiently, clearly, notably, visibly, expressively, meaningfully, characteristically) differ from other works of a similar kind.[419]

Also, in the legal literature it was noted that

> overly generous protection of industrial design, especially in its less prominent edition . . . may contribute to the degeneration of copyright protection. It should not be the purpose of the latter to facilitate the monopolization of utilitarian solutions intended for industrial use and at the same time sterilization of the element of creative individuality.[420]

TABLECLOTH PACKAGING

In 2001, in the Opole District Court,[421] a plaintiff filed a case against the copying of the packaging of his "stain-resistant tablecloth" and demanded that the defendant be prohibited from offering packaging with a "stain-resistant tablecloth" label on the market.[422] Based on the assumption that the *packaging* was *a literary-artistic work of authorship*, the plaintiff sought relief. The plaintiff claimed that his packaging included a special graphic design that was well received by its clientele and that led to high demand for its products. The defendant was accused of offering his products of worse quality in slavishly similar packaging, thereby misleading clients and exploiting the plaintiff's good reputation.[423] The plaintiff claimed that his tablecloth's packaging was the only instance in Europe of such a design that he had personally designed in

418 Case file, p. 234.
419 V CSK 202/13.
420 D. Flisak, komentarz do art. 1 ustawy o prawie autorskim i prawach pokrewnych, lex/el. 2015.
421 Case files no. I C 430/01. Jankowska, Meghaichi, Pawełczyk, *Illustrated* . . . .
422 Case files, p. 131.
423 Case files, p. 37.

February 2000 based on extensive market research. The plaintiff, recognising that in Poland tablecloths were packaged much worse than in Western Europe, wanted to increase his competitiveness by offering better packaging. He focused on three elements: the size of the package, the stiffness of the package and the fact that both sides would not slide down (to sell them in hypermarkets) as well as the use of a transparent and durable foil bag.[424] He claimed that the fanciful wrapper improved his sales, and that the defendant's copying of his design coincided with this improvement. Distributors were supposedly confusing the packaging of both products, which was detrimental to the plaintiff, especially in view of the lower quality of the defendant's product. The defendant's fabric texture was alleged to be looser, therefore less enduring and offering worse stain resistance. As for the packaging, it was of the same format, consisted of a cardboard interleaf, and had a graphical logo in the same place. The defendant's label consisted of identical elements as the plaintiff's with the same combination of symbols in the same locations. The label's colouring and reproduction technique were also claimed to be the same. The defendant argued they offered their product on the market long before the plaintiff and pointed out that the plaintiff did not provide any evidence as to which label was the original and which the knock-off. It was the court that ordered the plaintiff to deliver this proof. (The defendant's label was not available in the case files.)[425]

In the courtroom, the plaintiff showed samples of the two labels and testified to their similarity based on the fact that they have a similar graphical layout, shape, form and characteristic "bubbles".

The plaintiff stated that his idea to create a label and to include "bubbles" was to suggest that the tablecloth he was offering for sale would not soak up liquid. The photograph on his label shows a cup with spilled liquid, from which it can be inferred that the spilled liquid has beaded to form a "convex meniscus" has not been absorbed by the tablecloth. The packaging was designed so that it could be displayed in a vertical position during sale and the tablecloth in the packaging does not slide downwards, which, in the absence of the stiffener, it would, to the detriment of the aesthetic appearance of the retail package. Beside the cardboard with a description, inside there is a cardboard interleaf that strengthens the stiffness of the entire package. The defendant's previous packaging was alleged not to have had these advantages. The defendant had then changed the packaging by introducing a green colour, which he had never used before and which was not related to his company's logo. By using the same colours, the products came to be confused on the market, especially as the packages had the same dimensions. The plaintiff pointed out that the defendant's previous packaging had placed its elements in different places to the new label, whose placement exactly matched that of the plaintiff. The plaintiff also argued, with regard to the relative quality of the

424 Case files, p. 158.
425 Case files, pp. 38–41.

tablecloths, that his products were better because they were produced entirely in Poland, whereas the defendant used Turkish textiles.[426]

The defendant claimed to have used its graphic design since 1998 and also to have had a cardboard interleaf to make the packaging stiffer.[427] He claimed that, whereas previously the plaintiff had used labels of different colours, he himself had used only two: green (for single-coloured tablecloths) and yellow (for multi-coloured tablecloths). Its manufacturer claimed that the lettering used was taken from widely available computer graphics programs and that the fonts on both labels were different, despite their similarity for laypeople. The background was also taken from a computer graphics program that offers a variety of these for free use. The construction of the packaging is generally simple and well known. According to his testimony, the spherical elements on the dust jackets are called "radial tonal transitions", they are used on a variety of products, e.g. washing powders or mineral waters, and are also easily generated in computer programs. The defendant contested the claim that its product was of worse quality and gave evidence to a claim that he had used similar packaging imported from Turkey which was green and contained circular elements. At some point, it was offered for sale in these original packagings.[428] The District Court in Opole dismissed the case in a verdict of 31 October 2002. The court found that the defendant imported its products from Turkey in packaging having a picture of a set table with tableware on it and with circular elements around it. The defendant used different colours of label but that all bear a picture of a set table and a "stain-resistant tablecloth" label. The court pointed out that despite the fact that the plaintiff was represented by a professional counsel, the proof of evidence was conducted by the court itself. The counsel did not provide any specific proof to substantiate its claims, implicitly the court must have meant the proof of expert's opinion that could have been of importance for this case. The court having only the packaging as exhibits of proof and witness testimonies, not all of which were found reliable, dismissed the case. The court noted that

> by carrying out the evidentiary proceedings ex officio, the court would replace the parties themselves in the initiative of collecting evidence, it could also expose itself to the accusation of a lack of impartiality by seeking evidence in favour of one or other party. This would violate the adversarial principle which governs the civil process.

It was in the second instance that the plaintiff's counsel submitted a motion for an expert's opinion, which was obviously submitted too late. The motion read:

> allowing evidence of the opinion of an expert in the field of production technology and accounting as well as computer graphics on the occasion of obtaining special knowledge about the technological process of

426 Case files, pp. 54–55.
427 Case files, p. 105.
428 Case files, p. 159.

> developing the labels in question, putting them into production, reflecting it in the relevant documentation, as well as for an opinion on the possibility of developing very similar projects with existing technical conditions.[429]

The Court of Appeals in Wrocław, in the verdict of 28 February 2003,[430] upheld the first judgement. It pointed out that the plaintiff did not provide substantial evidence, including that he did not prove his authorship of the label. Neither did he prove he was the first to use it on the market. As for the claim that the court should invoke proofs ex officio based on Article 232 of the Polish Code of Civil Procedure, the court noted:

> the author of the appeal, the professional counsel, should be reminded that, after the amendments to the provisions of civil procedure introduced by the Act of March 1, 1996 on the amendment of the Code of Civil Procedure (Journal of Laws No. 43, item 189), the adversarial principle was fully restored, which freed the Court adjudicating on a case from liability for the result of the evidentiary proceedings. As for the admission of ex officio evidence by the court, it is inferred from the wording of Article 232 of the Code of Civil Procedure, including the second sentence of the same provision, that the court takes such an initiative only in special situations. This applies to any type of evidence, including expert opinions.

Discussion The case proves a lack of understanding of the basics of copyright on the part of the counsels leading the case. Copyright law was never intended to secure one's reputation or repute in the first place. On the contrary to the plaintiff's argument, reputation is of the least importance. The plaintiff did not deliver any substantiation for his claim, which was a specific comparison of the two designs, making their similarities clear, why the similarities constituted a copyright infringement.

COOKING CLOTHING, *BI-WEAR CLOTHING COMPANY B.V. VS. PIOTR MIKA AND RENATA MIKA*, PRZEDSIĘBIORSTWO PRODUKCYJNO-USŁUGOWE

In 2010, the District Court in Poznań decided a case related to the infringement of economic copyrights belonging to Bi-Wear Clothing Company B.V. The copyrights concerned cooking clothing designs, including chefs' blouses and aprons.[431] The plaintiff demanded withdrawal from the market and

429 It had been claimed that the motion should have been admitted based on Article 232 sentence 2, Article 278 § 1 in connection with Article 227 and 233 § 1 of the Polish Code of Civil Procedure.

430 Case files no. I ACa 72/03.

431 District Court judgement in Poznań as of 27 December 2012; case files no. IX Gc 433/10. Jankowska, Meghaichi, Pawełczyk, *Illustrated* . . . .

destruction of the defendant's 18 designs that were a part of the 'Kokswinkel' collection. The plaintiff submitted a motion to allow an expert's opinion as to 1) how the plaintiff's kitchen clothing differed from the defendant's and how they were an example of individual industrial design, in no way banal or formulaic; and 2) how the defendant had taken over a number of elements from the plaintiff's designs.[432]

In November 2009, the plaintiff noticed a collection on the Dutch market offered by "De Culinaire Makelaar" under the brand name "Chefs-Fashion", which was identical to his collection, "Chaud Devant", in terms of its design, materials (combination thereof), colours, haberdashery elements and other areas. The plaintiff obtained a favourable preliminary judgement from a Dutch court,[433] which found that the plaintiff's collection was subject to copyright and that there was an infringement. This case is of extreme importance for this study, because it hinges on identical fashion designs.

In this disputed case in Poland, the defendant was sub-commissioned by the plaintiff's contractor to sew its designs according to its 'design project' and 'pattern'. The plaintiff noted that the process of creating and sewing clothes takes place in two stages. The first step is to create a 'design project' for the collection. In practice, the 'design project' takes the form of drawings, sketches visualising future clothing. The second stage is the creation of 'patterns' based on the submitted project, which are in the form of specific material patterns. In practice, such patterns are in the form of pieces of fabric pinned together on a mannequin. The patterns are then transferred to the sewing room, where the production of the kitchen clothes takes place. In order to enable the defendant to properly perform its commissioned work, B-Wear had been organising a series of regular training meetings for the defendants' employees since 2003, during which very detailed instructions were given on the diligent production of kitchen clothes. This included step-by-step instructions for sewing sweatshirts, trousers and kitchen aprons. The plaintiff claimed that the sub-contractor sewed knock-off for the above-mentioned Dutch company and its "Chefs-Fashion" brand, including the use of the plaintiff's original haberdashery elements that were delivered to the defendant as a sewing accessory.[434] The plaintiff asserted that by producing and marketing kitchen clothes confusingly similar to Bi-Wear garments, the defendant infringed proprietary copyrights. The plaintiff claimed that the defendant infringed on its designs in many aspects. The external form of individual clothes was copied, especially the features that increase the usability of the clothes, the sewing method and aesthetic elements, e.g., a two-colour tape sewn on the sleeves and sides of some models.

432 Op. cit., p. 5.

433 Preliminary judgement of Dutch district court in Zwolle-Lelystad, as of 3 August 2011, case file no. 181699, HA ZA-11–168; Op. cit., Case files no. IX Gc 433/10 p. 1349–1355.

434 Op. cit., p. 11.

The plaintiff, making the copyright claim, asserted that fashion design is similar to architectural works, where there can be differentiation between a building project plan on paper and the actual three-dimensional building.

The plaintiff claimed that its work

> is an example of successful industrial design. The individual kitchen clothes are designed in such a way as to create a positive aesthetic impression. None of the garments considered is a simple conglomeration of materials sewn together. Creative effort should be estimated after successful combination of individual parts of the material making the creation, their combination, cut, look, use of accessories (buttons, hooks, metal inserts, longitudinal stripes on the sleeves), finishing elements (shape, format, size of collars, shape and location) trouser pockets, or other elements – e.g., pleats). The claimant's collection of kitchen clothes is austere, but at the same time attracts attention with its characteristic cut line. Each chef's outfit contains a number of specific, very characteristic elements resulting from the individual preferences of the designer, and is the implementation of his individual vision. The individuality and originality of Bi-Wear clothing is also determined by the fact that the defendants found it so attractive that they imitated it. . . . It is also worth adding that the models of the claimant's clothing, implementing a specific creative idea, together constitute a specific collection, e.g., a set of outfits united by one common idea.[435]

The plaintiff also submitted an expert's opinion on the originality and individuality of the Bi-Wear collection and on the similarities of the alleged copies. This was a private opinion. Irrespective of that, the plaintiff submitted a motion to allow a new opinion in the court to prove the first right. The plaintiff also invoked the presumption expressed in Article 8, section 2 of the PCL, which says that "it is assumed that the author is the person who is named as such on the copies of a work or whose authorship has otherwise been communicated to the public in association with the distribution of a work".[436] Based on this wording, the plaintiff asserted that the tags sewn into the clothing identify him as the copyright holder. Its name is made known to the general public in close connection with the work that has been disseminated.

Both 'Bi-Wear' and 'Kokswinkel' were subject to meticulous comparison that proved nearly identical material side incisions (cuts), snaps and size tags, packaging, cleaning instruction tags, location of pockets and elastics, pocket

435 Case files, p. 17.

436 Cf. Article 15 of the Berne Convention. This rule has been also adopted into European law, see point 19 of the Preamble to Directive 2004/48/EC of the European Parliament and of the Council of 29 April 2004 on the enforcement of intellectual property rights, OJEC as of 30.04.2004, L 157/45.

trims, hook and eye closures, press studs in the middle of the collar, concealed fastenings, vents and trims.

The plaintiff submitted a private opinion as to whether the 'Bi-Wear' kitchen clothing was distinguished by the designer's individual vision and whether the two collections at issue show the similarity of original and individual solutions. The expert noted that designing work clothes (including kitchen clothes) requires increased creativity of authorship from the designer to create forms that differ from routine and template. She went on to note that

> a designer of a concise clothing form must carefully work out the details of the outfit. The cut, collar, cuff, clasp, cut, tape or trim used have an undeniable impact on the overall perception of the form, and at the same time demonstrate the creativity of the designer.

The expert made a comparative analysis of nine garments from the collection, taking into account three aspects: 1) general modelling of the form, 2) elements resulting from the cut and 3) added elements. She found that most of the defendant's designs were in all three respects identical to the plaintiff's. She determined that the plaintiff's collection was original and individual due to the use of the discussed elements of the form in a non-routine and non-formulaic manner. The expert decided that the general feel of the plaintiff's collection made it distinctive. Furthermore, she decided that the collections at issue were "essentially identical" in terms of the fabric slot, cut, added details (fasteners, decorative tapes, trimmings, snaps, pockets), which served to prove that the similarity between the two collections was not accidental but the result of imitation. The 'De Kokswinkel' collection did not demonstrate its own creativity, and slight size changes to the detailed elements did not blur the impression of the identity of both collections.[437]

The defendants counterclaimed that they were a well-reputed sewing company with a long tradition of equipping the gastronomy and medical sectors with clothing of the highest quality and standards, including outfits for international contests and championships. They claimed it was their company that possessed intimate knowledge about sewing and that it was they who provided their clients with schooling and experience. They asserted that although they were provided with intermediate products for production, they did not offer these to competition. With regard to the Dutch judgement made by the court in Zwolle-Lelystad, this was not valid in Poland, as it was made based on the preliminary procedure and therefore had no extended binding effect in Poland.[438] The projects for the designs of kitchen blouses and trousers were created by the defendants, and they provided evidence that they had offered

437 Expert's opinion on the identity of the collections prepared by professor at the Academy of Fine Arts in Poznań as of 25 May 2010, Case files, pp. 424–631.

438 Case files, p. 633.

them for sale as early as 1998. They did not contain a high standard of authorship. They were classical models available on the market for many years.

These garments were offered by all producers of workwear (in particular those serving the needs of chefs) because they were the result of many years of tradition and adopted solutions that were purely functional and utilitarian in nature. Commonly accepted solutions for this type of clothing were, among others, a double-row type of fastening (providing protection from burns to the chest), an easy unfastening system (press studs – due to the need to allow the garment to tear off quickly in the event of its ignition), sleeves with a finish that ensures fast and secure tucking in order to avoid it getting dirty, etc. The solutions adopted are not to any extent the result of authorship of a particularly creative nature but are a manifestation of the thoughtful use of existing solutions considered practical and an indication in this type of clothing.[439]

Two experts were appointed to this case by the court. The first, Msc ing. Jerzy Łuczak, noted that the canon of kitchenwear is generally well known and that many elements are constant, if not identical. Some changes can be introduced using haberdashery, however compilations of these have been known for years. In his opinion, defendant's models differed from the plaintiff's only in minor details, such that an 'informed user' could be misled. However, in his mind, neither collection at issue bore a stamp of creativity, artistry or individuality that would make them distinctive on the market when compared with the competition.[440] There was also an extensive opinion from Professor Bogumiła Jung, working with the University of Arts in Poznań.

Item of note 4.17 Expert's opinion on kitchenwear's creativity

Professor's Bogumiła Jung's opinion on kitchenwear and its creativity:

1 In practice, the complexity of issues and, at the same time, usually the desired simplicity of solutions, e.g., usually reducing production costs – lead people who are not oriented in the matter to hasty conclusions that only some spectacular, unique creations are the result of the work of a designer, and (often only seemingly) simple things, having a modest appearance, seemingly only performing their function, that is, working well – do not belong to the area of "design". Meanwhile, quite the opposite is the case, and, in countries where the advancement of market processes and the development of the economy is higher, the knowledge that even (or actually: especially) seemingly simple objects/products are the work of designers who devoted a great deal of their time to create a form of a product that

(*Continued*)

439 Case files, p. 638.
440 Op. cit., pp. 1447–1448.

Item of note 4.17 (Continued)

stands out from the competition in an obvious – but subtle – way, so as not to obscure the basic aim, which is to perform a specific function;

2 In case of kitchenwear, its purpose should be taken into account: protection of the employee in the kitchen, difficult operating conditions and workplace hygiene;
3 An important element affecting the form of designed clothing is:

high-volume production forces such decisions on designers that the designed elements allow minimisation of production costs, which translates into a lower price for the offered product. Therefore, actions are usually taken to make considerable savings: desisting from unnecessary decorations and maximum simplification of the form of individual elements, facilitating the industrial production process;

4 "in highly competitive markets – it is natural that a conscious producer looks for its own distinctive features, individual traits, diverse detailed solutions or main construction elements, specific 'identification signs' ";
5 for many design areas, a specific "code" has emerged, associated with the high adherence of recipients (users) to the use of existing solutions, attachment to tradition – as a system, among others expressing specific messages through the possessed items. For example, just to simplify: the white colour of kitchen clothes is associated with the signal "clean" – it is an echo of the common belief that traditional methods of washing and disinfecting were the most effective for white clothes. Hence a strong feeling that whiteness equals "a guarantee of cleanliness". Today this is almost exclusively a cultural code[441];
6 making a product that is both functional and unconventional, individual but suitable for bulk production, is compared to merging "fire with water";
7 apart from the designer's vision, some part of the product is reliant on a brand's technology and its willingness to push the product forward;
8 in case of dress codes, only the most distinctive brands can let themselves step beyond certain conventions; one of the important factors is how clients receive the outfit especially when the outfit should be part of building a relationship based on trust and pre-existing client expectations. A flamboyant outfit could be perceived as a misstep, "an 'overdressed' employee may cause adverse publicity for its employer";

441 Case files, pp. 1638–1641.

9 in some situations, being "too original" works adversely and therefore there is a certain *cultural code* that should be followed, e.g. by the kitchenwear; therefore, experimentation with new forms should be moderate.[442]

In the pundit's opinion, the items at issue were identical as to the construction of the models, element fabrics, colours and details. Even the item names overlapped: 'Lady White' – 'First Lady White'; 'Sport White' – 'Active White'. It would have been impossible to create the copycat models unwittingly and by coincidence.

The District Court in Poznań, in its judgement of 27 December 2012, acknowledged that the plaintiff's collection at issue was individual and creative and therefore merited copyright protection. The court took this stand based on Bogumiła Jung's extensive opinion that all of the plaintiff's models of clothes constituted a coherent whole and made up one collection. It proved that these clothes were created as the result of a conceptual plan. Based on this conception, the court asserted that the premise of individuality was met. It stated that since the collection constitutes a whole, the creator was not acting in a random way, and that he used the freedom of creativity in his choices and in the ordering of elements. The court admitted that

> the expert pointed out that the choice of individual elements making up all the clothes presented by the claimant was neither accidental nor typical, but constituted an original composition. In the opinion of the Court, when assessing the individual character of a design, one should take into account the type of product for which the design was made, the industry to which it belongs and the designer's degree of freedom in creating the design. With a small margin of creative freedom, relatively small differences will be noticed by an informed user and will be sufficient to establish the individual character of the design. The court found no grounds to refuse the credibility and professionalism of the expert's opinion, since she is an outstanding specialist in the field of design.[443]

The court vehemently emphasised that the defendant had access to the plaintiff's designs for eight years and that the designs at issue were nearly identical. However, it rejected the claim on the ground that the plaintiff did not demonstrate that he had acquired the copyright. Although the in-house designer's contract included a stipulation in this regard, the projects were created before the designer joined the firm. The designer also testified that she had created delineators (pl. wykroje) based on the prior prepared project of

442 Case files, pp. 1642–1643.
443 Case files, p. 1697.

the model. She admitted that this process did not include any creative, aesthetic or utilitarian decisions, as this only requires technical knowledge. Obviously, the designer could introduce changes that merit copyright protection, but this was not demonstrated in this case. The claim made by the plaintiff based on the 'assumption of authorship' in Article 8 of PCL was rejected as the court pointed out that it does not introduce an 'assumption of a licence'. The designs were not credited to the designer's name and, as for the brand name that was claimed to be sewn into the clothes, the brand is not an author. Indeed, first, only some of the collection had such designation tags, and second, said tags did not contain the name of the company, only the name of the collection line and the website 'www.ChaudDevant.com'. The court pointed out that Article 8, section 2 of PCL requires the firm's name and not a collection name. The website name is also not sufficient, as it only provided part of the firm's name. The plaintiff appealed, pointing to Article 231 of the Polish Civil Proceeding Code that allows for *prima facie* evidence based on the fact that the plaintiff had been openly offering his product on the market for many years, which introduced a high level of certainty of the copyright ownership.[444] The Court of Appeals in Poznań in its judgement of 8 May 2013[445] upheld the verdict of the District Court based on the contention that the plaintiff did not demonstrate the acquisition of the copyrights.[446] The Court of Appeals did not explicitly address Article 231 of the Polish Civil Proceeding Code, but gave a detailed explanation as to the acquisition of copyrights. The evidence had demonstrated that the author of the designs was Bianca van der Lee, the plaintiff's CEO and the only shareholder and board member of the firm "Robia Holding P.U.", that was in turn the only shareholder and board member of the plaintiff. Factually, she and her firm are the same person, but legally, these are two different entities. Despite her testimony that it was the plaintiff that held the copyright, the court made clear that the transfer of copyrights must be made in writing to be valid according to Article 53 of PCL.

Discussion A basic line of kitchen clothing was introduced by Marie-Antoine Carême, a reputed French chef living in the 19th century. Many elements of the garments, including their shape, are dictated by their function. Also, a delineator and size table should be differentiated from the primary project. The first two kinds of work cannot be intrinsically subjective or original. Elements such as cuffs, collars, matching patterns across the collection, side cuts, elasticated waists, perforations in the material under the armpits, covered fasteners, sleeves with press-studs to secure the sleeve when rolled up, trimmings or stripes do not bring a new creative approach to the designed clothes. Comparing the location of tags or clasps does not add anything to the copyright discussion. These are elements positioned according to the norms

444 Polish Supreme Court judgement of 5 July 1967, case file no. I PR 174/67, lex no. 15128.
445 Case file no. I Aca 211/13.
446 Case files, p. 1838.

of economic trading and of culture.[447] These elements are commonly available at any tailor's wholesalers and constitute a standard solution, to which the plaintiff did not add any creative spark. Comparing the disputed models with others available on the market proves their formulaic nature.

One of the interesting takeaways from this case is that there was a dispute between the parties related to the scope and character of the expert's opinion given that, not being not a lawyer, he would not have a legal understanding of the premises for a work of authorship, namely "creativity" and "individuality".

According to the defendant, only works that incorporate the personality of the author, his "genius" or "creative tension" would benefit from copyright protection, effectively leaving a large portion of fashion design beyond copyright protection, with the exception of ***haute couture*** works. Interestingly, the defendant was not incorrect, despite the fact that, presumably, his reasoning was not based on extended research and expertise in fashion law.[448]

The plaintiff argued that 'individuality' should be assessed in this case with reference to works created by machine versus humans, bearing in mind that 'tiny load of individual creativity' brings copyrightable merit. The plaintiff gave an extensive description of ***technical elements*** of the works that, in his opinion, substantiated the copyright protection, such as

- waistline emphasising the feminine shape,
- location and length of the folds increasing the comfort of the clothes,
- selected number of snaps and the distance between them,
- width of the collar adjusted so as not to cause irritation,
- choice of perforated material with antibacterial properties,
- quilting of the pen pocket,
- placement of additional material under the clasp to strengthen it,
- quilting on the seat and side seams.

Besides the technical elements, the plaintiff listed elements that he claimed to be of an aesthetic nature, such as

- rectangular symmetrical collar 3 cm high,
- finishing overlock stitch, 1 cm wide,
- method of stitching the cuff and its processing,
- width and length of sleeves giving the design a better look,
- blind clasp allowing for elegance,
- front rise of women's trousers,
- choice of ribbon colours,
- choice of thin and shiny piping.[449]

447 This author supports opinion of R. Sroka, case files, p. 642.
448 Case files, p. 1135.
449 Case files, p. 1152–1171.

By the time an author discloses his identity, he is represented by his producer or publisher in enforcement of his copyright, or if he has no producer or publisher – a competent collecting society.

The major takeaway from this ruling is the fact that kitchenwear can be subject to copyright protection despite the fact, which at the first look may come as a surprise. This approach makes perfect sense on examination of the copyright character of the work, which shows that not only the purely aesthetical nature of the work is gauged, but also its technical aspects. This proves that fashion design is a specific type of work. Despite its mixed (aesthetic-technical) nature, it is often taken for granted that only the appearance makes a *fashion design* creative. In fact, behind the appearance of a product there may be a lot of technical and intimate knowledge or a sophisticated technological solution, aspects invisible to the eye but which make the fashion design what it is in terms of its utilitarian, structural and even aesthetic aspects. It is too often overlooked that fashion design is in the first instance utilitarian in its nature.

4.4 Conclusions: US, Italy, France, Netherlands, Germany, Poland

A deeper analysis of the mix of approaches from the US to the EU national regimes gives a better understanding of how copyright protection can work differently for fashion design in each country, despite the fact that all seem to be based on the same 'internationally acknowledged' copyright premises (Explanatory item no. 4.1). From the comparative research, it is clear that some legal regimes do not require a fashion good to be of high quality or extensive intellectual value, while some others situate fashion at the level of works of art, making the copyright premises nearly impossible to meet. National courts are seen to vary widely in their perspective on what threshold to apply for the premise of originality, and they cover the full gamut from very low to very high. Each jurisdiction chooses its own point on the originality spectrum, and some national copyright acts even insist on additional prerequisites.

The analysis of the US system shows that in order to benefit from copyright protection, a work must be proved to be original. This premise consists of two elements: 1) independent creation and 2) having at least some minimal degree of creativity.[450] The approach to this threshold is sometimes summed up with the observation that "combination of unoriginal component parts is itself original so as to merit copyright protection".[451] This approach, easy and simple as it may seem, is however not that generous for fashion design. Fashionable items are perceived as different types of works. This results from the fact that fashion designs are considered *useful articles* mostly unprotectable by

450 Re: Second Request for Reconsideration for Refusal to Register Nexus; Correspondence ID: 1-1IV50Q3; SR# 1-2500688671, 24.01.2017, p. 4, www.copyright.gov/rulings-filings/review-board/docs/nexus.pdf (accessed: 18.12.2021).

451 *Diamond Direct, LLC v. Star Diamond Group, Inc.*, 116 F. Supp. 2d 525, 529 (S.D.N.Y. 2000).

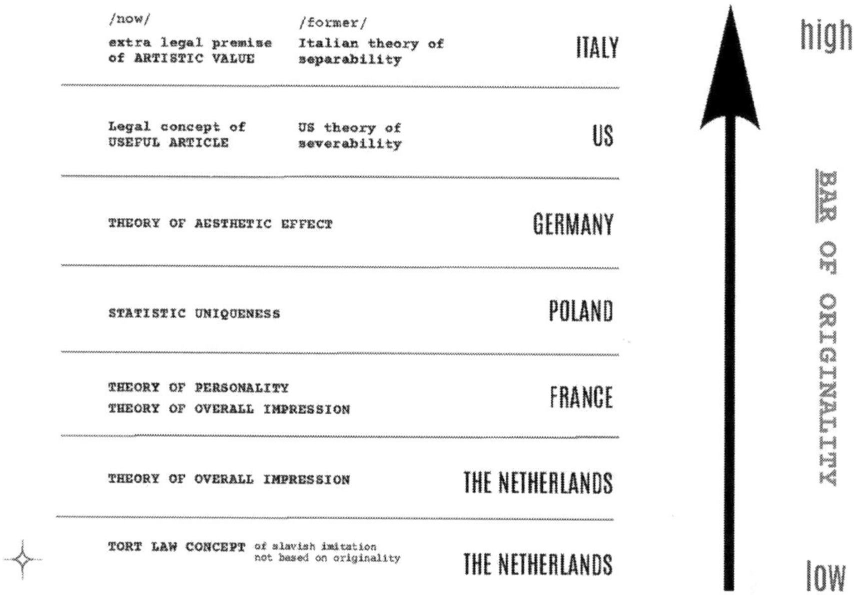

Explanatory item no. 4.1 Juxtaposition of differentiated rungs of creativity for design reflecting various theories of originality in the US, Italy, France, the Netherlands, Germany and Poland. Own study

Source: Created by author

the copyright system. In the US legal doctrine, it is believed that their purpose is to clothe people, making them utilitarian in nature. Therefore, fashion and design are subject to the Copyright Act's separability test, which is hard for them to pass.[452] Therefore, only those aspects of garments can be deemed copyrightable that constitute *works of art* by themselves. On the other hand, it is interesting that fabric designs are considered *writings* for purposes of copyright law and are accordingly protectible.[453]

452 "Fashion designs do not meet the conceptual separability test because it is hard to distinguish their expressive and functional components", A. Mitrani, *How Rings . . .*, cf. Hemphill & Suk, *The Law, Culture, and Economics of Fashion*, "Stanford Law Review", 2009, vol. 61, no. 1147, p. 1185.

453 United States Court of Appeals, Second Circuit from Nov 13, 1995, *Knitwaves, Inc. v. Lollytogs, Ltd.*, 71 F.3d 996 (2d Cir. 1995). David Nimmer opined that "fashion designs, i.e., the particular manner a garment is assembled and tailored". On this basis he differentiated between *fashion designs*, *fabric designs* and *dress designs*. The last one he defined as "graphically sets forth the shape, style, cut, and dimensions for converting fabric into a finished dress or other clothing garment", that does not constitute a work of authorship. D. Nimmer, *Nimmer on Copyright*, cyt. za: F. Montalvo Witzburg, *Protecting Fashion: A Comparative Analysis of Fashion Design Protection in the United States and Europe*, https://cardozoaelj.com/2016/12/01/protecting-fashion-comparative-analysis-fashion-design-protection-united-states-europe/#_ftn22 (accessed: 16.12.2021).

Jewellery pieces are often lumped together with fashion articles and accessories, leading some to question their status as purely ornamental sculptures.[454] Under the Copyright Act of 1976, many courts consider jewellery *ornamental sculptures* eligible for copyright protection as *pictorial, graphic or sculptural (PGS) works.* With the objective of protecting artistic works and excluding functional designs from protection, the Copyright Act explicitly distinguishes useful articles. If a PGS qualifies as a 'useful article', then it is subject to a separability test. While courts have differed in their analysis in applying separability, the test will essentially render the functional aspects of a PGS unprotectable.[455]

According to the general rule, the greater the number of options and the amount of material from which to select, coordinate or arrange, the more likely it is that a compilation will be creative.[456] With regard to jewellery and fashion, this assumption is overruled by the *doctrine of garden-variety configuration.* In other words, elements that are combined in a way that does not differentiate them from their basic shape and design components or are arranged in *garden-variety configurations* do not contain a sufficient amount of originality. This proves that fashion is not assessed in the same way as any other work of authorship. What appears irrelevant to copyrightability is whether a work exhibits a *'fresh take'* on a design, its attractiveness, symbolic meaning or the overall impression of the work, nor is a design's *success in the marketplace* deemed relevant.[457] It was observed in one of the cases that "even if accurate, the fact that the Works have been copied by competitors only indicates that others believe it to be profitable design, not that it possesses copyrightable authorship".[458] Therefore, *aesthetic qualities and commercial success* are not factors that would add to originality.[459] It is believed that "all creative works draw

454 It is taken as "undisputed that jewelry is included within the sculptural works classification of Section 102 (a) (5)", Donald Bruce Co. v. B.H. Multi Com Corp., 964 F.Supp. 265, 266 (N.D. Ill. 1997); *Donald Bruce & Co. v. B. H. Multi Com Corp.*: "It is undisputed that jewelry is included within the sculptural works classification of Section 102(a) (5)" US District Court for the Northern District of Illinois from May 15, 1997, *Donald Bruce & Co. v. BH Multi Com Corp.*, 964 F. Supp. 265 (N.D. Ill. 1997).

455 A. Mitrani, *How Rings Fit into the Copyright Scheme: Assessing Their Intrinsic Utilitarian Function*, "The NYU Journal of Intellectual Property and Entertainment Law", 2016, vol. 5, no. 2.

456 *Matthew Bender & Co. v. W. Pub. Co.*, 158 F.3d 674, 683 (2d Cir. 1998).

457 Re: Second Request for Reconsideration for Refusal to Register Arms of Love – LAR08–08C3-1, Arms of Love – LAR08–08C3–3, Arms of Love – LAR08–08C3–4, and Arms of Love – LAR08–08C3-S; Correspondence ID t -108JOER, 20.10.2016, p. 5, www.copyright.gov/rulings-filings/review-board/docs/arms-of-love.pdf (access: 19.01.2023).

458 Op. cit., p. 5; *See Paul Morelli Design, Inc. v. Tiffany & Co.,* 200 F. Supp. 2d 482, 488–89 (E.D. Pa. 2002).

459 Re: Second Request for Reconsideration for Refusal to Register Naga Gold & Silver (Season XX); Correspondence ID: l-1EY2QAE, 3.10.2016, p. 5, www.copyright.gov/rulings-filings/review-board/docs/naga-gold-and-silver.pdf (access: 19.01.2023); COMPENDIUM (THIRD)§§ 310.2 (aesthetic value, artistic merit and intrinsic quality), 310.3 (symbolic

on the common wellspring that is the public domain",[460] which for fashion sets the copyright bar high with a lot of creative effort required.

In Italy, both the copyright doctrine and jurisprudence surprisingly set the *niveau* for copyright protection very high and offer many theories that substantiate why design should be of an artistic nature. In the past, there was the concept of separation (It. *scindibilità*) that is a similar idea to the one supported in the US. In 2001, the Italian lawmaker abrogated the original formulation of Article 2, point 4 of the ICL and introduced a new unit, point 10 in the aforementioned article, discarding separability and bringing to the front the premise of an "inherent artistic value". It allowed the copyrightability of a work of applied art to be gauged from a new perspective based on several different concepts of art: *aesthetical*, *institutional* and *historical-cultural*. The requirement of the 'artistic value per se', standing beside the premise of creativity is understood in the sense that in order to grant copyright protection to an industrial product, it is necessary that the product show a prevalence of *artistic value over practical usefulness*.

Despite the variety of approaches taken in the Italian literature and jurisprudence, it is agreed that the protectable work should be a "high-end" object. Therefore, in addition to being a personal author's manifestation, it should also be regarded as an *art object*, with an *intrinsic autonomous value* recognised within the author's peer group. It has been generally agreed, that, since a work of applied art directly addresses the market, a long-lasting copyright monopoly should be given circumspectly. The threshold of originality for protection may be dependent on the kind of a work, its functionality and predestined shape. Jewellery, for example, can more easily secure copyright protection as it can be rendered using many methods and exhibit aesthetic value in many ways. It was noted in the Italian literature that the *Moon Boots* case was a flagship decision significant for court verdicts and the future approach to copyright protection in Italy.[461]

It is interesting that France, being next to Italy, the centre of fashion and design, offers an extremely different take on the copyrightability level. It sets the bar low with an expectation that a new fashion design offers a new perspective that is individual and fresh. It is surprising, in a very positive sense, how easily French courts manage to gauge fashion design using the *very idea of originality* to grant or refuse protection. French jurisprudence proves that copyright protection for fashion is an easily applicable tool that fits it very well. Studying this approach triggers a thought that the heated discussion about

meaning and impression), 310.7 (time, effort or expense), and 3 10. I 0 (commercial appeal and success).

460 *Kay Berry, Inc. v. Taylor Gifts, Inc.*, 421 F.3d 199, 207 (3rd Cir. 2005).

461 Lucrezia Palandri, *Fashion as Art: Rights and Remedies in the Age of Social Media*, Laws, 2020, vol. 9, p. 10; cf. Sara Caselli, *Le ultime tendenze sulla tutela autorale del design e sul requisito del "valore artistico"*, "Rivista di Diritto Industriale", 2017, no. 2, p. 333; S. Barabino, E. Varese, *In Fashion Law. Le problematiche giuridiche della filiera della moda* [in:] B. Pozzo, J. Valentin (eds.), *Fashion Law*, Giuffrè, 2016, pp. 93–108.

fashion protection is truly "much ado about nothing". It comes as a surprise, since the French copyright doctrine, the scholarship and philosophers, put a person of 'genius' at the heart of copyright protection, substantiating it with a *personality theory*. The idea goes back to 1793 and the French Revolution, that constituted the bedrock for modern copyright protection in France. The French concept of work is based on the premise of *originalité* that is encapsulated in Article L111–1 of FCL, but the French law does not impose a minimum artistic threshold for a work to qualify as original. But France is nowhere close to the strict Italian approach. It is significant that French copyright law protects fashion design without delving deeply into the differentiation between fine arts and applied arts.

Both design and fashion are included in the listing of Article L112–2, no. 10 and 14 of the FCL that includes the categories of copyrightable works. It is exceptional at the world level but makes perfect sense if we put this phenomenon into its historical, social, cultural (*haute couture*) and economic perspective.

The premise of originality in French law does not distinguish itself with a high threshold of originality that a work requires in order to merit copyright protection. As to fashion design, a good many cases regarding many different garments prove that the French concept of originality is very capacious and rather predictable. But copyright protection is not granted to any garment that is just a result of choice and selection. As also noted in some of the following cases, courts judge on originality based on the *doctrine of overall impression* (Fr. *impression d'ensemble*).

Another jurisprudence that builds on the doctrine of overall impression is that of the Netherlands. That country is known for a liberal approach to copyright protection with the bar set low. In the Dutch legal doctrine as well, as in the jurisprudence, it is observed that a work, in order to merit copyright protection, must be original (Dutch *oorsponkelijkheid*); that is, it must meet the criteria of individual character and the personal stamp. This level or creativity was also adopted for designs and models in the flagship case *Screenoprints*, that confirmed that applied art does not need to meet any higher standard. There is an opinion that the Dutch Copyright law does not set a high threshold of creativity and the Dutch Supreme Court has been known for a couple of judgements proving its easy-going approach to the premise of originality. The Dutch threshold was set based on reasonably simple ideas about creativity, and there was never any consideration of 'artistic value'. It was stressed many times that the *boundary line for copyright protection in fashion (design) is not something that can be learned or hammered out, it has to be felt.*

In the Dutch case law, there is a lot of emphasis on the *'total impression' approach* (or 'overall impression' approach), meaning that protection is subject to the court's investigation of whether a defendant has distanced themself sufficiently from existing works and expressed themself in an individual way that is protected as an original combination of free elements.[462] Therefore, a work of applied art may benefit from copyright protection even if its design is minimalistic.

Moreover, the concept of 'overall impression' has been borrowed from the Dutch design law and the doctrine of slavish imitation.

Interestingly and importantly, the Dutch jurisprudence of tort law developed a *theory of slavish imitation* to handle cases where *look-alikes* are put on the market by competitors. Slavish imitation is a form of wrongful act of essentially sponging off someone else's distinctive product by offering a virtually identical copy. However, it is based on different premises than the originality and individuality of a work: 1) the product must have its own, distinctive position on the market; 2) the claimant needs to make sufficient efforts to prevent the marketing of imitations on the market; 3) there is room for differences in the product that can be made without detrimental effect on the product; 4) there must be a risk of confusion between the products on the market; and 5) the infringement must be based on fault, that is, the perpetrator must know of the previous design.

On top of the previous discussion, there is an analysis of German law that shows another, specific, strict approach to originality that narrows down the scope of copyright protection for fashion design. German copyright protection is based on the prerequisite that a work be a *personal spiritual creation* (Ger. persönliche geistige Schöpfung), also translated as '*own intellectual creation*' (§ 2 Sec. 2 UrhG). The German courts have exerted some influence on the interpretation of § 2 Sec. 2 UrhG to interpret it as referring to a creation of an individual character, whose *aesthetic content* is of such a degree that, in the understanding of artistic circles as well as people reasonably familiar with artistic views, one can speak of an 'artistic' achievement. It is believed that the *aesthetic effect* of the design can only justify copyright protection if it is based on an artistic achievement and expressed in physical form. It is important to note that, until the *Geburtstagszug* case, the level of originality required from works of applied art was higher than for other genres of works. The long-standing contemporary German standpoint on fashion design was that, in theory, it could be qualified as a work of applied art and therefore enjoy copyright protection. However, in practice, it was hard to prove the *essential modicum of originality* to exercise that protection. In the German legal system, the overall effect achieved by the combination of several concrete designing elements does not reach the level of an artistic-individual creation. The focus is not primarily on individual design elements but on the overall impression that the work conveys to the viewer.

The Polish doctrine and jurisprudence seem to be very open-minded with regard to the scope of subject matter entitled to copyright protection and

462 Antoon Quaedvlieg, p. 58. A.A. Quaedvlieg, *"Style Is Free": Designs Beware*, EIPR, 2001, pp. 445–453.

when gauging the required criteria.[463] The Polish approach can be described as *semi-liberal* compared to the systems analysed in this chapter, fitting somewhere between Germany and France. The concept of *selection, arrangement and layout* resembles the *total impression* concept applied in France and the Netherlands.

This chapter, however, allows for an observation that is examined in greater detail with regard to the Polish jurisprudence: that obtaining copyright protection involves a great deal of argument, proof and expert opinions before the court. Finally, the outcome of court proceedings is dependent on many factors; therefore, it is often impossible to make simple assumptions based on different cases adjudicated in different legal regimes.

463 See J. Barta, R. Markiewicz, A. Matlak [in:] J. Barta (ed.), *System Prawa Prywatnego, t. XILI, Prawo autorskie,* 2013 CH BECK, p. 41 and ff.; E. Wojnicka, *Ochrona autorskich dóbr osobistych*, Łódź, Wydawca: Wydaw. Uniwersytetu Łódzkiego, 1997, p. 200; J. Barta, R. Markiewicz, *Prawo autorskie i prawa pokrewne. Komentarz*, Wolters Kluwer Poland, 2005; A. Kopff, *Utwór architektoniczny i jego autorstwo*, Nowe Prawo, 1970, no. 9, p. 1241; J. Barta, R. Markiewicz, *Dokumentacja techniczna w świetle prawa autorskiego*, ZNUJ, Prace z Wynalazczości i Własności Intelektualnej 1988, no. 47, pp. 61–87; P. Podrecki, J. Raglewski, S. Stanisławska-Kloc, T. Targosz, *Prawo autorskie i prawa pokrewne. Komentarz*, LEX 2015.

5 Coloured by emotions

Craft quality and seductive quality. Originality test revisited

5.1 Introduction: copyrightability spin

It was already argued in this book that fashion design involves *two aspects of the creative work*: the *craft quality* and *seductive quality* (comprising both the *artistic character* and the ability to trigger *emotions*). It cannot be understated that the things that make a fashion design marketable, competitive and simply beautiful (to the extent that it is permissible to use this term in the copyright context), alongside the purely *aesthetic* aspects, are its *shape*, *construction* (e.g. cuts) and *features* (e.g. choice of fabrics, choice of material having specific parameters). The major observation is that a *work of fashion design* is a mix of both *artistic work* and *technical work*. Therefore, copyrightability can be achieved through elaborating on at least one of these features. It seems important to include this aspect of the work since the *de minimis quantum of creativity/artistic character in the fashion business* (not to be used interchangeably with a *de minimis quantum of creativity/artistic character* in copyright law) is surprisingly low. This observation is of profound importance, because without knowing the codes of conduct on copying in the fashion business (social norms), it is impossible to enjoy copyright protection (legal norms). The copyrightability spin of fashion design as a function of craft quality (the technical touch) and the seductive quality (creativity, understood as the artistic and emotional touch) was established in Chapter 1 (see Explanatory item no. 1.3).

This chart shows the scheme of copyrightability of work, which arises as a result of many factors. As shown, higher craft quality can help the work attract copyright protection. It is also advocated here that the quantum of creativity should not only be estimated through formal gauging premises of individuality and originality, but that consideration should also be given to a *modicum of emotions* that are triggered by designers in customers, thereby stimulating the purchasing process. One should not forget that the first thing that designers are taught in fashion schools is how to work on client emotions. A good design is saleable because of the emotions it evokes in the buyer. Fashion and design as such are designed and received through emotions. This fact is unquestionable. The issue is whether the *theory of emotions* can be included in the copyright discourse.

DOI: 10.4324/9781003376033-5

5.1.1 High quality threshold. Utilitarian or highly technical character of fashion design

As shown in Chapter 4, a fashion design can benefit from copyright protection based on the technical character of the work. As in the Polish jurisprudence it has been noted that

> a work is not a work of authorship if it is only the application of even highly specialised technical knowledge, if its content is predetermined by objective technical conditions and requirements as well as the nature of the technical problem (task) being realized (solved).[1]

Therefore, determining whether a work has features that give it the character of a work of authorship is sometimes possible only with reference to specialist knowledge in the field. In connection with the above, it should also be noted that

> although the result of the work is partially determined by its subject and research methods, i.e., elements common to all potential authors, if the choice, layout and form of the study are independent and lead to an individual shaping of the work, it is possible to regard it as a work of authorship within the meaning of copyright law. The assessment – taking into account the indicated general assumptions – is always made on the basis of an analysis of specific features of the work.[2]

When both the form and content of a work are simply the result of a routine process, be it of the highest technical standard, it cannot be considered to be a manifestation of creativity. However, it was noted in the Polish jurisprudence that

> the fact that the author, as part of his regular professional activity, carries out work of the same type, using these research methods themselves and relying on certain solid foundations, does not automatically exclude all his subsequent works from the circle of works within the meaning of copyright law. In other words, not only the first work of a given kind can be a work of authorship; each subsequent work is subject to individual qualification, taking into account its specific features essential for determining whether the creation owes its origin to the author's independent creative effort, whether it differs from other results of an analogous action, or is merely a repetition of what others or the same author created previously.[3]

1 Judgement of Court of Appeals in Poznań of 9.11.2006, case file no. I Aca 490/06.
2 Supreme Court judgement of 30.06.2005, case file no. IV CK 763/04.
3 Op. cit.

It was shown in Chapter 1 that technical undertakings, such as the choice of textile for a fashion design, can be of significance in terms of the outer appearance and reception of a design. Construction is beyond important but surely cannot serve as proof of copyrightability without intimate knowledge from an expert.

5.1.2 High versus low threshold of artistic character

The research in the area of fashion styles, trends and creativity shows that fashion design does not comply with typical facets of copyright law in the same way as other works benefitting from copyright protection. It is plain to see that trends and forms introduced by big fashion players are subject to instant incorporation by minor fashion brands. Therefore, claiming that any form of work can be subject of copyright protection as long as it is creative is a contradiction of the basic rules of the fashion business. It is asserted in this book that typical copyrightability tests do not address the problem of originality with regard to fashion.

This author conducted extensive research into the area of fashion creativity, employing her own observations from fashion shows, shopping malls and discussions with fashion designers. One of the most distinctive, Dominika Nowak (owner of the brand Vanda Novak), shared her understanding of the creative process in fashion. The approach she outlined is beyond interesting and important. Even without including social and business norms in the discourse, the legal norms stand out as skewed. Dominika Nowak, who is an alumnus of Studio Bercot in Paris, shared the view that the *de minimis* quantum of creativity in the fashion business is set extremely low. It allows for ***numerous variations and combinations of ready forms*** observed in the designs of other brands.

According to the best practices learnt at fashion schools, ***it is absolutely legitimate to be inspired by product's ready elements***, and to incorporate these into one's own design (as reported by fashion designers from French fashion schools). Obviously, this is startling when gauged from the perspective of works of literature or pure arts. There are, however, some types of work that escape the perspective of a typical copyrightability test and need a specific approach to originality (e.g. websites), which is discussed later in this chapter.

As much as the perspective given by Dominika Nowak may baffle, it offers a compelling explanation of why it is so hard to fight against knock-offs and look-alikes. This approach is in line with the business practices that govern in the world of fashion. She points out that "fashion is a reflection of common taste and not a form of individual expression". This approach has its consequences. She asserts that fashion designers "create what they know will become subject to interest, in other words what will sell". It is a general observation and common knowledge that fashion houses and minor fashion brands are inspired by culture, vintage goods and travel. Often, they also include forms created by young designers. The inspiration/appropriation/copyright process permeates fashion in many directions, downwards and upwards.

The major fashion houses are naturally followed for inspiration but are also among the biggest users of the design forms of other players. It is also varied extend of copying that makes it hard to make general assumptions as to the quantum of creativity that can be copied.

Smaller players' fearless copying of ready elements from big fashion houses comes back around like a boomerang when it is the esteemed fashion house copying a smaller brand. This figure shows the NUNC design (by Dominika Nowak) as copied by MIU MIU, leaving an open question as to the line separating legitimate inspiration from infringement.

Therefore, it seems that traditional copyrightability tests need a missing element that would make fashion design copying better understood and more approachable.

Based on a review of cases (cf. Chapter 4, section titled "Christian Dior sneakers B 18"), it can be claimed that the fashion design at issue is copyrightable. Obviously, this standpoint would need an extensive explanation, but with the help of *expert opinions*, it is feasible to imagine how this design could meet the criteria of originality. However, plenty of cases are not easy to defend with regard to copyright protection. This sneakers shoe model designed by Vanda Novak is very simple in its form, rather typical for sneakers, but sublime and elegant at the same time.[4] The differences between the Vanda Novak sneakers and their copycats seem to be hardly noticeable on the one hand but paramount on the other. For a fashion lover, there is a gap between these two models. This example proves that if fashion design were to be gauged only by its artistic representation, it would often be extremely hard to prove its copyrightable character. However, if we look at a piece of fashion design as a mix of artistic and technical work, then the copyrightability may result from the technical aspects making the shoe model unique as to *shape, touch, look* and *feel.*

5.1.3 Theory of emotions versus facets of copyright

Recent scholarship has offered many perspectives on *emotional energy permeating the intellectual property (IP)* community and intellectual property rights (IPRs). The lingering question of whether cognition and emotions are separable leaves room for many approaches and perspectives.[5] Among the variety of contradictory views, some make clear that IP scholars have systematically

4 https://vandanovak.com/produkt/grace-white/.

5 Phoebe C. Ellsworth, Adrienne Dougherty, *Appraisals and Reappraisals in the Courtroom*, "Emotion Review", 2016, vol. 8, pp. 20, 21. This paper explores four basic theories of emotions, including basic emotions theory, valence/arousal emotions theory, constructivist theory and appraisal theory. Kathryn Abrams, Hila Keren, *Who's Afraid of Law and the Emotions?*, "Minnesota Law Review", 2010, vol. 94. pp. 1997, 2021; Terry A. Maroney, *A Field Evolves: Introduction to the Special Section on Law and Emotion*, "Emotion Review", 2015, vol. 8 pp. 3, 4; Terry A. Maroney, *Law and Emotion: A Proposed Taxonomy of an Emerging Field*, "Law and Human Behavior", 2006, vol. 30, p. 119.

overlooked the fact that IP discourse relies heavily on emotions.[6] At the heart of this claim is the assumption that affective responses and cognition can influence each other and that the degree of separability is not easy to ascertain. Margaret Chon pointed out that "unsurprisingly, trademark law includes more analysis of emotion than do the other areas of IP, due to the clear linkages between trademarks and marketing".[7] She also rightly advocates that "*all* areas of IP, and all heuristics that IP legal actors employ, involve emotion, to a greater or lesser extent".[8] This argumentation also includes the true point that it is not only the legal concepts that are applied using an emotional approach, but it is also jury or judge making decisions based presumably on the letter of the law.

In the Polish scholarship, the precursor of emotional approach to IPRs was Aleksandra Nowak-Gruca, who argues that

> in a cognitive sense, a work of authorship is a perceptual entity, established in any form, regardless of value, purpose or manner of expression, which has its physical representation in the form of specific states of neural activity and the distribution of neural networks in the brains of recipients recognizing a specific object as an individual object.[9]

Reception of a work of authorship is possible through the *physiological, neural representation* of the work, i.e. a manifestation (within the meaning of copyright law). The manifestation of a work is a concretisation of an idea in terms of a form that allows perception of the work, assuming that copyright only protects the manner of expression. In turn, the "manner of expression" is the manifestation of the work that has specific content in the sense that the perceptible form can be specified in the mind of the recipient of the work. This concept seems to rely on the assumption that a "manifestation" is therefore a recipient-oriented concept.

The author notes that the classification of a work as a work of authorship is determined by the psychophysiological reaction to a given object, and not by its other features. Deciding if something is truly original (see the concepts of personal stamp, novelty, creativity, originality, statistical uniqueness, creative choices, cultural significance), has until now been a matter of personal opinion. It is primarily about basing the court's decision on knowledge obtained and confirmed in an intersubjective manner.

In the light of this concept, it is only possible to determine whether an object is copyrightable with the help of the premise of aesthetic reaction

6 M. Chon, *Emotions and Intellectual Property Law*, "Akron Law Review", 2020, vol. 54, p. 531 and ff.

7 Chon, *Emotions* . . . , p. 535.

8 Chon, *Emotions* . . . , p. 535.

9 A. Nowak-Gruca, *Przedmiot prawa autorskiego (utwór) w ujęciu kognitywnym*, Difin, 2018, pp. 220 and ff., 275 and ff.

(experience).[10] The aesthetic response is an emotionally specific stimulus (super-stimulus). Emotions arise in the subcortical parts of our brain and may remain inaccessible to our consciousness. According to the theory of the embodiment of emotions presented by A. Nowak-Gruca, the reactions that arise during the experience of an emotional stimulus and the processing of emotional information are very fast, non-specific and non-voluntary at the same time.[11] Nevertheless, importantly, emotions are not only expressed in the states of the body but are also read from it.

On the basis of the *cognitive approach* to the work of authorship presented by that author, she clearly distinguishes between an *aesthetic experience* and an *aesthetic judgement* and addresses the chronological order of these reactions (first experience, then aesthetic judgement). On the basis of legal assessments, only emotional experience will be important. An aesthetic judgement, understood, for example, by Jean-Marie Schaeffer, as an expression of reconciliation of values with the object of aesthetic experience, remains irrelevant for legal assessments. In this sense, an object subject to legal qualification possesses creativity of an individual character as long as it can have its physiological representation in the form of specific states of neural activity and the distribution of neural networks in recipients' brains, regardless of aesthetic judgements about it (i.e. in accordance with the normative rule of so-called artistic neutrality).

According to the methodology adopted in copyright law, protection rests on the facets of creativity and individuality.[12] The cognitive approach looks for these features in a tested object on the basis of the recipient's reaction, with the criteria fulfilled provided that at least three reactions appear in the body, such as

- focus of attention;
- rejection by the perceptual system of conventional object reception;
- evoking aesthetic emotions.

Neuroaesthetics assumes that man has an innate ability to perform aesthetic evaluation, and the feelings/states on which art historians' research focuses can be studied and measured using the latest technologies and scientific experiments. Nevertheless, its assumptions and approaches to research are sometimes criticised. In particular, it is questioned whether a biological definition of art really creates tools for a scientific, objective view of what art is. The approach is also accused of excessive reductionism and determinism. There is also a visible criticism of the fact that works are perceived through the same mechanisms as everyday phenomena. However, while art critics or theorists

10 A similar approach can be seen in German doctrine, where attention is paid to communication with the recipient in order to induce an experience, K.-N. Peifer, *"Individualität" or Originality? Core Concepts in German Copyright Law*, "GRUR International", 2014, no. 12, p. 1102.

11 Cf. L. Feldman-Barrett, P. Niedenthal, P. Winkielman, *Emotion and Consciousness*, Guilford Press, 2007, s. 23; Damasio, *Błąd Kartezjusza*, Seria: Nowe Horyzonty Poznań, 1999, p. 157.

12 Nowak-Gruca, *Przedmiot . . .*, pp. 220–222.

may agree that this concept is very broad, the language of law should develop instruments allowing for the classification of certain phenomena.[13]

It is worth noting that according to the eminent brain researcher V. S. Ramachandran, it is possible that we all have elementary neural circuits in the visual systems that react with increased stimulation to the sculptures of Henry Moore, as they consist of certain elementary forms, particularly effective in activating selected parts of brain. But perhaps many of us engage in other higher cognitive processes (using, e.g. the language or thinking systems in the left hemisphere) and censor or deny the verdicts of the former.[14]

Item of note no. 5.1 Aleksandra Nowak-Gruca's theory of a cognitive approach to works of authorship

> Therefore, it should be clearly emphasized at this point that the limits of legal interpretation are set by the provisions creating the legal concept of a work. Thus, the assessments important from the perspective of the theoretician of art (aesthetic judgment, Kantian taste) remain irrelevant for a lawyer, because authors' protection arises "regardless of the value or purpose of the work". Neurobiologically rooted concepts of a work of art as a super-stimulus that weighs heavily on human cognitive structures, as well as legal conclusions built around a legal definition of a work, are distracted from assessments undertaken with varying degrees of success by other disciplines, traditionally recognized as humanistic. The concept of universal laws of aesthetics, each of which has some evolutionary roots, does not mean that all people will like the same objects or works of art, because categorized judgments in the context of beauty, value, and other qualities are made by means of higher cognitive functions in relation to whose so-called aesthetic emotion remains primal. Thus, a cognitive descriptive theory formulated on the basis of the normative concept of a work does not have to deal with problems that, in connection with the so-called cognitive turn clearly resonate in other disciplines dealing with the broadly understood creative activity of man. In line with the methodological approach presented here, necessarily naturalistically oriented, legal reasoning on the basis of which legal theories and assessments are built can therefore remain free from the allegations of determinism or excessive reductionism.[15]

13 A.G. Maglione, A. Brizi, G. Vecchiato, D. Rossi, A. Trettel, E. Modica, F. Babiloni, *A Neuroelectrical Brain Imaging Study on the Perception of Figurative Paintings against Only Their Color or Shape Contents*, "Frontiers in Human Neuroscience", 2017, vol. 11, p. 378. www.ncbi.nlm.nih.gov/pmc/articles/PMC5524918/ (accessed: 19.02.2022).

14 Ramachandran, *Neuroestetyka* . . ., p. 232.

15 Nowak-Gruca, *Przedmiot* . . ., p. 220.

The *cognitive concept* of a work of authorship proposed by Aleksander Nowak-Gruca allows for the assessment of objects subjected to copyright qualification according to the *criterion of aesthetic emotion* (experience), which is a reaction to the object of perception of a pre-reflective and emotional nature (aesthetic experience), anticipating a reflective aesthetic judgement, assuming that in the near future – precisely on the basis of the super-stimulus concept – this reaction can be empirically verified on the basis of specific methods of measuring physiological or neurophysiological parameters, possibly with the use of appropriate psychological tests. Such empirical verification will be important, specifically in *borderline cases*, where, not being able to say that a work exhibits creativity based on an individual character, we today rely only on subjective judgements. The criterion of aesthetic emotion indicated here, as it is based on subconscious processes that may not even penetrate into the consciousness of the recipient of the work, breaks away from evaluation of the value or purpose of the work. According to the author, especially in borderline cases, such as, for example, fashion design, copyright protection requires establishing and explaining that a given object possesses "creativity of an individual nature". Although we do not have to look for features that characterize a work of art (the concept of which remains undefined), we cannot completely decouple copyright protection from the premise of the creative character, which must be fulfilled, although only to a minimal extent. According to the cognitive concept, the level of intensity of this feature in borderline cases is determined by the emotional experience upon contact with the object – which, for works that deserve copyright protection, burdens the resources of our cognitive system.[16]

The important part of this theory is that defining an empirical meaning for the copyright concept of a work of authorship requires determination of a set of *observable indicators* that allow for inference about the occurrence of the phenomena aesthetical differential. Giving empirical meaning to theoretical concepts is often referred to as the "selection of indicators". The author assumes that a helpful tool in this case may be the semantic differential, also known as the Osgood scale.[17] It is used to measure the connotative meaning of concepts. The connotative meaning is understood as a set of features defined jointly by a given name but not clearly defining its scope. Therefore, the differential enables a psychological analysis to be carried out, the purpose of which is to determine the emotional relationship of an individual or a group to a specific concept. In other words, the Osgood scale is a quantitative method of

16 Nowak-Gruca, *Przedmiot . . .*, p. 220; W. Kemp, *Dzieło sztuki i widz: metoda estetyczno-recepcyjna* [w:] M. Bryl, P. Juszkiewicz, P. Piotrowski, W. Suchocki (red.), *Perspektywy współczesnej historii sztuki-Antologia przekładów*, WYD UAM, 2009, pp. 139–154.

17 C.E. Osgood, *Where Do Sentences Come From?* [in:] D.D. Steinberg, L.A. Jakobovits (eds.), *Semantics: An Interdisciplinary Reader in Philosophy, Linguistics and Psychology*, Cambridge University Press, 1971.

Table 5.1 Semantic scale to measure the connotative meaning of objects subject to copyright qualification

Sample instruction: Please rate on a five-point scale which pairs of adjectives, in your opinion, best describe the concept of a work: 1. definitely yes, 2. somewhat yes, 3. difficult to say, 4. somewhat no, 5. definitely not.

Opposing adjectives			*1*	*2*	*3*	*4*	*5*
Original	/	Unoriginal	□	□	□	□	□
Repetitive	/	Unrepetitive	□	□	□	□	□
Creational	/	Uncreational	□	□	□	□	□
Creative	/	Uncreative	□	□	□	□	□
Unique	/	Standard	□	□	□	□	□
An outcome of creative choices	/	Not an outcome of creative choices	□	□	□	□	□
Personal	/	Someone else's	□	□	□	□	□

Source: Own study of Aleksandra Nowak-Gruca.

examining the assessment of the impression of a phenomenon or object that is evoked in a subject.[18]

The basics of constructing a technique for measuring the connotative meaning of the concepts of semantic differential are as follows:

- the process of describing or judging can be understood as placing each concept on an empirical (conditioned experience) continuum delineated by a pair of opposing adjectives;
- many such scales are strongly correlated with each other and they form a correlation beam – one dimension;
- these dimensions define the semantic space within which the connotative meaning of the concept under study can be located.[19]

Following, there is an example of a survey which, using a five-point bipolar ordinal scale, allows measurement of the meaning (connotational) that the object under assessment (a potential copyright subject) has for different people, by obtaining their judgements about the object on a descriptive set of scales. The selection of the pairs of contradictory adjectives indicated here was

18 T. Skowroński, *Znaczenie – interpretacje psychologiczne* [in:] I. Kurcz (ed.), *Psychologia a semiotyka. Pojęcia i zagadnienia*, Polskie Towarzystwo Semiotyczne, 1993, pp. 169 and ff.; J. Czapiński, *Dyferencjał semantyczny. Materiały do nauczania Psychologii, t. 3*, Wydawnictwo Naukowe PWN, 1978, pp. 257–275.

19 D. Śleszyński, A. Wiśniewski, *Dyferencjał Semantyczny jako metoda pomiaru preferencji dążeń życiowych (problem teoretyczne i propozycje badawcze)*, Studia Philosophiae Christianae, 1977, vol. 13, no. 2, p. 198.

made using the procedure of competent judges (nine lawyers, specialists in the copyright field) who, on a five-point Likert scale, awarded a certain number of points with the usefulness of 20 hundred categories of antonymic adjectives that best describe the concept of a work. Statistically, the most homogeneous responses with the highest mean and median, highest first quartile and lowest variability were left. On this basis, seven subjective estimates concerning a normative notion of the work were obtained.

5.2 Theory of structure of the work of authorship

The cognitive concept of works of authorship, allowing for qualification of objects for copyright protection based on the criterion of an aesthetic reaction, which is evoked and shared by all people, coincides with Ingarden's intuitive (in the sense that it is not confirmed empirically) approach. It is worth pointing out that in his opinion, a *work is an intentional object*, the perception of which triggers the recipient's mental experiences aimed at making it more concrete. Ingarden also pointed out that different people are equally able to understand a given message and agree on its meaning, which proves the existence of an objective foundation for the work. It can therefore be admitted that many fragments of Ingarden's concepts are confirmed today by research on the brain and in the results of signal measurements of important physiological and neurophysiological parameters. According to Aleksandra Nowak-Gruca, in the light of the discoveries of neuroscience, claims that Ingarden's eidetic reduction made it possible to grasp the "essence of things" today, and is confirmed by empirical research.[20]

The creativity test should be applied with a diligent understanding of the work, its *structure*, *kind* (independent, derivative, co-authored, joint) and *type* (in other words genre: literature, music, fashion design, etc.). The world literature has offered at least a few approaches to decoding a work in order to ease the difficult task of finding out where its creative elements lie. In the continental European doctrine, there have been two major approaches: Roman, according to which a work is the sum of its interrelated elements, and Germanic, which reflected the stages of creating a work.[21] The former was represented by H. Desbois, who distinguished the following components of the work:

- idea (topic),
- theme composition
- a means of expressing the work to the public (external form).

20 A.A.A. Salah, A.A. Salah, *Technoscience Art: A Bridge Between Neuroesthetics and Art History?*, Review of General Psychology, 2008, t. 12, no 2, s.6; Nowak-Gruca, *Przedmiot . . .*, p. 220; D. Ulicka, *Ingardenowska Filozofia Literatury*, Polskie Wydawnictwo Naukowe, 1992, pp. 30–31.

21 J. Błeszyński, *Tłumaczenie i jego twórca w polskim prawie autorskim*, Wydawnictwo Prawnicze, 1973, ss. 33–34; A. Kopff, *Dzieło sztuk plastycznych i jego twórca w świetle przepisów prawa autorskiego*, "ZNUJ", 1961, Nr. 36, ss. 47–65; A. Kopff, *Autorskie prawa zależne*, "SC", 1978, t. XXIX, ss. 135–175.

The Germanic model was represented by J. Kohler, who pointed to three major facets of the work:

- content (individualised image),
- internal form (relations between individual means of expression),
- external form (the selection of specific means of expression makes it possible to communicate the work).

In the Polish doctrine, there is a concept authored by Andrzej Kopff that advocated for a *three-layered structure of the work*. He made this observation with regard to artistic work and, as much as he pointed out that it may not find application to all genres of work (e.g. musical work), this concept can easily be applied to fashion design. Kopff's approach rests on the juxtaposition of 'content' and 'form'. He followed Roman Ingarden's understanding of these terms: the content is what has been presented or expressed, and the form is a factor representing (expressing) something. The content covering the subject (topic) of an artistic work does not itself fall under copyright protection. According to A. Kopff, not only the entire work can be the subject of copyright, as the sum of its layers, but also each of the layers it distinguishes. Thus, each individual layer may be a subject of economic exploitation,[22] including its first layer of 'individualized image', which is the content. This layer is of paramount importance here, as, by including it in this discourse, the author questions leaving the 'idea' outside the copyright protection. He seems to follow the approach that it is possible to make a distinction between a 'general idea' and a 'specific idea', which gains form and is therefore subject to copyright protection.

He noted that in a finished work, the idea is understood as a "topic subjectively shaped (organized) by the artist (individualized image)".[23] But he also agreed that it is an issue of the utmost difficulty to make a precise description of a 'personalized image', as it is a mental construct not formed physically. It is only received through this physical form. Kopff wrote "the aesthetic values active, firmly related to the function of the work, exist in both the internal form and the personalized image and accurately grasped relation between these two".[24] The 'individualised image' is therefore a creative concept individualising an act of a general kind, whereas the internal form allows the equipping of this concept artistically. It is important to stress that this approach is, according to its author, free of artistic and aesthetic gauging, as these should be left outside the legal reasoning. In my view, it is fully possible to apply the theories pertaining to emotions (cf. Aleksandra Nowak-Gruca approach), as they also rest on the same facet. My own understanding, however, is that any process of assessing a creative act from the copyright perspective includes subjective presumptions and subjective utterances from artists, lawyers, judges and juries.

22 Kopff, *Dzieło sztuk plastycznych . . .*, pp. 100 and 107.
23 Kopff, *Dzieło sztuk plastycznych . . .*, p. 61.
24 Kopff, *Dzieło sztuk plastycznych . . .*, p. 61.

Kopff's approach also covers the issue of *protection of style*.[25] He advocated protection for the individual style of an artist. This standpoint has been widely criticised in the Polish literature.[26] I believe Kopff makes a good point, but it is a matter of explicit description what really qualifies as individualised style of an artist, which at some point can be equated with 'specific idea', that as a matter of law is a subject of protection as something that constitutes the so called manner of expression. One of the misunderstandings is a misplaced approach to the concept of style as such. Authors give it too little attention and do not relate style specifically to the genre of work to which it pertains. It is clear that style, in fashion, would enjoy a more relaxed comprehension and approach.

One of the major opponents of this approach in the Polish doctrine is Jan Błeszyński, who stresses the interrelations between the internal elements of a work. He noted that "work is a unity of elements of content and form . . .. The content of work is delineated by its form, therefore these two are correlating concepts".[27] He argues that the elements of a work cannot be regarded as "Lego bricks" and that each work of authorship is an *organic unity*. Its elements are not its sum, but a *composition*.[28] Błeszyński himself named this approach a unitary concept, but it is also known as the organic concept of the structure of a work of authorship. The same account was given by Ryszard Markiewicz and Janusz Barta as well as by Aleksandra Sewerynik.[29]

This author supports Andrzej Kopff's approach for many reasons. Foremost among these is that the extensive account of legal cases from many countries of various legal traditions prove that a work of fashion design is not only *artistic* in nature, but also *technical*. From the body of cases reported in this book that have been successfully fought in court, it can be seen that the more meticulous the description of the work, the greater is the chance to prove the copyrightability of that work. The elements of a work that are checked are not only those of a purely artistic nature but also the technical aspects. It has been pointed out many times in this book that overlooking the technical component of fashion design can be very detrimental to an overall copyright assessment. However,

25 M.M. Bieczyński, *Plagiat jako immanentna granica wolności*, "Studia Prawnicze", 2011, z. 2, no. 188, p. 7.

26 J. Barta, *R. Markiewicz: Prawo autorskie*, Wolters Kluwer, 2008, pp. 73 and ff.

27 Błeszyński, *Tłumaczenie . . .*, pp. 33–34.

28 J. Błeszyński, *Plagiat a naruszenie autorstwa utworu* [in:] W. Lis, G. Tylec (eds.), *Działalność naukowo-dydaktyczna w świetle prawa autorskiego*, Wydawnictwo KUL, Lublin, 2015, p. 15; J. Błeszyński, *Twórczość jako przesłanka ochrony w polskim prawie autorskim w świetle doktryny i orzecznictwa* [w:] J. Gołaczyński, P. Machnikowski (red.), *Współczesne problemy prawa prywatnego, Księga pamiątkowa ku czci profesora Edwarda Gniewska*, C.H. Beck, 2010, pp. 36, 52 Błeszyński, *Tłumaczenie . . .*, p. 38.

29 A. Sewerynik, *Utwór muzyczny jako przedmiot prawa autorskiego*, C.H. Beck, 2020, pp. 13 and ff.

this does not mean that copyright covers technical aspects that receive protection from patent law.

Item of note no. 5.2 Construction theories in fashion

As to the technical side, there are two basic methods of creating forms in fashion design. The first involves ***pinning on the silhouette*** a substitute fabric (e.g. raw cotton), reproducing the design. All cutting lines, seams and assembly points are marked on this, so that later, after disassembling all elements, the design can be reproduced. The second method involves ***mapping of the human figure*** on the basis of its dimensions, that is, drawing a basic construction grid and its subsequent modification (according to the design), in other words modelling. As noted by A. Pyrkosz

> the silhouette of a human is a spatial figure. Its complexity in terms of shape often discourages designers from delving into the garment construction process. . . . if . . . we look at a human through the eyes of a cubist, we can conclude that, in a certain generalization, the silhouette of a human is a geometrical solid, or more precisely – a set of mutually intersecting geometric solids. This is the most important assumption . . .. When comparing the figure of a human to a geometric figure, the clothing that wraps the body can be interpreted as the exterior surface of this body (packaging). The development of templates for this outfit will thus be a mesh mapping of the outer surface of the solid.[30]

Some of the technical elements of fashion design that seem to be of importance for copyright discourse are

- construction;
- finishings (e.g. stitches, seams, darts, cuts) that are a major factor in a garment's quality;
- choice of practical elements.

This author believes that the ***overall impression approach*** is valid with regard to fashion design, but breaking a work down to elements as described by Kopff makes it easier to address the general impression of a work.

30 Pyrkosz, *Projektowanie ubioru*, Pracownia Projektowania Tkaniny i Ubioru, Wydział Architektury Wnętrz, Akademia Sztuk Pięknych im. Jana Matejki w Krakowie, 2018, p. 136.

5.3 Fashion design versus interior design. Overall impression approach

The concept of 'overall impression', discussed in the Dutch[31] and French literature, is juxtaposed in this book with Josef Kohler's *layer theory* (Ger. Stufentheorie) and Andrzej Kopff's *layer theory*. These approaches comprise external form, internal form and most importantly, the 'imaginary image' (Ger. *imaginäres Bild*). This last concept was criticised with the argument that the understanding of the 'imaginäres Bild' is subject to constant mutability, and that it is therefore too vague and elusive. Kohler opposed that argument, saying: "Wer zu wenig philosophischen Geist hat, um sich auf solche Weise über das Alltägliche zu erheben, auf den brauchen wir keine Rücksicht zu nehmen! Er ist ja nach seiner eigenen Behauptung gar nicht vorhanden". (We need not heed those who have too little philosophical spirit to lift themselves above the everyday in this way! According to their own assertions, they don't exist at all.)[32] This reasoning was supported by M. R. de Zwaan, who asked "is not after everything organic subject to constant change?".[33] With regard to the concept of 'overall impression', he notes that, due to terminological and systematic flaws, it may not be an adequate criterion, but that, in some cases, it can still serve to indicate infringement, even if it cannot be decisive by itself. When the corresponding impression is invoked by unprotected elements, and the work is missing the sufficient creative choices, selection and application of elements, one cannot speak about an infringement.[34] Similarly, there might be an infringement in case of the reproduction of a copyrighted work's features without invoking an overall impression of similarity. In the Netherlands, several authors have, because of their reservations as to the complexity of the concept of 'overall impression' and its methodology, suggested limiting the application of the 'overall impression' doctrine to works of applied art only and/or exclusively to 'simple works'. Is it, however, possible to delineate simple works from complicated ones? M. R. de Zwaan argues that any sensory or reasoned impression and the total impression concept (in other words "estimation space") used to assess a work's originality uncovers the unexplainable differences between the linguistic and legal meaning of this term.[35] Interestingly, Spoor argues in favour of the concept of total impression finding it "an appealing, attractive and well-arranged criterion" only to discover that it is a curious, somewhat unpolished phenomenon which in fact is not a criterion at all, but a formula or a guidepost for how the originality assessment or comparison should proceed.[36] If one agrees that comparison is an activity, and not

31 After the *Decaux v. Mediamax* case of 1995.

32 J. Kohler, *Urheberrecht an Schriftwerken und Verlagsrecht*, Verlag Ferdinand Enke, Stuttgart: Verlag von Ferdinand Enke, 1907, Neuausgabe 1980, Scientia Verlag Aalen, p. 150.

33 M.R. de Zwaan, *De totaalindruk: onjuist maar niet onbruikbaar*, AMI, 2016, no. 5, p. 113.

34 J.H. Spoor, D.W.F. Verkade, D.J.G. Visser, *Auteursrecht*, Kluwer, 2005, p. 158.

35 de Zwaan, *De totaalindruk* . . ., p. 120.

36 J.H. Spoor, *Hoezo, totaalindrukken?*, [in:] N.A.N.M. van Eijk, P.B. Hugenholtz (red.), *Dommeringbundel*, Otto Cramwinckel, 2008, pp. 321–333.

itself a criterion, then what is being done is comparing the overall impressions of the works at issue, which results in a 'similar overall impression' (Dutch *overeenstemmende totaalindruk*). However, this is not a stand-alone criterion. It allows differentiation of the unprotected elements from the copyrightable ones and observation of how the unprotected elements are expressed or combined. It lines up with the methodology for deciding whether an infringement took place. Therefore, the approach is not about an impression, as much as it is about a judgement.[37] The term itself only suggests, wrongly, that the judge is allowed to make his own decisions based on the sensory stimulation triggered by the author's individual way of expressing the current fashion or style. As interestingly noted by Koelman in his comment regarding the *Stokke* case, the judge asked that the elements that were not protected be "Photoshopped" away and then juxtaposed the result with the full picture. That action allows the judge to form his own idea about the creative process employed in the making of the chair, see it in its entirety and get the 'total impression', which becomes a legal construct.[38] What is striking, though, is that this concept and the methodology of its application strongly resemble the US way of dealing with its concept of a 'useful article'.

This discussion does not prove fruitful with regard to minimalist design. The sheer will of granting copyright protection to pieces of applied art sounds just and plausible. But when the work is a piece of minimalist design and copyright exclusions (e.g. ideas, functions, trends and styles) come into play, copyright protection no longer seems that legitimate or reasonable. This is where the heated discussions about the protectability of style come to the forefront. Administering justice in such cases always arouses biased opinions. By example of the Tripp Trapp chair, the Dutch Supreme Court found that the merger doctrine (dilution doctrine, 'leer van de verwatering') did not apply. It found that a mere "cursive L-shape that forms the carrier of the chair" had no effect on the functionality of the chair and therefore was original.[39] Once a decision had been made on the scope of protection of the Tripp Trapp, the overall impressions of the Tripp Trapp and Carlo chair were compared. It was recognised that both forms have an open and floating character and that this is part of the overall impression. However, only the protected elements in this matter were assessed in order to establish a possible infringement. Since the Carlo design resembled a letter S, it was found to keep a sufficient distance.[40] Helen Maatjes noted that

> not only must a judge, on the basis of established case law, compare the overall impression of a design or copyright-protected work with the

37 de Zwaan, *De totaalindruk . . .*, p. 117.

38 de Zwaan, *De totaalindruk . . .*, p. 117.

39 HR 22 February 2013, nr. 11/02739, see p. 21.

40 Stefanie Chrisiaens, *De bescherming van designmeubelen door het intellectueel eigendomsrecht*, master's thesis, 2017/2018, pp. 21–22, https://libstore.ugent.be/fulltxt/RUG01/002/479/295/RUG01-002479295_2018_0001_AC.pdf (accessed: 04.03.2022).

> overall impression of a potentially infringing product, . . ., but also give consideration to the type of elements that have been adopted. If differences are made, which relate exclusively to functional elements, but the creative choices are the same, then there is still infringement. If it is precisely functional elements that are adopted and a strikingly characteristic creative part is different, then it is obvious that there is no infringement.[41]

The *overall impression doctrine* was itself subject to criticism in the Dutch literature for going beyond the essence of copyright law, whose core purpose should be to protect elements that are original. It is sometimes argued that non-original elements should not play a role in the assessment of infringement; however, the doctrine admits the non-original elements and their creative combination that are given a fair share in the copyright examination.[42] With minimalist products, it is difficult to determine where the originality of the product lies. Since minimalist products usually consist of few original elements, the judge will look more quickly at arrangements of non-original items. These orderings will be difficult to establish objectively, and the judge will then switch more quickly to a feeling. Moreover, protecting these combinations, whether original or not, can border on idea protection.[43]

Landerbarthold stated, somewhat jokingly and quite metaphorically, that copyright has been expanding and becoming like a corpulent old aunt. He contested,

> If I were to continue talking in this metaphor now, and see myself as a copyright health specialist, I would want to give the tip to this aunt to get a little more "in shape". I would like to recommend copyright to exercise more, and consume less and healthier. Copyright is needed to accommodate the imbalance. The movement should then move more towards the freedoms of others and less towards the maker. Consuming less and healthier could be done by skipping minimalist products a bit more. This is simply not good for copyright health. The combination of these elements will lead to a healthy and balanced copyright and will allow the aunt to flourish as before.[44]

41 Helen Maatjes reveals that, in the Dutch practice of law, there is *a concept of seven differences* that is more a myth than a legal theory. Helen Maatjes, *Bescherming tegen 'namaak' in de meubelbranche*, IEF 11619, 26 July 2012, https://intellectueeleigendomsrecht.nl/bescherming-tegen-namaak-in-de-meubelbranche-2/ (accessed: 04.03.2022).

42 Landerbarthold, *Minimalistisch ontwerp*; cf. P.B. Hugenholtz, 'Gezamenlijke noot onder Stokke/H3, Stokke/Fikszo en Hauck/Stokke', Amsterdam: IVIR 2013, NJ 2013, afl. 46, no. 503, pp. 5896–5900.

43 Landerbarthold, *Minimalistisch ontwerp*, p. 47.

44 Landerbarthold, *Minimalistisch ontwerp*, p. 60.

He is a strong proponent of dilution, in which it is possible that the scope of protection of a work can be reduced if elements of it are frequently imitated by others. He therefore sees dilution as something that is logical and desirable for several reasons, and advocates that "dilution be accepted in copyright law".[45] He points out that slavish imitation can first and foremost act as a safety net where copyright is not applicable.[46]

5.4 Fashion design versus industrial works. Significant differences approach

The prerequisites of design protection in Poland on the basis of Polish Copyright Law (PCL) and Polish Industrial Property Law (PIPL), despite some terminological convergence, are actually different. Not every industrial design exhibits features that would allow for copyright protection. Therefore, it is unsubstantiated to assume that every industrial design would *ex iure* be copyrightable, however as noted by Elżbieta Traple, that would very much come as a rule in Poland.[47] It is believed that otherwise it would not make any sense to keep dual protection, especially since industrial designs require registration. It is therefore argued that the interpretation of the premise "creative" must be deliberate.

The Court of Appeals in Warsaw, in a judgement of 1 February 1995, discussed the overlapping protection of 'container especially for bread' with regard to three legal regimes: utility design, unfair competition and copyright. By example of this work of applied art, it expressed its understanding of creativity (as a premise for copyright protection):

> assessment of the extent to which the product features in question prove its creative character and to what extent it has the features of novelty, originality, artistry as for its form, requires proving that a specific product (especially in the case of ordinary, everyday items) significantly differs from other products of this type especially with regard to solutions bearing the hallmarks of expressive, individual (also for certain types of objects) creative features.[48]

Based on this understanding, it found the container not copyrightable.[49] This case proves that the category of industrial design is analysed in a very meticulous

45 Landerbarthold, *Minimalistisch ontwerp*, p. 59.
46 Landerbarthold, *Minimalistisch ontwerp*, p. 59.
47 E. Traple, *Umowy o eksploatację utworów w prawie polskim*, Wolters Kluwer, 2010, p. 234.
48 Judgement of Court of Appeals in Warsaw as of 1 February 1995, case files no. I Acz 1208/94, lex no. 62645; cf. M. Balicki, *Ochrona wzorów użytkowych*, 2020, lex/el. 2020.
49 The container's features were mostly about:

> Reducing the number of container components, in addition to simplifying assembly, contributes to a significant reduction in the manufacturing costs of the container due to

way with regard to the premises of creativity and originality, which implies higher standards for this category of works than for the others.[50]

The 'bread container' case proved to be valid more recently when copyrightability of a countertop washbasin[51] and 'DS3 pen body' were considered.[52] In the latter case, the court asserted that proving originality "requires showing that a *specific product differs from other previously created products of a given type in a significant way due to the adopted solutions*, bearing the hallmarks of expressive, individual features of creativity" (emphasis mine – MJ). It was interestingly noted by the court in the first instance that the creativity level in works of this kind should be respectively high and show essential significant differences.[53] The dispute regarded the pen clip bridge that was claimed to be creative due to its elliptical form. The plaintiff asserted that copyright merit was based on the simple line of the corpus as "in the late eighties the simple body line, cleared of any additions and containing one clip in the form of a bridge, was a manifestation of the high originality and innovation of the disputed object".[54]

With regard to the 'DS3 pen body' case in the Polish legal literature, Ewa Laskowska-Litak took the approach that

> thus, the premises of creativity and individuality are *sought in comparison with products already existing in the market*, in addition, it is required to demonstrate the existence of significant (individual, artistic or expressive) differences between them. While the need to search for a *slightly higher threshold of creativity and individuality for copyright protection cannot be denied in general, its overestimation in relation to only one of the categories of protected works is not justified*. In particular, an argument

---

reducing the number of expensive specialty tools such as injection moulds as well as reducing the number of injection moulding machines involved in the production of containers. The ribbing on the bottom of the container allows for adequate stiffness despite using less plastic. The use of feet, made of rubber or fabric-like-rubber, prevents the container from slipping when opening or closing it;

utility model registration no. W.097296 as of 11 March 1993, right specification at https://ewyszukiwarka.pue.uprp.gov.pl/search/pwp-details/W.097296 (accessed: 07.01.2022).

50 See Laskowska-Litak, side note 97.

51 Judgement of Court of Appeals in Kraków as of 21 January 2016, case files no. I Acz 2544/15, lex no. 1966358 (judgement of District Court in Kraków as of 20 October 2015, case no. IX GCo 234/15). The Court of Appeals noted that

> The solutions used in each of the projects are based on the simplicity of shape and finishings. The lack of any characteristic elements, such as non-standard material, dimensions, bowl shape, additional decorations, etc. make these projects show a certain degree of routine and typicality for objects of their kind, and thus are deprived of an individual and unique character.

52 Judgement of Court of Appeals in Poznań as of 25 September 2007, case files no. I Aca 618/07, lex no. 370729 (Judgement of District Court in Zielona Góra as of 27 January 2006).

53 Op. cit.

54 Op. cit.

> about the utilitarian nature of the protected goods or the cumulative nature of protection of industrial designs cannot substantiate this practice. Such an interpretation contradicts not only the literal interpretation of the act (which by no means introduces any differences of the level of creativity of particular types of works), but also the principle of protection of all intellectual products, regardless of their presentation, form or value. Interpretation of the constitutive premises for the subject of copyright cannot therefore differ from the general principles adopted for all types of works (emphasis mine – MJ).[55]

According to Radomir Sroka, comparing works with those already on the market is part of checking of the premise of individuality (***significant differences approach***).[56]

In the Polish jurisprudence,[57] it was reasonably pointed out that the criterion of 'originality' of work may vary ***casu ad casum*** given the different, theoretically infinite, types of work. There are different elements proving 'creativity' of literary works (poetical layer, stylistic devices, figures of speech) and referential works. This approach goes along with the liberal approach in the Polish legal literature.[58]

According to Damian Flisak, "the quality of the work measured its professional making, artistic taste and assumed functionality has no significance".[59] He also points out that "under both Polish and European copyright law, both kitsch and high quality creation are genres equally eligible for its protection".[60] This author does not contest this account but believes that this is not the core of the problem in the case of fashion design.

Having analysed many examples of cases regarding industrial designs and especially fashion, I would rather say that, although there are no higher statutory standards or burdens for copyright protection of applied art in Poland, the assessment of the quantity of creativity and individuality may differ compared to "typical" works of authorship such as paintings or writings. As applied art

55 E. Laskowska-Litak [w:] *Komentarz do ustawy o prawie autorskim i prawach pokrewnych [w:] Ustawy autorskie. Komentarze. Tom I*, red. R. Markiewicz, Wolters Kluwer, 2021, Article 1, side note 97; A. Tischner, *Kumulatywna ochrona wzornictwa przemysłowego w prawie własności przemysłowej*, C.H. Beck, 2015, p. 218–219.

56 Sroka, legal paper in the case . . . ; p. 639, cf. d. Flisak, *Pojęcie utworu w prawie autorskim – potrzeba głębokich zmian*, "Przegląd Prawa Handlowego", 2006, vol. 12, pp. 35–36; M. Poźniak-Niedzielska, *Wzory zdobnicze i ich ochrona*, Wydawnictwo Prawnicze, 1978, p. 144–149; W. Machała, *Wzornictwo przemysłowe – miedzy własnością przemysłową a prawem autorskim*, "PPWI UJ", 2007, z. 100, pp. 248–250.

57 Polish Supreme Court judgement of 27 February 2009, case file no. V CSK 337/08, lex no. 488738; Polish Supreme Court judgement of 22 June 2010, case file no. IV CSK 359/09, "Biuletyn SN" 2010/7/12.

58 Błeszyński, *Twórczość jako . . .*, p. 28.

59 D. Flisak's legal paper, p. 1135; Polish Supreme Court judgement of 26 May 1988, case file no. IV 122/88; Anna Korpała [in:], Andrzej Matlak, Sybilla Stanisławska-Kloc (eds). *Prawo autorskie. Orzecznictwo*, Wolters Kluwer, 2010, p. 86.

60 Op. cit.

is meant to be useful or functional, it is often hard to find the legally relevant line between elements that are just useful and those that are actually creative. The simpler the form is, the harder the issue at stake. Therefore, I would rather argue that Polish courts do not introduce the additional burden of comparing existing works but take a shortcut to understanding the artistic and industrial nature of these works, as well this is one of the easiest ways to gain some understanding about industrial creativity. Fashion, with many examples from the area of jewellery, proves that designers use standard forms and ideas that are part of the public domain, then mould them into something new. This author contests the pure juxtaposition of form and content. For fashion, this distinction does not help to identify elements that make work creative and therefore copyrightable. In case of fashion, form and content should be gauged differently than with respect to other genres of works, such as literature, pictures or music.

Assessing originality always involves comparison and the assessment of existing standards in the creative area, even if this is not openly admitted. In the case regarding the flush-mounted junction box, the court noted that

> it was necessary for the claimant to prove that no similar works had been created before and that it is not statistically probable that another specialist undertaking a similar task in the future would achieve a similar effect (the so-called statistical uniqueness measure), or that her works were not the result of work determined by the function of the object, practical assumptions to be met, technical requirements or other objective factors (the so-called measure of creative freedom).[61]

5.5 Fashion design versus website design. Look and feel approach

This author also proposes to look at fashion design from a slightly different perspective. Multimedia works, such as websites, have also triggered a lot of discussion in the past, allowing for the conclusion that they are creative. This takeaway was possible only based on a delicately changed approach to originality that takes place in a multimedia environment. Having analysed the technique of creating websites, including the entire website's look and feel, it has been concluded that the individual elements such as font, photographs, animations, colours and graphic design may be protected.[62] A particularly important element here seems to be the observation expressed in the literature regarding the principle of the "unity of a work" such as a website, which consists of a multiplicity of fragments of various kinds. Therefore, it may wonder whether, in such a complex form, a work may be assessed as a work.[63]

Interestingly, a website is characterised by the fact that it exists in a digital form in a digital environment, and it can be perceived using digital devices,

61 Judgement of Court of Appeals in Warsaw as of 22 April 2022, case file VIII AGa 851/21.

62 D. Flisak, *Utwór multimedialny w prawie autorskim*, Oficyna, 2008, lex.

63 Flisak, *Utwór.*

including computers. The website does not have a classic fixed medium in the form of a "corpus mechanicum", and this does not affect the copyright protection, its content or scope.

It seems relevant that work becomes complete in a closed form with the possibility of delineating its boundaries. As noted by D. Flisak, the schematic complexity in this respect provides various qualifications due to the fact that

> the protection of the entire work does not mean that any section of it itself must also be subject to copyright protection. This only happens if it itself meets the general criteria of protection. The same counts the other way round. The fulfilment of the premise of protection by a fragment of the work does not extend that protection to the whole.[64]

The rules of objective experience will help to determine whether a given website is the result of template, routine and diagram-based work, or has the value of a unique selection of elements allowing qualification of a given component of the work for copyright protection. Determining these properties becomes possible by comparing the analysed object with others already in existence. Also, the Court of Appeal in Poznań, in its judgement of 18 May 2006,[65] held that "furniture as a work may be considered an object of copyright (work), as long as it is distinct and individual in nature, against other furniture available on the market".

It should also be noted that a website will almost always consist of some permanent elements allowing users to use it by default and with well-known applications. This is achieved by windows, specific fields, a specific structure (often similar) or the so-called pull-down menu. It is noted in the literature that such additions with a purely functional application are in principle exempt from copyright protection. In addition, it should be determined to what extent the form of the expression is determined by professional terminology and the entrepreneur's dealings with a specific field. On a side note, it should be mentioned that a website, as a combination of individual components or works, may acquire a creative character by the way these elements are combined, allowing for a new aesthetic dimension. This is a situation in which a website ceases to be the sum of its individual components. In the literature, attention is paid to the so-called layout, i.e. the recognition of a given product, also known as *look and feel*, consisting of a characteristic background, colours, typeface, links, headers, cursor, spacing between lines of text, a characteristic format or spatial arrangement of photos. In this regard, attention is paid to the interaction between individual elements, which is definitely more than a simple selection and compilation of components by combining them on the page in a specific schematic relationship.

64 Flisak, *Utwór*.

65 Case file no. I ACa 1449/05.

It is noteworthy how a website and fashion design have so many aspects in common. It is also true for fashion that certain forms simply cannot look different, just as a blouse must have two sleeves. It is nevertheless up to the author whether they will make it plain or puffed, will introduce a specific pattern, ribbing or sleeve length.

Websites are created according to a similar pattern, which is the result of the work of psychologists and sales specialists. For web design, we can mention, for example, J. Nielsen who proposes that there are ten rules for creating a home page:

1. placing an advertising slogan next to the logo at the top on the left, briefly describing the message of the website;
2. starting the main page with issues important to the website;
3. providing links to sections such as "Company", "About us";
4. creating so-called Starting points on the website from which users can quickly view the website resources;
5. placing a search engine in a visible place on the website;
6. revealing portions of real site content directly on the home page;
7. using relevant keywords in link text;
8. using the home page to post links to the most important products;
9. avoiding overly elaborate presentation of important content – users may confuse such content with advertisements;
10. ensuring graphics used are relevant to your content, not generic.[66]

It follows from this discussion that the layout and schematic connections may be similar and will not constitute an infringement of copyright. This is confirmed by the rules of copyright, which place general ideas outside the scope of protection.

5.6 Summary: power to attract. Mind energy. Emotional approach

Interestingly, this research proves that fashion itself has not stirred as much debate on this matter as has design in general. Design as a wider concept is a part of the ongoing discussions of the overlap between copyright and industrial property protection. The variety of legal systems analysed in Chapter 4 show that there is a wide range of approaches and interpretations regarding the copyrightability of design, including fashion. The in-depth analysis of legal regulations and case law brings this author to the simple conclusion, that, from the legal point of view, ***fashion is*** part of the broader concept of ***design***. In other words, the standpoint taken with regard to the legal protection of design is also valid for fashion.

66 J. Nielsen, Top Ten Guidelines for Homepage Usability, www.useit.com/alertbox/20020512.html (accessed: 02.10.2023); J. Nielsen, K. Pernice, *Eyetracking Web Usability*, New Riders Pub, 2010.

An account given in the Polish literature of philosophy draws on the philosophical approach of W. Tatarkiewicz, according to which not every new scheme or layout can be held to be "creative", but only those that demonstrate higher levels of skill or that have a significant effect. Therefore, it is not enough that the work be "new", it should be brought about using a "higher level of activity, bigger effort and greater efficacy. Therefore, authors should not be considered those, whose works are new, but those whose output are proof of special skill, tension, talents or genius". This account gives way to the idea of "mind energy".[67] This approach is not followed in the Polish legal doctrine, as it is deemed too restrictive and sets too high a threshold, but the idea of mind energy is an appealing starting point for further discussion.

In design practice, it is observed that people without professional training are not able to appreciate that the simplicity of the expected solutions is a result of a complex thought and production process (whether hand- or machine-made). This leads people who are not well versed in the matter to hasty conclusions that the result of a designer's work should be spectacular and unique. Therefore, the lingering question is whether 'simple design' is still protected by copyright. According to Prof. Bogumiła Jung, the expectation of 'creativity', which is based on art and on clear differences between two fashion designs and the analysed product is a result of a lack of understanding for this area of work.[68] In her opinion, in the practice of creating fashion, it is extremely rare for an employer or contracting authority to expect the creator to prepare a project that will be an expression of their own 'ego', including their 'individual character'. Bogumiła Jung, in her opinion on kitchenware, stated that

> a design creator solves the client's problems, without looking for artistry. These problems include, for example, the desire to increase sales, optimize production, better use machinery and raw materials, reduce waste, optimize transport, lower energy consumption during production, more easily dispose of the product after use, and finally lower the final price – all this can be "achieved" by a good designer.

Sometimes a 'brief' defines a precise design task in such a way as to emphasise the importance of differences from competitors' designs. As B. Jung rightly points out, the spectacular differences arise for *haute couture* collections but not for workwear. Quaedvlieg, in his Dutch approach states: "Contemporary design wants to maximally integrate beauty and function: function is the creator

67 D. Flisak's legal paper in the case IX Gc 433/10, District Court judgement in Poznań as of 27 December 2012, p. 639; W. Tatarkiewicz, *Dzieje sześciu pojęć*, ed. 5, Polskie Wydawnictwo Naukowe, 2006, pp. 309–311.

68 District Court judgement in Poznań as of 27 December 2012; case files no. IX Gc 433/10, case files, pp. 1648–1649.

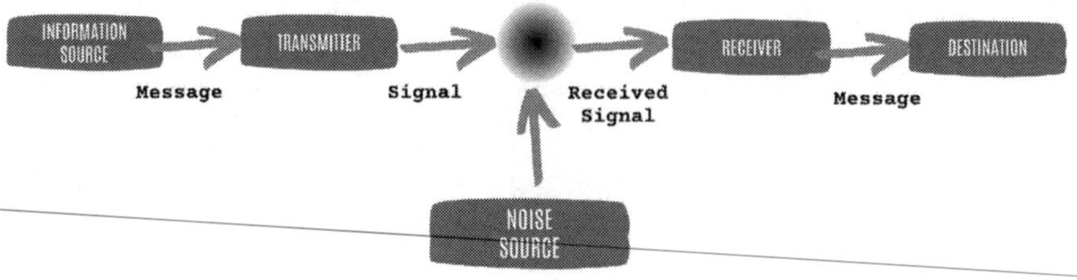

Explanatory item no. 5.1 Illustration of the source of authorship using C. Shannon's information theory

Source: Created by author

of the design and design is the expression of function".[69] It can be argued that with the introduction (almost a century ago) of minimalism in design ("less is more"), separation between form and function has become a considerably more complicated exercise. Should the copyright lawyer's answer also be "less is just less", therefore meaning that not everything will be copyrightable?

The creative process, which has fascinated scholars for centuries, cannot, however, be encapsulated into simple concepts, tests and thresholds, despite what copyright lawyers might wish for. For many years, a starting point in my copyright endeavours was the test formulated by A. L. Durham, who used C. Shannon's information theory to explain the copyrightability process.[70]

Explanatory item no. 5.1 should be provided with a brief explanation. The transmitter is an author who draws from a generally understood information source. It may be the author's own inspiration, a more or less concrete idea appearing in the imagination or some aspect of reality (e.g. the sunset the author observes). By creating a work, the author sends (in schematic terms) to the receivers of the work a signal in the form of a message (e.g., a song) into which the author, intentionally or not, puts the characteristics of their individual personality. Exactly these features, such as characteristic expressions or even imperfections in presenting the author's inner image projection, represent the so-called noise source through which the author reveals their mark in the work's personality. Figuratively speaking, the noise source is the source of authorship.

I have used Shannon's theory of information in my research and teaching activity, and it was always very useful in understanding the romance between copyright and aesthetics. Creativity lies at the intersection of these scientific domains, and it is clear that it involves concepts from both fields, which need to be examined from these respective perspectives. Nevertheless, it has to be

69 A.A. Quaedvlieg, *Ideas, Technique and Style as Dark Matter of the Scope of Copyright Protection*, "AMI", 2015, vol. 2, pp. 29–37.

70 A.L. Durham, *Copyright and Information Theory: Toward an Alternative Model of Authorship*, "BYU Law Review", 2004, no. 69, p. 74; por. A.L. Durham, *The Random Muse: Authorship and Indeterminacy*, "William & Mary Law Review", 2002, no. 44, p. 634.

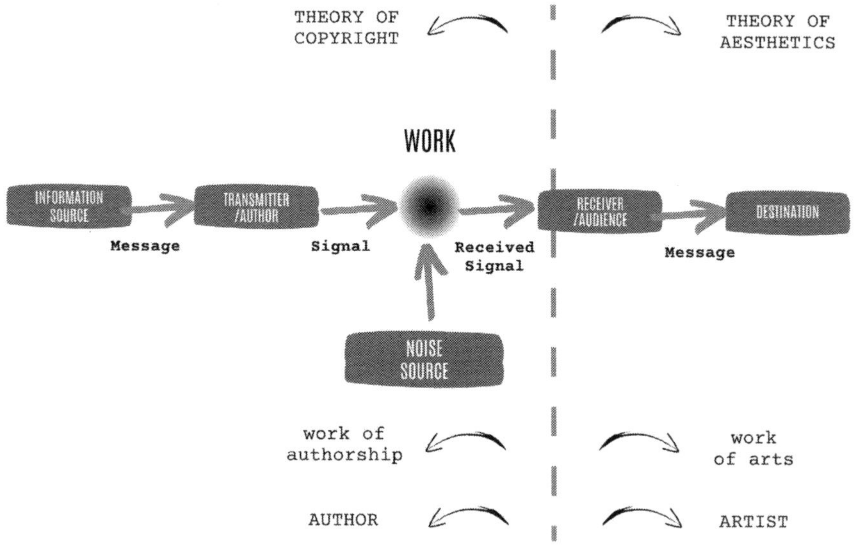

Explanatory item no. 5.2 Theory of copyright explained using C. Shannon's theory. Own reinterpretation

Source: Created by author, own reinterpretation

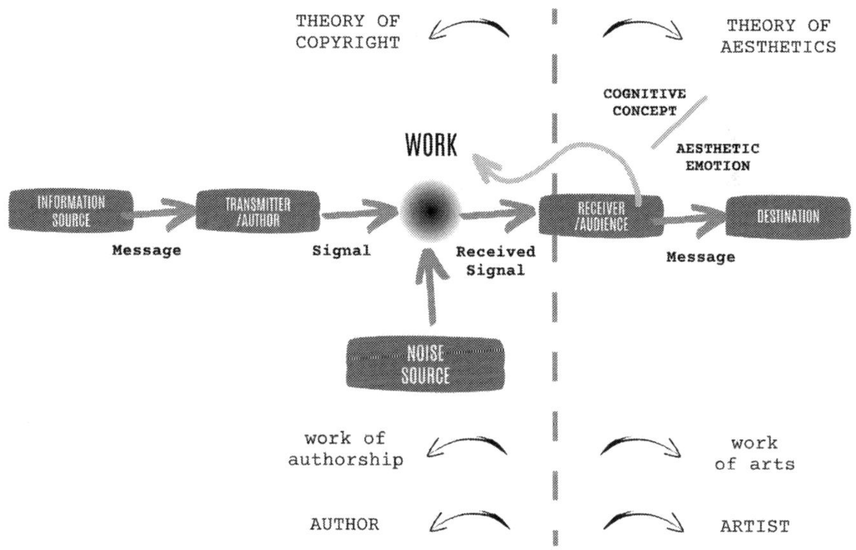

Explanatory item no. 5.3 Theory of copyright law revisited. Own reinterpretation

Source: Created by author, own reinterpretation

done with a certain care, because relying too heavily on an aesthetic understanding of originality could be at odds with the fundamentals of copyright. This concept, C. Shannon's theory applied to copyright law, allows a line to be drawn between copyright and aesthetics and an understand of the premises on which copyright rests (Explanatory item no. 5.2). A work of authorship, in general, does not seek attention from the audience the way a work of art does. The idea of an author in copyright law and that of an artist in the arts are also somehow different. For a good many years, I believed that the line delineating copyright law lay just in front of the audience, whose attitude to or comprehension of a work does not matter. Obviously, from an aesthetic point of view, there is a special relationship between an author and a receiver or audience, but that is unrelated to copyright premises.

The research undertaken for this book proves that fashion design challenges this overgeneralisation, since fashion is made from emotions (Explanatory item no. 5.3). The cognitive concept, developed by Aleksandra Nowak-Gruca, among others, allows a marrying of some of the concepts that inherently belong to both copyright and aesthetics, in order to better understand the creative process and reward accordingly. This new emotional approach to copyright law also makes room for a very close relationship between an author and the audience through the author's work (of authorship).

Index

Made in the USA
Las Vegas, NV
19 September 2026

e03f8a71-4fd2-40b1-95ce-acecf7cc058aR01